THE
THEATREGOER'S
ALMANAC

THE THEATREGOER'S ALMANAC

A Collection of Lists, People, History, and Commentary on the American Theatre

THOMAS S. HISCHAK

GREENWOOD PRESS
Westport, Connecticut • London

Library of Congress Cataloging-in-Publication Data

Hischak, Thomas S.
   The theatregoer's almanac : a collection of lists, people,
history, and commentary on the American theatre / Thomas S. Hischak.
     p.   cm.
   Includes bibliographical references and index.
   ISBN 0–313–30246–4 (alk. paper)
   1. Theater—United States—Dictionaries. 2. Theater—New York
(State)—New York—Dictionaries. 3. Theater—United States—
Biography—Dictionaries. 4. American drama—20th century—Bio-
bibliography—Dictionaries. 5. American drama—19th century—Bio-
bibliography—Dictionaries. I. Title.
PN2266.H53   1997
792′.0973—dc21   96–43782

British Library Cataloguing in Publication Data is available.

Library of Congress Catalog Card Number: 96–43782
ISBN: 0–313–30246–4

First published in 1997

Greenwood Press, 88 Post Road West, Westport, CT 06881
An imprint of Greenwood Publishing Group, Inc.

Printed in the United States of America

The paper used in this book complies with the
Permanent Paper Standard issued by the National
Information Standards Organization (Z39.48–1984).

10 9 8 7 6 5 4 3 2 1

For Alan Hanson, Christian Moe and Gerald Bordman,
three teachers who have guided me with patience and humor

CONTENTS

PREFACE

If you asked the average theatregoer in New York City in the 1870s what was the matter with the American Theatre, he or she would probably mention high ticket prices, an excess of English and French plays, too many revivals and not enough new plays, and a surplus of melodramas and vehicles that were not worthy of their stars. Forty years later, the same question would bring hostile remarks about high ticket prices, too many revivals, too few American plays, talented stars in tawdry plays, and how this new craze of automobiling was keeping people from the theatre. A decade later, films would be the culprit, along with high ticket prices and too few notable American plays. By the 1970s the fault was with the unions, the decaying Theatre District, the British invasion, and high ticket prices, of course. The cry of "What's happening to the Theatre?" can be heard echoing down through the decades, whether it was a season with hundreds of productions and new plays by O'Neill or a season of a few dozen new shows and a phalanx of long-running mega-musicals intended to boost box office figures to new heights.

Watching the "fabulous invalid" that is the American Theatre as it struggled through the past two centuries is fascinating, if for no other reason than that these echoes from the past seem vividly familiar to us. The invalid seems to have had the same symptoms for decades, and a series of physicians have diagnosed alarmingly similar remedies. What was recommended for the theatre in 1870 is what most feel we need today: lots of great new American plays at inexpensive prices. It did not happen then, and we are still waiting for it to happen now. But, surprisingly, the patient did not die. So the remedies continue and the theatre struggles on.

This is a book about that invalid, taking bits and pieces from its history and its present condition to try and highlight what makes it so stubbornly interesting. It is not an encyclopedia because its subject matter is selective. Nor is the book a history because it does not try to survey the art form or outline it chronologically. Instead it is a compendium, a pulling together of various features from a vast subject. I have called the book *The Theatregoer's Almanac* because it moves from topic to topic just as a theatregoer's curiosity moves from one idea to a related one. Sometimes these ideas present themselves in the form of lists, sometimes they are objective statistics, and other times they are very selective and subjective observations.

The series of complaints mentioned earlier form the path that this book takes. Ticket prices, revivals, number of productions in a season, American versus foreign plays, and other topics have been of concern to theatregoers ever since there first was an American Theatre. Then there are the people, the plays and the places where theatre happens. Add awards and other odds and ends to this, and the scope of the book is complete. Because no particular subject in the book can be dealt with in great detail, each section ends with suggestions for further reading.

There is little in this work that cannot be found in a collection of other reference books and theatre chronicles. But, I believe, no other work arranges the myriad bits of information in the same way presented here. Like an eccentric collector who arranges his personal museum of art in his own unique way, *The Theatregoer's Almanac* hopes to take you on a personal and distinctive tour of the American Theatre.

I wish to acknowledge the continued help of the staff at the Cortland Free Library and the Memorial Library of the State University of New York College at Cortland. Thank you to Alicia Merritt, my enthusiastic editor at Greenwood. I offer special thanks to Gerald Bordman for reviewing the manuscript and for his many suggestions. And, as always, I present my public appreciation for the encouragement of my wife Cathy and my family.

THE
THEATREGOER'S
ALMANAC

1

BROADWAY

WHAT IS BROADWAY?

Broadway is a street, a district, a form of theatre, a union classification and a state of mind. The street runs the length of Manhattan, continuing north, all the way to Albany, New York. As a district, it originated in lower Manhattan with the first theatre built on the thoroughfare in the 1730s. Today the district is centered near Times Square with theatres on the street itself and on the side streets east and west of Broadway. A "Broadway play" or "Broadway musical" is that highly polished, highly publicized kind of theatre that once meant the finest to be found in America. Contractually, a "Broadway house" is one of forty theatres designated by the unions for a "Broadway contract." The size of the house and its contractual obligations rather than location determine which theatres are classified as "Broadway." For example, the Vivian Beaumont Theatre at Lincoln Center on 66th Street is a Broadway house; the smaller Mitzi Newhouse Theatre in the same building is classified as an "Off-Broadway" house. And Broadway as a "state of mind"? It is the illusion that Broadway represents the American Theatre. Fewer and fewer people feel that such a sentiment is an accurate one, but there is still a glamour to the expression that has not been replaced by theatre elsewhere.

Off Broadway, as we know it today, was born in the late 1940s as an alternative to Broadway. There had been non-Broadway theatre in New York as early as the 1910s with such experimental theatre groups as the Neighborhood Playhouse and the Provincetown Players. But in the post-war years, a new theatre venue surfaced with small, independent productions in a new atmosphere of theatregoing. Off Broadway has smaller houses, less expensive budgets, lower ticket prices and, hopefully, more experimental and challenging fare. An Off-Broadway theatre can be located anywhere in New York but the cluster of intimate theatres in Greenwich Village is considered the heart of Off Broadway.

In the 1970s a further alternative was born: Off Off Broadway. These houses (often not formal theatres but sometimes churches, storefronts, and other "found" spaces) are even smaller and the products even more adventurous. Sometimes catering to specific sociopolitical groups or causes, Off Off Broadway in the 1970s was often abrasive and even anti-theatre. Today the uniqueness is usually ethnic, sexual, or philosophical. The dream of every Off-Off-Broadway production? To be so successful that it moves to Off Broadway or even Broadway. Some shows have actually done it. The Broadway state of mind continues on.

THE BROADWAY SEASON

In the nineteenth century, and for much of this century, the traditional Broadway season officially began in June, started to gain steam in late August, peaked around New Year's Eve, and wound down in April and May. This pattern was not dictated by any philosophical or artistic ideals but was a practical approach to the lack of air-conditioned theatres during the summer. While some theatre producers braved the hot weather and opened shows in July and August, most theatres were dark. This gave rise to the popularity of rooftop garden theatres in the late 1800s, which offered audiences temporary relief from the heat. The September to May pattern held out through the 1950s, even though many theatres were "air cooled" by World War Two. But traditions die hard on Broadway, and it was not until the 1970s that producers saw the market of summer tourists at the theatre. Now business booms in June, July, and August (at least for musicals; serious dramas still do best in the cooler months), and shows are opened year round. But Broadway still uses June as the start of the season; officially, June 1 is the date that the *Best Plays* volumes chronicling New York theatre has used since 1946.

TICKET PRICES

Critics, patrons, and producers have been complaining about the steep price of theatre tickets since before the Civil War. One thing has remained constant: legitimate theatre has always been expensive. Even before film, radio, and television, there were always cheaper forms of entertainment, such as vaudeville or the neighborhood theatres, nicknamed "ten-twent'-thirt'" houses because tickets ranged from thirty cents down to a dime. But even in the late 1700s, legitimate theatres charged seventy-five cents for a ticket. Around the late 1800s the top price rose to $2.00 but it stayed there for many decades. It was not until World War One that theatre tickets rose steadily, though not as quickly as we have seen in the past few decades. During the Depression, average ticket prices actually went down a bit to adjust to the lower demand and disastrous financial state of the arts.

Theatre in New York has always been elitist; "popular" prices were reserved for other forms of entertainment. And there have always been special attractions that demanded outrageous prices because of the unique nature of the production. In 1864, for example, Edwin Booth and his brothers appeared in *Julius Caesar* and were able to charge $5.00 for the best seats. Today's Broadway prices are high but probably not any higher proportionally than Broadway prices ever were. What has changed for the worse has been the scaling of prices. For example, when *Bells Are Ringing* opened on Broadway at the Shubert Theatre in 1956, ticket prices ranged from $7.90 for the best seats on a Saturday night to $1.50 for second balcony seats on a Wednesday matinee. When the musical *Big* opened in the same theatre in 1996, the ticket prices ranged only from $70 to $42.50. There is no such thing as the "cheap seats" on Broadway today.

BROADWAY OVER THE YEARS

The chart below compares the Broadway seasons over the past 125 years, looking at the number of productions and the typical top price for every fifth season.

Theatre Season	Number of Productions	Ticket Prices
1870-71	94	$1.50
1875-76	78	$1.50
1880-81	113	$1.50
1885-86	148	$1.50
1890-91	153	$1.50
1895-96	171	$2.00
1900-01	111	$2.00
1905-06	168	$2.00
1910-11	157	$2.00
1915-16	117	$3.50
1920-21	157	$3.50
1925-26	265	$6.00
1930-31	190	$4.00
1935-36	155	$4.00
1940-41	75	$4.40
1945-46	98	$6.60
1950-51	88	$7.20
1955-56	73	$7.50
1960-61	63	$8.60
1965-66	76	$11.90
1970-71	56	$15.00
1975-76	65	$17.50

1980-81	63	$32.00
1985-86	42	$43.00
1990-91	27	$55.00
1995-96	38	$75.00

The number of productions is a deceptive and inaccurate figure because everyone counts the entries differently. In the nineteenth century, for example, stars would bring their repertory of plays to New York and perform seven or eight different plays in a week's time. Other plays opened on Broadway, played their modest run and then, later in the season, returned to fill an empty theatre that had just housed a flop. There are attractions that played Broadway that were not plays but were termed "specialty" programs and were deemed Broadway entries. Finally, before the concept of "Broadway" was established, any legitimate theatre in Manhattan was included in the final tally. But even with these inconsistencies, one can see the pattern of the rise of numbers of productions until the Depression and the gradual but definite diminishing of that number since World War Two.

BROADWAY'S BUSIEST SEASON

The 1927-1928 theatre season was a highwater mark for the American theatre. That season 270 plays, musicals, and revivals opened on Broadway. Flush from the prosperity of the Roaring Twenties and (unknowingly) on the eve of talking pictures and the Great Depression, the 1927-1928 season was the American theatre's last hurrah. It was healthy in quantity and quality. New American plays seen on Broadway that season included *Burlesque*, *The Trial of Mary Dugan*, *Coquette*, *Porgy*, *Marco Millions*, *The Royal Family*, *Diamond Lil*, *Strange Interlude*, as well as the foreign imports *Plough and the Stars*, *Escape*, *Fallen Angels*, *The Letter*, and *Dracula*. Among the musicals that premiered included *Good News*, *The Five O'Clock Girl*, *Funny Face*, *A Connecticut Yankee*, *The Three Musketeers*, *Blackbirds of 1928*, *Rosalie*, and *Show Boat*.

BROADWAY'S BUSIEST NIGHT

In the midst of its busiest season, Broadway had its busiest night ever: eleven shows opened on Monday, December 26, 1927. Nine of the offerings were new plays, one was a revival of a French play, and the last was a musical. Here is what Broadway offered on that historic night:

Excess Baggage, a play by John McGowan about various characters who worked in vaudeville (219 performances)
Behold the Bridegroom, one of George Kelly's lesser efforts with a strong per-

formance by Judith Anderson (88 performances)

Mongolia, a melodrama by Conrad Westervelt about White Russian military in Northern China (48 performances)

It Is to Laugh, Fanny Hurst's play about an American Jewish family (32 performances)

Bless You, Sister, a flop drama about a female revivalist preacher that boasted a strong performance by Alice Brady (24 performances)

Celebrity, a short-lived boxing drama by Willard Keefe (24 performances)

Restless Woman, a potboiler about disillusioned housewives in America (24 performances)

Venus, an interesting futuristic drama by Rachel Crothers about the battle of the sexes (8 performances)

Paradise, a weeper by William Hurlbut about a small-town spinster (8 performances)

L'Aiglon, a revival of Sarah Bernhardt's famous vehicle but starring the less fascinating actress Michael Strange, John Barrymore's wife at the time (8 performances)

White Eagle, a Rudolf Friml musical version of the popular melodrama *The Squaw Man* (48 performances).

While only the first two shows ran long enough to be considered hits, the diversity of theatre available to playgoers in the 1927-1928 season is illustrated by this famous night's varied offerings. The next night the original *Show Boat* opened and the season had its greatest classic.

BROADWAY PLAYHOUSES TODAY

New York City as the center of theatre in America is a relatively recent distinction. During colonial days and in the first decades of the new nation, Boston, Philadelphia, and Charleston were, along with New York, considered the most important cultural centers. There was a theatre on the thoroughfare called Broadway as early as 1735. By 1860, Manhattan had only six theatres, although there were additional vaudeville houses and concert halls. But by 1868 there were twenty-one playhouses including four in Brooklyn. By 1894, with thirty-nine operating theatres, New York was clearly the theatrical center of the country and in 1901 it boasted more theatres than any other city in the world: forty-one. (London had thirty-nine and Paris only twenty-four.)

The center of theatregoing in Manhattan has been slowly moving uptown since the mid-1800s and today seems firmly settled in the Times Square area. Here are the existing, operating theatres in the Broadway district in order of their completion:

The **New Victory Theatre** (West 42nd Street) is Broadway's newest and oldest theatre. As the Republic Theatre, it was the first legitimate theatre built on 42nd Street. Impresario Oscar Hammerstein I built it in 1900 along with another house called the Victoria Theatre next door; on top of both he then added his Paradise Garden rooftop theatre. Producer David Belasco renamed the theatre after himself when he took over management in 1902, but it later became the Republic again. During the Depression the house was used for burlesque, and in 1942 it became the Victory movie house and continued as such until 1995 when it reopened, after extensive renovation, as the New Victory Theatre. With only 500 seats and two balconies, it is one of Broadway's most intimate houses but too small to be economically successful for most plays; its future will be mostly as a recital hall and home for specialty programs.

The **Lyceum Theatre** (West 45th Street), completed in 1903, was the oldest operating legitimate theatre in New York for many years. The name had been used for several earlier Manhattan playhouses, including a lovely theatre built by Daniel Frohman on Fourth Avenue in 1885. When that was demolished in 1902, Frohman moved uptown, starting a new trend, and built the present theatre with his offices and apartment situated above the auditorium.

The **New Amsterdam Theatre** (West 42nd Street) opened the same day as the Lyceum but it has not been an operating theatre for many years. It is included here because the New Amsterdam is currently being restored and will be presenting live theatre in the near future. The New Amsterdam was the flagship for the vast Erlanger empire and for many years was a favorite house for musicals, the *Ziegfeld Follies* in particular. The theatre also had a roof garden theatre, which was later turned into a rehearsal hall.

The **Belasco Theatre** (West 44th Street) is named after the dynamic producer-author-director David Belasco who built it as the Stuyvesant Theatre in 1907 but renamed it after himself in 1910. Not used much today, it is nonetheless a marvelous playhouse.

The **Lunt-Fontanne Theatre** (West 46th Street) was built by producer Charles Dillingham in 1910 as the Globe Theatre and was considered the finest of its day. The Depression eventually turned the theatre into a movie house, but it was revived as a legitimate theatre in 1958 and renamed after the distinguished acting couple Alfred Lunt and Lynn Fontanne.

The **New Apollo Theatre** (West 43rd Street) opened in 1910 as the Bryant Theatre, a vaudeville and movie house, then went legitimate. It has gone under a series of names over the years and has been at times a burlesque house, a cabaret, and a movie house again. Its recent history has been just as irregular; it is dark more often than not.

The **Winter Garden Theatre** (Broadway at 50th Street) has been a favorite home for musicals since it was built by the Shuberts in 1911 on the site of the old American Horse Exchange. Besides being a gem of a theatre, it is unusual for its very wide auditorium.

The **Helen Hayes Theatre** (West 44th Street) is not the glorious old theatre torn down in 1982 but the renamed Little Theatre that has sat on this site since 1912. At 499 seats, the theatre is indeed little, but that makes it special in the midst of the big auditoriums on Broadway.

The **Cort Theatre** (West 48th Street) also opened in 1912 and is also one of the district's smaller theatres. It is ideal for intimate dramas and comedies, but small musicals have also been known to do well here.

The **Palace Theatre** (Broadway at 47th Street) is still remembered as the "Valhalla of Vaudeville" even though for much of its history it has been a movie house and a legitimate theatre. Martin Beck built the elaborate theatre in 1913, but he soon lost ownership and it became the flagship for the Keith circuit. The theatre did not start housing legitimate Broadway productions until 1966, but it has been a busy house ever since.

The **Longacre Theatre** (West 48th Street) was built by baseball magnate H. H. Frazee in 1913. It was named after the nearby Longacre Square, now the site of the *New York Times* tower.

The **Sam S. Shubert Theatre** (West 44th Street), situated on Shubert Alley across from Sardi's, is what many think of when they picture a Broadway theatre. The Shubert Brothers built the theatre in 1913 as the flagship for their considerable empire and named it after their deceased brother Sam. The Shubert Organization still has their offices in the building.

The **Booth Theatre** (West 45th Street) was designed and built as part of the Shubert Theatre in 1913 and sits elegantly at the other end of Shubert Alley. One of the smaller Broadway houses, this intimate space named after actor Edwin Booth is a theatregoer's favorite.

The **Broadhurst Theatre** (West 44th Street) opened in 1917 and has rarely been unoccupied since then. It was named after the turn-of-the-century playwright George Broadhurst and some of his later plays were presented here.

The **Plymouth Theatre** (West 45th Street) was built by the distinguished producer Arthur Hopkins in 1917. Like most of the plays he presented here, the Plymouth is known for its good taste and architectural restraint.

The **Ambassador Theatre** (West 49th Street) has been a legitimate theatre, a movie house, and a radio and television studio since it opened in 1921. An unusual feature of the theatre is its angled auditorium designed to best utilize the limited space.

The **Walter Kerr Theatre** (West 48th Street) began as the Ritz Theatre in 1921 but was renamed after the influential critic in 1989. After being dark for quite some time, the Jujamcyn Organization carefully restored it to its original 1921 design, right down to the original color scheme and light fixtures.

The **Nederlander Theatre** (West 41st Street) has had so many names since it was built in 1921 (the National, Billy Rose Theatre, Trafalgar) that it still suffers from an identity crisis. It is the only legitimate Broadway theatre today below 42nd Street, another reason it is often neglected.

The **Music Box Theatre** (West 45th Street) is yet a fourth theatre that opened in 1921 and the most beloved of the group. Irving Berlin and his producing partner Sam H. Harris built the modest-sized theatre to house a series of Berlin revues appropriately called the *Music Box Revues*. It is a jewel of a house and one that is perfect for comedy, drama, or musicals.

The **Imperial Theatre** (West 45th Street) was built in 1923 as a musical house, and it has been happily occupied with them ever since. Many argue that it has the best sight lines of any large Broadway house.

The **Martin Beck Theatre** (West 45th Street) was built by and modestly named after the vaudeville czar in 1924. Beck broke tradition by building the theatre west of Eighth Avenue. But tradition held strong; no other theatre was ever built so far west.

The **Broadway Theatre** (Broadway at 53rd Street) opened in 1924 as a movie palace, the Colony. It went legitimate in 1930 and for nearly fifty years was the largest house in the theatre district. Too big for anything but large musicals, the Broadway Theatre has had more than its fair share of hits.

The **Richard Rodgers Theatre** (West 46th Street) opened as Chanin's 46th Street Theatre and for most of its existence was known simply as the 46th Street Theatre. It opened in 1925 with a musical and has been presenting mostly musicals ever since. The theatre is unusual in that it seems to be larger than it actually is. The Nederlanders changed the name in 1990 to honor the great theatre composer, but only one Rodgers show (*Do I Hear a Waltz?* in 1965) ever played the old 46th Street Theatre.

The **Virginia Theatre** (West 52nd Street) was designed and built to house the repertory system of the Theatre Guild. It opened in 1925 as the Guild Theatre. Twenty-five years later it became home to the American National Theatre and Academy and was simply called the ANTA Theatre. The theatre has one of the largest and most unusual backstage areas of any Broadway house and has been renovated twice over the years to try and make it work. It was renamed the Virginia Theatre in 1981.

The **Eugene O'Neill Theatre** (West 49th Street) was built in 1925 as the Forrest Theatre, was renamed the Coronet twenty years later, and finally called the O'Neill in 1959. Primarily a house for dramas over the years, it is appropriate that it is named for America's greatest dramatist (although it is a pity for Edwin Forrest, the popular nineteenth-century actor who inspired the original name).

The **Biltmore Theatre** (West 47th Street) was yet another theatre built in 1925, this one by the Chanin Brothers. The theatre gained notoriety when the police closed Mae West's *The Pleasure Man* here in 1928; a checkered history of flops and hits followed. During the Depression the Biltmore was home to some notable Federal Theatre Project productions. The theatre last presented a show in 1977, and in 1987 it suffered internal damage as a result of a fire. But the house has been designated an historical landmark, and it is hoped that it will be restored and used again.

The **Brooks Atkinson Theatre** (West 47th Street) was built in 1926 as the Mansfield Theatre (after the distinguished actor Richard Mansfield) and was renamed in 1961 (after the just-as-distinguished critic Atkinson). Surprisingly, Actors Equity did not complain when a critic stole a theatre from an actor.

The **Royale Theatre** (West 45th Street) is a mid-sized theatre owned by the Shuberts. It opened in 1927 and usually hosts plays rather than musicals; however, this theatre was home to *Grease* during its record-breaking run.

The **John Golden Theatre** (West 45th Street) is an intimate theatre in the Spanish style. It opened in 1927 as Theatre Masque then in 1937 it was bought by lyricist-turned-producer Golden who renamed it after himself.

The **Neil Simon Theatre** (West 52nd Street) was built in 1927 by producers Alex Aarons and Vinton Freedley who combined their first names and called it the Alvin Theatre. It has been the home for several Gershwin successes and continues to present musical hits. It was renamed after America's most popular contemporary playwright in 1983.

The **St. James Theatre** (West 44th Street) began as the Erlanger Theatre, built by Theatrical Syndicate emperor Abraham Erlanger in 1927. It was renamed after London's St. James Theatre in 1932. It ought to be called the Rodgers and Hammerstein Theatre, so many of their long-running hits played here.

The **Ethel Barrymore Theatre** (West 47th Street) was built for and named for the great American actress by the Shubert Brothers in 1927 as a way to seduce her into signing with them. It worked; she appeared in the first production here. The theatre is an ideal house for nonmusicals.

The **Mark Hellinger Theatre** (West 51st Street) is currently leased by a church, but it remains one of Broadway's finest musical houses; it will hopefully return to that use someday soon. It was built as the Hollywood Theatre, a Warners movie theatre, in 1930 and was known as the 51st Street Theatre when it went legitimate. In 1949 it was renamed after the Broadway columnist Hellinger.

The **Vivian Beaumont Theatre** at Lincoln Center (West 65th Street) was built in 1965 as a repertory house, but the Repertory Theatre of Lincoln Center has had a controversial history. The Beaumont (named after the philanthropist who paid for half of the $9 million plus that it cost to build) is not geographically considered part of the Broadway theatre district, but in terms of contracts, unions, ticket prices, and Tony Awards, it is a full-fledged Broadway house. The theatre has a semi-thrust stage, which seems to have caused more problems than benefits over the years. But some notable productions have been seen here, such as the 1994 revival of *Carousel*, which seemed to blossom when confronting the difficulties of that round stage.

The **Gershwin Theatre** (Broadway at 50th Street) was the first new Broadway theatre to be built in the district in nearly fifty years, and it is currently the largest at 1,933 seats. It opened in 1972 as the Uris Theatre but was renamed after the great composer in 1983. It also houses the Theatre Hall of Fame in one of its huge lobbies.

The **Circle in the Square Theatre** (Broadway at 50th Street) is in the same building as the Gershwin Theatre and it also opened in 1972. It is the first and only "flexible" theatre on Broadway, offering productions in a thrust or a theatre-in-the-round setting. This odd little theatre is perhaps the least typical of any Broadway house.

The **Minskoff Theatre** (Broadway at 45th Street) is in a high-rise office building but its interior is a pretty traditional musical theatre house. It also boasts the largest backstage space of any Broadway theatre. It was built in 1973 on the site of the the old Astor Hotel and was named for its developer, Jerome Minskoff.

The **Marquis Theatre** (Broadway at 46th Street) was completed in 1986 despite protests that three old theatres had to be torn down to build it. Located in a gigantic hotel, the Marquis is a traditional musical house and has a short but impressive track record for hits.

Criterion Center/Stage Right (Broadway between 44th and 45th Streets) is a new theatre that sits on the site of many previous theatres, going back to Oscar Hammerstein I's Olympia Theatre in 1895. In 1988 the site was transformed into the Criterion Center, containing two theatres and several movie houses. The theatre called Stage Right is a legitimate Broadway house even though it has only 499 seats. It has housed plays and small musicals since 1988; in 1991 it became the home of the Roundabout Theatre Company.

A majority of the current Broadway theatres were built before 1930, the golden age of theatregoing when hundreds of productions opened each season. In those days new theatres were built or vaudeville houses were turned into legitimate theatres to keep up with the demand. In the years 1913, 1921, and 1925, four new theatres, which still exist, opened each year; in 1927 five opened. And this does not include those theatres since torn down. The building boom stopped with the Depression and not until 1972 did a new house open in the Broadway district.

PLAYHOUSES OF THE PAST

Because of New York City's inclination to keep building at all costs, many famous playhouses of yesteryear have disappeared, both in the present Theatre District and about town. More encouraging, there are several glorious theatres of the past that are still standing, but are hiding. Here are some of the most memorable New York theatres no longer in operation as legitimate theatres.

The **Bijou Theatre** on West 45th Street is remembered today as one of the three historic theatres torn down in 1982, amid much controversy, to make way for the Marquis hotel and theatre. The playhouse opened in 1917 but was always too small to house a major hit. During the Depression it became a movie house but returned as a legitimate house in 1973; its chief claim to fame was as home of the long-running *Mummenchanz* mime and mask attraction.

The **Bowery Theatre** opened in 1826 as the New York Theatre, Bowery, but it was commonly called the Bowery Theatre during its long life. The theatre was built on the site of the Bull's Head Theatre on the lower east side of Manhattan and, like many theatres of its day, it suffered a series of fires followed by a series of rebuilding. In its heyday, the Bowery Theatre was home to such popular stage personalities as Edwin Forrest and Charlotte Cushman. When the theatre was rebuilt for the third time in 1838, the theatre district had moved elsewhere and the Bowery became known for its low melodramas and rough clientele. By 1879 it was renamed the Thalia and catered to German, Yiddish, and other ethnic plays. When it burnt down once again in 1929 the theatre disappeared forever.

The **Casino Theatre** was built in 1882 to house musicals, the first theatre in America designed and erected with the new form of entertainment in mind. It was located on Broadway at 39th Street and had seats for 1,300 patrons. A roof garden was later added, the first in the city. *Florodora* was presented here as well as *The Passing Show*, the first American musical revue. By the 1920s all the new theatres were being built north of 42nd Street and the Casino was soon neglected. The Depression was the final blow and the theatre was demolished in 1930.

The **Comedy Theatre** was one of the Shubert Brothers' first properties in New York City. It was located on West 41st Street and opened in 1909. But once the theatre district moved north, the Comedy was hard to book, and by the Depression, it was closed. But the playhouse saw new life in 1935 when Orson Welles and the Federal Theatre Project took over and renamed it the Mercury Theatre. During his brief put potent reign there, Welles staged his landmark productions of *Doctor Faustus* and *Julius Caesar*. The Mercury Theatre became the Artef Theatre in 1939 and staged Yiddish plays until the playhouse was razed in 1942.

The **Earl Carroll Theatre** was located on Seventh Avenue at 50th Street and was managed by the famed producer-director-songwriter of the theatre's name. The playhouse opened in 1922 but was too small for the kind of musical productions Carroll had in mind. He razed the theatre in 1927 and built a larger one on the same site. The new Art Deco Earl Carroll Theatre had the most up-to-date air conditioning system of its day and even furnished small lights at each orchestra seat so patrons could refer to their programs during the show. The theatre's elevator stage, indirect lighting, and other features were all copied later when Radio City Music Hall was built. Carroll presented his lavish musical revues in the new theatre but the house was never a financial success. Later producers Florenz Ziegfeld, George White, and Billy Rose all attempted to make the ornate theatre work, changing the name and even turning it into a Folies

Begere-like casino cabaret. In 1939 a portion of the site was razed for the construction of an office building. Parts of the auditorium and stage still remain as renovated retail space.

The **Empire Theatre** was, for nearly sixty years, possibly Broadway's most prestigious house and more great stars performed here than perhaps any other Broadway theatre. It was built in 1893 by Charles Frohman and Al Hayman and stood on Broadway at 40th Street. Most of its productions during its first few decades were European imports; major works by Pinero, Shaw, Barrie, and others made their American debuts at the Empire. After Frohman's death in 1915, the theatre presented mostly American plays and performers from Ethel Barrymore to Katherine Cornell to Julie Harris graced the Empire's stage. In addition to being one of the most beloved playhouses in New York, the Empire was instrumental in many areas. It had an unusually large and elegant lobby and superb sight lines. It was the first theatre in New York constructed to use electricity rather than gas (though it also had a gas backup system) and, later, the first to have an outdoor electric sign. The Empire was also the first theatre built in New York after the passing of the 1892 fire code, making it the safest playhouse of its day. Among the famous productions that played the Empire were the original *Peter Pan* starring Maude Adams, John Guilgud's *Hamlet*, and *Life With Father*, the longest running play in Broadway history. *The Time of the Cuckoo* starring Shirley Booth was the last production presented at the Empire. It was demolished in 1953 and an office building now stands on the site.

The **Fifth Avenue Theatre** was actually located on 24th Street but named after the famous Fifth Avenue Hotel nearby. It was built in 1862 as a stock exchange but was turned into a theatre in 1865 where George Christy's Minstrels performed. Producer Augustin Daly took over the theatre in 1869 and it became home to his famous theatre company until the structure burnt down in 1873.

The new **Fifth Avenue Theatre** was a remodeled version of an earlier theatre, Gilsey's Apollo Hall on 28th Street, which producer Augustin Daly renovated in 1873 for his prestigious theatre company after the old Fifth Avenue Theatre burnt down. He retained the theatre's name even though it was not located anywhere near Fifth Avenue. Both the theatre and the company thrived here until 1878 when Daly retired and the Fifth Avenue went on to house various productions, the most famous being the world premiere of *The Pirates of Penzance*. When the Fifth Avenue Theatre suffered a fire in 1891, it was rebuilt as a vaudeville house, later a movie theatre, and finally a burlesque house before it was torn down in 1938.

The **Forty-Eighth Street Theatre** was built in 1912 and during the next fifty years changed names and venues many times. It was located on West 48th Street, a good location, but the theatre had a troubled history all the same. The most successful play to ever run here was the comedy *Harvey*. In 1955 the water tower on the roof collapsed and the water damage to the theatre was so great that the whole structure was torn down.

The **Forty-Fourth Street Theatre** was known as the Weber and Fields Music Hall when it opened in 1913 on West 44th Street and many of the theatre's great clowns, from Ed Wynn to the Marx Brothers, played here. It was named after its location when the Shubert Brothers bought it soon after it opened. The theatre was torn down in 1945 when the *New York Times* needed more space for its printing plant.

The **Gaiety Theatre** was built in 1909 by theatre czars Klaw and Erlanger for the showman George M. Cohan. The playhouse, located on Broadway between 45th and 46th Streets, boasted the first cantilevered balconies, which eliminated pillars and obstructed views. It was also notable for its sunken orchestra pit that allowed a lower stage and better sight lines. Despite some notable successes, the Gaiety became a movie house in 1926 and later a burlesque house. It was being used as a movie theatre again, called the Victoria, when it was torn down in 1982.

The **George Abbott Theatre**, named for the American theatre's most prolific and durable director-writer, opened as the Craig Theatre in 1928, just in time for the Depression. It took years for this theatre to pay off; as the Adelphi Theatre it saw some success in the 1930s and 1940s but by the 1950s it was a television and radio studio. Renamed the Fifty-Fourth Street Theatre (where it was located), the theatre returned as a legitimate house in 1958 but had no major hits before it was demolished in 1970. It was named after Abbott in 1968 but two years later it was gone. So sad for a theatre named after the man with the longest theatre career on record.

The **George M. Cohan Theatre** was built in 1911 by Cohan and his producing partner Sam H. Harris to house the great showman's works, and several of his plays and musicals were first produced here. The theatre was located on Broadway at 43rd Street and it housed all kinds of theatrical shows until it was demolished in 1938.

The **Harris Theatre** is another house that was run by Cohan and Harris and presented many of Cohan's shows. It opened on 42nd Street in 1914 as a movie house but almost immediately became the legitimate Candler Theatre. When Harris and Cohan ended their partnership in 1920, Harris renamed the theatre after himself. Perhaps the most famous production to play at the Harris Theatre was John Barrymore's *Hamlet* in 1922. The theatre became a movie house in the Depression and still stands today. Plans are to renovate it into a twin movie theatre.

The old **Helen Hayes Theatre** opened in 1911 as a nightclub that was quickly turned into the Fulton Theatre. Located on West 46th Street, the Fulton had a long history of hits when it was named after the beloved actress in 1955. Because Hayes was still alive in 1982 when a battle was waged to save the theatre from the wrecking ball, the theatre became the focal point of controversy and led the way to having historic theatres protected by the New York City Landmarks Preservation Commission. When the theatre was torn down in 1982 to make way for the Marriott Marquis Hotel, the developers offered to name their new theatre in the complex after Hayes. She declined and soon after the historic Little Theatre was given her name instead.

The **Hippodrome Theatre** was the largest and most modern theatre of its day, a huge 5,200-seat auditorium that could accommodate legitimate theatre, circuses, vaudeville, even aquatic entertainments. Located on Sixth Avenue between 43rd and 44th Streets, the colossal theatre opened in 1905 with great fanfare. The stage was 200 feet wide and could hold 600 performers. Beneath the stage were offices, costume shops, compartments for a whole menagerie of animals and a water tank above to provide a lake and a waterfall. Musical plays were produced at the Hippodrome, but the theatre was more successful with its spectacular entertainments and vaudeville programs. Because it was so expensive a house to operate, the theatre often had financial problems despite being one of the city's most popular entertainment attractions. The last success the Hippodrome saw was Rodgers and Hart's circus musical *Jumbo* in 1933. The theatre was demolished in 1939 and a parking garage and office building now stand on the site.

The **Hudson Theatre** was a spacious playhouse built by producer Henry B. Harris in 1903 in a prime location on West 44th Street. But the theatre had a difficult history, especially after Harris died on the *Titanic* in 1912 and his widow had trouble managing the house. After some memorable productions, such as *Hot Chocolates* (1929), the Hudson ceased to be a legitimate house during the Depression. It was a radio studio for awhile in the 1930s, returned as a theatre venue in 1937, was sold as a television studio in the 1950s, and briefly housed live theatre again in the 1960s. The Hudson still exists and in recent years has been a disco and a concert space. Because it was declared a landmark in 1987, it is hoped that the theatre will soon return to its rightful use.

The **John Street Theatre** was the first permanent playhouse in New York, opening in 1767 on John Street in lower Manhattan and remaining the premiere theatre in the city for thirty-one years. Patterned after the English playhouses, the John Street Theatre was constructed of wood and featured European imports for Loyalist New Yorkers. During the American Revolution, the theatre's name was changed to the Theatre Royal but reverted back to its original name after the war. The John Street Theatre housed the first truly American play, *The Contrast*, and was the home of Lewis Hallam's famous American Company. It was demolished in 1798.

Jolson's 59th Street Theatre experienced more name changes in its forty-year existence than perhaps any other Broadway theatre. It was built in 1921 by the Shuberts to feature their biggest star, Al Jolson. A few hits followed but not nearly as many as new names for the theatre. Located on Seventh Avenue between 58th and 59th Streets, the house was also known as The Shakespeare Theatre, the Venice Theatre, the Yiddish Art Theatre, the Molly Picon Theatre, the New Century Theatre, the NBC Theatre (as a television studio) and, in 1959, the odd but prophetic name the Video Tape Center. The multi-titled playhouse was demolished in 1961.

The **Lafayette Theatre** was the most famous theatre in Harlem and the home to important early productions in the history of black theatre. It opened in 1912 as a musical house but soon was the home for the innovative Lafayette Players who presented plays in repertory, ranging from Shakespeare to contemporary dramas about African-Americans. The company disbanded in 1932 but the Lafayette became an important center for the Federal Theatre Project and saw the mountings of several landmark productions in the 1930s. After years of hard times and occasionally being used as a church, the Lafayette burned down in 1968. An unusual feature of the theatre was a huge elm tree that stood in front of the theatre; black performers called it the "Tree of Hope" and touching it was supposed to bring luck.

The **Liberty Theatre** is not gone but has not been in operation as a legitimate theatre since 1932. Located on West 42nd Street, the Liberty opened in 1904 as a musical house and had a string of hits, such as *Little Johnny Jones*, *Lady, Be Good!* and editions of the *George White Scandals*. When the Depression hit, the Liberty became a vaudeville house, then a movie theatre, and then a porno film house. But still it sits there, waiting to be reborn. If the Times Square Development Plan has its way, it will be.

The **Lyceum Theatre** predates the present day Lyceum, though both were managed by producer Daniel Frohman. The old Lyceum was located on Fourth Avenue between 23rd and 24th Streets and was built in 1885 by producer-playwright Steele MacKaye who briefly presented plays there until Frohman took over. The electric lighting in the Lyceum Theatre was supervised by Thomas Edison himself and was considered the most modern of its day. When the theatre district moved uptown, the old Lyceum was neglected and was demolished in 1902.

The **Lyric Theatre** is another 42nd Street gem waiting to be rescued. The Renaissance-style theatre opened in 1903 and housed many famous operetta hits in the 1910s and 1920s. It became a movie house in 1933 and, except for removing the theatre boxes to add a wider screen, the Lyric is pretty much in tact. Like the Liberty, it is slated for restoration in the Times Square Redevelopment Plan.

The **Madison Square Theatre** was located on 24th Street and was built in 1879 by the ambitious Steele MacKay on the ruins of the recently burned old Fifth Avenue Theatre. The Madison Square Theatre was one of the most unique houses of its and any other era. It seated only 700 people and had the look and intimacy of a drawing room rather than a public theatre. The stage moved up and down for quick set changes, the orchestra was located in a box above the proscenium, and it even boasted an early form of air conditioning. Despite some early successes, MacKay lost the theatre and it was later managed by such figures as Daniel Frohman, Charles Hoyt, and Albert M. Palmer. The Madison Square

Theatre was torn down in 1908.

Maxine Elliott's Theatre was the most expensive theatre of its time, just as its namesake was considered the most ravishing beauty of her day. The actress, known as the "Venus de Milo with arms," commissioned the elaborate theatre and Lee Shubert paid the bills. The 1908 playhouse was located on West 39th Street between Broadway and Sixth Avenue, and featured such extravagances as running water, full carpeting, and full length mirrors in the dressing rooms. After a shaky start, the Elliott had its share of hits and saw such beloved actresses as Jane Cowl, Jeanne Eagels, and Helen Hayes on its stage. The theatre became a radio studio in 1941, then later a television studio before it was demolished in 1959.

The **Morosco Theatre** was home to such distinguished dramas as *Death of a Salesman* and *Cat on a Hot Tin Roof* and was a favorite of both actors and audiences. Built in 1917 by the Shubert Brothers, it was located on West 45th Street and named in honor of West Coast producer Oliver Morosco. Used almost exclusively for non-musical plays, the Morosco was still a very marketable house when it was razed, against much protest, with the Bijou and old Helen Hayes theatres in 1982 to make way for the Marquis hotel and theatre.

The **New Theatre** was built in 1909 in the hopes of establishing a home for a national theatre company. J. P. Morgan and Otto Kahn were among the entrepeneural citizens who backed the venture and built the large and ornate theatre on Central Park West between 62nd and 63rd Streets. Despite some memorable productions, the repertory idea was soon scrapped and the theatre, now called the Century Theatre, housed musicals by Florenz Ziegfeld and Charles Dillingham, as well as mammoth dramatic productions by Max Reinhardt. But its odd location and expensive operating costs forced the theatre to close down and it was demolished in 1930.

The **Olympia Music Hall** was responsible, more than any other theatre, for establishing Times Square as the theatre center in New York. Impresario Oscar Hammerstein I built the huge complex on Broadway between 44th and 45th Streets in 1895. It contained three theatres seating over 6,000 people, a Turkish bath, billiard rooms, a restaurant, a bowling alley, and New York's first roof garden. The enterprise was never a financial success and it changed ownership several times, ending up as a movie house in 1914. The entire complex was demolished in 1935 and the Criterion Center now stands on the site.

The **Park Theatre** was, more than any other theatre, responsible for making New York the theatrical center of America. It was located on Park Row and opened in 1798 to replace the John Street Theatre. For twenty-five years it was the only playhouse in New York, but as the city grew and other theatres were built the Park remained the center of attention with a series of successes and long runs. Under the management of Stephen Price, the thriving theatre represented New York theatre, featuring the premiere productions of such plays as *Fashion* and *London Assurance*. Although the Park Theatre had been previously reconstructed after several minor fires, it burnt to the ground in 1845 and never rose again.

The **Princess Theatre** was an intimate little playhouse on 39th Street that became famous for the series of sophisticated and innovative musicals that premiered here. The theatre was built in 1913 as a venue for one-act plays, but Jerome Kern and Guy Bolton (and later P. G. Wodehouse) found the space ideal for the small-scale, contemporary musicals that they started presenting in 1915. The popularity of shows such as *Very Good Eddie* and *Oh, Boy!* made the series (dubbed the Princess Theatre musicals) and the theatre famous. During the Depression the theatre became a movie house; in 1937 it was renamed the Labor Stage and housed the long-running musical revue *Pins and Needles*. After reverting back to a movie house in the 1950s, the Princess Theatre was torn down in 1955 and an office building was constructed on the site.

The **Punch and Judy Theatre** was a small (and usually unsuccessful) theatre that producer Charles Hopkins built on West 49th Street in 1914. Despite a few hits, the little playhouse floundered so Hopkins renamed it the Charles Hopkins Theatre in 1926 to capitalize on his name recognition with the public. It did little good and the Depression finished the theatre off. It became a movie house and eventually a porno film house until it was demolished in 1987.

The **Selwyn Theatre** is another elegant 42nd Street theatre waiting to be rescued. It opened in 1918 and was named after its builder, the producer Arch Selwyn. Designed in the Italian Renaissance style, the lovely theatre has a terra-cotta facade that covers the exterior of the theatre as well as the office building adjoining it. The Selwyn is a musical house with excellent sight lines and a spacious lobby. It housed legitimate theatre productions until the Depression when it became a movie house. It may yet return as a legitimate theatre if the Times Square Redevelopment Plan is carried out.

The **Times Square Theatre** enjoyed thirteen years of hit plays and musicals. The 42nd Street playhouse opened in 1920 and featured a silver, black, and green auditorium in the Adam style. It was a legitimate house until 1933 when it became a movie house and remains one to this day, although there are plans to refurbish it back into a theatre.

The **Union Square Theatre** was the home of some of the most popular romantic dramas of the late 1800s. The playhouse was located on 14th Street between Broadway and Fourth Avenue and opened in 1871 as a variety house. But producer A. M. Palmer turned it into a legitimate theatre with productions that rivaled the best in town. *The Two Orphans* and *Camille* were among the most popular attractions before Palmer brought his company uptown and the Union Square Theatre floundered. After a fire in 1888, the theatre was rebuilt as a vaudeville house, later reduced to burlesque and movies. The Union Square Theatre is not totally gone today; the shell of the structure still stands on 14th Street.

The **Victoria Theatre** was the most famous vaudeville house in New York until the Palace Theatre stole its thunder. The theatre, located at 42nd Street and Seventh Avenue, opened in 1899 as a legitimate theatre but producer-manager Oscar Hammerstein I had more success with it as a home for original (and sometimes notorious) specialty acts. The structure has been a movie house since 1935.

The **Ziegfeld Theatre**, with its sleek and modern design by Joseph Urban and spacious egg-shaped auditorium devoid of boxes and right angles, was one of the most unique and beautiful theatres ever built in New York. The new theatre was financed by William Randolph Hearst who owned the Sixth Avenue and 54th Street site, and producer Florenz Ziegfeld brought in his favorite scenic designer Urban as architect. The theatre opened in 1927 after much publicity and hype. Among the many distinguishing features of the large house was the gigantic mural, "The Joy of Living" by Lillian Gaertner, which was said to be the largest oil painting in the world. While Ziegfeld continued to present his annual *Follies* at the New Amsterdam Theatre, he used his namesake theatre to present book musicals, the most famous among them being *Show Boat*. After Ziegfeld's death the theatre became a movie house, but producer Billy Rose restored the Ziegfeld as a legitimate theatre in 1944 and it went on to house more famous musicals. The theatre struggled through the 1960s, operating briefly as a television studio in 1965; when Rose died, it was sold as part of his estate and torn down in 1967 to make way for a skyscraper.

DEPARTED THEATRE DISTRICT LANDMARKS

There were many non-theatre structures in the Times Square area that were famous nationwide and did much to create the Broadway mystique. Here are some of the most memorable; all, alas, are now gone.

Astor Hotel   During its heyday, this eleven-story luxury hotel on Broadway between 44th and 45th Streets was the most famous hotel in New York. The lovely Times Square landmark opened in 1904 and lodged and entertained the world's celebrities for over half a century. During its existence the hotel was renovated several times to keep up with the changing tastes of the rich and famous. The Grand Ballroom, built during a 1944 renovation, was the largest in New York for many years. By the 1960s the hotel became a financial burden and it was demolished in 1967. The Minskoff Theatre and skyscraper now stand on the site.

The Automat   An innovative new concept in dining out graced the theatre district for over half a century and many thought of it as the food service of the future. Entrees, desserts, salads, and other selections were kept in coin-operated glass cubicles and the patrons helped themselves without the need of menus or waiters. The idea originated in Germany and the first successful Automat opened in Philadelphia in 1902. But it was the Times Square Automat, opening in 1912 with much fanfare, that was the most famous. Located on Broadway between 46th and 47th Street, the Automat catered to businessmen, theatre and movie patrons, tourists, and families. The food was wholesome and inexpensive and the variety was quite extensive. The Automat craze reached its peak of popularity during the 1940s when there were nearly fifty Automats in New York City. By the 1960s the introduction of fast food chains and the deterioration of the Times Square area hurt the Automat and by 1969 the last one was gone.

Cafe de L'Opera Before World War One, this cabaret on the corner of 42nd Street and Eighth Avenue was one of the most celebrated in the country. The intimate club, patterned after Paris's Cafe de Paris, was particularly famous for the dances, such as the Castle Walk, that were introduced here and soon spread across the country.

Diamond Horseshoe Impresario Billy Rose operated this cabaret-theatre on West 46th Street and produced the Gay Nineties-style shows that played there. The intimate theatre opened in 1938 and operated successfully until 1951 when it was turned into a traditional theatre, first called the Mayfair and later the Century Theatre. The space still exists in the basement of the Century-Paramount Hotel.

Lambs Club The oldest theatre club for actors in America, the Lambs was founded in 1874 and was housed in various locations until the club opened a permanent home in 1904 on 44th Street. The new home had facilities for the club as well as a small theatre, both designed by Stanford White. The Lambs Club still exists but financial difficulties forced the sale of the building in 1974.

Latin Quarter This nightclub on Broadway between Seventh Avenue and 48th Street went by several names over its long history but it was always in the news. From 1936 to 1940, it housed the downtown version of the Cotton Club, featuring the greatest black entertainers of the day. It became the Latin Quarter in 1942 and was considered the most sophisticated of New York nightclubs, famous for its celebrities in the house and chorus girls on the stage. The club dwindled in the 1950s and closed for good in 1969. The space was turned into a small theatre in the 1970s but had little success and the whole block was demolished in 1990.

Leblang's Ticket Office Hungarian immigrant Joe Leblang owned a tobacco shop downtown and started selling the ticket passes that he and other merchants got from producers for posting advertisements in their windows. The business grew, and in the 1910s Leblang opened up Times Square's first ticket agency in the basement of Gray's Drug Store on Broadway and 43rd Street. Soon theatre box offices were sending him unsold tickets a few hours before curtain, and Leblang sold them on commission. The establishment continued after Leblang's death in 1931 and existed until the late 1940s.

Lindy's The theatre district's most famous delicatessen, this eatery located on Broadway at 51st Street was a favorite of theatre stars as well as theatre patrons. Lindy's was famous for its cheesecake and its humorously rude waiters. The owner Leo Lindy was also a local favorite, catering to the odd requests of his beloved patrons and not charging actors who were on the outs. The restaurant was in operation from 1921 until 1957.

Mamma Leone's Ristorante This popular eatery existed for decades in three different locations. The original site in 1906 was in the Leone family's living room on West 34th Street and seated only twenty people. When the business moved to West 48th Street in 1926, it occupied eleven dining rooms and could accommodate 1,250 patrons. This was the Mamma Leone's that New Yorkers and tourists patronized for over sixty years. Filled with statues, fountains, and other kitschy items, the festive restaurant was reminiscent of Murray's Roman Gardens. In 1988 Mamma Leone's moved to Eighth Avenue and 44th Street and was part of the Milford Plaza Hotel until it folded in 1994.

Murray's Roman Gardens This 42nd Street restaurant was a big hit in the 1910s and early 1920s. The classy eatery was decorated in pseudo-Roman decor with dozens of statues and a revolving floor. In 1925 the restaurant closed and the space became the home of the famous Hubert's Flea Circus, a bizarre attraction that lasted until 1975.

Rector's Restaurant At the turn of the century, there was no New York restaurant more elegant than this fine institution located on Broadway at 44th Street. Covered with mirrors and chandeliers, Rector's opened in 1899 and for the next decade it was the most famous "lobster palace" in the city. But its success was short-lived. A hit play in 1909 titled *The Girl From Rector's* told a fictional tale of a married woman who lived a life of sin and patronized the restaurant, and soon Rector's had a reputation for catering to loose women. Prohibition also hurt the restaurant and it closed in 1919.

Ripley's Wax Museum A popular Times Square attraction in the 1950s and 1960s, Ripley's was located on Broadway at 43rd Street and was a tourist favorite. Its chamber of horrors, known as the Odditorium, was a particular favorite. The museum closed in 1971 but outlets in Niagara Falls, Los Angeles, and other tourist meccas still exist.

Roxy Theatre The largest and most opulent movie theatre of its day, the Roxy was located at 50th Street and Seventh Avenue and had seats for over 6,000 patrons. It opened in 1927 as "the Cathedral of the Motion Picture" and featured stage spectaculars as well as films. Like all movie palaces, the Roxy struggled through the 1950s and the interior was renovated to accommodate various wide-screen experiments. The famous landmark closed and was demolished in 1960.

Stage Door Canteen The American Theatre Wing operated eight Stage Door Canteens to serve food and provide entertainment for servicemen during World War Two. But none was as famous as the New York Stage Door Canteen, located underneath Sardi's Restaurant on 44th Street. Between 1942 and 1945, the Canteen was hosted by hundreds of volunteers from the theatre, many of them stars, who catered to as many as 4,000 enlisted men each night.

Wiennig and Sberber's Restaurant A favorite eatery for actors and other theatre district personnel, this restaurant located on 45th Street was a bit rowdy but much loved. Like Lindy's, the establishment was as famous for its colorful proprietors, the two men of the restaurant's name, and its comical waiters as it was for its food. Weinnig and Sberber's flourished from the 1910s to the late 1920s.

OTHER LOST LANDMARKS

Although not in the Theatre District, some structures were closely connected to the theatre business. Here are some departed theatrical landmarks that were located outside the Times Square area.

American Museum More a lecture hall than a traditional museum, this institution on Chambers Street opened in 1810 and offered lectures and performances of various types. The museum relocated several times and became most famous as Barnum's American Museum at Broadway and Ann Street. In addition to Barnum's display of oddities, the museum also had a 3,000-seat auditorium that presented shows, most memorably *The Drunkard*, which ran over 100 performances in the 1850s. After a fire in 1865, the museum was rebuilt but an 1868 fire destroyed the building forever.

Cain's Warehouse From the 1890s until 1938, this warehouse specialized in storing scenery from Broadway shows that had closed until it could be rented to stock or touring companies. Hence, the expression "go to Cain's" became a euphemism for closing a show.

Dazian's Theatrical Emporium What started out as a dry goods supplier in 1842 became the leading costumer for Broadway for many years. Dazian's supplied the costumes for *The Black Crook* (1866) and other famous shows up until 1919 when owner Wolf Dazian died and the company began to supply the fabrics for other costume houses to construct.

Little Church Around the Corner This Episcopal church on 29th Street has been the sight of many marriages and funerals of actors and other theatre personnel since the 1870s. The church got its nickname in 1870 when friends of actor George Holland went to arrange funeral services at a nearby church and were refused on the grounds of the deceased's profession. But they were recommended to try the "little church around the corner."

Niblo's Garden What started as an outdoor garden theatre in 1828 eventually became New York's premiere home for musical entertainment. The original garden theatre was located at Broadway and Prince Street. The enterprise was so successful that owner William Niblo built a larger, permanent structure on the site and called it Niblo's Garden and Theatre. Because it was located in what was considered a northern suburb at the time, Niblo ran stagecoaches from the Battery to the Garden for his patrons. It was at Niblo's Garden that *The Black Crook* (1866), America's first musical, was presented and it made the theatre famous. After some fires and rebuilding, Niblo's was demolished in 1895 when it was still the oldest playhouse in New York.

Pfaff's Restaurant   A small saloon on lower Broadway built in the late 1850s and owned by Charles Pfaff, this popular watering hole soon started attracting theatre celebrities as well as writers and intellectuals so Pfaff expanded the place into a legitimate restaurant. When the Theatre District moved uptown, Pfaff also moved, opening a new restaurant on West 24th Street where it operated successfully as the Sardi's of its day until it closed in 1887.

Rehearsal Club   More a boarding house than a club, this establishment was founded in 1913 as a place where young actresses could find food and lodgings at a reasonable rate. The Club served as the inspiration for the Footlights Club in the hit play *Stage Door* (1936). The Club closed in 1980.

EXISTING THEATRICAL LANDMARKS IN NEW YORK

It is comforting to realize that some equally famous establishments are still around to be enjoyed and treasured. Here are some favorite theatre-related structures.

Algonquin Hotel   A favorite theatre district fixture since 1902, the Algonquin was not only a popular hotel but also the permanent home for many famous theatre and literary folk. Located on West 44th Street, the European-style hotel still exists pretty much as it did in the legendary days of the Algonquin Round Table in the 1920s. The dining room where the great American wits met for lunch is also intact, as is the comfortable lobby that seems not to have changed with time.

Brill Building   This art deco-style building completed in 1930 was the center of music publishing in America until the 1960s. Located at Broadway and 49th Street, the building housed all the major publishers of sheet music and was the headquarters for the popular music industry known as Tin Pan Alley. Most companies relocated to other parts of town or to the West Coast in the 1960s but the elegant building remains and is still in use.

Friars Club   Although this private theatrical club has been in existence since 1904, it did not move into its present home on East 55th Street until 1958. In its heyday the Friars presented annual shows called the Frolics to raise money for charity. Today's members come from all branches of the entertainment business.

Players Club   The Players Club was founded in 1888 by Edwin Booth as a private club for actors and dramatists, similar to the Garrick Club in London.

Architect Stanford White redesigned a house on Gramercy Park into the home of the Players Club and it has been there ever since. Among the features at the club is the Walter Hampden Memorial Library, one of the largest theatre research libraries in the country.

Roseland There used to many dance halls up and down Broadway but only one is left today: Roseland, the largest of them all. The first Roseland dance hall opened in 1919 and was located on 51st Street and Broadway. It was an immediate success and managed to withstand Prohibition and the Great Depression. In 1956 the new Roseland opened on 52nd Street with an even bigger dance floor and a restaurant that could seat 700. In the basement of Roseland is a Wall of Fame featuring displays on the many great dancers who graced the famous dance floor in the past.

Sardi's Restaurant The most famous of all theatre restaurants, Sardi's has been open to the public at its location on West 44th Street since 1927. The tradition of gathering at Sardi's on opening nights to party and await the reviews only began in 1950 with the play *Come Back Little Sheba* and still continues to this day. The tradition of putting caricatures of famous theatrical folk on the walls goes back to 1929 and also continues today.

Times Tower No building symbolizes Times Square more than this 1904 building used as the focal point of the annual New Year's Eve celebration. Wishing to copy the *Herald*'s location on Herald Square, the *New York Times* build this twenty-five story headquarters on 42nd Street and Broadway, which was known as Longacre Square, and renamed the crossroads Times Square. The early skyscraper (only the Flatiron Building predates it) towered above the other buildings in the area for many years. In 1913 the *Times* moved to larger quarters on 43rd Street but retained ownership of the tower until 1961. In 1966 the Times Tower was renovated with a marble exterior and was known as the Allied Chemical Building after its new owners. When it was sold again in 1974 the build was renamed One Times Square.

TKTS Booth This small structure located on a traffic island in Duffy Square (between Seventh Avenue and 47th Street) has sold millions of dollars of discount theatre tickets since it opened in 1973. Operated by the non-profit Theatre Development Fund, the TKTS Booth sells reduced-price tickets for shows not sold out that day.

COLORFUL BROADWAY CHARACTERS

Not all of the theatre district's memorable personalities were on the stage. Here are some of the more colorful people not necessarily in the theatre profession who made Broadway distinctive.

Bugs Baer (1886-1969) was one of New York's most popular and funniest columnists, a sly reporter who covered the Times Square district for various newspapers. Arthur Baer got the nickname "Bugs" from the cartoons he drew for the *Washington Times*, but he was mostly known for his columns in *The New York World*, *The New York American*, and the *World Journal Tribune*. At one time he was writing columns for competing newspapers, using the pseudonym Graham Wire so that tycoon publisher William Randolph Hearst would not find out. Perhaps Bugs Baer's most famous quote: "Paying alimony is like buying oats for a dead horse."

Robert Benchley (1889-1945) wore so many hats it's hard to know how to classify him. He was one of America's greatest humorists with hundreds of short stories and essays to his credit. He was also theatre critic for *The New Yorker*, the old *Life Magazine* and others, as well as an editor for *Vanity Fair*. Benchley occasionally performed on stage and in film and was one of the brightest wits at the Algonquin Round Table in the 1920s. He was consistently beloved by the theatre community even though he served as a critic for many years.

Diamond Jim Brady (1856-1917) was one of New York's most colorful millionaires and such a favorite in the Theatre District that he was dubbed the King of the Great White Way. Brady made his money in railroads and enjoyed displaying his wealth and high style of living more than anyone else. In the 1890s he was often seen at the best restaurants and theatre openings, always with a beautiful bejeweled woman. Lillian Russell was his favorite companion for several years. His nickname came from his love of diamonds; it was rumored that he owned 26,000 of them, and he was never seen without a diamond pin or cuff link or shirt stud. Brady was also a notorious glutton, known to eat thirty-six oysters just for lunch. He died of an intestinal ailment at the age of fifty-seven.

Legs Diamond (1896-1931) was a notorious gangster who owned the Hotsy Totsy Club in the Theatre District and used it as a front for his illegal operations. Generally hated, Diamond murdered his rivals and innocent witnesses. He, in turn, was murdered in Albany by his enemies. He was the subject of the unsuccessful 1988 musical *Legs Diamond*.

Abraham Ellis (1901-1985) was a self-made millionaire who was known as the Hatcheck King. Born in poverty, Ellis worked his way up by buying the concessions at theatres and hotels and instituting the idea of hat check girls and numbered claim checks. Many of the Times Square establishments were supplied by Ellis and he eventually bought property in the area as well. He served as the inspiration for a character in Damon Runyon's *Little Miss Marker*.

William J. Fallon (1886-1927) was a famous New York criminal lawyer and a flamboyant playboy who frequented the Times Square district with celebrities, most often with Texas Guinan. In the practice of law, Fallon was unscrupulous; he bribed jurors, sought publicity for his clients, and arranged for hung juries to delay verdicts. None of his 100 plus clients was ever executed, but

Fallon himself died of alcoholism at the age of 41.

Don Freeman (1908-1978) was a popular illustrator and newspaper cartoonist who depicted the hustle and bustle of the Theatre District. Freeman's sketches in *The New York Times* and the *Herald Tribune* in the 1930s and 1940s are vibrant portrayals of the theatre world. He was also a successful book illustrator and author of children's books.

Waxy Gordon (1888-1952) was a bootlegger and gangster who operated in the Times Square area and was a frequent investor in Broadway shows. Much as in the old cliché, Gordon would see that his latest girlfriend was placed in the chorus of the show he was backing.

Texas Guinan (?-1933) ran such successful speakeasies during Prohibition that she earned the title "Queen of Whoopee." Born in Texas, Guinan worked as a bronco buster and made some silent Western films before coming to New York as a chorus girl. After entertaining troops overseas during World War One, she became a favorite performer in clubs and eventually ran her own place. She counted among her close friends journalists, gangsters, and political figures, and she was such a beloved favorite that at her funeral 2,000 fans marched down Broadway as part of the procession.

Mark Hellinger (1903-1947) was one of New York's most popular columnists and the first to write exclusively about the Broadway scene. His writing was seen in several New York newspapers before he left for Hollywood in 1937 to write screenplays. Hellinger also wrote some 4,500 short stories and occasionally contributed sketches for Broadway revues. Much loved in the theatre community, a theatre was named in his honor after his death.

Abe Hummel (1850-1926) was one of the most famous of all New York City criminal lawyers and a favorite attorney for theatrical folk in the last decades of the nineteenth century. Born Abraham Henry Hummel in a Jewish neighborhood of Boston, Hummel worked his way through law school in record time and, together with famous lawyer William H. Howe, their firm became known as New York's cleverest and most successful. Although Hummel always wore black, he was a colorful character who befriended theatre celebrities such as Edwin Booth, Lillie Langtry, Henry Irving, and Maurice Barrymore, representing them in notorious legal cases. But Hummel's sometimes unethical practices eventually caught up with him and he was disbarred in 1905.

Lucky Luciano (1897-1962) was a famous gangster and one of the prime figures of the Broadway Mob who provided liquor to all the speakeasies in the Times Square district. Luciano was a very public celebrity and was seen in all the area's clubs and theatres.

Maury Paul (1890-1942) was the real name of Cholly Knickerbocker, the society columnist who covered the New York scene for twenty-five years. Although Paul wrote for a variety of New York newspapers, his syndicated column was popular across the nation. He was greatly responsible for how the country viewed Broadway during the 1920s and 1930s.

Damon Runyon (1884-1946) created a mythical Times Square in his stories that was so endearing that it's hard to believe it was not real. As a newspaper columnist with Broadway as his beat, Runyon took the real gangsters, prizefighters, show girls, gamblers, and other colorful Times Square types and gave them a comic-romantic edge that can only be described as Runyonesque. Runyon was known primarily as a sports writer but he covered the nightlife of Manhattan for various newspapers and sold his stories to the best magazines of the day. Aside from inspiring the musical comedy classic *Guys and Dolls* (1950), Runyon's stories were turned into no less than sixteen movies.

Ed Sullivan (1902-1974) is remembered for his long-running television variety show, but in the 1930s and 1940s he was one of New York's most influential newspaper columnists, powerful enough to make or break shows and stars. Never a formal drama critic, Sullivan expressed his opinions freely in his column and later produced some Broadway revues himself. By 1947 he was on television, but he always kept his eye on the theatre scene and, through his Sunday television show, brought Broadway to the rest of America more than any one individual ever has.

Walter Winchell (1897-1972) was the most powerful of all the New York columnists and a very controversial figure because of his ability to create or destroy careers. Writing for various newspapers and then later on the radio, Winchell waged celebrated feuds in public; some genuine, others pure publicity ploys. He enjoyed his celebrity and was very visible at the Stork Club and other sophisticated New York haunts. As the number of New York newspapers diminished in the 1960s and his kind of column disappeared, Winchell fought to remain in the public eyes but he eventually faded from sight.

Alexander Woollcott (1887-1946) was a notable drama critic but such a flamboyant character that he became a Broadway legend in his time. Remembered today as the inspiration for the character of Sheridan Whiteside in *The Man Who Came to Dinner* (1939), Woollcott was also one of the famous wits at the Algonquin Round Table in the 1920s and a very popular radio personality in the 1930s. Often accused of being a sentimental or narrow-minded critic, he was ruthless in his opinions and even fought the powerful Shubert syndicate in his early years as a reviewer. There is no question his writing style was of days past but Woollcott had a vitality that was found in few writers of the day.

NEW YORK THEATRE COMPANIES PAST AND PRESENT

While most think of Broadway shows when they think of theatre in New York, there have been many theatre companies, both commercial and non-profit, that presented quality theatre over the decades. It is rare for one company to last very long but the impact of these groups was often quite significant. Here is a selective list of some of the more notable New York theatre companies of this century that no longer exist.

The **Actor's Workshop** was very popular in the 1950s as a home for political plays and modern avant-garde classics. Founded by Herbert Blau and Jules Irving in 1952, The Actor's Workshop encouraged each actor in the company to pursue his or her own individual approach to performance. The company folded after its originators left to head the new Lincoln Center Theatre in 1965.

The **American Repertory Theatre** only lasted one season but it was a bold attempt to establish a national theatre on the order of London's Old Vic. Cheryl Crawford, Eva Le Gallienne, and Margaret Webster founded the company in 1946 and attracted distinguished actors for an ambitious season. But its odd location on Columbus Circle and lack of audience interest did not allow it to continue.

ARTEF is an acronym from the Yiddish for "Workers' Theatre Group," an ethnic company that flourished in the 1930s. Most of the theatre's plays were political in nature and used non-professional actors, usually laborers, who brought a powerful vitality to the agitprop productions. The group officially disbanded in 1937 but some members continued to present productions under the ARTEF name.

Association of Producing Artists was more popularly known for its acronym APA and under this name presented some of New York's most memorable revivals of the 1960s. Director Ellis Rabb founded the company in 1960 and it was housed in various cities across the nation before settling in New York in 1964. With Rabb directing most of the productions and Rosemary Harris as its principal actress, APA presented striking revivals of both American and foreign classics. The company's last hit, *The Show-Off* (1967) with Helen Hayes, was popular on Broadway and on the road.

Cafe Cino was not a formal theatre company but a coffee house in Greenwich Village that owner Joe Cino used to feature new playwrights in the avant-garde movement. The little venue flourished from 1959 to 1967 and is considered the first Off-Off-Broadway theatre.

The **Circle Repertory Company** was one of the most respected of the New York companies dedicated to new works and, from its establishment in 1969 to its demise in 1996, it sent many plays on to Broadway and the West End in London. The company was founded by an actress (Tanya Berezin), an actor (Rob Thirkield), a director (Marshall W. Mason), and a playwright (Lanford Wilson). Mason was the Artistic Director for many years and Wilson had no less than twenty of his plays premiered at the Circle Rep.

The **Civic Repertory Theatre** was an ambitious venture started by actress/director Eva Le Gallienne in 1926 to establish a true repertory company in New York City. The actors played a variety of roles during one season and a mixture of American and foreign plays were rotated at the 14th Street Theatre. Despite several fine productions over the years, the company's low ticket prices, the expense of repertory, and the Depression forced the theatre to close in 1933.

Dramatists' Theatre, Inc. was a short-lived theatre company founded in 1923 by Owen Davis, Arthur Richman, and other playwrights as a venue for their work. After a promising start the company floundered and in fours years it was gone.

The **Equity Library Theatre** presented free performances of plays in libraries throughout the city to offer a training ground for young actors and directors and to foster new audiences for live theatre. The company was founded in 1943 by Sam Jaffe and George Freedley and in 1949 they added the Lennox Hill Playhouse as their home base. After hundreds of productions that gave many artists their start in the profession, the company folded in 1990.

Equity Players was a theatre company founded by the young Actors' Equity union in 1922 as a showcase for their members. The group presented several interesting revivals in the 1920s then was absorbed by Kenneth MacGowan's theatre company in Greenwich Village.

The **Experimental Theatre** was an early non-profit theatre that was launched in 1940 but did not start presenting plays until 1947. The company was under the direction of the American National Theatre and Academy (ANTA) and presented top actors who worked at reduced salaries. Some of the early productions were quite impressive but the company lasted only a few seasons.

The **Federal Theatre Project** was a national relief program established in 1935 by an act of Congress. There were theatres established across the country but much attention was put on the New York branch, which included such famous companies as the Living Newspaper (documentary dramas about issues in the news) and several black theatres that performed in Harlem. The whole program was closed by Congress in 1939 because of the leftist nature of some of the projects and the fear of propaganda in the arts.

The **Group Theatre** was founded in 1931 by Harold Clurman, Cheryl Crawford, and Lee Strasberg, three members of the Theatre Guild who hoped to present more politically oriented plays. The company was dedicated to leftist ideas but managed to attract some of the most potent playwrights and actors of the day. Before the Group Theatre disbanded in 1940, it had produced dozens of important works, most memorably *Awake and Sing!* (1935), *Waiting for Lefty* (1935), *Johnny Johnson* (1936), *Golden Boy* (1937), and *My Heart's in the Highlands* (1939).

The **Lafayette Players** was an adventurous company of black actors, directors, and playwrights housed in Harlem's famous Lafayette Theatre from 1915 to 1932. The company staged plays about contemporary black life as well as the classics, and some distinguished African-American actors first made a name for themselves there.

The **Living Theatre Company** was a controversial ensemble founded in 1947 by Julian Beck and Judith Malina that presented challenging theatre with sociopolitical beliefs. While many of the European avant garde writers were often revived, the company's most famous production was Jack Gelber's *The Connection* (1959), a searing look at drug addition done in an environmental setting. The company folded in 1963 but Beck and Malina resurfaced under the name of the Living Theatre several times since then.

The **Mercury Theatre** was an exciting classical theatre company founded by Orson Welles and John Houseman in 1937. The repertory company sometimes chose unusual pieces from world literature, such as *The Shoemaker's Holiday* and *Danton's Death*, but the results were always fascinating. The Mercury's most famous production was the modern dress *Macbeth* that Welles directed and starred in. The theatre disbanded in 1938 when Welles and other members moved on to radio and film, but most of the company was seen in the film *Citizen Kane* (1941).

The **Neighborhood Playhouse** was an amateur theatre company founded in 1915 that went professional in 1920 and presented productions by the best contemporary playwrights. The company was disbanded in 1927 but productions under the Neighborhood Playhouse appeared occasionally for years after. The Neighborhood Playhouse School of Theatre, one of the finest training programs in the city, is still in existence.

The **New Theatre** was a highly ambitious attempt to create a permanent repertory company in New York on a grand scale but, despite the money and prestige behind the venture, the project failed. J. P. Morgan and Otto Kahn were the New Theatre's principal backers and in 1909 they hired the finest architects, Carrere and Hastings, to build a large and lavish theatre on Central Park West, far from the traditional Theatre District of the time. The playhouse was a marvel and the company's opening production, Julia Marlowe and E. H. Sothern in *Antony and Cleopatra*, was a class act. But the theatre's awkward location and the expense of operating the huge playhouse soon forced the New Theatre to abandon repertory and, eventually, to fold completely.

The **Phoenix Theatre** was an admirable theatre company that, like its name suggested, rose from financial difficulties on a couple of occasions to survive yet another season. The company was founded in 1953 by T. Edward Hambleton and Norris Houghton and in its own theatre space, the old Yiddish Art Theatre, they staged classic revivals, new American plays, and even original musicals. In 1961 financial pressures forced the Phoenix to abandon its home base and move into a smaller space. The theatre resurged again in the mid-1960s under the direction of Ellis Rabb and offered many notable revivals. By the 1970s its troubles returned and the theatre struggled on until it finally closed in 1982.

The **Playwrights' Company** was founded in 1938 by five prominent playwrights (Maxwell Anderson, S. N. Behrman, Sidney Howard, Elmer Rice, and Robert E. Sherwood) as a venue where their work could be produced without the interference of commercial producers. For the next twenty years some of the finest plays by these and other playwrights were first seen at the Playwrights' Company. By 1960 most of the founders were deceased and the theatre company was dissolved.

The **Provincetown Players** originated in the Cape Cod town of its name in 1915 by summering New Yorkers who wanted to experiment with new forms of playwriting and design. The group relocated to their own home in Greenwich Village in 1917 and, presenting the early works of Eugene O'Neill and the scenic designs of Robert Edmond Jones, the little theatre became famous. Many renowned one-acts and full-length plays premiered at the Provincetown throughout the 1920s, and by the time it folded in 1929 it had initiated the Little Theatre movement in America. The historic theatre still sits on MacDougal Street and retains the old name.

The **Theatre Guild** was perhaps the most successful and influential of the New York theatre companies, presenting the best of old and new plays and musicals from 1919 up through the 1950s. Lawrence Langner, Theresa Helburn, and others founded the company in order to offer challenging theatre not normally seen on Broadway. Most of the productions during the early years were foreign plays but, with *The Adding Machine* in 1923, the group showed they could present the most innovative of American plays as well. The 1920s and early 1930s was the heyday of the Theatre Guild with dozens of famous productions written by the best American playwrights and some of the finest acting, direction, and design seen in this century. The Guild was facing financial ruin in the 1940s when its bold decision to invest everything in *Oklahoma!* (1943) saved the theatre and allowed it to continue. In 1950 the Theatre Guild was merged with the American National Theatre Academy (ANTA). A program called "Theatre Guild on the Air" presented acclaimed radio and television broadcasts of plays from 1945 to 1963.

The **Theatre Union** was a short-lived non-profit theatre company that produced leftist plays about strong social issues. The company lasted from 1932 to 1937 and often used the Civic Repertory Theatre's space for performances.

The **Washington Square Players** was begun in 1914 to foster new American playwrights, and early one-acts by Eugene O'Neill and Elmer Rice were first done here. During its short reign, the Washington Square Players gave several later-prominent actors and designers their start. The group disbanded in 1918 and several of its members helped start the new Theatre Guild.

The **Yiddish Art Theatre** survived from 1918 to 1950, presenting both classics and contemporary works in Yiddish. Founded by distinguished Yiddish actor Maurice Schwartz, the company was successful enough to build its own theatre on Second Avenue and was home to the very best Yiddish actors and directors.

Currently there are dozens of theatre companies in New York and, since the institution of Off Off Broadway in the 1970s, these little groups can be found throughout the city in a variety of spaces, from church basements to traditional theatres to warehouses. Few companies continue on for very long but several have presented a play or season that was the talk of the city. Here is a highly arbitrary list of some of the finest theatre companies currently operating in New York.

The **Acting Company** is one of the country's most respected professional touring companies. Founded in 1972 by John Houseman and Margot Henley as an offshoot of the drama division at Juilliard School, the Acting Company is based in and performs in New York and features young actors in the classics and, occasionally, new works.

The **Actor's Studio** is more a place for workshops than traditional performances but this home of Lee Strasberg's famous method acting does public presentations, usually by invitation only. The company was founded in 1947 by Cheryl Crawford, Elia Kazan and Robert Lewis to provide a place for professional actors to experiment and grow. From this little space on West 44th Street have come some of the most dynamic actors of the post-war American theatre.

The **American Jewish Theatre** has had a couple of different homes since it was founded in 1974 by Stanley Brechner but its goal to present Yiddish classics in translation, as well as new plays featuring Jewish themes, has been consistently fulfilled.

The **American Place Theatre** is dedicated to new works by American playwrights and many early works of Sam Shepard, Ed Bullins, Joyce Carol Oates, and others were first produced here. Founded in 1963 by Wynn Handman and Sidney Lanier, the theatre moved into its own home on the Avenue of the Americas in 1971. The American Place Theatre is not as active today as it was in the 1960s but it does house The Women's Project and hosts performance art pieces and theatre soloists.

Circle in the Square was founded in 1950 by Theodore Mann and José Quintero as a home for revivals of neglected American classics, and no other theatre company did more to bring about a reevaluation of Eugene O'Neill's works than this little arena stage on Sheridan Square. With their renowned revivals, such as *Summer and Smoke* (1952) and *The Iceman Cometh* (1956), the Circle in the Square brought respectability to Off Broadway and launched the careers of Quintero, George C. Scott, Geraldine Fitzgerald, Jason Robards, Jr., and others. The company moved to a new home on Bleecker Street in 1960 and in 1972 they opened an uptown theatre under the Uris (today the Gershwin) Theatre on 50th Street.

The **Ensemble Studio Theatre** is a true studio operation, letting plays develop over a period of time and using workshop performances to let playwrights revise their work. The company is most famous for its annual Marathon Festival of One-Act Plays, a popular event since 1976 that has attracted the finest American playwrights, both new and established.

Folksbiene is New York's only surviving Yiddish theatre company and it has not missed a season since its founding in 1915. The company (the name translates as "People's Theatre" in Yiddish) has always had leftist political sympathies but the productions are often more than mere agitprop. Folksbiene is housed in its own space on East 55th Street and performances are usually in Yiddish with simultaneous live English translations on earphones. Because the actors are amateurs, the company only performs on weekends.

The **Glines** was the first and is probably still the best legitimate theatre company in New York dedicated to gay theatre. Some famous gay plays, such as *Torch Song Trilogy* (1982) and *As Is* (1985), have come from the Glines and gone on to Broadway, and the company maintains its excellence in a genre of theatre too often subject to trends.

The **Jean Cocteau Repertory** has been presenting the best of the bizarre and the daring since 1971. The repertory models itself after the famed Berliner Ensemble and usually presents European plays in bold new interpretations.

The **Jewish Repertory Theatre** was founded by Ran Avni in 1974 as a showcase for plays in English with Jewish themes. Situated in a small theatre inside a temple in Gramercy Park, the Jewish Rep has had many acclaimed productions over the past few years.

La Mama Experimental Theatre Club is the oldest and most consistently experimental theatre company in New York, shocking and delighting audiences since 1962. The theatre, sometimes called La Mama ETC or Café La Mama, is housed in an offbeat space on East 4th Street and is still run by its founder Ellen Stewart.

Mabou Mines is the world-famous avant garde company that radically reinterprets the classics and creates original performance pieces using modern music and the latest technology. The company was founded in 1970 by JoAnne Akalaitis, Philip Glass, Lee Breuer, and others and, although the troupe is often touring around the world, has kept New York as its home base.

The **Manhattan Theatre Club** is one of New York's favorite theatre companies with a large subscription audience and the best actors, playwrights, and directors in the city anxious to work there. Founded in 1970, the company has sent many plays to further success Off Broadway and on Broadway. Terrence McNally is the playwright most associated with the Manhattan Theatre Club these days but over the years many fine artists were first produced here. The artistic director for many years and the driving force behind the successful company is Lynne Meadow.

The **National Actors' Theatre**, founded by Tony Randall in 1991, offers revivals of American and world classics on Broadway. Most of the productions feature stars and, after a shaky start, the group has offered some very satisfying productions.

The **Negro Ensemble Company** did more than any other black theatre group to recognize and promote works by African Americans in the 1960s and allow black plays to enter the mainstream of the American theatre. Founded in

1967, the company has presented many original plays that have gone on to Broadway, including works by Charles Fuller, Samm-Art Williams, Joseph A. Walker, and Charles Gordone. The company has long been under the leadership of co-founder Douglas Turner Ward.

The **New York Shakespeare Festival** was started by Joe Papp in 1954 to tour the city boroughs with free productions of Shakespeare. In 1962 the non-profit theatre got a permanent home, the Delacorte Theatre in Central Park, for summer productions and in 1966 the organization took over the old Astor Library and turned it into the most vital Off-Broadway theatre complex in New York. Over the years the Public Theatre, as the Astor location is called, has nurtured new playwrights, promoted plays by and for minorities, developed new musicals, and sent several shows on to Broadway and worldwide fame. *Hair* (1967), *The Basic Training of Pavlo Hummel* (1971), *Sticks and Bones* (1971), *That Championship Season* (1972), and *A Chorus Line* (1975) are among the productions the New York Shakespeare Festival presented during its heyday. Since the death of Joe Papp in 1991, the theatre has suffered from unsteady leadership and given us fewer notable productions but the organization is still very much alive and remarkable theatre is always a strong possibility at the Public.

The **Pan Asian Repertory Theatre** has been presenting new and old plays with Asian subject matter and themes for twenty years and the productions have been so well received that today nearly half of its audience is non-Asian. This exciting company, founded and managed by Tisa Chang, is also well known from touring across the country and overseas.

The **Paper Bag Players** is one of New York's oldest and favorite children's theatre companies. For over thirty years the theatre has been presenting original, innovative works for children that rely on improvisation and creativity rather than spectacle and special effects.

Playwrights Horizons, as its name suggests, is committed to nurturing new American playwrights, composers, and lyricists. This little theatre has sent many plays and musicals on to Broadway, Pulitzer Prizes, and renown. Andre Bishop, who guided Playwrights Horizons for many seasons, managed to seek out new talent that was the envy of all Off Off Broadway.

The **Puerto Rican Traveling Theatre** has presented works by Puerto Rican writers for over twenty years, offering some performances in English and others in Spanish. The company travels the five boroughs of New York each summer, playing to thousands of New Yorkers.

The **Repertory Theatre of Lincoln Center** has been enjoying so much success the past few years with both revivals and new works that one almost forgets what a troubled history this theatre has. A repertory was founded in 1960 while Lincoln Center for the Performing Arts was still in the planning stages. In 1964 the new company, under the direction of Robert Whitehead and Elia Kazan, presented their first production at a temporary location and then moved into the completed Vivian Beaumont and Forum (later Mitzi Newhouse) Theatres in 1965. Troubles plagued the company for the next decades, artistic directors came and went, and the place was actually dark for a few seasons in the early 1980s. Since Lincoln Center Theatre (as it is now called) reemerged in 1986 under the direction of Gregory Mosher and Bernard Gersten, the place has become a vital and thriving theatre with acclaimed productions not only in their two theatres at Lincoln Center but in traditional Broadway houses as well.

The **Ridiculous Theatrical Company** has been offering New York the best in theatre travesty since 1966. Although its figurehead and primary playwright Charles Ludlam is gone, artistic director Everett Quinton has seen to it that the outrageous parodies of theatre and opera classics continue on.

The **Roundabout Theatre Company** claims the largest subscription audience in New York and it is not difficult to believe when one considers how many hits it has had over the past decade. The company was founded in 1965 by Gene Feist as a home for revivals. After some bumpy seasons and different locations, the Roundabout moved into the Criterion Center on Broadway in 1991 and has enjoyed amazing success, usually selling out most performances and sending several popular shows on to Broadway houses.

The **Second Stage Theatre** was created in 1979 to offer a second mounting to recent American plays that failed. Some of the company's rediscoveries over the years have been quite revealing and successful. Today the theatre also presents new American plays.

Theatreworks/USA has been presenting original and often musical adaptations of classic tales for children for over thirty years. The company presents many productions each season and in the summer offers free performances of selected works.

The **Wooster Group** is a small but dedicated band of artists who explore performance art and performance monologues. The company evolved from the earlier Performance Group in 1975 and has since presented intriguing theatre pieces for a cult audience.

For further reading: Louis Botto's *At This Theatre*, Ruth Leon's *New York's Guide to the Performing Arts*, Ken Bloom's *Broadway: An Encyclopedic Guide to the History, People and Places of Times Square*, and Gerald Bordman's three-volume *American Theatre: A Chronicle of Comedy and Drama*, *Oxford Companion to the American Theatre*, and *American Musical Theatre: A Chronicle*.

2

PLAYS

BROADWAY'S LONG RUNS

As recently as the 1920s, a play's one hundredth performance was considered a milestone. Today, even a small-cast play that runs only 100 times is probably a financial disaster. So comparing the number of performances from era to era is a deceiving business at best. Also, many plays in the nineteenth century played as part of a repertory of some half dozen other works so it was difficult to chalk up a large number of performances for any one play. But there is something impressive about a play in any period running for a couple of years. Here are the top twenty longest-running non-musical plays in Broadway history:

Life with Father (1939) by Howard Lindsay and Russel Crouse (3,224 performances)
Tobacco Road (1933) by Jack Kirkland (3,182 performances)
Abie's Irish Rose (1922) by Anne Nichols (2,327 performances)
Deathtrap (1978) by Ira Levin (1,793 performances)
Gemini (1977) by Albert Innaurato (1,788 performances)
Harvey (1944) by Mary Chase (1,775 performances)
Born Yesterday (1946) by Garson Kanin (1,642 performances)
Mary, Mary (1961) by Jean Kerr (1,572 performances)
The Voice of the Turtle (1943) by John Van Druten (1,557 performances)
Barefoot in the Park (1963) by Neil Simon (1,530 performances)
Brighton Beach Memoirs (1983) by Neil Simon (1,530 performances)
Same Time, Next Year (1975) by Bernard Slade (1,453 performances)
Arsenic and Old Lace (1941) by Joseph Kesselring (1,444 performances)
Mummenschanz (1977)* (1, 326 performances)
Angel Street (1941) by Patrick Hamilton (1,295 performances)
Lightnin' (1918) by Winchell Smith and Frank Bacon (1,291 performances)
Cactus Flower (1965) by Abe Burrows (1,234 performances)

*Mummenschanz was an Italian-Swiss mask and mime troupe and the show had no
        dialogue or plot; hence, no author is listed.

Sleuth (1970) by Anthony Shaffer (1,222 performances)
Torch Song Trilogy (1982) by Harvey Fierstein (1,222 performances)
Equus (1974) by Peter Shaffer (1,209 performances)

All of the plays are American except *Sleuth* and *Equus* by the Shaffer brothers, the London hit *Angel Street* and the foreign import *Mummenchanz*. Each decade this century has offered a long-run record holder except the 1950s and, so far, the 1990s. In fact, 1983 was the last year to offer a substantial long-run hit (*Brighton Beach Memoirs*) and these days, with fewer non-musicals running very long, it seems unlikely that a new play will come on the scene that will hope to run over a thousand performances. On the other hand, musicals seem to be breaking records all the time. (See the MUSICALS section for those long-running record holders.)

Most of the plays listed above are either comedies or seriocomic plays emphasizing comedy. However, the adage that serious drama never runs as long as comedy or musicals is not always true. Here are Broadway's twenty longest-running serious dramas on record:

Tobacco Road (1933) by Jack Kirkland (3,182 performances)
Deathtrap (1978) by Ira Levin (1,793 performances)
Angel Street (1941) by Patrick Hamilton (1,295 performances)
Sleuth (1970) by Anthony Shaffer (1,222 performances)
Equus (1974) by Peter Shaffer (1, 209 performances)
Amadeus (1980) by Peter Shaffer (1,181 performances)
Anna Lucasta (1944) by Philip Yordan (957 performances)
Dracula (1977 revival) by Hamilton Deane and John Balderston (925 performances)
The Elephant Man (1979) by Bernard Pomerance (916 performances)
Children of a Lesser God (1980) by Mark Medoff (887 performances)
The Bat (1920) by Mary Roberts Reinhart and Avery Hopwood (867 performances)
A Streetcar Named Desire (1947) by Tennessee Williams (855 performances)
The Subject Was Roses (1964) by Frank D. Gilroy (832 performances)
Inherit the Wind (1955) by Jerome Lawrence and Robert E. Lee (806 performances)
The Ladder (1926) by J. Frank Davis (789 performances)
M. Butterfly (1988) by David Henry Hwang (777 performances)
Two for the Seesaw (1958) by William Gibson (750 performances)
Death of a Salesman (1949) by Arthur Miller (742 performances)
for colored girls who have considered suicide when the rainbow is enuf (1976) by
        Ntozake Shange (742 performances)
The Diary of Anne Frank (1955) by Frances Goodrich and Albert Hackett (717
        performances)

Again, all the entries are American except for the three British plays by the Shaffer brothers and the London import *Dracula*. Six of the above are mystery or suspense plays, leaving eleven American dramas that ran without benefit of thrills or chills. *Tobacco Road*, the longest-running American drama, is sometimes revived, but due to its outrageous characters and blatant plot, it plays more like a comedy today.

OFF BROADWAY'S LONG RUNS

Off Broadway has always served as an alternative to Broadway, providing smaller and more intimate theatres for plays considered too risky for the Great White Way. Some of the theatres Off Broadway have a very small seating capacity so it is sometimes difficult to equate these figures with those for a Broadway house. Here are the twenty longest-running non-musical plays in Off-Broadway history:

Perfect Crime (1987) by Warren Manzi (3,500+ performances; still running)
Tony 'n Tina's Wedding (1988) by Artificial Intelligence (2,500+ performances; still running)
Vampire Lesbians of Sodom (1985) by Charles Busch (2,024 performances)
Vanities (1976) by Jack Heifner (1,785 performances)
The Blacks (1961) by Jean Genet (1,408 performances)
Driving Miss Daisy (1987) by Alfred Uhry (1,195 performances)
The Hot l Baltimore (1973) by Lanford Wilson (1,166 performances)
Steel Magnolias (1987) by Robert Harling (1,126 performances)
Beau Jest (1991) by James Sherman (1,069 performances)
Tamara (1987) by Richard Rose and John Krizanc (1,036 performances)
One Flew Over the Cuckoo's Nest (1971 revival) by Dale Wasserman (1,025 performances)
The Boys in the Band (1968) by Mart Crowley (1,000 performances)
Fool for Love (1983) by Sam Shepard (1,000 performances)
Other People's Money (1989) by Jerry Sterner (990 performances)
Cloud 9 (1981) by Caryl Churchill (971 performances)
Sister Mary Ignatius Explains It All for You & *The Actor's Nightmare* (1979) by Christopher Durang (947 performances)
The Effect of Gamma Rays on Man-in-the-Moon Marigolds (1970) by Paul Zindel (819 performances)
A View from the Bridge (1965 revival) by Arthur Miller (780 performances)
True West (1982 revival) by Sam Shepard (762 performances)
Isn't It Romantic (1983) by Wendy Wasserstein (733 performances)

Not included in the above, but arguable cases nevertheless, are *The Proposition*, an improvised theatre piece that ran 1,109 performances in the 1960s, and the specialty piece *Tubes*, which has played over 1,500 performances so far. All of the above are American works except the British import *Cloud 9* and the French *The Blacks*. Some of our finest young or experimental playwrights are found on this list, which is what Off Broadway is all about.

FORGOTTEN NINETEENTH-CENTURY HIT PLAYS

Because long runs in one theatre are a twentieth-century phenomenon, none of the titles in the lists above represent the previous century's theatrical hits. A popular play in the 1800s was not merely a New York success. A play (or favorite star) could tour across the country for years on end, racking up as many and even more performances than noted in the list of Broadway and Off-Broadway long runs. It is impossible to determine just how many performances *Uncle Tom's Cabin* or *East Lynne* finally played but there is no question the number would be impressive.

While very few nineteenth-century plays could hold the stage today (*Fashion* is a notable exception), this is no judgment of their powerful craftsmanship and ability to thrill audiences across the nation. Here, in chronological order, is a very selective list of some of the most popular plays from the 1800s that were written by Americans or first presented in an American production.

The Drunkard (1844) by W. H. Smith. Starting in Boston as part of a temperance crusade, this melodrama favorite held the boards for the rest of the century and even made successful return appearances in the 1900s. Family man Edward Cribbs is led to drink and decay by a villainous lawyer, only to be saved at the last moment by a foster brother and a beneficent philanthropist. The melodrama broke records in Boston and later several productions played simultaneously in New York. The play was no less successful on the road and a 1933 revival in Los Angeles ran an astounding twenty years. Smith was a transplanted Englishman but *The Drunkard* was an American classic in temperament and theme.

Fashion (1845) by Anna Cora Mowatt. This popular comedy, which broke records for a play in New York, is perhaps the finest comedy of manners of the century and still a witty and satisfying stage piece. The ambitious but foolish Mrs. Tiffany tries to climb the ranks of high society in New York, even going so far as scheming to marry her daughters off to well-placed snobs. But Yankee common sense wins out in the end and the frivolity of fashion is exposed. It is a classic American theme and in *Fashion* it still plays beautifully.

Uncle Tom's Cabin (1853) from Harriet Beecher Stowe. There were many unauthorized stage versions of Stowe's inflammatory novel but one by George L. Aiken was considered the best adaptation of this tale of life in the South. All of the vivid characters from the novel were retained, as well as such memorable scenes as Eliza's escape across the icy river, the slave auction, and Little Eva's ascent into heaven. From 1853 to 1930 there was not a season that there was not at least one touring company of *Uncle Tom's Cabin* on the road.

Ten Nights in a Barroom (1858) by William W. Pratt. While this prohibitionist play did not have the craftsmanship of the earlier *The Drunkard*, it certainly knew how to move an audience to tears, especially when little Mary arrives at the bar and pleads with her alcoholic father: "Father, dear father -- come home!" Big cities gave the melodrama modest runs but few shows were more popular in rural America than *Ten Nights in a Barroom*.

The Colleen Bawn (1860) by Dion Boucicault. The Irish Boucicault was truly a transatlantic playwright with hits in both New York and London. This popular play was written for the American producer Laura Keene and premiered here, becoming one of the most successful of all Irish-flavored plays. The fair-haired Eily is secretly married to an impoverished aristocrat and is nearly done in by the hunchback villain Danny Mann. The play was later a hit in London but Americans kept it a favorite here on the road for many years.

East Lynne (1863) by Clifton W. Tayleure. The actress Lucille Western paid Tayleure $100 to adapt Mrs. Henry Wood's popular Victorian novel for the stage because she saw in it a vehicle for herself. Western played the heroine Lady Isabel for several years and the melodrama was also a huge success with other actresses in the role. The tearjerker was about the plight of a good woman who is deceived in love and only on her deathbed is reunited with her faithful husband and loving children in the homestead called East Lynne. This play was so popular and returned to touring cities so many times that the expression "Next week, *East Lynne*" became a catch phrase for the predictability of theatre bills.

Rip Van Winkle (1866) by Dion Boucicault and Joseph Jefferson. There had been stage versions of the Washington Irving tale since soon after its publication in 1819 but this adaptation, which Jefferson played for decades, was the most satisfying. Jefferson's performance as the dissolute Rip who returns from the Kaatskill Mountains after a nap of several years was one of the comic gems of the century, but the play was popular even without Jefferson.

Under the Gaslight (1867) by Augustin Daly. This melodrama was very popular not only for its own sake but also for dozens of other successful melodramas and even, years later, early films that copied it. In the most famous scene the villainous Byke ties the one-armed Snorkey to a railway track, who is then rescued from an approaching train by the heroine. Daly had gotten the train idea from a British play but audiences did not care about its origins and the play remained popular for decades.

Kit, the Arkansas Traveler (1871) by T. B. DeWalden and Edward Spencer. An epic tale filled with adventure and woe, this play was a hardy vehicle for Frank Chanfrau who played the title role for years. But with or without Chanfrau, the melodrama thrilled audiences for over twenty years.

Davy Crockett (1873) by Frank Murdoch. America's fascination with frontier life helped keep this play popular for decades and Frank Mayo, who played the title character, was an audience favorite across the country because of his portrayal of the legendary hero. Davy battles hungry wolves, exposes blackmailing villains, and finally gets his childhood sweetheart in this perennial hit.

The Two Orphans (1874) by N. Hart Jackson. Although it originated as a French play by Adolphe D'Ennery and Eugene Cormon that took Paris by storm, Jackson's terse adaptation was equally successful in America, appearing on the boards for over twenty-five years. The heart-wrenching story about a waif and her blind sister adrift on a sea of troubles was the basis for the later silent film classic *Orphans of the Storm* (1922) starring the Gish sisters.

Hazel Kirke (1880) by Steele MacKaye. This popular melodrama was unusual in that it had no distinct villain and the dialogue avoided sensationalism and opted for a more naturalistic flavor. When Hazel Kirke goes against her father's wishes and marries the man she loves, forces conspire to destroy the marriage and push Hazel toward suicide. Audiences responded to the more realistic approach: the New York production broke records and five road companies were sent out immediately to meet the demand for tickets across the country.

The White Slave (1882) by Bartley Campbell. While critics sneered at this weepy tale of the quadroon Lisa whose own stepbrother tries to sell her to slavery, audiences loved it and kept it popular for twenty-five years. The play was no doubt helped by Lisa's famous exclamation, "Rags are royal raiment when worn for virtue's sake."

The Old Homestead (1887) by Denman Thompson and George W. Ryer. This play may seem like a giant cliché now but it is the melodrama that established the idyllic rural farm as the heart of the American way of life. Farmer Joshua Whitcomb leaves his New Hampshire homestead to go to decrepit New York City and rescue his derelict son from a life of regret. Thompson played Joshua for twenty-four years and the play was around even long than that.

Shenandoah (1889) by Bronson Howard. One of the finest plays ever written about the Civil War, this drama about two West Point friends torn apart by opposing loyalties had a complicated plot and plenty of suspense. Howard, one of America's most influential playwrights, had his greatest success with *Shenandoah*, which ran 250 performances in New York alone.

Secret Service (1896) by William Gillette. This exciting melodrama was also set during the Civil War but it centered on espionage and the use of the telegraph for its thrills. Gillette played the double agent Lewis Dumont in the original production and returned to it off and on for many years after. The tightly-constructed drama is still revived on occasion and its original popularity is easily understood.

FORGOTTEN TWENTIETH-CENTURY HIT PLAYS

A long run on Broadway is not always a guarantee of immortality. Many a long run hit has quickly vanished, rarely to be revived or thought of again. Each decade has its share of embarrassments: plays that ran and ran and it is hard now to figure out why. Others, for some reason or other, have been forgotten despite their high quality. Here, in chronological order, are some plays from this century that were extremely popular in their day but have been rarely or never revived.

The Lion and the Mouse (1905) by Charles Klein (686 performances). This melodrama about wealth and greed is a step above the clichés of a "mellerdramer"; but neither is it a lost gem of a play. The tyrannical millionaire in the piece was patterned after John D. Rockefeller so eyebrows were certainly raised. But 686 performances in 1905 is a run equivalent to several years today. Ironically, *The Lion and the Mouse* opened about the same time as *Peter Pan* but completely overshadowed it in popularity; time has given us a different perspective.

Lightnin' (1918) by Frank Bacon and Winchell Smith (1,291 performances). The long run for this affable but uninspired comedy is explained by the popularity of co-author Bacon who starred in the piece and stayed with it for every one of its 1,291 performances. In fact, four years later he was still touring with the play when he died. The plot centers on the misadventures of "Lightnin'" Bill Jones and how he outwits a bunch of city slickers. When the play was revived in 1938 without Bacon, it quickly folded.

Abie's Irish Rose (1922) by Anne Nichols (2,327 performances). People still laugh at how popular this Jewish-Catholic comic romance was, for fewer plays ever received worse reviews and went on to a long run anyway. The play is still done on occasion and its heart is in the right place. But the writing is amazingly stilted and the characters are rather offensive stereotypes, even in a 1922 context. Nichols herself produced and directed revivals of *Abie's Irish Rose* in 1937 and 1954 but both failed.

The Ladder (1926) by J. Frank Davis (789 performances). Some shows the critics like but the audiences stay away from; others are taken up by audiences despite a roasting from the critics. *The Ladder* is unique in that both critics and audiences disliked it. This elaborate melodrama about reincarnation was backed by millionaire Edgar B. Davis who kept it running even when the cast outnumbered the audiences. After a year of this, Davis made the play a free show and still it had trouble limping along for another season. All in all, Davis lost about one and a half million dollars on the project but, as a confirmed believer in reincarnation, he felt he had done his part in spreading the message. Perhaps in another life this play will be a success.

Tobacco Road (1933) by Jack Kirkland (3,182 performances). Just to mention the title of this long-running drama was guaranteed a laugh for many years. It was based on Erskine Caldwell's novel about a steamy bunch of Georgia crackers and their down-and-dirty dealings. Critics scoffed or were shocked, ministers condemned it from their pulpits, and mayors and congressmen refused to let the tour come into their hometowns. Is it any wonder it ran for eight years on Broadway and played in 327 cities, some as many as eight times? The play is produced today on occasion and it is actually quite fun, in an unintentional way. *Tobacco Road* returned to Broadway four times after its initial record-breaking run.

Junior Miss (1941) by Jerome Chodorov and Joseph Fields (710 performances). The popularity of this play is not hard to understand when you consider the Gidget movies and the numerous TV shows with a spunky teenage heroine. Coming at a time when America was dealing with Pearl Harbor and the onset of a world war, *Junior Miss* was a delightful look at innocence and youth. It still pleases and a revival for this endearing piece of triviality is not hard to imagine.

Anna Lucasta (1944) by Philip Yordan (957 performances). This original drama had many similarities to O'Neill's *Anna Christie* but the story was told with African-American characters and the script was quite ahead of its time. Yordon had originally written the drama about Poles in America but, unable to find a producer, gave it to the American Negro Theatre Company to produce in a black context. While much in *Anna Lucasta* might disturb modern audiences (particularly the narrow view of black Americans that white audiences found believable in 1944), the original cast and staff introduced such future celebrities as Ruby Dee, Earle Hyman, Alice Childress, and Rosetta LeNoire and it was hardly a *Blackbirds on Broadway* kind of venture. The production started out in Harlem then transferred to Broadway where it ran nearly a thousand performances, much longer than O'Neill's original version.

Happy Birthday (1946) by Anita Loos (564 performances). The very grand, very serious "first lady of the American Theatre," Helen Hayes, let her hair down in this silly farce and charmed audiences, if not the critics. Loos wrote the part of a repressed librarian who gets drunk and cuts loose especially for Hayes, more as a bet that she would not dare play it. But Hayes did and got a Tony Award in the bargain. Today an alcoholic stupor played as a great comic adventure would not go over very well and it is doubtful if the original would have taken off without Hayes in it.

The Moon Is Blue (1951) by F. Hugh Herbert (924 performances). Most remember this title as a movie of 1953 that caused an uproar with the Catholic Legion of Decency. The original play raised eyebrows as well but it was tame enough to run nearly 1,000 performances and generate eight road companies. What was the fuss all about? The young lady in the play actually discussed the idea of losing her virginity with a man she meets in the Empire State Building. Today it would cause yawns but, with the original cast of Barbara Bel Geddes, Barry Nelson, and Donald Cook, it was an entertaining enough night of Broadway comedy.

Anniversary Waltz (1954) by Jerome Chodorov and Joseph Fields (615 performances). This popular comedy centers on a nice sitcom-like couple dealing with the crisis of having their sexual past announced on television. Many of the play's jokes centered on the strange new box that had invaded the family's apartment. Critics yawned but audiences laughed; after all, they were all purchasing their first television set as well.

The World of Suzie Wong (1958) by Paul Osborn (508 performances). Western artist meets Asian prostitute with a heart of gold in Hong Kong and they fall in love. What worked for *Madame Butterfly* and still works for *Miss Saigon* was turned into a popular melodrama based on a novel by Richard Mason. It is hard to say what audiences would think of this play today. At least it ends more happily than the other two examples cited.

A Majority of One (1959) by Leonard Spigelgass (556 performances). New York City widow and Japanese businessman with a grudge meet and fall in love on an ocean cruise. The 1958-1959 season was ripe with Asian plays (it also produced *Flower Drum Song*, *Rashomon*, and *The World of Suzie Wong*), but this was the only one to confront the issue of racial prejudice. Radio and television favorite Gertrude Berg played the Jewish widow, which accounted for much of the play's success, and the Japanese love interest was played by Sir Cedric Hardwicke, which would not go over very well today.

Come Blow Your Horn (1961) by Neil Simon (677 performances). If any Neil Simon play seems dated, this first theatrical effort of his is definitely it. While it is an amusing diversion in summer stock today, it is hard to imagine Broadway embracing a revival of this silly comedy about a bachelor and his pad. It is quite interesting to note that the play ran as long as it did when no one yet knew that Neil Simon was our funniest playwright.

Never Too Late (1962) by Sumner Arthur Long (1,007 performances). This one-joke comedy about two middle-aged parents who find themselves expecting a baby was very popular and one has to credit the strong cast (Paul Ford, Maureen O'Sullivan, Orson Bean) and George Abbott's razor-sharp direction over the script. It was a nice 1940s comedy that just happened to be a hit in the 1960s.

The Impossible Years (1965) by Bob Fisher and Arthur Marx (670 performances). People who feared the effect that television was to have on playwriting pointed to this comedy as the handwriting on the wall. Another one-joke show (famous child psychiatrist who cannot control his teenage daughter), *The Impossible Years* was a good vehicle for Alan King who everybody knew from . . . well, television. Even summer stocks theatres cannot get away with this one anymore.

THE MOST POPULAR PLAYS: SCHOOLS

Tabulating New York successes and failures is all very well but the American Theatre is not Broadway and Broadway is not what most theatre is in this country. Going by the numbers, there are more high school play productions than any other kind. The International Thespian Society keeps track of which plays high schools are producing each year and they publish annual survey results of nearly 1,000 schools polled. With a few exceptions, most non-musical plays being produced are old established American classics. Year in and year out, certain non-musicals consistently appear high on the list. Here, in chronological order of their original productions, are the most popular school plays.

You Can't Take It With You (1936) by George S. Kaufman and Moss Hart
Our Town (1938) by Thornton Wilder
The Man Who Came to Dinner (1939) by George S. Kaufman and Moss Hart
Arsenic and Old Lace (1941) by Joseph Kesselring
Harvey (1944) by Mary Chase
The Curious Savage (1950) by John Patrick
The Crucible (1953) by Arthur Miller
The Diary of Anne Frank (1955) by Frances Goodrich and Albert Hackett
The Miracle Worker (1959) by William Gibson
The Odd Couple (1965) by Neil Simon

Also high on the list of high school favorites are two plays that were never seen on Broadway: *Cheaper By the Dozen* by Frank Gilbreth, Ernestine Gilbreth Carey, and Christopher Sergel, and *Up the Down Staircase* by Bel Kaufman and Christopher Sergel. The only non-American plays to show up on the list frequently were Shakespeare's *A Midsummer Night's Dream* and Agatha Christie's *The Mousetrap*. (See Chapter 6 for the most often produced musicals in high schools.)

THE MOST POPULAR PLAYS: REGIONAL THEATRE

The League of Resident Theatres keeps track of the productions by regional or repertory theatre companies across the nation. The results vary so much from year to year that a clear list of recurring titles is hard to come by. A new Mamet or McNally play may be presented dozens of times the first year it is released to regional theatres, only to fall off the list completely as the circuit exhausts the new plays from New York.

Two conclusions can be drawn, though: Shakespeare is the single most produced playwright in regional theatre with *Twelfth Night*, *Romeo and Juliet*, *Macbeth*, and *A Midsummer Night's Dream* among the most recurring titles. But even the choice of which Shakespeare plays are done goes in cycles; one season everybody seems to be doing *The Winter's Tale* and then years may go by before it even appears on the survey list again. The other clear conclusion to be drawn is that Charles Dickens' *A Christmas Carol* (in a variety of dramatizations) reappears more often than any other title on the lists of regional productions. If you add all the school and community theatre productions (as well as the occasional Broadway version), the Dickens Christmas classic is the most often produced theatrical property in America today.

AMERICA'S MOST POPULAR PLAY

But today is not yesterday and a look at the nineteenth century changes the picture. *Cats* may claim to be "for now and forever" but there was a lot of theatre in America in the 1800s and the statistics there are far from puny. True, a run of several months on Broadway was considered colossal in the nineteenth century but when you consider how comprehensive "the road" was then, you get a better idea of who was seeing what on stage. A hit play would run possibly five months in New York but it would then go on the road for two or three years. Major hits usually spawned more than one road company, each one returning to some cities several times.

Looking at the American Theatre this way, it is probable that the most popular play ever produced in this country was Harriet Beecher Stowe's *Uncle Tom's Cabin*. The dramatization was popular across the country not for a season or two but for decades throughout the later half of the century. The 1853 dramatization by George L. Aiken ran a record-breaking 100 performances when it tried out in Troy, New York, before coming to Broadway for an astounding 325. In 1879 there were no less than fifty touring companies of *Uncle Tom's Cabin* on the road; as late as 1927 there were still a dozen troupes touring the country. *Cats* will have to run many decades in New York and on the road to try and come close to the number of tickets that were sold for *Uncle Tom's Cabin*, America's most popular play.

MEMORABLE PLAY REVIVALS ON AND OFF BROADWAY

A true revival is an old play that is re-examined and re-imagined rather than just revived or reproduced. In earlier centuries, theatre companies kept favorite vehicles in their repertory for decades. Many revivals then were actually returns of former productions with little or no cast changes. Another common practice was to take a Broadway hit, tour it across the country for several months, then bring the same production back to New York for a second run.

Today we expect a revival to be a new theatre experience. In most cases the director, designer, and actors go out of their way *not* to reproduce the original production in look and interpretation. This sometimes makes for some wildly inappropriate or "deconstructed" productions that are almost unrecognizable. But when a bold, new production of an older play makes us see it with fresh eyes and brings an even greater understanding to the original, then the product is as satisfying and important as the heralding of a new work. Here are some memorable New York revivals of American plays from the past fifty years.

The Front Page (1946) When this Ben Hecht-Charles MacArthur comedy opened in 1928 it was a hit but many felt the colorful conversation and humor of the newspaper reporters too vulgar for public performance. But no one seemed to mind eighteen years later with this successful revival featuring Lew Parker and Arnold Moss, directed by MacArthur himself. (79 performances)

Burlesque (1946) Bert Lahr scored an acting triumph as the burlesque comic Skid Johnson in this extremely popular revival of the 1927 comedy by George Manker Wattes and Arthur Hopkins. Movie actress Jean Parker was applauded for her portrayal of the wife Bonny and co-author Hopkins directed the large cast expertly. (439 performances)

Twentieth Century (1950) José Ferrer directed and starred in this popular revival of the Ben Hecht-Charles MacArthur comedy about show business. The American National Theatre and Academy (ANTA) produced the revival in their playhouse then moved it to a Broadway theatre for an extended run. Ferrer's co-star was Gloria Swanson. (233 performances)

The Children's Hour (1952) Lillian Hellman herself staged this popular revival of her disturbing drama of 1934. Patricia Neal and Kim Hunter played the two teachers accused of lesbianism. (189 performances)

The Male Animal (1952) Most critics applauded this revival of the 1940 play by James Thurber and Elliot Nugent as the best comedy of the season, and it was so successful it transferred to Broadway after its sold-out run at the City Center. Nugent recreated his role as the college professor Tommy Turner and movie actor Robert Preston gave his career a new start playing the ex-football hero Joe Ferguson. (317 performances)

Summer and Smoke (1952) When this sensitive Tennessee Williams drama opened on Broadway in 1948, it was greeted with faint praise and only managed to run 100 performances. It was this Off-Broadway revival that established the play as one of Williams' finest, and it launched the career of Geraldine Page who played the fragile heroine. José Quintero directed the Circle in the Square production, which ran for a year. (356 performances)

Desire Under the Elms (1952) The American National Theatre and Academy (ANTA) produced this O'Neill classic with a superb cast headed by Karl Malden as the crusty old farmer Ephraim Cabot. Harold Clurman directed and Mordecai Gorelik's set was as stunning, if different, from Robert Edmond Jones' original in 1924. Douglas Watson played the youngest son and Carol Stone portrayed the young stepmother who falls in love with him. In the small part of a neighbor was Colleen Dewhurst who would later develop into one of America's finest interpreters of O'Neill. (46 performances)

On Borrowed Time (1953) A sparkling comic performance by comic Victor Moore as Gramps distinguished this revival of the 1938 comedy by Paul Osborn. Also in the cast were Beulah Bondi, Kay Hammond, and Leo G. Carroll as the Angel of Death. (78 performances)

The Skin of Our Teeth (1955) Thornton Wilder's 1942 dark comedy continued to bewilder audiences in the 1950s and this revival was no exception.

Alan Schneider directed the comedy and the fine cast included Mary Martin, George Abbott, Helen Hayes, and Florence Reed. Though not a box office hit, the ANTA production was fondly remembered by many for years after. (22 performances)

The Iceman Cometh (1956) This Off-Broadway production may be the most important revival in the history of the American theatre. It re-established the significance of Eugene O'Neill, launched the career of actor Jason Robards, secured José Quintero's reputation as one of America's finest directors, and, more than any other non-musical, validated the new venue called Off Broadway. While the original 1946 Broadway production was greeted with mild praise and only 136 performances, this vibrant revival at the Circle in the Square Theatre was a major critical and financial hit. It was also the beginning of the long-term teaming of Quintero directing Robards in O'Neill's works. (565 performances)

The Crucible (1958) This was another Off-Broadway revival that was more successful than its Broadway original. Arthur Miller's 1953 drama seemed even more potent when removed from the McCarthy era in which it was first seen on Broadway for only 197 performances. This theatre-in-the-round production directed by Word Baker featured Michael Higgins, Barbara Barrie, Ann Wedgeworth, Noah Curry, Barbara Stanton, and Vinnette Carroll. (571 performances)

Desire Under the Elms (1963) José Quintero directed two successful revivals of Eugene O'Neill plays during the 1962-63 season, making it clear that he was the definitive interpreter of the great playwright. George C. Scott, Colleen Dewhurst, and Rip Torn headed the cast of this powerful Off-Broadway production. (380 performances)

Strange Interlude (1963) A few months later, Quintero's revival of this lengthy O'Neill drama opened on Broadway presented by the Actors Studio. The superb cast included Geraldine Page, Ben Gazzara, Franchot Tone, Pat Hingle, Betty Field, William Prince, a young Jane Fonda, and an even younger Richard Thomas. (97 performances)

You Can't Take It With You (1965) This APA Repertory revival of the Kaufman and Hart comedy classic was directed by Ellis Rabb and proved so popular that the company put it back in the repertory the next season. The fine cast included Donald Moffat, Rosemary Harris, Dee Victor, Patricia Connolly, Keene Curtis, and Rabb. (255 performances)

The Glass Menagerie (1965) Tennessee Williams' memory play returned to Broadway in this fine revival that featured Maureen Stapleton as Amanda. Also in the cast were George Gizzard, Piper Laurie, and Pat Hingle. (175 performances)

A View From the Bridge (1965) Like the 1958 Off-Broadway revival of Arthur Miller's *The Crucible*, this Miller revival was more successful than the original Broadway run in 1955. Ulu Grosbard directed Robert Duvall, Jeanne Kaplan, Jon Voight, Susan Anspach, and Ramon Bieri in a full-length version of the one-act play and the gripping production ran two years. (780 performances)

The Show-Off (1967)   Helen Hayes starred in this revival of George Kelly's 1924 comedy, shifting the focus from the boastful Aubrey Piper to the fussy Mrs. Fisher. Stephen Porter directed the smart production presented by the APA Repertory that later toured the country. (81 performances)

The Little Foxes (1967)   This star-studded revival of Lillian Hellman's biting melodrama started at Lincoln Center then moved into a traditional Broadway house. Mike Nichols directed a cast that included Anne Bancroft, George C. Scott, Margaret Leighton, E. G. Marshall, Austin Pendleton, and Maria Tucci. (100 performances)

The Front Page (1969)   This Broadway revival of the 1928 comedy classic was successful enough that it ran out the 1969-70 season then reopened the next season for another four months. Robert Ryan and Bert Convy led the large cast as a parade of stars (Helen Hayes, Molly Picon, Paul Ford, Dody Goodman, Jules Munchin, Maureen O'Sullivan, Peggy Cass, Robert Alda, Butterfly McQueen, John McGiver) took minor roles for limited times.   (222 performances)

Harvey (1970)   It is difficult to believe that this production, co-produced by ANTA and the Phoenix Theatre, was the first Broadway revival of Mary Chase's beloved 1944 comedy. James Stewart, who had played the tipsy Elwood P. Dowd on film, recreated his role and Helen Hayes shone as his sister Veta. Stephen Porter directed a cast that also included Henderson Forsythe, Marian Hailey, and Jesse White. (79 performances)

One Flew Over the Cuckoo's Nest (1971)   Dale Wasserman's 1962 adaptation of Ken Kesey's cult novel only only 82 performances on Broadway and did not impress audiences or critics (despite Kirk Douglas starring as the volatile leading character). But this Off-Broadway revival was a long-run hit, with William Devane and Janet Ward leading the fine cast. (1,025 performances)

Mourning Becomes Electra (1972)   The Eugene O'Neill trilogy, which takes five and a half hours to perform, seemed an unlikely candidate for revival, but this edited version done uptown at the Circle in the Square ran a reasonable three and a half hours and proved rather popular. Colleen Dewhurst, Pamela Payton-Wright, and Stephen McHattie led a memorable cast directed by Theodore Mann. (55 performances)

A Moon for the Misbegotten (1973)   José Quintero, America's finest director of Eugene O'Neill's plays, scored another triumph with this Broadway revival. Jason Robards and Colleen Dewhurst played the unusual lovers, to great acclaim. (313 performances)

A Streetcar Named Desire (1973)   The Repertory Theatre of Lincoln Center had a success with this Williams classic, which featured Rosemary Harris as Blanche and James Farentino as Stanley. Ellis Rabb directed and Patricia Connolly and Philip Bosco were also in the cast. (110 performances)

Sweet Bird of Youth (1975)   Tennessee Williams' 1959 drama seemed excessive to many and the original production probably ran on its sensational elements. But this tender revival, directed by Edwin Sherin, opened up new possibilities for the play. Memorable performances by Irene Worth and Christopher Walken were also a plus. (48 performances)

The Royal Family (1975)   Many wondered if this 1927 comedy about the thinly-disguised Drew-Barrymore family of actors would play today but this sterling revival from the Brooklyn Academy of Music was a Broadway hit and revived interest in the old play. Ellis Rabb directed smashingly a cast that included Rosemary Harris, Eva Le Gallienne, Sam Levene, George Gizzard, Joseph Maher, Mary Louise Wilson, and Rosetta LeNoire. (232 performances)

Death of a Salesman (1975)   George C. Scott directed and played Willy Loman in this powerful revival at Circle in the Square. The rest of the Loman family was played by Teresa Wright, James Farentino, and Harvey Keitel. (64 performances)

Dracula (1977)   This popular revival of the 1927 Hamilton Deane-John L. Balderston potboiler ran three times the length of the original, which starred Bela Lugosi. Frank Langella was the star in 1977 and his interpretation could not have been more different from Lugosi's. Dennis Rosa directed and Edward Gorey designed the distinctive costumes and scenery. (925 performances)

Anna Christie (1977)   Swedish film and stage star Liv Ullman was the attraction behind this Broadway revival of the 1921 drama. O'Neill expert José Quintero directed and the cast also included John Lithgow, Robert Donley, and Mary McCarty. (77 performances)

The Basic Training of Pavlo Hummel (1977)   David Rabe's Viet Nam play was a hit Off Broadway only six years earlier but this Boston revival came to Broadway because Al Pacino played the title character. David Wheeler directed the large cast. (107 performances)

Morning's at Seven (1980)   Paul Osborn's gentle comedy ran only 44 performances in its initial 1939 production but this superior revival, lovingly directed by Vivian Matalon, made the old piece seem new; a tour and many stock productions followed. The cast consisted of Teresa Wright, Elizabeth Wilson, Nancy Marchand, Maureen O'Sullivan, Gary Merrill, David Rounds, Maurice Copeland, Lois de Banzie, and Richard Hamilton in one of the best ensembles seen on Broadway in many a season. (564 performances)

The Philadelphia Story (1980)   Ellis Rabb, who has brought more successful revivals of American plays to Broadway than anyone else, directed this 1980 production of Philip Barry's 1939 comedy of manners. Blythe Danner, Edward Hermann and Frank Converse made up the romantic triangle. (60 performances)

The Little Foxes (1981)   Elizabeth Taylor made her Broadway debut in this popular limited-run revival of Lillian Hellman's Southern drama and got generally good reviews for her efforts. Austin Pendleton directed a cast that also featured Maureen Stapleton, Tom Aldridge, and Anthony Zerbe. (126 performances)

American Buffalo (1981)   The early David Mamet drama managed a modest 135 performances in 1977, but with Al Pacino playing the burglar Teach this revival ran out its limited run with full houses. Arvin Brown directed the production that originated at the Long Wharf Theatre in New Haven and Pacino's colleagues on stage were Thomas Waites and Clifton James. (262 performances)

True West (1982)   The original New York Shakespeare Festival production of Sam Shepard's sinister comedy was a matter of such disagreement that the director quit, the playwright disavowed the production and Shepard and producer Joseph Papp never spoke to each other again. But this Off-Broadway revival, originally from Chicago's Steppenwolf Theatre and directed by Gary Sinise, was a critical and popular success. Sinise and John Malkovich played the odd brothers, launching their New York careers. (762 performances)

A View From the Bridge (1983)   This Broadway revival also originated at the Long Wharf Theatre with Arvin Brown as director. The Arthur Miller drama featured Tony Lo Bianco, Rose Gregorio, and Robert Prosky in the cast. (149 performances)

You Can't Take It with You (1983)   What was particularly enjoyable about this Broadway revival of the Pulitzer Prize comedy was the opportunity to see Jason Robards and Colleen Dewhurst, two of America's finest tragic actors, give high-flying comic performances. Ellis Rabb directed the production, which also featured Elizabeth Wilson, Bill McCutcheon, and James Coco. (312 performances)

Death of a Salesman (1984)   Dustin Hoffman returned to the stage to play Willy Loman in this successful revival of Arthur Miller's acclaimed play. Physically and vocally different from previous Willys, Hoffman gave a fascinating performance and was supported by John Malkovich, Kate Reid, and Stephen Lang. (158 performances)

Strange Interlude (1985)   Glenda Jackson was the star of this revival of Eugene O'Neill's psychological drama, which originated in England and arrived on Broadway with a mixture of American and British actors in the cast. The nine-act drama was cut but the production retained much of the interior soliloquies that make the play so unique. (63 performances)

The Odd Couple (1985)   Neil Simon rewrote his 1965 comedy hit to accommodate two women and made some other sex changes in the supporting cast but basically it was the same farcical tale of mismatched roommates. Rita Moreno and Sally Struthers were the stars and Gene Saks directed. The play was a modest success but since then has done very well with stock and community theatre groups. (295 performances)

The House of Blue Leaves (1986)   Lincoln Center Theatre's revival of John Guare's 1971 dark comedy opened in their smaller Mitzi Newhouse Theatre but proved so popular that it soon transferred upstairs to the Vivian Beaumont

Theatre. Director Jerry Zaks found just the right tone for this difficult piece and got sterling performances from John Mahoney, Stockard Channing, and Swoozie Kurtz. (398 performances)

Long Day's Journey Into Night (1986)   This controversial but acclaimed production of Eugene O'Neill's great domestic tragedy used overlapping dialogue and a rapid delivery of lines at times to give the play a more conversational feel. British director Jonathan Miller got marvelous performances from actors Jack Lemmon, Nethel Leslie, Kevin Spacey, and Peter Gallagher. (54 performances)

Orpheus Descending (1989)   This problematic Tennessee Williams play ran only 68 performances in its original 1957 production and was always a play that caused mixed reaction. Many did not like the play any better in this British production directed by Peter Hall but there was no question about Vanessa Redgrave's dynamic performance. Also in the British-American cast were Kevin Anderson, Anne Twomey, and Tammy Grimes. (97 performances)

Cat on a Hot Tin Roof (1990)   Movie actress Kathleen Turner as Maggie was the draw behind this successful Broadway revival, which used Tennessee Williams' preferred ending rather than the one Elia Kazan insisted on in the original Broadway production. Howard Davies directed the revival and the cast also featured Daniel Hugh Kelly as Brick, Polly Holliday as Big Mama, and Charles Durning as Big Daddy. (149 performances)

A Streetcar Named Desire (1992)   Film stars Jessica Lange and Alec Baldwin made this limited-run revival a hot ticket on Broadway. Gregory Mosher directed the production of Tennessee Williams' masterpiece and opinions ranged from raves to polite dismissal. Amy Madigan and Timothy Carhart were also in the cast. (137 performances)

Anna Christie (1993)   Eugene O'Neill's powerful love story was revived on Broadway with British actors Natasha Richardson and Liam Neeson as the tormented lovers. Americans Rip Torn and Anne Meara were also featured. (54 performances)

Abe Lincoln in Illinois (1993)   This large-cast historical drama by Robert E. Sherwood was quite an economic gamble in these days of frugal non-musical productions; but Lincoln Center Theatre's presentation, directed by Gerald Gutierrez, was rich in production and in performance. Sam Waterson played the title character and he was ably supported by a large cast that included Lizbeth Mackay, David Huddleston, Robert Joy, Robert Westenberg, George Hall, and Nesbitt Blaisdell. (40 performances)

The Heiress (1995)   Gerald Gutierrez also directed this sensitive adaptation of Henry James by Ruth and Augustus Goetz and found exciting drama in the period piece. Lincoln Center Theatre presented the multi-award winner in a Broadway house and the superb cast included Cherry Jones, Philip Bosco, Frances Sternhagen, and Jon Tenney. (340 performances)

Inherit the Wind (1996)   Jerome Lawrence and Robert E. Lee's 1955 drama, based on the "Monkey" trial in Tennessee over the teaching of evolution in schools, has never really dated became and this satisfying revival produced by the National Actors Theatre was solid proof of the play's durability. John Tillinger directed the large cast that featured sterling performances by George C. Scott as the Clarence Darrow-like Drummond and Charles Durning as the William Jennings Bryant-like Brady. Due to illness, Scott was often replaced by producer-actor Tony Randall who had played a supporting character in the 1955 original. (45 performances)

A Delicate Balance (1996) Lincoln Center, director Gerald Gutierrez and a splendid cast joined together again for this acclaimed revival of Edward Albee's 1966 drama. Although the original won the Pulitzer Prize, it ran only 132 performances and was perceived as a chilly, intellectual exercise in playwriting. But Gutierrez's brilliant direction revealed the play to be alarmingly funny and potent. The dynamic cast consisted of George Gizzard, Rosemary Harris, Elaine Stritch, Elizabeth Wilson, John Carter, and Mary Beth Hurt. (186 performances)

Buried Child (1996) After thirty years of writing plays and having them produced around the world, Sam Shepard got his first Broadway production with this revised revival of his 1978 Pulitzer Prize-winning drama. Gary Sinise directed the Steppenwolf Theatre Company production from Chicago and emphasized the play's dark humor. James Gammon and Lois Smith headed the fine cast. (45 performances)

PLAY SERIES, CYCLES, AND SEQUELS

Most plays are meant to be viewed singly as a self-contained entity. But there are others that are part of a more ambitious undertaking. In ancient Greek theatre, a trilogy of plays covering the same family or series of events was common. In the Middle Ages, a long cycle of short plays based on Bible stories was the accepted theatre format. Shakespeare wrote sequels to some of his popular works, as did Beaumarchais and others. American playwrights have sometimes written with a similar purpose. Here are some well-known play trilogies in the American theatre.

Eugene O'Neill (1888-1953), our most ambitious playwright, adapted Aeschylus' *Oresteia* into an American idiom and called it *Mourning Becomes Electra* (1931). The three plays of the trilogy, *The Homecoming*, *The Hunted*, and *The Haunted*, told the story of a New England family after the Civil War who destroy and are destroyed through love, jealousy, and revenge. The trilogy takes about five and a half hours to perform and Broadway audiences saw it in a single sitting with a dinner break after the first play. The trilogy was successfully revived on Broadway in 1972 but all three plays were edited into a more conventional playing time of three and a half hours.

David Rabe (1940-) wrote three plays that were thematically tied together and unofficially called it the "Viet Nam War Trilogy." *The Basic Training of Pavlo Hummel* (1971) followed an American soldier's career from induction into the Army to his death in Viet Nam, all in the form of quick and potent flashbacks. Rabe's *Sticks and Bones* (1971) was an expressionistic look at a typical American family and how it is affected when one of the sons returns home from Viet Nam. A few years later *Streamers* (1976) completed the trilogy. It was a more naturalistic view of life in an Army barracks with symbolic overtones about racial disharmony in America. All three plays were successfully produced by the New York Shakespeare Festival and later were seen on Broadway.

Lanford Wilson (1937-) wrote three plays about the fictional Talley family in rural Missouri, where Wilson was born and raised. *The 5th of July* (1978) was the first to be produced but it told the end of the story. A group of odd but likable friends gather on the Talley farm in this Chekhov-like piece. During the course of the play, the aged Sally buries her husband's ashes on the farm and recalls events from the past. In *Talley's Folly* (1980), we meet the young Sally on the night she accepted a marriage proposal from the Jewish Matt Friedman. *Talley & Son* (1985) takes place in the Talley farmhouse while the events of *Talley's Folly* are occurring down by the river. The first two plays of the trilogy were the most successful, both moving from Off Broadway to Broadway for profitable runs.

Harvey Fierstein (1954-) took three of his one-act plays about the tragicomic aspects of the homosexual lifestyle and put them together into a full-length play called *Torch Song Trilogy* (1982). More than a bill of one-acts, *Torch Song Trilogy* was a funny and passionate panorama of gay life in the age before AIDS. *The International Stud* introduces the drag queen Arnold and his new affair with Ed. *Fugue in a Nursery* explores the complications that occur when Ed marries Laurel but is attracted to Arnold's new lover Alan. *Widows and Children First!* occurs later when Arnold adopts a teenager, is reunited with Ed, and has to deal with his own confused mother. The plays range from cinema-like scenes in the first play, expressionism in the second, and realism in the third. The trilogy was very successful first Off Broadway and later on Broadway where it won the Tony Award for Best Play.

Neil Simon (1927-) wrote his most autobiographical plays when he delved into his own youth in Brooklyn and came up with the trilogy consisting of *Brighton Beach Memoirs* (1983), *Biloxi Blues* (1985), and *Broadway Bound* (1986). In the three plays, Simon's alter ego Eugene Jerome moves from his teen years during the Depression to his Army training days in Mississippi to his breaking into television writing in the early 1950s. Each play holds up on its own and each was successfully produced on Broadway and across the country.

Preston Jones (1936 - 1979) wrote his three-play *A Texas Trilogy* for the Dallas Theatre Center and the acclaim was so great that the trio played at the Kennedy Center in Washington and eventually on Broadway in 1976. All three plays take place in Bradleyville, Texas, and various characters appear in some or all of the plays.*The Last Meeting of the Knights of the White Magnolia* (1973) is a wry look at a Southern society that started as a political KKK-like band but has decayed into a collection of the town's misfits. *Lu Ann Hampton Laverty Oberlander* (1974) follows a high school cheerleader from her eager youth through her two marriages into a resigned middle age. *The Oldest Living Graduate* (1974) is about a senile World War One colonel who relives the past when he is presented an award by a military school. While the run of the trilogy on Broadway was disappointing, the plays were successful in regional and educational theatres across the country.

While a series of three plays may seem ambitious enough, some American playwrights have attempted even longer cycles of play. Here are some of the more notable play cycles.

Horton Foote (1916-) has written several full-length and one-act plays set in his fictional Harrison, Texas, but his most comprehensive series of works is his ***Orphans' Home Cycle***, nine full-length plays that follow a Harrison family starting at the turn of the century and ending in 1928. The plays were produced Off Broadway in the 1980s and some of them were filmed for television. The cycle's most memorable plays are *Lily Dale*, *The Widow Claire*, *Valentine's Day*, and *1918*.

Robert Scenkkan (1953-) won the Pulitzer Prize for ***The Kentucky Cycle*** in 1992 before the play had even been produced in New York. The cycle consists of nine plays that are presented in two parts taking two evenings to perform. Set in the Appalachian portion of Eastern Kentucky, the series follows three families from 1775 to 1975. With events ranging from Indian attacks to the Civil War to coal miners' strikes, *The Kentucky Cycle* has an epic sweep few American plays have ever attempted. The 1993 Broadway run was a critical success but a financial disappointment.

August Wilson (1945-) is currently in the midst of his cycle of full-length plays dealing with African-Americans in the twentieth century. Wilson plans one play for each decade and, while characters or families do not cross over from one play to another, most of the plays are set in Pittsburgh (Wilson's hometown) and are unified by the unique sounds, music, and dialogue that is so distinctive of Wilson's craftsmanship. The completed plays include *Ma Rainey's Black Bottom* (1984), *Fences* (1985), *Joe Turner's Come and Gone* (1988), *The Piano Lesson* (1990), *Two Trains Running* (1992), and *Seven Guitars* (1996).

Perhaps the most ambitious cycle ever attempted by a major American playwright was the unfinished ***Tales of Possessors Dis-Possessed*** by **Eugene O'Neill**. This eleven (some say thirteen) play cycle about an

American family from Revolutionary War days to the 1950s was a passion with O'Neill, and he struggled to complete it before he died. But his grave illness in the 1950s made him realize that the task was impossible and, not wanting anyone else to complete the plays after his death, he destroyed the handful of scripts that were complete. One play, *A Touch of the Poet*, survived and was produced in 1957; from the surviving fragments, *More Stately Mansions* was pieced together and produced in 1967. Judging from the quality of the writing in *A Touch of the Poet*, O'Neill's cycle would have been a major literary accomplishment and one can only wonder what was lost to us forever.

Theatre sequels are not as common as movie sequels but they do show up on occasion. Some plays are planned as having two parts (e.g. *Angels in America*), whereas in other cases the success of one play spurns a playwright to pen a sequel (e.g. *Life With Mother*). Here are some sequels to famous plays of the American theatre.

Lillian Hellman returned to the Hubbard family of ***The Little Foxes*** (1939) with her prequel ***Another Part of the Forest*** (1946), which took place several years before the events of the first play.

Howard Lindsay and **Russel Crouse** adapted a series of *New Yorker* stories into the long-running hit ***Life With Father*** (1939) and for years audiences could not get enough of the Day family. When the authors presented their sequel ***Life With Mother*** (1948) about the same family, notices were warm but audiences seemed to have lost interest.

William Gibson had great success with ***The Miracle Worker*** (1959) about Helen Keller and her teacher Annie Sullivan. His sequel ***Monday After the Miracle*** (1982) looked at the characters' later years but failed to win an audience.

John Patrick wrote many plays for Broadway but none brought him more wealth than his comedy ***Everybody Loves Opal*** (1961). Actually, the play received poor notices and closed after 21 performances but Opal Kronkie was a hit across the country where hundreds of community theatres and schools produced the play for years after. So Patrick skipped Broadway altogether for its many sequels: *Opal's Husband*, *Opal Is a Diamond*, *Opal's Baby*, and *Opal's Million Dollar Duck*.

Frank D. Gilroy won the Pulitzer Prize for ***The Subject Was Roses*** (1964) but when he returned to the Cleary family in ***Any Given Day*** (1993) there was little interest. The sequel was actually a prelude to the events depicted in *The Subject Was Roses*, showing the beginnings of what would result five years later.

Tony Kushner planned both parts of ***Angels in America*** (1993) together but the first play, ***Millennium Approaches***, was produced and revised before the second part, ***Perestroika***, was written. Both were critical successes and the two plays are now thought of as a single entity rather than a play and its sequel. (See Chapter 6 for musical sequels)

CONTROVERSIAL AND CENSORED PLAYS

Considering that this country was first settled by Puritans, Pilgrims, Quakers, and Dutch, all strongly anti-theatre in their sentiments, it is not surprising that the history of the American Theatre is filled with bouts with censorship. Basically a rural culture, the colonies were not receptive to theatricals and only when cities grew in size and culture did theatre get a foothold in the new land. Yet the Puritanical streak held strong for many years. Even as late as the 1890s, theatre buildings were often called halls or opera houses or museums in order to escape the theatre stigma. Performances were often billed as concerts, lectures, or even dissertations so as not to offend the more sensitive members of the public.

Each colony and later each state or city had its own restrictions regarding theatricals. Boston had the most rigid laws, hence "banned in Boston" was more than a cliché; well into the 1900s, Broadway hits with questionable subject matter had to play in the Boston suburbs. New York City was the most liberal city but even Manhattan had more than its fair share of ministers, newspaper editors, and drama critics who ranted about the promiscuity of the modern theatre.

Here are some of the more famous American plays over the past three hundred years that have had problems with censorship or, at the least, aroused some controversy. Notice how few involve political issues. Americans have always been more concerned with matters of sex, race, and morals rather than political ideas. That Puritan streak never left us.

The Bear and the Cub (1665) may be the earliest record of a play in the colonies and it was greeted with accusations of licentiousness. We do not know the author or the subject matter of the play but it was brought before the court in the Virginia colony and the three major actors were required to perform sections in costume in order for the judge to determine a verdict. The charge of wickedness was dismissed and the actors, probably amateurs, were released.

Mazeppa (1861) was a typical action-packed melodrama of the period but a scene with Adah Isaacs Menken (in a trouser role; that is, a male character usually played by a female), supposed nude and tied to a runaway horse, was a little too action-packed for some. Despite the initial controversy, Menken stuck with the play, performing it in London, Paris, and across this country for eight years.

The Black Crook (1866), generally accepted as the first American musical, was astoundingly popular for many reasons, not the least for the chorus of girls wearing flesh-colored tights. The girls were supposedly Amazons and residents of Fairyland but preachers and politicians found nothing fantastical about their appearance and denounced the newfangled entertainment. *The Black Crook* was the first show to run longer than a year in one theatre and grossed over a million dollars for its producers.

Divorce (1871) had only to announce its title and controversy erupted. Augustin Daly adapted and Americanized an Anthony Trollope novel into this very popular play about marriage, infidelity, and ultimately divorce. Many felt that it was not an appropriate subject for a play; others disagreed and it ran a sensational 200 performances.

Margaret Fleming (1891) was never a major success but in terms of theatre history it was a major milestone for the developing American drama. James A. Herne's drama was one of the first American plays to model itself on the Ibsen problem play that was just starting to be seen on this side of the Atlantic. The title character is a wife who learns of her husband's infidelity, goes blind and only years later is reconciled to the situation. Because the unfaithful husband was not depicted as a villain and the issues raised were not easily resolved, critics called the play immoral and no theatre in New York or Boston would book the piece. Only after a private performance and praise from prominent writers did the play open for a short run.

Sapho (1900) did more than raise eyebrows; prompted by yellow journalists such as William Randolph Hearst, the play was closed by the police and its stars and manager were brought to court. The scene in the Clyde Fitch drama that brought them there was one in which a courtesan (Olga Nethersole) is seduced and carried up a flight of stairs to her bedroom in the arms of her lover (Hamilton Revelle). All were acquitted and the play reopened for another scintillating 80 performances.

The Easiest Way (1909) by Eugene Walter dealt with a kept woman (Frances Starr) who falls and fails in love, but returns to a life of sin rather than starve. Her line to her maid ("I'm going to Rector's to make a hit, and to hell with the rest") was proclaimed as the first honest ending to an American play by some; others saw it as a new low for the theatre. The play was banned in several places but managed to run out the season on Broadway.

The City (1909) was Clyde Fitch's last and perhaps most potent play. When a family from the country moves to a big city, drug addiction, an illegitimate child, and blackmail result. But what caused the greatest uproar on opening night was when a principle character shouted "You're a God damn liar!" and several members of the audience, including some critics, fainted. "Damn" had been heard on stage before but never with "God" in such a blatant expletive. *The City* was praised and reviled on Broadway for 190 performances but it had a lot of trouble on the road.

The Lure (1913) was about about a young girl lured into the life of prostitution and was written by George Scarborough, a former Secret Service agent who based his play on a white slave case he had investigated. After complaints about the lewd subject of the play, city officials closed the production and only after the producing Shuberts agreed to some revisions in the script was it allowed to reopen for a moderate run.

All God's Chillun Got Wings (1924) is not one of Eugene O'Neill's most remembered plays today but in its day it was very much in the news. The drama is about a black law student (Paul Robeson) and a white girl (Mary Blair) who, friends since childhood, fall in love after a disastrous affair that she has had with another man. Before the play opened, word got out that a black actor kisses a white actress on stage and the city commissioner closed the theatre. Also upsetting to the authorities was the presence of young children in the cast of such an immoral show. So the producer cut the children's roles and the actors performed the play with scripts, thereby getting around the injunction and running a profitable 43 performances.

Desire Under the Elms (1924) is one of O'Neill's finest works and one of the most sensual of all American plays. District Attorney Joab H. Banton, fuming from his inability to stop *All God's Chillun Got Wings*, did not sit still for this play either and tried to close it as well. The story (a farmer falls in love with his young stepmother, they have a child together, and then she kills the baby to prove her love) owed more than just its plot to *Phaedre* but O'Neill set the play in contemporary New England and the loss of a classical buffer made the play uncomfortable for many. The issue went to a jury that acquitted the players and the management but *Desire Under the Elms* was banned in Boston, Los Angeles, and England.

What Price Glory? (1924) was another 1924 play that raised eyebrows even in the liberated Jazz Age. This fine war drama by Maxwell Anderson and Laurence Stallings was admired (and reviled) for its honest depiction of war and the way soldiers actually speak and behave. Some of the salty language had to be softened before the play opened but what remained was still pretty potent and opened the door for more realistic dialogue in future plays. But even critics could not agree on how far the stage presentation of real life should be allowed to go and *What Price Glory?* was denied the Pulitzer Prize that year by a narrow margin of votes.

Sex (1926) is the play that made Mae West famous and infamous. She played a prostitute who helps an ungrateful socialite out of a tricky situation, then seduces the socialite's son to get even. West wrote the play (under the pen name Jane Mast), filling it with sly humor and double entendres that were obvious enough to get the play raided by the police. Hauled into court on a wave of publicity, West was fined $500 and sentenced to ten days in the workhouse. But the play had already managed to run 375 profitable performances, making West's famous reputation.

Lulu Belle (1926) by Edward Sheldon and Charles MacArthur was an ambitious play about a black prostitute and her tragic end after getting involved with wealthy white society. Some complained about the play's blatant handling of the profession and black groups protested the depiction of their race (Lulu was played by the white actress Lenore Ulric in blackface) but the play was one of the great successes of its day.

The Captive (1926) was the first Broadway play to allude to lesbianism, though the reference was obscure and the heroine's supposed lover never appeared in the play. The Arthur Hornblow, Jr., drama, closely based on a French play, received favorable notices and was playing to profitable houses when the District Attorney stepped in and closed it. Gilbert Miller, the play's producer and director, fought to bring the issue to court but the backers wanted no trouble and *The Captive* never reopened. In the play the lover sends a bouquet of violets as a secret way to communicate with the heroine. Because of the controversy, the sale of violets and even purple clothing plummeted in New York.

Strange Interlude (1928) was a complex, psychological epic tale that utilized a lot of Freudian ideas. But what upset audiences most in Eugene O'Neill's nine-act drama was the incident when the heroine (Lynn Fontanne) agrees to an abortion when she learns that her husband's family has a history of insanity. Although the play ran 426 performances and was debated heatedly in New York, *Strange Interlude* was banned in Boston and several other major cities.

The Children's Hour (1934) caused quite a sensation that season because it alluded to the subject of lesbianism. Lillian Hellman's play is about a vindictive school girl who accuses two of her teachers of unnatural affection for each other and destroys their careers. The play was about the power of rumor and accusation but the subject of the rumor was what all the commotion was about. When the Pulitzer Prize committee refused to acknowledge the play, there was an outcry from several critics who established the New York Drama Critics Circle. Yet *The Children's Hour* was refused in Chicago, Boston, and other cities.

The Cradle Will Rock (1938) was one of the most famous of the politically controversial plays to come out of the Federal Theatre Project. This musical drama by Marc Blitzstein was a seething attack on greed and capitalism with the unions and laborers as the only hope for the future. When government officials got wind of it, they placed an injunction on the theatre before it opened. But producers John Houseman and Orson Welles led the cast and audience to an empty theatre some distance away where they did an improvised performance without using the stage. Eventually the play found a home and played a controversial 108 performances.

Trio (1944) by Dorothy and Howard Baker was about a man who tries to break up a lesbian relationship by marrying one of the women, causing the other woman to commit suicide. The producer first ran into trouble during the Philadelphia tryouts and lost his New York theatre when the theatre owners panicked. Eventually another theatre was secured but religious groups and reformers protested and the play was shut down by the police after 67 performances. The case went all the way to court but the verdict was not favorable and *Trio* closed for good

Tea and Sympathy (1953) was no more about homosexuality than *The Children's Hour* was about lesbianism but audiences were exposed to the subject in a serious and thoughtful manner for the first time. The prep school student Tom (John Kerr) is more sensitive and shy than the other boys and soon, fueled by the insecure masculinity of the headmaster, suspicion of homosexuality arises. Playwright Robert Anderson ends the play affirming the boy's heterosexuality (he makes love with the headmaster's wife) but the very mention of the topic of homosexuality caused a stir at the time.

Cat on a Hot Tin Roof (1955) was a much-awarded and successful play by Tennessee Williams but its theme of latent homosexuality and its graphic language was a matter of concern at the time. Two weeks into the run, Edward T. McCaffrey, Commissioner of Licenses, acted on complaints by the Children's Aid Society and other groups. The main objection was to the language, especially since the cast included some children. Once a few lines were deleted and it was assured that the children were in their dressing rooms during the play's more offensive passages, *Cat on a Hot Tin Roof* was allowed to continue.

Who's Afraid of Virginia Woolf? (1962) by Edward Albee received much acclaim by critics and audiences alike when it opened but the abrasive language and, in particular, the many expletives using "Jesus Christ" offended some powerful people. The Pulitzer Prize committee issued a "no award" decree that year, a decision that was an obvious criticism of Albee's play. Two out-voted members of the committee resigned over the decision. The drama received a great deal of opposition when it planned to play in Boston and was only allowed to open after Albee made some cuts in the script. And, because Albee insisted that his play only be performed for nonsegregated audiences, some Southern cities refused productions, citing the foul language as their reason.

The Dutchman (1964) was perhaps the most powerful and controversial of the protest plays penned by African-American playwrights in the 1960s. This short drama by Leroi Jones (later Imamu Amiri Baraka) was about the violent confrontation between a sluttish white girl and a middle-class black man on a subway. The play was an allegory for racial strife in America and inspired more arguments than most any other play in its day.

The Boys in the Band (1968) made no secret of the sexual preference of its characters. This Mart Crowley play was the most blatant and uncompromising mainstream play about homosexuals yet seen and, while many were put off by its bitchy and hysterical aspects, it allowed for fully-developed gay characters in future plays. Although it may seem dated and rather mechanical today, *The Boys in the Band* played 1,000 performances Off Broadway.

Hair (1967) gained its notoriety by attacking the established theatre community on two fronts: nudity and politics. The "tribal love-rock musical" started Off Broadway where its rock score, youthful abandon, and uncompromising sense of protest caught everyone's attention. The show was then restaged, rewritten, and reshaped into a powerful anti-establishment celebration, complete with a short nude scene that merrily offended Broadway for 1,836 performances.

Oh! Calcutta! (1969) was the brainchild of the British critic Kenneth Tynan and consisted of sketches about sex written mostly by American authors. Because of the large amount of nudity in the show, protests were heard but the show continued on for 704 performances without legal trouble. But in 1976, when a revival of *Oh! Calcutta!* was planned, there was a great deal of opposition from the League of New York Theatres and Producers who were in the midst of an effort to clean up Times Square of massage parlors and X-rated movie theatres. They felt the presence of such an "adult" entertainment in a legitimate Broadway theatre would undermine the pressure they were putting on the city to save the Theatre District. Because no first class house would book *Oh! Calcutta!*, the show opened in the small Edison Theatre and it ran there for a surprising 5,969 performances.

THE GREAT AMERICAN PLAY?

Audiences and critics have been waiting for the Great American Play as long as they have been waiting for the Great American Novel. And while *Moby Dick*, *Huckleberry Finn*, and other works over the years have been proclaimed the greatest novel, there has been much less common consent about one single American play. The whole idea of the Best or the Greatest is a literary fantasy because no one play (or novel, for that matter) can hope to capture the many diverse aspects of the American character. But fantasy or not, here are fifteen of the more likely candidates, presented in chronological order, for this phantom award.

The Contrast (1787) by Royall Tyler is the first comedy written by an American to be professionally produced and, more importantly, one that was distinctly American in tone and temperament. The comedy deals with class barriers and models itself after *The School for Scandal*, but the character of Jonathan, the first stage Yankee, laid the foundation for that most American of personas: the rugged individual. Jonathan is honest, a bit crude, down to earth, proud of his simple heritage, and servant to no man. He is the forefather of the stage Davey Crockett and Rip Van Winkle, as well as filmdom's cowboy heroes and tough private eyes. But, despite its historical importance, *The Contrast* is rarely revived and its dramaturgy is not especially notable.

Fashion; or, *Life in New York* (1845) by Anna Cora Mowatt is often revived and its dramaturgy is remarkable. Mowatt draws vivid, funny characters and the theme of honest values versus put-on airs is beautifully handled. When Mrs. Tiffany tries to break into high society by using her fractured French and marrying her daughters to men of class rather than their devoted beaux, the satire on "fashionable" ways is wickedly accurate. The play was a record-breaking hit in 1845 and has delighted audiences ever since.

Show Boat (1927), with music by Jerome Kern and book and lyrics by Oscar Hammerstein, is perhaps our greatest musical. Because the musical form is America's one unique contribution to world theatre, perhaps the Great American Play should be a musical play. The libretto alone is one of the strongest pieces of drama ever written by an American and Kern's music is world class. *Show Boat*'s broad spectrum, its potent use of several characters growing and changing over a substantial length of time, and its sweeping themes of family, racial dignity, and the power of love make it a strong candidate.

Ah, Wilderness! (1933) by Eugene O'Neill is his least typical work, but this idealized vision of what American life could be like is a vivid contrast to O'Neill's usual tragic point of view. Few American works capture the themes of family strength, young love, and the bittersweet pains of growing up better than *Ah, Wilderness!* Set on the Fourth of July, the gentle comedy also celebrates America as a land of dignity and hope. It was not a world that O'Neill (and most of America) ever experienced but he captured it vividly all the same.

Porgy and Bess (1935) is probably our greatest opera but it was conceived and written by its authors as a theatre work and it still holds forth as beautifully in a theatre as it does in an opera house. Based on DuBose Heyward's play *Porgy*, the musical expands on its themes and captures the sound of a people better than any non-musical play can. Heyward wrote the libretto and some of the lyrics with Ira Gershwin's help and set them to George Gershwin's music. By taking one small ghetto neighborhood as its focal point, *Porgy and Bess* encapsulates the anguish of thousands of Americans over many decades and today.

You Can't Take It With You (1936) by George S. Kaufman and Moss Hart is one of America's finest comedies and there is no reason that the Great American Play's approach should not be a comic one. While the play celebrates the warm and wacky qualities of a family that is distinctly atypical, it captures the inner spirit of revolt in each one of us. There is also something so characteristically American about the comedy's take on conventionality and unconventionality that it is endearing in a very democratic way.

Our Town (1938) by Thornton Wilder is perhaps the most universal of all American plays. It deals with life's most insignificant details as it tackles the world's most complex issues. No American play is more personal and, at the same time, so abstract. The town of Grover's Corners is a microcosm of America, to be sure, but these are living, breathing characters rather than symbols. *Our Town* remains one of the most popular of American plays so it must still be touching audiences in a special way.

Life With Father (1939) by Howard Lindsay and Russel Crouse was a pleasing and nostalgic view of upper class life in the late 1800s and it remains the longest-running play on record. Its charm is of an escapist quality (the comedy opened on the eve of World War Two and ran through several of the war years) and its characters have a familiarity that breaks through the period costumes and mannerisms. Yet the play is not often revived today and the America it depicted seems very foreign to us now.

The Glass Menagerie (1945) by Tennessee Williams is perhaps the most fragile and delicate play ever written by an American yet it still is a powerful stage piece. The scope of the play is small but telling and the narration is dreamy and evocative. Williams captures much about America's hopes and dreams in the little drama and then surely and defiantly destroys them both. Perhaps the Great American Play should be a drama of regret and of a life haunted by the past.

A Streetcar Named Desire (1947) by Tennessee Williams is a louder and more violent play than *The Glass Menagerie* but no less poetic. The fiery battle for survival between Stanley Kowalski and Blanche Du Bois can be seen as anything from a symbolic Civil War to the destruction of beauty by crass American greed for power and wealth. But it is the poetry that counts; while not writing in actual verse, Williams has created America's great epic poem in these two plays.

Death of a Salesman (1949) by Arthur Miller seems an obvious candidate for the Great American Play because, from its first production, Miller and others have argued that it is a modern American tragedy. Willy Loman is symbolic of many Americans who had the wrong kind of dreams but the character is so vivid and so powerfully written that he transcends any simple tokenism. Lacking the poetry of Williams or even O'Neill, *Death of a Salesman* is still a remarkable piece, a working man's tragic vision of America.

Long Day's Journey Into Night (1956) by Eugene O'Neill, probably his finest and most unrelentless work, is the flip side of his earlier *Ah, Wilderness!* While that play celebrated Americana by examining a happy Connecticut family, *Long Day's Journey Into Night* takes a tortured Connecticut family and looks at the four members with unsentimental honesty and truth. Although the play is largely autobiographical, it is also very universal with its themes of disillusionment, escape from reality, and the complex love-hate relationships found within a family.

A Raisin in the Sun (1959) by Lorraine Hansberry was applauded as an accomplished piece about "colored folk" in America when it opened, but now it is appreciated as one of the finest dramas ever written about the American family. Ostensibly about an African-American family living in the tenements of Chicago, the issue of race in the play has somewhat faded over the years and what remains is a taut, powerful drama about the American urge to break free and grow despite adversity. More hopeful than most plays about African-Americans, *A Raisin in the Sun* does not seem to date and, despite claims that it is too submissive a piece, the drama still plays beautifully on stage.

Who's Afraid of Virginia Woolf? (1962) by Edward Albee was a shocking and controversial hit in its day; looking back now, the shock is gone but a devastating drama still remains. Although small in scope, the play has a grandiose way of looking at tragedy and uses biting humor as few American dramas ever have. One can view the childless George and Martha as some sort of wicked joke by Albee to represent the Father and Mother of our country. But the play's power lies not in its mysteries or symbolism but in its savage honesty.

Angels in America, Parts One & Two (1993) by Tony Kushner is the only recent play on the list because the test of time is one of the most important ways to judge a play's greatness. But this two-part panorama of American life in the 1990s has such a wide range of ideas and such an all-encompassing grasp of what America is going through that it just may stand the test of time. More expressionistic than any other play on this list, *Angels in America* uses a nightmarish approach to its subject. Its characters are broadly drawn and its many plots are frenetic in their construction but the final effect is overwhelming. Will we look back at this twenty years from now and see explosive drama or just period angst?

For further reading: David Sheward's *It's a Hit: The Backstage Book of Longest-Running Broadway Shows*, Abe Laufe's *The Wicked Stage: A History of Censorship and Harassment in the United States*, Gerald Bordman's three-volume *American Theatre: A Chronicle of Comedy and Drama* and *Oxford Companion to the American Theatre*, and the *Best Plays* series.

3

PLAYERS

MEMORABLE BROADWAY DEBUTS

Few actors make a big splash with their first Broadway role. Most start out in the chorus, in the crowd, or as unnamed characters such as the Maid or the Wounded Soldier. Contemporary actor Jason Robards, Jr., and the popular nineteenth century-actor Henry E. Dixey, for example, each started his professional career playing a cow in a play. But once in a while an actor starts with a juicy role that brings him or her immediate attention. Here are some memorable Broadway debuts by American actors. Those who won a Tony Award for their initial effort are marked with an asterisk (*).

Edith Adams as Eileen in *Wonderful Town* (1953)
Robert Alda as Sky Masterson in *Guys and Dolls* (1950)
Jane Alexander* as Ellie Bachman in *The Great White Hope* (1968)
Woody Allen as Allan Felix in *Play It Again, Sam* (1969)
Pearl Bailey as Butterfly in *St. Louis Woman* (1946)
Kay Ballard as Helen in *The Golden Apple* (1954)
Anne Bancroft as Gittel Mosca in *Two for the See Saw* (1958)
Vivian Blaine as Adelaide in *Guys and Dolls* (1950)
Tom Bosley* as LaGuardia in *Fiorello!* (1959)
Betty Buckley as Martha Jefferson in *1776* (1969)
Carol Burnett as Princess Winifred in *Once Upon a Mattress* (1959)
Mrs. Leslie Carter as Kate Graydon in *The Ugly Duckling* (1890)
Brandon De Wilde as John Henry in *A Member of the Wedding* (1950)
Alice Ghostley in *New Faces of 1952*
Lulu Glaser in *The Lion Tamer* (1891)
Joanna Gleason as Monica in *I Love My Wife* (1977)
Cliff Gorman* as Lenny Bruce in *Lenny* (1971)
Robert Goulet as Lancelot in *Camelot* (1960)
Uta Hagen as Nina in *The Sea Gull* (1938)

Hal Holbrook as Mark Twain in *Mark Twain Tonight!* (1955)
Jennifer Holliday* as Effie Melody White in *Dreamgirls* (1981)
Kim Hunter as Stella Kowalski in *A Streetcar Named Desire* (1948)
Judith Ivey* as Josie in *Steaming* (1982)
Carol Lawrence in *New Faces of 1952*
Andrea Martin* as Alice in *My Favorite Year* (1992)
Mary Martin as Dolly Winslow in *Leave It to Me!* (1938)
The Marx Brothers in *I'll Say She Is* (1924)
Andrea McArdle as Annie in *Annie* (1977)
Ethel Merman as Kate Fothergill in *Girl Crazy* (1930)
Stephanie Mills as Dorothy in *The Wiz* (1975)
Liza Minnelli* as Flora in *Flora, the Red Menace* (1965)
Jerry Orbach as Paul in *Carnival* (1961)
John Raitt as Billy Bigelow in *Carousel* (1945)
Martha Scott as Emily Webb in *Our Town* (1938)
Vivienne Segal as Mizi in *The Blue Paradise* (1915)
Alexis Smith* as Phyllis Stone in *Follies* (1971)
Stephen Spinella* as Prior in *Angels in America, Part One* (1993)
Barbra Streisand as Miss Marmelstein in *I Can Get It for You Wholesale*
    (1962)
Nancy Walker as the Blind Date in *Best Foot Forward* (1941)

ACTORS AND THEIR FAMOUS ROLES

In the days before film and television, it was possible for an actor to play the same role for years, sometimes for a full career, and still attract audiences. While long runs in New York were not common until the 1940s, it was possible to take a play on the road and tour for several seasons. Here is a selective list of some actors who enjoyed a long association with a particular character in a play.

Frank Bacon (1864-1922) had a moderately successful career as a professional actor until he and Winchell Smith wrote the comedy *Lightnin'* (1918), which ran a surprising 1,291 performances on Broadway. Bacon played the shiftless hero Lightnin' Bill Jones for much of the run, as well as on tour and in revivals. All in all, he played the role over 2,000 times.

Henry Clay Barnabee (1833-1917) was a popular comic singer in Gilbert and Sullivan productions and other comic operettas. But he was best remembered for his dandy performance as the Sheriff of Nottingham in the musical *Robin Hood* (1891), a role he created in the original production and played over 2,000 times in various revivals.

Yul Brynner (1920-1985) was always identified with the role that made him famous, the King of Siam in *The King and I* (1951). Ironically, the role was considered a supporting one and Byrnner was billed below the title in the original production where Gertrude Lawrence was the box office draw. But soon it became the King's show and Brynner owned the role as few actors have ever inhabited a part. He played the King for most of the 1,246 Broadway performances, recreated it on film, toured with the show off and on over the next thirty years, and brought it back to Broadway on two other occasions. All in all, Brynner figured out that he played the King 4,631 times.

Frank Chanfrau (1824-1884) was a beloved comic actor who had the good fortune to find two roles that lasted him throughout his long career. In 1848 he first played the bigger-than-life fireman Mose in *A Glance at New York*, a part he played in revivals and sequels for twenty years. Just when he was outgrowing the youthful Mose, Chanfrau introduced his Kit Redding, the pioneer hero in *Kit, the Arkansas Traveller* (1870), and played the part until shortly before his death.

Carol Channing (1921-) has played Dolly Levi in *Hello, Dolly!* so many times it is questionable if even she knows the exact number; by 1996 she had tallied well over 4,000 performances. The 1964 musical provided her with her most beloved role and she toured extensively with it after her Broadway stint. In the late 1970s she returned to the role and toured again, bringing the show back to Broadway in 1978. She repeated the same feat again in 1995.

Kate Claxton (1848-1924) had her first (and only) major hit playing the blind waif Louise in *The Two Orphans* (1874) and she continued to play it for the next thirty years. Audiences so identified Louise with Claxton that in 1876, when the theatre she was performing in burned down, they believed the misfortunes of the fictional Louise and the actress were one and the same.

Katharine Cornell (1893-1974) played many famous roles during her illustrious stage career but the one she kept returning to was that of Elizabeth Barrett Browning in *The Barretts of Wimpole Street* (1931). After her successful Broadway engagement and revival, Cornell toured with the play across the country and around the world in a notable 1934 tour that took in seventy-seven cities.

William H. Crane (1845-1928), a favorite character actor on Broadway and on the road, had many popular comic roles but none more famous than the crusty horse-trader in *David Harum* (1900). Crane played the title role for the 148 New York performances then toured with the show for four seasons. He even made an early silent film version of his performance.

Henry E. Dixey (1859-1943) was a gifted comic actor who was unusual in that he was also extremely handsome. This attribute allowed him to play the comely statue-turned-human in the musical *Adonis* (1884) for a record-breaking run in New York and for several years on tour and in return engagements.

Jeanne Eagels (1894-1929), in her short and tragic life, managed to find the role of a lifetime and play it for many performances in New York and on the road. She originated the part of sultry Sadie Thompson who seduces a minister in *Rain* (1922) and played the part at one place or another for the next seven years.

J. K. Emmet (1841-1891) was a popular stage tenor and comic who was beloved by audiences in the late nineteenth century for his recurring role of Fritz in a handful of musicals. Emmet first played the part in *Fritz, Our Cousin German* in 1870 where, as an immigrant looking for his long-lost sister, he charmed audiences and sang "Emmet's Lullabye," one of the most famous lullabies ever written. He was so successful that Emmet played Fritz in several musical sequels and in other shows that were thinly disguised versions of the original. He was still playing Fritz when he died, still at the peak of his popularity.

Edwin Forrest (1806-1872), one of the greatest American actors of the nineteenth century, played many classical roles but there were two roles that he kept returning to throughout his career, performing them over 1,000 performances each. As the great Indian chief in *Metamora* (1829) and the rebellious Spartacus in *The Gladiator* (1831), Forrest filled playhouses in New York and across the country for many years.

William Gillette (1855-1937) appeared in many hits during his long career but the role he is most remembered for is that of *Sherlock Holmes* (1899), which he adapted himself from the Arthur Conan Doyle stories. The original production ran 256 performances and then, as was the custom, Gillette toured with it. Throughout the rest of his career, he returned to the role and thirty-two years later he was still reviving his Holmes because of public demand.

Charlotte Greenwood (1893-1978) was a musical comedy star who first played a character named Letitia Proudfoot in *Pretty Mrs. Smith* (1914). She so endeared audiences with the role that for the next twenty years she played Letty in a series of musicals, such as *Long, Lanky Letty* (1915), *So Long, Letty* (1916), *Linger Longer, Letty* (1919), *Let 'er Go, Letty* (1921), *Letty Pepper* (1922), and *Leaning on Letty* (1935). Not all of these made it to New York but all were successes on tour and Greenwood racked up well over 1,000 performances as Letty.

Joel Grey (1932-) originated the role of the Master of Ceremonies in the musical *Cabaret* (1966), toured with the show, and reprised his performance in summer stock for years. In 1972 he made the film version and in 1987 he returned to Broadway with a *Cabaret* revival. Another role Grey did on Broadway and toured with for years was that of showman George M. Cohan in *George M!* (1968). Rarely in the modern theatre have two roles provided steady work for an actor for over twenty years.

J. H. Hackett (1800-1871) first played the farcical Kentucky Congressman Colonel Nimrod Wildfire in *The Lion of the West* (1831) and the colorful backwoodsman was so popular with audiences that he recreated the character in *The Kentuckian* (1833). After a career of playing some of Shakespeare's most demanding roles, Hackett returned to Colonel Wildfire again and performed the famous role for years until he retired.

Richard Harrison (1864-1935) only played one role in his professional career, that of De Lawd in the fable fantasy *The Green Pastures* (1930), but he played it over 2,000 times and was forever identified with the heavenly character. Harrison originated the role on Broadway and for the next five years played it on tour and in revivals.

Matilda Heron (1830-1877) was not the first American to play *Camille* but the English version she commissioned and first performed in 1857 was considered the best and her Camille the definitive portrayal in America. Heron played the dying courtesan for many years after, returning to the role during her frequent financial troubles.

Hal Holbrook (1925-) is a versatile actor with a variety of roles in his credits but most theatregoers will always remember him for his one-man show *Mark Twain Tonight!* Holbrook first presented his unforgettable portrayal of the American author in 1955 and for the next forty years played it hundreds of times on Broadway, on tour, and on television.

Edward Everett Horton (1886-1970), one of the movies' most distinctive character actors, appeared in several plays but was seen most often in a role that he did not originate. *Springtime for Henry* was a popular comedy on Broadway in 1931 but in 1932 Horton played the role of the aging playboy Henry Dewlip in Southern California. He was so popular in it that he toured in the comedy season after season and brought his interpretation to Broadway for a revival in 1951. All in all, it is estimated he played Henry over 1,700 times.

Joseph Jefferson (1829-1905) was one of the nineteenth century's greatest comic actors and of all his memorable roles none approached the popularity of his *Rip van Winkle*. Jefferson first adapted the Washington Irving story as a stage piece in 1859, but in 1866 an adaptation co-authored by Dion Bouicault opened on Broadway and it established Jefferson forever after as the colorful Rip. Jefferson revived the role on tour for many years after, racking up well over 1,000 performances.

Doris Keane (1881-1945) was a dark-eyed beauty who was an audience and critic favorite for many years, although she was most well known for only one role: the opera star Margherita Cavallini in the popular melodrama *Romance* (1913). Keane played the passionate Italian lady on Broadway, across America, and in Europe for five years, then returned to the role again in the 1920s. All in all, it is estimated she played Margherita over 1,000 times.

Laura Keene (1826?-1873), the first female theatre manager in America, was known and beloved first and foremost for her acting. Her most popular role was that of Florence Trenchard in Tom Taylor's comedy *Our American Cousin*, which she produced in 1858. Keene played the role in New York and across the country for years, and on April 14, 1865 she was celebrating her one thousandth performance of the part in Ford's Theatre in Washington, D.C. when she and her cast were interrupted by the assassination of Abraham Lincoln.

Larry Kert (1930-1991) originated the role of Tony in the Broadway musical *West Side Story* (1957) and, plagued by a career of flop musicals, he returned to the role on tour and in summer stock until he was too old to play the street gang leader. It is estimated he played Tony over 1,000 times.

Wilton Lackaye (1862-1932) was a popular actor in many successful comedies and dramas but by far his most acclaimed role was that of the mesmerizing Svengali in *Trilby* (1895). As the villain who uses his hypnotic powers to turn Trilby into a great opera star, Lackaye thrilled audiences and he played the part off and on for the next thirty-five years.

Paul Lipson (1913-) is hardly a household name but it has been determined that he played Tevye in *Fiddler on the Roof* more than any other actor. Lipson played a supporting role in the original 1964 production on Broadway then toured as Tevye in one of the major road companies. Later in the Broadway run, Lipson returned to the original production and played Tevye for hundreds of more performances during the historic run.

Richard Mansfield (1854-1907), the most successful stage actor of his day, was the first American to play several famous roles, including some by Shaw. But his most popular role, and one that he played off and on for years, was the flamboyantly careless dandy *Beau Brummell* (1890). The part was one that brought Mansfield wealth and attention until his death.

Frank Mayo (1839-1896) was a renowned Shakespearean actor but spent much of his career playing the rugged frontiersman in *Davy Crockett*. Mayo first played the Kentucky hero in 1872 on the road and, despite initial lackluster business, he stuck with the role and eventually he and the play became perennial favorites. He first played Davey in New York in 1873 and returned often. Mayo was still playing it two days before his death in 1896. While no accurate number of performances exists, it is well known that the active Mayo played in little else for 25 years.

Maggie Mitchell (1832-1918) was a child actress who grew up to play several beloved heroines, from Jane Eyre to Mignon; but the role her audiences always demanded again was her bewitching country girl Fanchon in *Fanchon, the Cricket* (1862), based on a George Sand story. As part of the play, Mitchell presented an alluring "shadow dance" that Fanchon uses to win over her future father-in-law. Mitchell played the gamesome heroine off and on for the next twenty-five years.

James O'Neill (1847-1920) was one of the nineteenth century's most promising Shakespearean actors and played many of the great classical roles. But the part that endeared him to the public was the dashing Edmund Dantes in *The Count of Monte Cristo* (1883), making him a matinee idol and very wealthy. Ironically, it was the role that ruined his career as well. Whenever he needed money, O'Neill revived *The Count of Monte Cristo* and soon audiences would not accept him in the great tragic roles that he wanted to play. He was the father of Eugene O'Neill who wrote about his father's tortured relationship with his famous role in *Long Day's Journey Into Night* (1956).

John Owens (1823-1886) was a promising nineteenth-century actor who found his goldmine in the part of Solon Shingle, the crusty country bumpkin in *The People's Lawyer* (1856). Owens was so popular in the role that many subsequent productions were titled *Solon Shingle* and he played it until he retired in 1885.

Richard Sterling (1880-1959) was never a famous name on Broadway but he had the distinction of appearing in *Life With Father* (1939) for its entire seven-year run. Sterling played the supporting role of Rev. Dr. Lloyd for all of the comedy's 3,224 performances.

David Warfield (1866-1951) was a popular character actor with several famous roles to his credit but his most memorable was in *The Music Master* (1904). As the conductor Anton von Barwig looking for his long-lost daughter, Warfield moved audiences to tears of happiness and the play proved his biggest hit. He played the conductor on Broadway and on tour for three years then returned to it throughout his career, racking up well over 1,000 performances.

When discussing prolific performers, there are three contemporary examples that come to mind. Marian Seldes played the victimized wife Myra for much of *Deathtrap*'s 1,793 performances. Davis Gaines has played the title role in *The Phantom of the Opera* for over six years on tour and on Broadway. Cathy Russell has played in the Off-Broadway thriller *Perfect Crime* for over 4,000 performances. And singer/dancer Marlene Danielle has played Bombalurina in the Broadway cast of *Cats* for over fourteen years, racking up over 5,000 performances.

RENOWNED ACTING TEAMS

There are no famous acting partnerships in the theatre today but in the past the dynamics created when two beautifully matched actors performed together could create a box office sensation. Here are some beloved acting teams from the past.

Adele (1898-1981) and **Fred Astaire** (1899-1987) were Broadway's favorite brother-sister team, starring in sixteen musicals in New York and London. Both were accomplished singers, but it was their dancing and comic talents that endeared them to audiences. *Lady, Be Good!* (1924), *Funny Face* (1927), and *The Band Wagon* (1931) were among their hit shows. The team broke up after Adele retired in 1931 to marry the British Lord Cavendish.

Bobby Clark (1888-1960) and **Paul McCullough** (1883-1936) worked together as a comedy team for thirty-one years in circuses, minstrel shows, vaudeville, and eventually on Broadway where they were featured in *The Ramblers* (1926) *Strike Up the Band* (1930), and other musicals and revues. After McCullough's suicide, Clark continued to appear solo in musicals and remained one of Broadway's favorite clowns through the 1940s.

William Crane (1845-1928) and **Stuart Robson** (1836-1903) were the most celebrated comic acting team of their day. Starting with *Our Boarding House* in 1877, the two comedians enthralled audiences with numerous plays for the next dozen years. The two actors had successful individual careers after their parting in 1889 but audiences always fondly remembered their dual comedic genius in plays such as *A Comedy of Errors* (1878) and *The Henrietta* (1887).

Hume Cronyn (1911-) and **Jessica Tandy** (1909-1994) each had distinguished careers separately (she was the original Blanche DuBois in *A Streetcar Named Desire* in 1947), but the married couple is often remembered for their co-acting in such plays as *The Fourposter* (1951), *A Delicate Balance* (1966), *The Gin Game* (1977), and on the screen.

John Drew (1853-1927), **Ada Rehan** (1860-1916), **James Lewis** (1838-1896), and **Mrs. G. H. Gilbert** (1821-1904) were the mainstays of Augustin Daly's famous repertory, so respected by audiences, critics, and fellow actors that the quartet was known affectionately as the Big Four. Drew and Rehan played the young couple in both classical and new plays while Gilbert and Lewis excelled in character roles. From 1879 to almost the end of the century, the foursome presented the most deft and polished comic acting seen on Broadway and on the road.

Edward Gallagher (1873?-1929) and **Al Shean** (1868-1949), the renowned comedy team from vaudeville, appeared intermittently on the Broadway stage, most memorably together in *The Ziegfeld Follies of 1922*, and separately in a variety of shows.

William Gaxton (1893-1963) and **Victor Moore** (1876-1962) were first cast together to play the President and Vice President in *Of Thee I Sing* (1931) and the comic rapport was so electric that they later appeared in five more musicals together. While each had many Broadway credits separately, it was in their musicals together, such as *Anything Goes* (1934), *Leave It to Me!* (1938), and *Louisiana Purchase* (1938), that they were most fondly remembered.

Edward Harrigan (1844-1911) and **Tony Hart** (1855-1891) starred in seventeen Broadway musicals between 1878 and 1885, which they produced and wrote themselves. Harrigan and Hart were most known for their seven *Mulligan Guard* musicals, knockdown musical farces about brawling immigrants in the slums of New York City. Harrigan specialized in ethnic types and Hart often played female roles with outrageous sincerity.

Willie (1886?-1949) and **Eugene Howard** (1880-1965) were two gifted comic singers who starred in vaudeville before going on to do seventeen Broadway musicals. The brothers were featured in several editions of *The Passing Show* and *George White's Scandals* before going on to such revues as *Ballyhoo of 1932* and *The Show Is On* (1937).

Alfred Lunt (1892-1980) and **Lynn Fontanne** (1887-1983) were unquestionably the most famous and beloved acting couple in the American theatre. The British-born Fontanne met the American Lunt when they acted together on stage in 1916 but their first important production together was *The Guardsman* (1924). They went on to perform in comedies, dramas, and classics together, reigning as the undisputed masters of comic timing, subtle nuances, and electric co-acting. Among their many critical and popular hits together were *Elizabeth the Queen* (1930), *Design for Living* (1933), *Idiot's Delight* (1936), *There Shall Be No Night* (1940), *The Great Sebastians* (1956), and *The Visit* (1958).

Frederic March (1897-1975) and **Florence Eldridge** (1901-1988) were wed in 1927 and, in between successful careers apart (mostly in Hollywood for March), they played husband and wife in such memorable plays as *The Skin of Our Teeth* (1942), *Years Ago* (1946), and *Long Day's Journey Into Night* (1956).

The **Marx Brothers** were major vaudeville and Broadway stars before going on to movie fame. Chico (1887-1961), Harpo (1888-1964), and Groucho (1890-1977) were the primary members of the team, sometimes assisted by brothers Gummo (1895-1977) and Zeppo (1901-1979). They made a sensational Broadway debut with their musical *I'll Say She Is* (1924) and went on to the hits *The Cocoanuts* (1925) and *Animal Crackers* (1928) before going to Hollywood.

Ole Olsen (1892-1963) and **Chic Johnson** (1891-1962) were the madcap vaudeville team of comics who appeared on Broadway in musicals, most memorably *Take a Chance* (1933) and the long-running *Hellzapoppin* (1938).

E. H. Sothern (1859-1933) and **Julia Marlowe** (1866-1950) were America's premiere Shakespearean acting couple. Each of them performed the Bard's famous roles with their first spouse but when Sothern married Marlowe and they started performing together with *Romeo and Juliet* in 1904, audiences and critics were enthralled. They performed most of the major plays on Broadway and on tour until Marlowe's retirement due to ill health in 1924.

Fred Stone (1873-1959) and **Dave Montgomery** (1870-1917) first teamed up in vaudeville but by 1901 were on Broadway where they became the most popular comedy team in the musicals of their day. Their most beloved performances together were in *The Wizard of Oz* (1903) and *The Red Mill* (1906).

Joe Weber (1867-1942) and **Lew Fields** (1867-1941) co-starred in fifteen Broadway musicals during a ten-year period at the turn of the century. The team played "Dutch comics" in a series of musical burlesques that parodied the plays of the day. They were so successful that Weber and Fields were able to build their own Broadway theatre and produce their own shows there. Dressed in outrageous check suits and exaggerated whiskers, the two comics played Dutch immigrants and established a form of ethnic humor that would be seen later in vaudeville, film, and television.

OTHER POPULAR ACTORS OF YESTERDAY

In addition to those mentioned above for their famous roles or memorable teams, here is a very selective list of some other beloved actors and actresses from the past. (While this list includes male favorites from the musical stage, famous actresses from musicals are listed as "Broadway Divas" in the Chapter 6.)

Maude Adams (1872-1953) endeared herself to audiences and critics with her gentle manner and heartwarming portrayal of wistful characters. Adams started her acting career as a child and became a star with her performance of Lady Babbie in J. M. Barrie's *The Little Minister* (1897). Barrie wrote *Peter Pan* (1905) for her and it became her most famous role. In 1918, at the peak of her popularity, Adams retired from the New York stage.

Jacob Adler (1855-1926) was the most famous star of the American-Yiddish theatre, appearing on Broadway later in his career. The Russian-born Adler emigrated to America in 1887 and toured extensively before founding his own theatre company in New York. In addition to many roles in Yiddish plays, his Shylock was considered one of the most powerful performances of his day.

Ira Aldridge (1804?-1867), America's first important African-American actor, was the toast of Europe in the mid-nineteenth century but did little performing in his American homeland. Sources vary on when or where he was born but Aldridge began performing in New York with black theatre ensembles. He was soon discouraged because most serious roles for blacks were played by white actors in blackface, so he relocated to England where he became famous for playing Romeo, Othello, and other roles that he toured with across the Continent.

Judith Anderson (1898-1992) was one of America's finest actresses of tragedy; her *Medea* (1947) ranked as a highlight of classical acting. The hard-faced Australian-born actress first made a name for herself in *Cobra* (1924) and appeared as dark and often sinister characters on stage and in film for over sixty years.

Mary Anderson (1859-1940) was considered the most beautiful actress to grace the stages of America around the 1880s though critics were divided regarding her acting abilities. She became an audience favorite playing Juliet, Pauline in *The Lady of Lyons* (1877), *Meg Merrilies,* and Perdita in *The Winter's Tale.* Anderson retired at the peak of her popularity to marry and was fondly remembered for years after.

George Arliss (1868-1946) was a character actor whose portrayal of diabolically haunting characters made him a star on stage and in Hollywood. Among his Broadway hits were *The Darling of the Gods* (1902), *The Devil* (1908), *Disraeli* (1911), and The *Green Goddess* (1921).

Anthony Aston is believed to have been the first professional actor in America but we only have his word for it. Little is known about Aston except that he performed during the first half of the eighteenth century. In an autobiographical preface to a play that he wrote, Aston describes some of his acting experiences and the many places he performed.

Tallulah Bankhead (1903-1968), the highly-mannered actress from Alabama who called everybody "dahling," was a popular favorite on stage and screen. Her most memorable Broadway roles were the conniving Regina Giddens in *The Little Foxes* (1939), the seductive Sabina in *The Skin of Our Teeth* (1942), and the feisty Amanda in *Private Lives* (1946).

Lawrence Barrett (1838-1891) was one of the finest tragedians of the nineteenthth century, an actor who often played opposite Edwin Booth and held his own. Barrett was more ambitious than Booth, trying new roles all the time and exploring different staging techniques. He was also a noted theatre historian, writing about Booth, Edwin Forrest, and other actors of the day.

Ethel Barrymore (1879-1959) became a star with *Captain Jinks of the Horse Marines* (1901) and remained one of the grande dames of the American theatre for fifty years. Perhaps the most subtle of the famous Barrymore acting clan, she was influential in bringing a more natural style of acting to the American stage. In addition to several classical roles, Barrymore was acclaimed for her performances in *Our Mrs. McChesney* (1915), *The Lady of the Camellias* (1917), *Déclassée* (1919), *The Constant Wife* (1926), and *The Corn Is Green* (1940).

John Barrymore (1882-1942) was the most electric actor of the Barrymore family and one of the most exciting stage performers of his day. Before he succumbed to films, he offered dynamic stage performances as *Richard III* (1920) and *Hamlet* (1923), as well as memorable roles in *The Yellow Ticket* (1919), *Justice* (1916), and *Redemption* (1918).

Lionel Barrymore (1878-1954), the character actor of the Barrymore family and perhaps the finest craftsman of the clan, found uneven success on stage and so went to Hollywood rather early in his career. His most famous stage roles include the suspected spy Milt Shanks in *TheCopperhead* (1918) and the radical politician Achille Cortelton in *The Claw* (1921).

Blanche Bates (1873-1941) was a passionate beauty whose finest stage performances were in David Belasco productions: Cho-Cho-San in *Madame Butterfly* (1900), Yo-San in *The Darling of the Gods* (1902), and Minnie in *The Girl of the Golden West* (1905).

Sam Bernard (1863-1927), one of the stage's favorite comedians at the turn of the century, got his start as a featured player in Joe Weber and Lew Fields' celebrated travesties in the 1890s. Playing a variety of dialect roles such as the silly Mr. Hoggenheimer, Bernard appeared in both comedies and musicals until he retired in 1927.

Edwin Booth (1833-1893), arguably the finest classical American actor of the nineteenth century, played most of the major Shakespearean roles but was most beloved for his *Hamlet*, which he first played in 1860 and was still performing as late as 1891. His other notable stage performances include *Richelieu, King Lear, A New Way to Pay Old Debts, The Lady of Lyons,* and *Othello,* all of which he kept in his repertory for many years.

Shirley Booth (1898?-1992) was equally adept at performing in comedies, serious dramas, and musicals. The talented character actress appeared in such American classics as *Three Men on a Horse* (1935), *The Philadelphia Story* (1939), and *Come Back, Little Sheba* (1950). Booth also starred in *A Tree Grows in Brooklyn* (1951) and *By the Beautiful Sea* (1954), two musicals that allowed her to play wistful comic spinsters, as well as other musicals and plays.

Mrs. Leslie Carter (1862-1937) was an infamous divorcee who turned to the stage to make her fortune after good society had shunned her. Under the tutelage of David Belasco, she had her greatest triumphs in his productions of *The Heart of Maryland* (1895), *Zaza* (1899), *Du Barry* (1901), and *Adrea* (1905).

Ina Claire (1892-1985) was one of the finest stage comediennes of the 1920s and 1930s, specializing in sophisticated but spirited heroines. Among her many notable Broadway credits were *Polly With a Past* (1917), *The Awful Truth* (1922), *The Last of Mrs. Cheyney* (1925), *Biography* (1932), *The Fatal Weakness* (1946), and *The Confidential Clerk* (1954).

George M. Cohan (1878-1942) was the musical theatre's leading dynamo (author, songwriter, director, producer) and one of Broadway's most popular actors for over thirty years. Cohan first gained attention in vaudeville but he became a full-fledged Broadway star in his own *Little Johnny Jones* (1904). In addition to his performances in his own plays and musicals, Cohan is also remembered for his paternal Nat Miller in *Ah, Wilderness!* (1933) and his singing-dancing FDR in *I'd Rather Be Right* (1937).

Thomas Abthorpe Cooper (1776-1849) is considered America's first major tragedian, an actor who tackled the most difficult of roles and usually succeeded. The British-born Cooper first made his name in the Philadelphia theatres then conquered New York, managing the Park Theatre for a time. He became an American citizen and later was appointed by President Polk to a goverment post but continued to perform until 1838.

Jane Cowl (1884-1950) was a dark-eyed beauty who mesmerized audiences during the first half of the twentieth century. A discovery of David Belasco, she appeared in several of his productions from 1903 to 1910, then went on to play tragic waifs in a variety of melodramas, some of which she co-wrote.

Charlotte Crabtree (1847-1924) was the perpetually young entertainer known and beloved by thousands as simply "Lotta." While none of her vehicles were very noteworthy, her charm, youthful beauty, and singing and dancing vitality made her a favorite with audiences for over thirty years. Lotta played youthful ingenues well into her forties and she left a $4,000,000 estate when she died.

Frank Craven (1875-1945) was a gentle and beloved character actor who often appeared in domestic comedies that he wrote, such as *The First Year* (1920) and *That's Gratitude* (1930). Perhaps his most remembered performance came near the end of his career: as the Stage Manager in *Our Town* (1938).

Charlotte Cushman (1816-1876) was not only America's first tragic actress to achieve national and international fame, she was in many ways the American theatre's first great female star. Cushman played in both the classics and in contemporary dramas, her portrayals of Meg Merrilies in *Guy Mannering* (1837) and Nancy in *Oliver Twist* (1839) being among her most popular roles. She even played several male roles, including Romeo and Hamlet.

Alfred Drake (1914-1992) was one of the Broadway musical's favorite leading men in the 1940s and 1950s. Among his many musical roles, he introduced the characters of Curly in *Oklahoma!* (1943), Fred/Petruchio in *Kiss Me, Kate* (1948), and the poet Hajj in *Kismet* (1953).

Ruth Draper (1884-1956) was a beloved performer who played in comic monodramas that she wrote herself. On a bare stage and with minimal props, Draper portrayed a variety of characters so succinctly and with such honesty that she charmed audiences worldwide from 1917 until her death in 1956.

Mrs. John Drew (1820-1897) was not only one of the nineteenth century's finest actresses, she was also one of the most respected and successful theatre managers, running the Arch Street Theatre in Philadelphia for over thirty years. Of her many memorable performances, her Mrs. Malaprop in *The Rivals* was the most beloved and she played it off and on for years. Drew was the grandmother of and responsible for raising Ethel, John, and Lionel Barrymore.

Maxine Elliott (1868-1940) may not have been the most versatile of actresses but her stunning beauty made her an audience favorite at the turn of the century. Many of her plays turned into showcases for her regal looks and dignified manner but audiences did not seem to mind. Of the many superlatives used to describe Elliott's beauty, the one that most people remembered: "Venus de Milo with arms."

Minnie Fiske (1865-1932) was perhaps the most ambitious, forward-looking and experimental actress the American theatre has ever seen. She started as a child actress, turned to playwriting for a while, then returned to the stage to champion plays by Ibsen and promising new American playwrights. In addition to all the major Ibsen heroines, Mrs. Fiske (as she was usually billed) gave unforgettable performances as *Tess of the D'Urbervilles* (1897), *Becky Sharp* (1899), *Salvation Nell* (1908), and *Mrs. Bumpstead-Leigh* (1911).

Henry Fonda (1905-1982) had such a remarkable film career that it is too often forgotten that he also had a memorable stage career before and after Hollywood discovered him. Fonda was featured in such Broadway plays as *New Faces* (1934) and *The Farmer Takes a Wife* (1934) before his film career took off, and he then returned to Broadway perhaps more than any other movie star. Among his many later stage credits were *Mister Roberts* (1948), *Point of No Return* (1951), *The Caine Mutiny Court-Martial* (1954), *Two for the Seesaw*

(1958), and *Clarence Darrow* (1974).

John Gilbert (1810-1889) was one of the most respected actors of the nineteenth century, a stiff, conservative actor who managed to excell in elderly comic roles even as a young man. Gilbert worked for various companies and was most remembered for his superb interpretations of such classic roles as Anthony Absolute in *The Rivals* and Peter Teazle in *The School for Scandal.*

Nat Goodwin (1857-1919) was a comic favorite on Broadway and on the road during the decades surrounding the turn of the century. Goodwin played rowdy, boisterous characters in forgotten low comedies for years but graduated to more sophisticated roles, such as Uncle Everett in *Why Marry?* (1917), near the end of his career.

Ruth Gordon (1896-1985) was one of the stage and film's most versatile actresses, playing everything from farce to Chekhov to fantasy. Perhaps her finest stage performance was as Dolly Levi in the original *The Matchmaker* (1955). Gordon was also a successful playwright and screenwriter.

Lewis Hallam, Jr. (1740-1808) was born in Britain but came to America with his theatre parents at a young age, spending much of his life acting throughout the colonies and founding the landmak American Company. Hallam played a variety of roles but was most known for his tragic characters, such as Arsaces in *The Prince of Parthia* (1767) and *Hamlet*, the earliest known record of an American playing the part.

Walter Hampden (1879-1955) was a distinguished actor known for his many performances in classical roles. Although his Hamlet, Romeo, Marc Antony, Shylock, and Othello were kept in his repertory for years because of audience demand, his most memorable roles were *Cyrano de Bergerac*, *Richelieu*, and Manson in *The Servant in the House* (1908)

Helen Hayes (1900-1993) was often proclaimed the "first lady of the American stage" for her long career of varied roles and many memorable performances. Hayes was equally adept at historical drama, such as *Mary of Scotland* (1933) and *Victoria Regina* (1935); broad comedy, such as *Happy Birthday* (1946) and *Mrs. McThing* (1952); Shakespeare, such as Viola in a 1940 revival of *Twelfth Night;* and contemporary drama, such as *A Touch of the Poet* (1958). Hayes started as a child actress and ended her career playing lovable little old ladies in plays, films, and on television.

De Wolf Hopper (1858-1935) was a deep-voiced musical comedy star who delighted audiences in New York and on the road in Gilbert and Sullivan operettas and in several early American musicals such as *Wang* (1891) and *El Capitan* (1896).

Josephine Hull (1886-1957) played loveable and looney old ladies better than anyone else. The popular character actress was seen in such American classics as *Craig's Wife* (1925), *You Can't Take It With You* (1936), *Arsenic and Old Lace* (1941), *Harvey* (1944), and *The Solid Gold Cadillac* (1953).

Walter Huston (1884-1950) was a dynamic presence on stage and in films with his gruff voice and talent for quirky characterization. Among this most remembered stage roles were the greedy Ephraim Cabot in *Desire Under the Elms* (1924), the pensive businessman *Dodsworth* (1934), and Pieter Stuyvesant in *Knickerbocker Holiday* (1938).

Al Jolson (1886-1950), considered by many to be the greatest all-around American entertainer, was a star in vaudeville, minstrel shows, and even burlesque before conquering Broadway, radio, and films. A passionate performer who seduced his audiences with his unabashed sentimentality, Jolson's vehicles were rarely noteworthy but the songs he introduced were as legendary as the stage persona he created.

Dennis King (1897-1971) was Broadway's favorite operetta leading man in the 1920s, staring in such musicals as *Rose-Marie* (1924), *The Vagabond King* (1925), and *The Three Musketeers* (1928). In the 1930s he turned to non-musicals and appeared in a variety of different plays through the 1960s.

Bert Lahr (1895-1967), one of America's most gifted clowns, lit up burlesque, vaudeville, Broadway, and films with a series of memorable comic performances for over fifty years. Equally hilarious in book musicals as well as in revues, Lahr also gave vibrant performances in works as varied as *Waiting for Godot* (1956), *A Midsummer Night's Dream* (1960), and *The Beauty Part* (1962).

Eva Le Gallienne (1899-1991) was an accomplished theatre manager as well as an adventurous actress. Her stage successes ranged from Ibsen heroines to fantasy figures, many in productions by her own Civic Repertory Theatre in the 1920s and 1930s. The British-born Le Gallienne was a small woman with unbounded energy and she performed on the boards for over sixty years.

Helena Modjeska (1840-1909) was a stage favorite across America in the later decades of the nineteenth century, known for her powerful performances in classical roles. The Polish-born Modjeska fled her native country for political reasons, settled in California, and mastered the language of her new homeland, becoming a beloved American original.

Geraldine Page (1924-1987) had a notable film career but it was her stage performances that were most enthralling; the versatile actress often found pathos in the most unlikely characters. Among her memorable stage credits were *Summer and Smoke* (1952), *The Rainmaker* (1954), *Sweet Bird of Youth* (1959), and *Agnes of God* (1982).

Robert Preston (1919-1987) left behind a mildly successful career in films and stage comedies when he created the role of Harold Hill in *The Music Man* (1957), becoming one of Broadway's favorite song and dance men for the next twenty years.

Paul Robeson (1898-1976) was a remarkable athlete, singer, actor, and political activist who enjoyed only sporadic success because of his race and political beliefs. Among his most memorable performances were those in renowned revivals of *The Emperor Jones* (1925), *Show Boat* (1932), and *Othello*

(1943).

Otis Skinner (1858-1942) was a distinguished figure on the American stage for many decades, first as a member of Augustin Daly's famous company in the 1880s, then as Helena Modjeska's leading man, then in a series of classical roles and popular melodramas. The dashing Skinner was also a prolific author of books about the theatre.

E. A. Sothern (1826-1881) was one of America's most popular comic actors, a tall and eccentric figure who delighted audiences first as a member of J. W. Wallack's famous company in the mid-nineteenth century. Of his many delightful performances, none was more popular than his lisping Lord Dundreary in *Our American Cousin* (1858).

Laurette Taylor (1884-1946) was a tragic figure who had two separate grasps at stardom in the theatre. She first dazzled audiences as a slender ingenue in such hit plays as *The Bird of Paradise* (1912) and *Peg o' My Heart* (1912). By the 1920s her career had faded and alcoholism caused her to retire. But in 1945 she returned to the stage as Amanda Wingfield in *The Glass Menagerie*, giving one of the theatre's legendary performances before her death soon after.

Ernest Truex (1889-1973) tread the boards for over seventy years, playing child roles well past his youth, then specializing in meek characters in plays and musicals such as *Very Good Eddie* (1915) and *George Washington Slept Here* (1940).

Lenore Ulric (1892-1970) specialized in exotic, passionate, and often destructive women in the 1910s and 1920s. Often under the tuteledge of David Belasco, she played sultry heroines in such play as *Tiger Rose* (1917), *Kiki* (1921), *The Harem* (1924), and *Lulu Belle* (1926).

Mrs. Vernon (1796-1869) was one of the finest comediennes of the nineteenth century. During a long career she played youthful comic beauties, mature ladies of wit, and later hilarious spinsters and dowagers.

Mrs. Vincent (1818-1887) restricted her career to the Boston theatres but there was nothing restrictive about the variety of roles she played at the Boston Museum and other theatres. During her forty-year career there, Mrs. Vincent played 444 different roles, from classical to contemporary.

Lester Wallack (1819-1888) created some 300 different characters as leading actor of the famous company that his father started in New York in 1851. Wallack played every sort of role that came along and was playing young heroes well into his seventies.

William Warren, Jr. (1812-1888) was an inspired actor who won plaudits all over the country for his classic comic roles. In 1846 he settled in Boston where he appeared in some 600 productions over the next forty years.

Clifton Webb (1893-1966), the debonair film star with a distinctive persona, played in many musicals and comedies before going to Hollywood in 1946. Among his many memorable credits were *The Little Show* (1929), *As Thousands Cheer* (1933), *Blithe Spirit* (1941), and *Present Laughter* (1946).

Bert Williams (1874?-1922) was not only the most popular black performer in America in the early decades of the century, he was one of America's most brilliant comedians as well. Williams started in minstrel shows, developing his shuffling onstage persona. His popularity rose with his appearance in such legendary black shows such as *In Dahomey* (1903) and *Bandanna Land* (1908) and peaked with his starring in several editions of the *Ziegfeld Follies*.

Ed Wynn (1886-1966), the unique American comic actor, created his fluttering, zany stage character in vaudeville and went on to conquer Broadway, radio, and film. Among his many starring stage vehicles were *The Perfect Fool* (1921), *Simple Simon* (1930), *The Laugh Parade* (1931), and several editions of the *Ziegfeld Follies*.

For further reading: Daniel Blum's *Great Stars of the American Stage*, Gerald Bordman's *The Oxford Companion to the American Theatre*, Don Wilmeth and Tice Miller's *Cambridge Guide to American Theatre*, Thomas Hischak's *Stage It With Music: An Encyclopedic Guide to the American Musical Theatre*, Mary Henderson's *Theatre in America*, Sheridan Morley's *The Great Stage Stars*, and Ian Herbert's *Who's Who in the Theatre*.

4

PLAYWRIGHTS

PRODIGIOUS PRE-O'NEILL PLAYWRIGHTS

Just as the vitality of the American Theatre is measured by the new plays it produces each season, the backbone of the theatre is its playwrights. Creative producers, fine acting, and distinguished direction and design can only mask the limitations of weak playwriting. The play still is the thing.

While we often chart the rise of the American drama with the debut of Eugene O'Neill, there were many accomplished playwrights who wrote exceptional plays in earlier times and prepared the way for serious American playwriting. Here are some of the recognized playwrights, librettists, and lyricists who made considerable contributions before O'Neill's career began.

David Belasco (1853-1931) had his hand in the creation of so many plays that it is difficult to determine how many he actually wrote or co-wrote and how many he just supervised, produced, or directed and took authorship credit for. He completed his first play at the age of twelve and throughout his long career he always seemed to have many projects going on at once. Of the some thirty plays it is clear that he actually did write (often with collaborators), most significant were *The Heart of Maryland* (1895), *Madame Butterfly* (1900), *The Darling of the Gods* (1902), *The Girl of the Golden West* (1905), and *The Return of Peter Grimm* (1911). Belasco was a much better playwright than he is often given credit for; his plays were melodramas but were well-crafted with solid writing, memorable characters, and a superb sense of locale.

Henry Blossom, Jr. (1866-1919) wrote plays and many librettos for musicals, most memorably Victor Herbert's *Mlle. Modiste* (1905) and *The Red Mill* (1906).

George Henry Boker (1823-1890) wrote romantic tragedies, often in verse, and usually in the European style. *Leonor de Guzman* (1853) and *Francesca da Rimini* (1855) were the most popular of his many hits.

Anne Caldwell (1867-1936) was a librettist-lyricist who wrote twenty-five Broadway musicals, collaborating with such composers as Victor Herbert and Jerome Kern. Her most notable shows include *The Lady of the Slipper* (1912), *Chin-Chin* (1914), *Good Morning, Dearie* (1921), *Stepping Stones* (1923), and *Criss Cross* (1926).

Bartley Campbell (1843-1888) wrote several melodramas that posed complex dilemmas for fully-realized characters. Campbell, because of the success and respect he received from his plays, is sometimes considered our first fully professional playwright. While his works are not much heard of today, Campbell's plays laid the groundwork for the serious problem play in America.

George M. Cohan (1878-1942) is remembered for the trunkful of song favorites he wrote for Broadway and Tin Pan Alley, but he also wrote over forty plays and musical librettos during his vibrant career. Cohan was actually the first to write tightly structured musical books and he saw a strong libretto as the backbone of a successful musical comedy. In shows such as *Little Johnny Jones* (1904), *Forty-Five Minutes From Broadway* (1906), and *George Washington, Jr.* (1906), there is a great deal of well-plotted story. His most durable non-musicals were *Seven Keys to Baldpate* (1913) and *The Tavern* (1920).

Paul Laurence Dunbar (1872-1906), the renowned African-American poet and novelist, wrote lyrics and librettos for such early pioneering black musicals as *Cloridy* (1898) and *In Dahomey* (1903).

William Dunlap (1766-1839), an important manager in the early days of the American theatre, wrote some sixty plays, many of them translations from the European theatre. *André* (1798) and *The Stranger* (1798) were the most famous of the many Dunlap scripts first produced at the Park Theatre in New York.

Clyde Fitch (1865-1909) wrote some sixty plays in a career that lasted only twenty years; about half of these scripts were translations or adaptations of European plays but the other half were well-crafted dramas that still read well. His first hit was the Richard Mansfield vehicle *Beau Brumell* (1890) but he really hit his stride with such gripping dramas as *Barbara Frietchie* (1899), *Captain Jinks of the Horse Marines* (1901), and *The City* (1909). The finest American playwright at the turn of the century, Fitch laid the groundwork for later dramatists such as Eugene O'Neill.

J. Cheever Goodwin (1850-1912) is the first American playwright to make his living writing librettos for musicals. Among his many Broadway successes were *Evangeline* (1874), *The Merry Monarch* (1890), *Wang* (1891), and *An Arabian Girl and Forty Thieves* (1899).

Edward Harrigan (1844-1911) is one of the grandfathers of the American musicals, writing librettos and lyrics for a series of musical comedies about immigrant life that were extremely popular. With his performing partner Tony Hart, Harrigan presented the famous *Mulligan Guard* musicals in the 1880s and laid the foundation for Broadway musical farce.

James A. Herne (1839-1901) was a talented author of plays that moved toward the naturalistic. While he was not as popular as most of his contemporaries, Herne made some bold strides in playwriting in *Hearts of Oak* (1880), *Margaret Fleming* (1891), *Shore Acres* (1893), and *Sag Harbor* (1900).

Avery Hopwood (1882-1928) liked to boast that he was "America's richest playwright" and his string of commercial hits backed up that claim. With little pretensions toward art, Hopwood wrote highly crafted formula plays, sometimes with a risqué element to help ensure box office success. While none of his some two dozen plays have stood the test of time, works such as *The Gold Diggers* (1919), *The Bat* (1920), and *Getting Gertie's Garter* (1921) were very popular and made Hopwood very wealthy.

Bronson Howard (1842-1908) was a drama critic who also wrote plays, but after the success of *Saratoga* (1870) and *The Banker's Daughter* (1878), he abandoned newspaper writing and became one of our first fully professional playwrights. With such outstanding plays as *Young Mrs. Winthrop* (1882), *The Henrietta* (1887), and *Shenandoah* (1889), Howard used American themes and characters to help establish a more mature style of American playwriting.

Charles H. Hoyt (1860-1900) was a brilliant satirist who poked fun at contemporary life in his plays and musicals in a way rarely seen in American drama. Among Hoyt's most celebrated works were *A Parlor Match* (1884), *A Midnight Bell* (1889), and the pioneering musical comedy *A Trip to Chinatown* (1891).

Joseph Stevens Jones (1809-1877) was a prolific author of romantic melodramas filled with all-American characters. It is estimated he wrote anywhere from sixty to 150 of these audience pleasers between 1832 and 1875. *The People's Lawyer* (1839) and *The Silver Spoon* (1852) were his biggest hits.

John Luther Long (1861-1927) was a gentlemanly author of romantic plays, often written with David Belasco. *Madame Butterfly* (1900), *The Darling of the Gods* (1902), and *Adrea* (1904) were his most successful ventures.

Glen MacDonough (1870-1924) was a reliable librettist and lyricist who wrote operettas and musicals with such composers as John Philip Sousa and Victor Herbert. Among his twentysome Broadway credits were *Chris and the Wonderful Lamp* (1900), *Babes in Toyland* (1903), and *It Happened in Nordland* (1904).

Percy MacKaye (1875-1956) was an oddly brilliant poet and playwright who experimented with all kinds of drama, from historical pieces to satires to fantasy. His allegorical *The Scarecrow* (1911) was MacKaye's only big success but his works have always proved fascinating reading.

Steele MacKaye (1842-1894) was an adventurous playwright and producer who promoted new forms of playwriting and unique arrangements for theatre playhouses. While his plays cannot be easily revived today, dramas such as *Hazel Kirke* (1880) and *Paul Kauvar* (1887) were important and innovative works at the time. He was the father of Percy MacKay.

J. Hartley Manners (1870-1928) was a reliable and polished playwright who created vehicles for famous actresses. His most lasting work was *Peg o' My Heart* (1912), which he wrote for his wife Laurette Taylor.

Langdon Mitchell (1862-1935) was a successful author who adapted several novels for the stage, but his original *The New York Idea* (1906), a sly comedy about divorce, remains one of our finest social satires.

William Vaughan Moody (1869-1910) managed, in his short life and few plays, to explore areas of American drama that O'Neill would continue to examine in his finest plays. Moody was a well-educated poet and playwright who had only two of his plays produced during his lifetime but both *The Great Divide* (1906) and *The Faith Healer* (1909) are uncompromising dramas about the search for fulfillment in America.

Anna Cora Mowatt (1819-1870) was a lady of society who turned to writing because her frail health left her with idle time. Her first play, *Fashion* (1845), was extremely popular and remains one of the finest satires ever written by an American. The success of the play encouraged Mowatt to start performing as well and she became a favorite, bringing a new respectability to the status of the actress in America. She managed to write a few more plays before remarrying and retiring from the theatre.

Susanna Haswell Rowson (1762-1824) was the first woman playwright to be produced in America and, although only fragments of her plays are extant today, she wrote several scripts that were presented by theatres in Philadelphia and Boston. Rowson was born in England but came over to America with her husband and child to act on the stage out of financial necessity. She wrote some very popular novels as well as plays but, because of the lack of any form of copyright protection, Rowson made little money from her writing and retired to run a school in Boston in 1802.

Edward Sheldon (1886-1946) wrote several highly theatrical dramas and adaptations despite an illness that eventually left him blind and paralyzed for many years. His first Broadway play, the social drama *Salvation Nell* (1908), was a critical and popular success, and he followed it up with such notable works as *The Boss* (1911), *Romance* (1913), *The Jest* (1919), and *Lulu Belle* (1926).

Augustus Thomas (1857-1934) was one of the earliest American dramatists to experiment with realism. During his career he wrote some 100 plays, more than half of them adaptations of European hits. But in his original efforts, such as *Arizona* (1900), *The Witching Hour* (1907), and *The Copperhead* (1918), he displayed a unique gift for serious American drama.

Royall Tyler (1757-1826) is America's first playwright, a gentleman scholar-writer, many of whose comedies are lost now but who used wit and satire in his plays. Tyler's *The Contrast* (1787) was the first comedy by an American to be professionally produced, and it remains a landmark work.

Eugene Walter (1874-1941) wrote some twenty melodramas for Broadway that were known for their hard-hitting realism. *Paid in Full* (1908) and *The*

Easiest Way (1909) were the best of his works.

Mercy Otis Warren (1728-1814) is considered the first American woman to write plays, though their popularity was more through reading than performance. Warren, the wife of the president of the Provisional Congress of Massachusetts, wrote two political satires during the Revolution: *The Adulateur* (1773) and *The Group* (1775). Although it is doubtful that either comedy was ever produced, both were printed and were widely read. Warren wrote a blank verse tragedy in 1790 and later other plays, though their authorship cannot be verified.

Rida Johnson Young (1875?-1926) was a society lady who went on the stage then later turned to writing plays and both lyrics and librettos for operettas. Her most remembered plays were *Brown of Harvard* (1906), *The Lottery Man* (1909) and *Little Old New York* (1920); her most famous operettas were *Naughty Marietta* (1910) and *Maytime* (1917).

MODERN AMERICAN PLAYWRIGHTS

Agreeing with the theory that modern drama in America begins with Eugene O'Neill, here is a selective list of playwrights, lyricists and librettists since 1920 who have gained some recognition in the theatre.

Lee Adams (1924-) wrote the lyrics for several Broadway musicals, such as *Bye Bye Birdie* (1960), *Golden Boy* (1964), and *Applause* (1970), with composer-partner Charles Strouse.

Richard Adler (1921-), a composer and lyricist, is remembered for his two hit musicals with Jerry Ross, *The Pajama Game* (1954) and *Damn Yankees* (1955), and his solo effort *Kwamina* (1961).

Zoë Akins (1886-1958) wrote many plays in a career that was uneven in quality but always interesting. Akins intrigued audiences in the 1910s and 1920s with her sharp commentary on contemporary morals, as in *Déclassée* (1919). She later did a series of stage adaptations of foreign plays and in 1935 she won the Pulitzer Prize for her dramatization of Edith Wharton's *The Old Maid*.

Edward Albee (1928-), America's premiere playwright of chilling and disturbing dramas about the American family, has remained one of our most puzzling and haunting playwrights for over forty years. Among his many notable plays: *The Zoo Story* (1960), *Who's Afraid of Virginia Woolf?* (1962), *Tiny Alice* (1964), *A Delicate Balance* (1966), *Seascape* (1975), and *Three Tall Women* (1994).

Maxwell Anderson (1888-1959) wrote some thirty plays, many of them verse dramas and a good number of them hits as well. Anderson was the most respected playwright of his day and his plays were cited by the *Best Plays* series more than any other American playwright. His career spans from 1923 to 1954, with such distinguished plays as *What Price Glory?* (1924) with Laurence Stallings, *Elizabeth the Queen* (1930), *Both Your Houses* (1933), *Winterset* (1935), *Key Largo* (1939), *Anne of a Thousand Days* (1948), *The Bad Seed* (1954), as well as the musicals *Knickerbocker Holiday* (1938) and *Lost in the Stars* (1949).

Robert Anderson (1917-) has authored many memorable American dramas, such as *Tea and Sympathy* (1953), *You Know I Can't Hear You When the Water's Running* (1967), and *I Never Sang for My Father* (1968).

Philip Barry (1896-1949) was a master of American high comedy and his plays *Paris Bound* (1927), *Holiday* (1928), *The Animal Kingdom* (1932), *The Philadelphia Story* (1939) and others are high points of sophisticated wit in the American theatre.

S. N. Behrman (1893-1973) wrote some of the most sophisticated of American comedies during a career that lasted forty years and produced nearly thirty plays. His most notable efforts include *Biography* (1932), *End of Summer* (1936), *No Time for Comedy* (1939), and the musical *Fanny* (1954).

Guy Bolton (1884-1979) wrote over fifty Broadway and London musical comedies and plays during a long and successful career. His most memorable musical librettos include *Very Good Eddie* (1915), *Leave It To Jane* (1917), *Sally* (1920), *Lady, Be Good!* (1924), *Oh, Kay!* (1926), and *Girl Crazy* (1930); his accomplished non-musicals include *Polly With a Past* (1917), *Adam and Eva* (1919), and *Anastasia* (1954).

Clare Boothe (Luce) (1903-1987) was active in publishing, politics, and writing books but the handful of plays she wrote were ripe with humor and revealing wit. Her most remembered Broadway credits were *The Women* (1936), *Kiss the Boys Good-bye* (1938), and *Margin for Error* (1939).

Lew Brown (1893-1958) was a lyricist for the team of DeSylva, Brown, and Henderson who scored such memorable 1920s musicals as *Good News!* (1927), *Hold Everything!* (1928), *Flying High* (1930), and editions of *George White's Scandals*.

Abe Burrows (1910-1985) was one of the best librettists of the post-war musical with such hit shows as *Guys and Dolls* (1950), *Can-Can* (1953), and *How To Succeed in Business Without Really Trying* (1963).

Mary Chase (1907-1981), who wrote the beloved comedy favorite *Harvey* (1944), penned many plays between the late 1930s and the late 1970s but only found additional success with *Mrs. McThing* (1952) and *Bernadine* (1952). Chase was an uneven playwright but her touch of whimsy and warm-hearted insanity is unique in the American theatre.

Rachel Crothers (1870?-1958) was the first and one of the best American playwrights to look at women and the roles society assigns to them. In such Broadway plays as *He and She* (1920), *Nice People* (1921), *Let Us Be Gay* (1929), *As Husbands Go* (1931), *When Ladies Meet* (1932), and *Susan and God* (1937), Crothers considered the issues of womanhood in a witty and thought-provoking manner.

Gretchen Cryer (1935-), a lyricist-librettist from the team of Cryer and Ford, wrote *The Last Sweet Days of Isaac* (1970), *I'm Getting My Act Together and Taking It on the Road* (1978) and other provocative musicals.

Owen Davis (1874-1956) wrote over 200 plays in a fifty-year seesaw career. Although he wished to write verse dramas, Davis started cranking out cheap melodramas in order to support his family. At the rate of a new script every other week, he made a name for himself for sensational, highly visual melodramas that were easily understood and enjoyed by immigrants. Later in his career he surprised critics with some powerfully written dramas such as *The Detour* (1921) and the Pulitzer Prize-winner *Icebound* (1923). But these promising works led to a series of more melodramas and many failures.

B. G. De Sylva (1895-1950) wrote librettos and/or lyrics for over twenty Broadway musicals. As part of the illustrious team of De Sylva, Brown, and Henderson, he wrote *Good News!* (1927), *Hold Everything* (1928), *Follow Thru* (1929), *Flying High* (1930) and others. His musical hits with other collaborators include *Take a Chance* (1932), *DuBarry Was a Lady* (1939), and *Louisiana Purchase* (1940).

Howard Dietz (1896-1983), one of Broadway's finest lyricists, often wrote with partner-composer Arthur Schwartz and together they scored some of the best musical revues ever seen on Broadway: *The Little Show* (1929), *Three's a Crowd* (1930), *The Band Wagon* (1931) and others.

Dorothy Donnelly (1880-1928) had a very successful career as an actress (she introduced roles by Shaw and Yeats to America) but turned to writing lyrics and librettos in 1916 and gave up acting. Her most remembered works were with Sigmund Romberg, and include *Blossom Time* (1921), *The Student Prince* (1924) and *My Maryland* (1927).

Fred Ebb (1932-) is the lyricist for the successful team of Kander and Ebb who have written such diverse musicals as *Cabaret* (1966), *The Happy Time* (1968), *Chicago* (1975), *Woman of the Year* (1981), and *Kiss of the Spider Woman* (1993).

Edna Ferber (1887-1968) was one of the most celebrated novelists of her day but she had just as notable a career writing plays, usually with collaborators. Her finest stage works were written with George S. Kaufman: *Minick* (1924), *The Royal Family* (1927), *Dinner at Eight* (1932), and *Stage Door* (1936).

Dorothy Fields (1905-1974) was one of America's finest lyricists, with a superb talent for slangy and vivid wordplay as well as insightful characterization. The youngest of the famous theatre family of Fields, she was equally adept at writing for revues, book musicals, and films. Collaborating with Arthur Schwartz, Sigmund Romberg, Jimmy McHugh, Cy Coleman, and her brother Herbert, Fields wrote the lyrics and/or librettos for such Broadway hits as *Blackbirds of 1928*, *Up in Central Park* (1945), *Annie Get Your Gun* (1946), *A Tree Grows in Brooklyn* (1951), and *Sweet Charity* (1966).

Horton Foote (1916-), a television and screenwriter who has been writing for Broadway, Off Broadway and regional theatres since the 1940s, has set almost all of his plays in his fictional town of Harrison, Texas. Among his many New York productions are *The Chase* (1952), *The Trip to Bountiful* (1953), *The Traveling Lady* (1954), *Lily Dale* (1986), *The Widow Claire* (1986), and the Pulitzer Prize-winning *The Young Man From Atlanta* (1995).

Rose Franken (1895-1988) was an oft-produced Broadway playwright whose plays about contemporary life were particularly popular with women audiences. Among her hits were *Another Language* (1932), *Claudia* (1941), and *Outrageous Fortune* (1943).

Zona Gale (1874-1938) was an accomplished novelist who also wrote many plays for Broadway and amateur groups in the early decades of this century. Although her work was respected at the time, only her Pulitzer Prize-winning *Miss Lulu Brett* (1920) is much remembered today.

Herb Gardner (1934-) is a comic playwright from television who has had intermittent hits on Broadway over the past thirty-five years: *A Thousand Clowns* (1962), *Thieves* (1974), *I'm Not Rappaport* (1985), and *Conversations With My Father* (1992).

Ira Gershwin (1896-1983), one of America's most beloved and versatile lyricists, wrote many shows with his composer-brother George as well as with other collaborators. From *Lady Be Good* (1924) and *Of Thee I Sing* (1931) to *Porgy and Bess* (1935) and *Lady in the Dark* (1941), it was a career filled with invention and genius.

William Gibson (1914-) has written several plays for Broadway and regional theatres that are varied in subject matter and tone. His most known plays include *Two for the Seesaw* (1958), *The Miracle Worker* (1959), and *Golda* (1977).

Susan Glaspell (1876?-1948) is one of the American masters of the one-act play and many of her telling short works were first presented at the Provincetown Players, which she co-founded. Glaspell also wrote several full-length dramas, most memorably *Alison's House* (1930), which won the Pulitzer Prize.

Paul Green (1894-1981) was a talented author of folk plays and dramas with strong messages. Among his Broadway credits were the Pulitzer Prize-winning *In Abraham's Bosom* (1926), *The House of Connelly* (1931), and *Johnny Johnson* (1936); as well as several outdoor historical dramas, most notably *The Lost Colony*, which has played summers on Roanoke Island, North Carolina, since 1937.

John Guare (1938-) has been writing dark comedies with fluctuating success since the 1960s. Among his many New York credits are *The House of Blue Leaves* (1971), *Two Gentlemen of Verona* (1971), *Bosoms or Neglect* (1979), *Lydie Breeze* (1982), and *Six Degrees of Separation* (1990).

A. R. Guerney, Jr. (1930-) began his playwriting career late in life but has been a prolific and successful author since 1971 with *Scenes From American Life*. Guerney is adept at capturing the American WASP in a bittersweet way, as seen in his *The Dining Room* (1982), *The Perfect Party* (1986), *The Cocktail Hour* (1988), *Love Letters* (1989), *Later Life* (1993), *Sylvia* (1995) and others.

Oscar Hammerstein II (1895-1960), the most influential man in the history of the American musical, penned the lyrics and nearly all the librettos for some forty-five Broadway shows. Between 1920 and 1959 he contributed to operettas, musical comedies, popular opera musicals, the influential musical play, and even the concept musical. The more than 1,500 songs he wrote for the theatre represent a panorama of theatrical lyric writing.

Lorraine Hansberry (1930-1965) only finished a few plays in her short life but *A Raisin in the Sun* (1959) remains one of the finest plays ever written by an African-American.

Otto Harbach (1873-1963) wrote the librettos and lyrics for over thirty Broadway musicals between 1908 and 1933, bringing a respectability to musical theatre writing that too often had been judged as hack work. Among his notable hits were *Madame Sherry* (1910), *The Firefly* (1912), *Rose-Marie* (1924), *No, No, Nanette* (1925), *The Desert Song* (1926), *The Cat and the Fiddle* (1931), and *Roberta* (1933).

E. Y. Harburg (1898-1981) was one of Broadway's most acerbic lyricist-librettists who wrote light musical comedies with often disturbing subtexts. *Hooray for What!* (1937), *Bloomer Girl* (1944), *Finian's Rainbow* (1947), and *Jamaica* (1957) are among his distinctive shows.

Sheldon Harnick (1924-), as the lyricist member of the team of Bock and Harnick, wrote the memorable musicals *Fiorello!* (1959), *She Loves Me* (1963), *Fiddler on the Roof* (1964), *The Rothschilds* (1970), as well as others with and without composer Jerry Bock.

Lorenz Hart (1895-1943), arguably Broadway's most agile and witty lyricist, worked with composer Richard Rodgers on a series of successful musicals between 1925 and 1943: *The Garrick Gaieties* (1925), *A Connecticut Yankee* (1927), *On Your Toes* (1936), *Babes in Arms* (1937), *The Boys From Syracuse* (1938), *Pal Joey* (1940) and others.

Lillian Hellman (1905-1984), perhaps America's premiere woman playwright, managed to create startling characters, dramatic situations, and explore social and moral issues in her plays. In addition to such well-known modern classics as *The Children's Hour* (1934), *The Little Foxes* (1939) and *Toys in the Attic* (1960), Hellman was also successful at writing quieter, Chekhov-like plays, such as *The Autumn Garden* (1951), and adaptations, such as *The Lark* (1955).

Sidney Howard (1891-1939) authored many plays for Broadway in the 1920s and 1930s, including *They Knew What They Wanted* (1924), *The Silver Cord* (1926), *The Late Christopher Bean* (1932), and *Dodsworth* (1934).

Tina Howe (1937-) has written some challenging plays that have received recognition Off Broadway and on: *The Art of Dining* (1979), *Painting Churches* (1983), *Coastal Disturbances* (1987) and others.

Langston Hughes (1902-1967), the acclaimed African-American poet, wrote plays, librettos and lyrics about black life for the theatre. *Mulatto* (1935), *Street Scene* (1947), *Simply Heavenly* (1957), and *Jerico-Jim Crow* (1964) were among his notable works, none of which were financial successes.

Zora Neale Hurston (1891-1960), the fascinating poet and novelist who was the most prolific black woman writer of her time, has only recently been rediscovered and her plays reevaluated. Working solo and in collaboration with Langston Hughes, Hurston wrote a dozen theatre pieces, most memorably *Mule Bone*, a folk comedy written in the early 1930s but not produced until 1991, and *Spunk* (1990), a dramatization of three of her short stories by George C. Wolfe.

William Inge (1913-1973) captured the lifestyle of everyday people in rural America in his realistic dramas such as *Come Back, Little Sheba* (1950), *Picnic* (1953),and *The Dark at the Top of the Stairs* (1957).

Albert Innaurato (1948-) received a lot of attention in the 1970s for his offbeat and dark comedies, such as *The Transfiguration of Benno Blimpie* (1973), *Gemini* (1976), *Ulysses in Traction* (1977) and others.

Georgia Douglas Johnson (1880-1966), a recognized poet of the Harlem Renaissance, is perhaps America's first notable black woman playwright. She wrote thirty plays, including *A Sunday Morning in the South* (1925) and *Plumes* (1927), and although only her poetry is much remembered today, she laid the groundwork for plays about women of color in America.

LeRoi Jones (1934-), the African-American playwright who later changed his name to Imamu Amiri Baraka, wrote explosive plays in the 1960s about racial strive, such as *Dutchman* (1964), *The Slave* (1964), *The Toilet* (1964), and *Slave Ship* (1967).

Tom Jones (1928-) is the lyricist/librettist who, with his composer-partner Harvey Schmidt, wrote the long-running Off-Broadway musical *The Fantasticks* (1960). The team's other musicals include *110 in the Shade* (1963), *I Do! I Do!* (1966), and *Celebration* (1969).

George Kelly (1887-1974) was a gifted play craftsman who often captured a zestful sense of character in his plays. *The Show-Off* (1924), *Craig's Wife* (1925), *Daisy Mayme* (1926), and *The Fatal Weakness* (1946) are among his best works.

Jean Kerr (1923-) wrote comedies and musical librettos over a forty-year stage career, as well as a series of humorous books that were bestsellers in their day. Kerr's best plays were *Jenny Kissed Me* (1948), *King of Hearts* (1954), *Mary, Mary* (1961), and *Finishing Touches* (1973), as well as her stage adaptation of Cornelia Otis Skinner's *Our Hearts Were Young and Gay* (1948) which was a favorite in educational theatre for many years.

Sidney Kingsley (1906-1995) wrote several hard-hitting dramas that still are of interest today: *Men in White* (1933), *Dead End* (1935), *The Patriots* (1943), *Detective Story* (1949), *Darkness at Noon* (1951) and others.

Arthur Kopit (1937-) has been writing plays with daring imagery and content since the 1960s when his avant-garde one-acts first gained attention. His varied playwriting credits include *Oh Dad, Poor Dad . . .* (1962), *Indians* (1969), *Wings* (1979), *End of the World* (1984), and the musicals *Nine* (1982) and *Phantom* (1983).

Norman Krasna (1909-1984) was a screenwriter who provided Broadway with several light comedies in the 1940s and 1950s: *Dear Ruth* (1944), *John Loves Mary* (1947), *Kind Sir* (1953) and others.

Clare Kummer (1873?-1958) is all but forgotten today but in the early decades of the century she had over a dozen plays produced on Broadway, many of them hits. Her biggest successes were *Good Gracious Annabelle* (1916), *A Successful Calamity* (1917), and *Her Master's Voice* (1933).

James Lapine (1949-) is the librettist and often director of innovative musicals such as *Sunday in the Park With George* (1984), *Into the Woods* (1987), *Falsettoland* (1990), *Passion* (1994), as well as some non-musical plays.

John Latouche (1917-1956) was an inventive lyricist-librettist who, during his short life, contributed to such memorable musicals as *Cabin in the Sky* (1940), *The Golden Apple* (1954), and *Candide* (1956).

Arthur Laurents (1918-) is the librettist of some of Broadway's most distinguished musicals, including *West Side Story* (19590 and *Gypsy* (1959), as well as a director and the author of several non-musical plays, such as *The Time of The Cuckoo* (1952).

Alan Jay Lerner (1918-1986), the celebrated lyricist-librettist of the team of Lerner and Loewe, has written some of Broadway's most beloved scores, including *Brigadoon* (1947), *My Fair Lady* (1956), *Camelot* (1960), and *On a Clear Day You Can See Forever* (1965).

Ira Levin (1929-), the successful novelist, has enjoyed success on Broadway over the years with various kinds of plays: *No Time for Sergeants* (1955), *Critic's Choice* (1960), *Deathtrap* (1978) and others.

Anita Loos (1893-1981) was one of the most famous authors in America as a result of her comic novel *Gentlemen Prefer Blondes*, which she dramatized in 1926 and helped musicalize in 1949. Loos' other works for the stage include *The Whole Town's Talking* (1932), *Happy Birthday* (1946), and the stage version of Colette's *Gigi* (1951).

Charles Ludlam (1943-1987) managed to write thirty plays in a career of only twenty years cut short by his premature death. Ludlam wrote outrageous comedies and bizarre adaptations of the classics for his Off-Broadway Ridiculous Theatre Company and often performed the leading role, male or female, himself. His most memorable works include *Camille* (1973), *Stage Blood* (1975), *Galas* (1983), and *The Mystery of Irma Vep* (1984).

Ken Ludwig (1950-) is the author of the recent Broadway hit comedies

Lend Me a Tenor (1989) and *Moon Over Buffalo* (1995), as well as the libretto for the musical *Crazy for You* (1992).

Richard Maltby, Jr. (1937-) has written lyrics and/or librettos for musicals, often with composer-partner David Shire. *Starting Here, Starting Now* (1977), *Baby* (1983), *Closer Than Ever* (1989), *Miss Saigon* (1989), and *Big* (1996) are among his notable credits.

David Mamet (1947-), one of the most distinctive of American playwrights writing today, hails from Chicago where some of his earliest works were first produced. Mamet is a master at lowlife characters and their particular speech patterns. Among his many notable plays are *Sexual Perversity in Chicago* (1976), *American Buffalo* (1977), *Glengarry Glen Ross* (1984), *Speed-the-Plow* (1988), *Oleanna* (1992), and *The Cryptogram* (1995).

Terrence McNally (1939-) has been writing for Off Broadway and Broadway since the early 1960s, presenting an array of funny and tragicomic characters often outside the mainstream of American life. *The Ritz* (1975), *The Lisbon Traviata* (1985) *Frankie and Johnny in the Clair de Lune* (1987), *Lips Together, Teeth Apart* (1991), *A Perfect Ganesh* (1994), *Love! Valor! Compassion!* (1995), and *Master Class* (1995) are among the most known, as well as the librettos for the musicals *The Rink* (1984) and *Kiss of the Spider Woman* (1993).

Mark Medoff (1940-) created dynamic tension in his plays about contemporary life, such as *When You Comin' Back, Red Ryder?* (1973), *The Wager* (1974), and *Children of a Lesser God* (1980).

Arthur Miller (1915-), one of America's premiere post-war dramatists, first gained attention with *All My Sons* (1947) and has remained a major creative force in the theatre ever since. Among Miller's many distinguished plays are *Death of a Salesman* (1949), *The Crucible* (1953), *A View From the Bridge* (1955), *After the Fall* (1964), *The Price* (1968), *The American Clock* (1980), and *Broken Glass* (1994).

Marsha Norman (1947-) is a bold and distinctive voice in the contemporary American theatre, as witnessed in her *Getting Out* (1977) and *'Night, Mother* (1983). She also authored the libretto for the musical *The Secret Garden* (1991).

Clifford Odets (1906-1963) was perhaps the best of the leftist playwrights who emerged in the 1930s. His dramas *Waiting for Lefty* (1935), *Awake and Sing!* (1935), *Golden Boy* (1937), *The Big Knife* (1949), *The Country Girl* (1950) and others are hard-hitting pieces with vivid characters placed in dynamic situations.

Eugene O'Neill (1888-1953), America's greatest playwright, wrote some thirty full-length and one-act plays; the number is considerable when one takes in account that O'Neill wrote very slowly and that he sometimes destroyed scripts before they could be produced or published. From his first successful full-length play, *Beyond the Horizon* (1920), to his posthumously produced *Long*

Day's Journey Into Night (1956), it was a towering career by a giant among playwrights.

Paul Osborn (1901-1988) wrote many different kinds of plays but is best remembered for his gentle portrayal of everyday people in such comedies as *The Vinegar Tree* (1930), *On Borrowed Time* (1938), and *Morning's at Seven* (1939). Among his other notable Broadway productions, most of which were adaptations, were *A Bell for Adano* (1944), *Point of No Return* (1951), and *The World of Suzie Wong* (1958).

John Patrick (1907-1995) was the author of some thirty Broadway plays; many of these were not hits but have become staples in community theatres, such as *The Curious Savage* (1950) and *Everybody Loves Opal* (1961). His most successful Broadway plays were *The Hasty Heart* (1945) and *The Teahouse of the August Moon* (1953). He penned several films as well.

David Rabe (1940-) mixes both expressionism and realism in his potent dramas about dysfunctional people caught in crisis: *The Basic Training of Pavlo Hummel* (1971), *Sticks and Bones* (1971), *In the Boom Boom Room* (1973), *Streamers* (1976), *Hurlyburly* (1984) and others.

Samson Raphaelson (1896-1983) was a journeyman playwright and screenplay author who had some Broadway successes spread throughout his long career. *The Jazz Singer* (1925), *Accent on Youth* (1924), *Skylark* (1939), and *Jason* (1942) are his most remembered works.

Elmer Rice (1892-1967) wrote some thirty plays that were produced on Broadway, among them the most notable expressionistic plays ever written by an American: *On Trial* (1914), *The Adding Machine* (1923), and *Dream Girl* (1945). Rice was also adept at realism, as witnessed in such plays as *Street Scene* (1929) and *Counsellor-at-Law* (1931).

Morrie Ryskind (1895-1985) co-authored some of Broadway's most satirical musical comedies, including *Animal Crackers* (1928), *Strike Up the Band* (1930), *Of Thee I Sing* (1931), and *Louisiana Purchase* (1940).

William Saroyan (1908-1981) was a unique author of plays and stories that had a wistful, unreal quality to them. Among his best one-act and full-length plays were *My Heart's in the Highlands* (1939), *The Time of Your Life* (1939), *The Beautiful People* (1941), *Hello, Out There* (1942), and *The Cave Dwellers* (1957).

Sam Shepard (1943-) has been writing plays since 1964 and, despite a successful film acting career, has found time to pen over thirty plays. After many surreal one-act plays in the 1960s, Shepard moved into full-length tragicomedies that slyly expose the decay of the American dream. *The Tooth of Crime* (1973), *Buried Child* (1978), *Curse of the Starving Class* (1979), *True West* (1980), *Fool for Love* (1983), and *The Lie of The Mind* (1985) are among his notable works.

Robert Sherwood (1896-1955) was a distinguished playwright who received the Pulitzer Prize three times for his insightful dramas and dark comedies. *The Road to Rome* (1927), *Reunion in Vienna* (1931), *The Petrified Forest* (1935), *Idiot's Delight* (1936), *Abe Lincoln in Illinois* (1938), and *There Shall Be No Night* (1940) are among his memorable works.

Neil Simon (1927-) has had some thirty plays produced on Broadway; more importantly, nearly all of these have been hits. The most successful American playwright of his era, Simon has moved back and forth between comedy, farce, and more serious autobiographical plays. His first Broadway comedy was *Come Blow Your Horn* (1961), followed by such perennial favorites as *Barefoot in the Park* (1963) and *The Odd Couple* (1965). Starting with *Chapter Two* (1977), his plays usually have a more sober subtext and often are based on his own life, as in his trilogy *Brighton Beach Memoirs* (1983), *Biloxi Blues* (1985), and *Broadway Bound* (1986). He has also written several films and the librettos for musicals, most memorably *Sweet Charity* (1966) and *Promises, Promises* (1968).

Noble Sissle (1889-1975), the pioneering black lyricist, worked with composer Eubie Blake on such groundbreaking musicals as *Shuffle Along* (1921) and *Chocolate Dandies* (1924).

Cornelia Otis Skinner (1901-1979) was a popular actress who came from a famous theatrical family and between 1924 and 1958 she wrote many plays, most memorably *The Pleasure of His Company* (1958). Skinner also wrote one-woman character sketches for herself, which she performed to great renown. Her books include the autobiographical *Our Hearts Were Young and Gay* (1942), which was adapted by Jean Kerr into a play in 1948.

Edgar Smith (1857-1938) wrote the librettos and/or lyrics for some 150 Broadway musicals, many of them Weber and Fields burlesques. His most accomplished credits were *Fiddle-Dee-Dee* (1900), *Tillie's Nightmare* (1910), and *The Blue Paradise* (1915).

Harry B. Smith (1860-1936) wrote more lyrics and librettos for musicals than any other American on record, some 6,000 songs heard in 300 musicals produced across the country and in Europe. Smith collaborated with such composers as Reginald De Koven, Victor Herbert and Jerome Kern, actively writing musicals between 1887 and 1932; in 1899 alone he had eight new shows on Broadway. Among his 123 Broadway musicals are *Robin Hood* (1891), *The Fortune Teller* (1898), *The Casino Girl* (1900), *The Girl From Utah* (1914), *Watch Your Step* (1915), and *Countess Maritza* (1926).

Robert B. Smith (1875-1951), the younger brother of the prolific Harry B. Smith, was fairly prolific himself, providing librettos and lyrics for twenty-seven Broadway musicals. *Twirly-Whirly* (1902) and *Sweethearts* (1913) are the most notable of his works.

Gertrude Stein (1874-1946), the controversial expatriate who wrote poetry, novellas, and criticism and who fostered the work of young writers and artists, wrote seventy plays between 1913 and her death. Many of these works were short curtain raisers; others were meant to be read only and were published but not produced. Her most familiar works were *Four Saints in Three Acts* (1934), an avant-garde opera-theatre piece with music by Virgil Thomson, and *In Savoy* (1949).

Joseph Stein (1912-) is an accomplished Broadway lyricist who has contributed to musicals since 1955. Among his shows are *Plain and Fancy* (1955), *Fiddler on the Roof* (1964), *Zorbá* (1968), *The Baker's Wife* (1976), and *Rags* (1986).

Michael Stewart (1929-1987) wrote several memorable librettos (and sometimes lyrics) for musicals, most notably *Bye Bye Birdie* (1960), *Carnival* (1961), *Hello, Dolly!* (1964), *Mack and Mabel* (1974), *I Love My Wife* (1977), *Barnum* (1980), and *42nd Street* (1980).

Peter Stone (1930-)has written librettos for many successful musicals, including *1776* (1969), *Sugar* (1972), *Woman of the Year* (1981), *My One and Only* (1983), and *The Will Rogers Follies* (1991).

Samuel Taylor (1912-), a radio writer who penned a handful of Broadway hits, wrote *The Happy Time* (1950), *Sabrina Fair* (1953), *The Pleasure of His Company* (1958), and the musical *No Strings* (1962).

Sophie Treadwell (1885?-1970) was an innovative playwright who had a half dozen challenging plays produced on Broadway, most memorably *Machinal* (1928). Treadwell was an experimentor in expressionism, terse dialogue, and bold themes.

Gladys Unger (1885?-1940) wrote some forty plays between 1903 and 1939 that were produced in New York and Chicago, many of them adaptations of foreign plays and some done in collaboration with others. Her comedies *The Goldfish* (1922) and *The Werewolf* (1924) were her most successful Broadway entries.

John Van Druten (1901-1957), a London playwright who settled in America, wrote several witty observations about society in such Broadway hits as *The Voice of the Turtle* (1943), *I Remember Mama* (1944), *Bell, Book and Candle* (1950), and *I Am a Camera* (1951).

Lula Vollmer (1898-1955) wrote a series of folk plays about life in the hills of her native North Carolina. Two of these, *Sun-Up* (1923) and *The Shame Woman* (1923), were major hits but all of her work was truthful and noteworthy.

Wendy Wasserstein (1950-) has been shrewdly depicting women in our time since her *Uncommon Women and Others* (1977). Her subsequent playwriting credits include *Isn't It Romantic* (1981), *The Heidi Chronicles* (1989), and *The Sisters Rosensweig* (1993).

Jerome Weidman (1913-), a successful novelist and screenwriter who also wrote musical librettos for Broadway, contributed to *Fiorello!* (1959), *Tenderloin* (1960), *I Can Get It for You Wholesale* (1962) and other plays and musicals.

Michael Weller (1942-) has written many plays that found favor Off Broadway and in regional theatre, most memorably *Moonchildren* (1972), *Loose*

Ends (1979), *Spoils of War* (1988), as well as several screenplays.

Mae West (1892-1980) is so well known for her sly, sexy film persona that it is often forgotten that she started in the theatre where she wrote plays produced on Broadway. *Sex* (1926) and *The Drag* (1927) both ran into censorship problems and were very controversial in their day. *Diamond Lil* (1928) and *Catherine Was Great* (1944) were West's best and most successful Broadway entries.

Thornton Wilder (1897-1975) was an acclaimed novelist who wrote only a few plays during his long career but each one is a masterpiece of its kind: the expressionistic-realistic *Our Town* (1938), the fantastical-allegory *The Skin of Our Teeth* (1942), the farce *The Matchmaker* (1954) and many superb one-act plays.

Tennessee Williams (1911-1983), perhaps the most poetic dramatist America has yet produced, had a long and uneven career filled with hits and misses. But even in his less satisfying plays Williams vividly captured the music of the disenchanted. *The Glass Menagerie* (1945), *A Streetcar Named Desire* (1947), *Summer and Smoke* (1948), *The Rose Tattoo* (1951), *Cat on a Hot Tin Roof* (1955), *Sweet Bird of Youth* (1959) and *The Night of the Iguana* (1961) are among the classic American dramas Williams created.

August Wilson (1945-) is the single most potent African-American voice in the theatre today. Highly poetic and almost Chekhovian in his presentation of characters in time, Wilson has written such stage successes as *Ma Rainey's Black Bottom* (1984), *Fences* (1987), *Joe Turner's Come and Gone* (1988), *The Piano Lesson* (1990), *Two Trains Running* (1992), and *Seven Guitars* (1996).

Lanford Wilson (1937-) is a character playwright who captures the language and subtle interplay of both rural and urban individuals. Since his early one-acts were first presented Off Off Broadway in the 1960s, Wilson has written *The Hot l Baltimore* (1973), *The Fifth of July* (1978), *Talley's Folly* (1980), *Angels Fall* (1983), *Burn This* (1987), *Redwood Curtain* (1993) and many others.

P. G. Wodehouse (1881-1975), the famous comic novelist, only spent a small portion of his long writing career in the theatre but he helped develop the American style of lyric writing in such musicals as *Oh, Boy!* (1917), *Leave It to Jane* (1917), *Sitting Pretty* (1924), *Rosalie* (1928) and others. Wodehouse also co-authored musical librettos, such as *Oh, Kay!* (1926) and *Anything Goes* (1934).

(For American composers of note, see Chapter 6)

PLAYWRITING TEAMS

While the teaming of writers and composers is usual in musicals, most plays are written by a single author. But there are cases throughout American theatre history when playwriting teams have enjoyed success because of the special magic that resulted from their working together. Here are some famous teams of playwrights, librettists and lyricists.

David Belasco (1853-1931) wrote with a variety of collaborators but none were as impressive as the promising playwright **Henry C. De Mille** (1855?-1893). Together they wrote four of the biggest hits at the end of the nineteenth century: *The Wife* (1887), *Lord Chumley* (1888), *The Charity Ball* (1889), and *Men and Women* (1890).

Guy Bolton (1884-1979), the prolific playwright-librettist, worked with just about everyone in the musical theatre profession but had particular success with two collaborators: **P. G. Wodehouse** (1881-1975) and **Fred Thompson** (1884-1949). With Wodehouse Bolton wrote such early musical gems as *Oh, Boy!* (1917), *Leave It to Jane* (1917), and *Sitting Pretty* (1924); with Thompson he wrote over a dozen musicals for Broadway and London, including *Tip-Toes* (1925), *Rio Rita* (1927), and *Follow the Girls* (1944).

Betty Comden (1915-) and **Adolph Green** (1915-) have the longest collaboration in the American theatre: from 1944 to the present. The team has written many musicals, sometimes providing the librettos, sometimes the lyrics, sometimes both. Among their many hits were *On the Town* (1944), *Wonderful Town* (1953), *Peter Pan* (1954), *Bells Are Ringing* (1956), *Applause* (1970), and *The Will Rogers Follies* (1991).

Herbert Fields (1897-1958) and his sister **Dorothy Fields** (1905-1974) wrote eight musical librettos together, with Dorothy often providing the lyrics as well. Their most remembered collaborations include *Let's Face It!* (1941), *Something for the Boys* (1943), *Up in Central Park* (1945), *Annie Get Your Gun* (1946), and *Redhead* (1959). Herbert Fields' teaming with lyricist **Lorenz Hart** (1895-1943) and composer **Richard Rodgers** (1902-1979) was one of the musical theatre's most innovative triumvirates.

Joseph Fields (1895-1966), unlike his siblings Herbert and Dorothy, concentrated on comedies rather than musicals and wrote several plays with **Jerome Chodorov** (1911-). Among their hits were *My Sister Eileen* (1940) and its musicalization *Wonderful Town* (1953), *Junior Miss* (1941), *Anniversary Waltz* (1954), and *The Ponder Heart* (1956).

Ruth Goodman Goetz (1912-) and **Augustus Goetz** (1901-1957) were a successful husband and wife team who are most remembered today for their intelligent stage adaptations, such as the sterling Henry James treatment *The Heiress* (1947), *The Immortalist* (1954), based on a Andre Gide novel, and

The Hidden River (1957), based on a Storm Jackson novel.

Frances Goodrich (1891-1984) and her husband **Albert Hackett** (1900-1995) were screenwriters who penned a handful of plays together, most memorably *The Diary of Anne Frank* (1955).

Fanny Locke Hatton (1870?-1939) collaborated with her husband **Frederic Hatton** (1879-1946) on several Broadway plays between 1912 and the late 1930s that were serviceable vehicles about interesting people with clever dialogue. The Hattons' most notable plays were *The Great Lover* (1915), *Upstairs and Down* (1916), and *Lombardi, Ltd.* (1917).

Ben Hecht (1894-1964) and **Charles McArthur** (1895-1956) were two Chicago newspaper writers who collaborated on a series of plays in addition to having successful careers separately. The best of the Hecht-McArthur plays were *The Front Page* (1928), *Twentieth Century* (1932), the musical *Jumbo* (1935), and *Ladies and Gentlemen* (1939).

George S. Kaufman (1889-1961), known as the Great Collaborator for his many successful teamings with playwrights, enjoyed many hits with three playwrights in particular. With **Marc Connelly** (1890-1981) he wrote the hit comedies *Dulcy* (1921), *Merton of the Movies* (1922), *Beggar on Horseback* (1924) and others. With **Edna Ferber** (1887-1968), he penned such hits as *The Royal Family* (1927), *Dinner at Eight* (1932), and *Stage Door* (1936). But Kaufman's most notable collaboration was with **Moss Hart** (1904-1961); the team wrote nine plays including such American classics as *Once in a Lifetime* (1930), *You Can't Take It With You* (1936), and *The Man Who Came To Dinner* (1939).

Jerome Lawrence (1915-) and **Robert E. Lee** (1916-1994) worked exclusively with each other on many plays and musical librettos. Their most accomplished works include *Auntie Mame* (1956), its musicalization *Mame* (1966), and the drama *Inherit the Wind* (1955).

Howard Lindsay (1889-1968) and **Russel Crouse** (1893-1966) were perhaps the most successful of all playwriting teams. Not only did they write *Life With Father* (1939), the longest running play in Broadway history, but they also won a Pulitzer Prize for their deft comedy *State of the Union* (1945). The team's other Broadway non-musicals include *Strip for Action* (1942), *Life With Mother* (1948), *The Prescott Proposals* (1953), and *The Great Sebastians* (1956). Their first collaboration was a matter of odd luck. Lindsay was slated to direct the new Cole Porter musical *Anything Goes* (1934) with a book by P. G. Wodehouse and Guy Bolton. The plot had to do with a shipwreck but, right before rehearsals were to begin, an actual ship, the *Morro Castle*, sunk with tragic loss of life. Using the same setting, Lindsay teamed up with press agent Russel Crouse and they wrote a totally new book that could utilize the already completed sets and costumes. The two later wrote the librettos for such musicals as *Red, Hot and Blue!* (1936), *Horray for What!* (1937), *Call Me Madam* (1950), *The Sound of Music* (1959), and *Mr. President* (1962).

Bella Spewack (1899-1990) and **Samuel Spewack** (1899-1971) were another husband and wife playwriting team who wrote several plays together, as well as the librettos for two Cole Porter hits: *Leave It to Me!* (1935) and *Kiss Me, Kate* (1948). Their comedy hits include *Boy Meets Girl* (1935) and *My Three Angels* (1953).

Robert Wright (1914-) and **George Forrest** (1915-) have only a handful of Broadway credits (plus many films) but they have one of the longest careers as a songwriting team: over 65 years. The team is best known for the musicals that they adapted from classic music pieces, such as *Song of Norway* (1944) and *Kismet* (1953), as well as original scores, such as the more recent *Grand Hotel* (1989).

THE NEW PLAYWRIGHTS

One interesting play makes for a promising playwright. Some writers go years before a second noteworthy play comes along. And too many, unfortunately, are one-play- only writers. Here is a highly arbitrary list of some of the new playwrights who are shaping up to be more than transitory.

Lynn Ahrens (1948-), a lyricist and librettist who began in television, has co-authored with composer Stephen Flaherty, the musicals *Lucky Stiff* (1988), *Once on This Island* (1990), and *My Favorite Year* (1992), as well as *A Christmas Carol* (1994) with composer Alan Menken.

Jon Robin Baitz (1961-) writes plays with an international consciousness, as in his *The Film Society* (1988), *The Substance of Fire* (1991), *Three Hotels* (1993), and *A Fair Country* (1996).

Lee Blessing (1949-) has written intriguing plays on varied topics, from *A Walk in the Woods* (1988) to *Cobb* (1989) to *Eleemosynary* (1989).

Eric Bogosian (1953-) is an actor who writes his own material, resulting in such dynamic one-man scripts as *Drinking in America* (1986), *Talk Radio* (1987), *Sex, Drugs, Rock & Roll* (1990), as well as the multi-character play *SubUrbia* (1994).

Charles Busch (1954-) has written and often played the female leads in outrageous Off-Broadway comedies, often as part of his Theatre-in-Limbo company. His most known works are *Vampire Lesbians of Sodom* (1984), *Psycho Beach Party* (1986), and *The Lady in Question* (1988).

Christopher Durang (1949-) is one of the sharpest satirists working in the theatre today, as witnessed by his comedies *Sister Mary Ignatius Explains It All for You* (1981), *Beyond Therapy* (1981), *Baby With the Bathwater* (1983), *The Marriage of Bette and Boo* (1985), *Sex and Longing* (1996), and several one-act plays.

Harvey Fierstein (1954-) has written a handful of one-act plays, some of which turned into the acclaimed modern gay epic *Torch Song Trilogy* (1982). Subsequent works include the libretto for *La Cage aux Folles* (1983), *Spookhouse* (1984), and *Safe Sex* (1987).

Richard Greenberg (1958-) first attracted attention with his one-acts, then later with such works as *Eastern Standard* (1988), *The American Plan* (1990), and *Night and Her Stars* (1995).

David Henry Hwang (1957-) has written about Chinese-Americans and issues of East and West in such plays as *FOB* (1980), *The Dance and the Railroad* (1981), *M. Butterfly* (1988), and *Golden Child* (1996).

David Ives (1950-) had written several superb one-acts that were produced over the years but not until six of them were combined under the title *All in the Timing* (1994) did they receive the recognition they deserved. Ives has also written full-length comedies, such as *Ancient History* (1989).

Larry Kramer (1935-) is a gay activist who has addressed the issue of AIDS in such potent dramas as *The Normal Heart* (1985) and *The Destiny of Me* (1992).

Tony Kushner (1956-) wrote some Off-Broadway plays and adaptations before gaining recognition for his two-part modern epic *Angels in America* (1993).

Craig Lucas (1951-), an actor who has turned to playwriting, has explored the fantastical in such plays as *Blue Window* (1984), *Reckless* (1988), and *Prelude to a Kiss* (1989), as well as the libretto for the musical *Three Postcards* (1987).

Donald Margulies (1954-) wrote several Off-Broadway scripts before gaining attention for *The Loman Family Picnic* (1989) and *Sight Unseen* (1992).

Richard Nelson (1950-) is an American playwright whose work has often premiered in England before reaching his homeland. Among his plays are *Principia Scriptoriae* (1986), *Some Americans Abroad* (1990), *Two Shakespearean Actors* (1992), *New England* (1995), as well as the libretto for *Chess* (1988).

Suzan-Lori Parks (1963-) is an African-American playwright who uses history and fantasy in her plays, such as *The Death of the Last Black Man in the Whole Entire World* (1990), *The America Play* (1994), and *Venus* (1996).

Paul Rudnick (1957-) is a novelist and playwright with an acerbic wit, as seen in his satiric comedies *I Hate Hamlet* (1991), *Jeffrey* (1993), and *The Naked Eye* (1996).

Nicky Silver (1961-) has gained attention recently for his wacky dark comedies, such as *Pterodactyls* (1993), *Raised in Captivity* (1995), *The Food Chain* (1995), and *Fit to Be Tied* (1996).

Anna Deavere Smith (1950-) is an actress-author who has turned the monologue form into the dynamic documentary-dramas *Fires in the Mirror* (1992) and *Twilight: Los Angeles, 1992* (1994).

John Weidman (1946-) has written the librettos for a handful of very different musicals, including *Pacific Overtures* (1976), *Assassins* (1990), and *Big* (1996).

George C. Wolfe (1954-) is an African-American playwright, director and producer who has contributed to both plays and musicals. He has written *The Colored Museum* (1986), *Spunk* (1990), and *Jelly's Last Jam* (1992).

MOST CITED PLAYWRIGHTS IN THE *BEST PLAYS*

The Burns Mantle *Best Plays* series has cited the ten best plays of each theatre season since 1919. Preceding the Tony Awards, New York Drama Critics Circle Awards and most other theatre honors, the citation of being a "best play" of the season provides perhaps the most comprehensive list of distinction in the American Theatre. The following are the fifteen playwrights most often cited as a "best play" author.

Maxwell Anderson	19 plays and musicals
George S. Kaufman	18 plays and musicals
Neil Simon	15 plays and musicals
Eugene O'Neill	12 plays
Moss Hart	11 plays and musicals
Philip Barry	10 plays
S. N. Behrman	9 plays
Lillian Hellman	9 plays
Robert Sherwood	9 plays
Tennessee Williams	9 plays
Terrence McNally	9 plays and musicals
Stephen Sondheim	8 musicals
Arthur Miller	7 plays
David Mamet	6 plays
Edward Albee	6 plays

For further reading: Oscar Brockett and Robert Findlay's *Century of Innovation*, Lehrman Engel's *Their Words Are Music*, Don Wilmeth and Tice Miller's *Cambridge Guide to American Theatre*, Gerald Bordman's *The Oxford Companion to American Theatre*, K. A. Berney's *Contemporary Dramatists*, Stanley Green's *The Encyclopedia of the Musical Theatre*, Ian Herbert's *Who's Who in the Theatre*, Philip Furia's *The Poets of Tin Pan Alley*, Thomas Hischak's *Word Crazy*, Mary Henderson's *Theatre in America*, and the *Best Plays* Series.

5

PLAYMAKERS

COLORFUL PRODUCERS

In the nineteenth century there were the great actor-managers and the playwright-managers. During the first half of the twentieth century there were colorful individual producers and impresarios. Today there are mostly theatre owner-production companies, conglomerates, and media giants. With few exceptions, Broadway plays are produced by large teams, some members of which are not in the theatre at all. Only in regional theatre does the idea of a producing director still exist. Here are some of the more famous of the old-time American producers, managers, and theatre owners.

Alex A. Aarons (1891-1943) with his partner **Vinton Freedley** (1891-1969) produced some of the best musicals of the 1920s, including the Gershwins' *Lady, Be Good!* (1924), *Oh, Kay* (1926), *Funny Face* (1927), and *Girl Crazy* (1930). Aarons was the son of Alfred E. Aarons (1865-1936), a successful producer and composer.

Winthrop Ames (1870-1937), a gentlemanly producer and director, built theatres, ran stock companies, and presented many Broadway plays in the 1910s and 1920s. With the Shuberts he built the Booth Theatre.

John Murray Anderson (1886-1954) was a multi-talented director and producer of musical revues, most notably the many editions of the *Greenwich Village Follies*.

Martin Beck (1865-1940) was an enterprising producer of theatre and vaudeville who built the Palace Theatre and the current theatre named after him.

David Belasco (1853-1931) wore many hats (actor, director, playwright) but his long career as a producer of plays by himself and with others was the most successful. He also created many stage stars, such as Mrs. Leslie Carter, Blanche Bates, and Frances Starr. Belasco did more than any other director to bring realism and naturalism to American theatre production, exploring the ways acting, scenery, and lighting could be used together to create life-like impressions on stage.

Kermit Bloomgarden (1904-1976) was a respected producer of very challenging plays on Broadway in the 1940s through the 1970s. Among his many distinguished productions were *Death of a Salesman* (1949), *The Diary of Anne Frank* (1955), *The Music Man* (1957), and *Equus* (1974).

William A. Brady (1863-1950) built theatres and produced plays in New York and on the road from 1888 through the 1920s. His productions include potboilers and melodramas, such as *Way Down East* (1898), *Sinners* (1915), and *Street Scene* (1929), and several comedies featuring his wife Grace George (1879-1961).

Earl Carroll (1893?-1948) was a colorful showman who built theatres and presented provocative musicals revues such as his *Earl Carroll Vanities* which had several editions in the 1920s.

George M. Cohan (1878-1942), in addition to writing, directing, and sometimes starring in his musicals and plays, produced them as well, sometimes with partner Sam Harris. Cohan was an active producer on Broadway from 1901 to 1940. He got so much attention for his songs, his performing and producing of Broadway comedies and musicals that it is often forgotten that he directed many of these productions himself. Cohan was instrumental in developing the tight, polished, and economic kind of staging that would identify the American style of production later seen in the work of George Abbott and other directors.

F. Ray Comstock (1880-1949) was a successful Broadway producer and presenter of foreign theatre companies but he is most remembered for presenting the landmark Princess Theatre musicals in the 1910s.

Cheryl Crawford (1902-1986) was a respected independent producer and director who founded or was associated with such important organizations as the Theatre Guild, Group Theatre, ANTA, and the Actors Studio.

Homer F. Curran (1885-1952) was an important West Coast producer and theatre owner who kept theatre alive in California during the Depression by presenting San Francisco versions of New York hits. He also co-founded the San Francisco Light Opera Company and sent a handful of shows to Broadway.

Jean Dalrymple (1910-) was a producer who is most famous for her many distinguished revivals at the New York City Center and the City Center Light Opera Company in the 1950s and 1960s.

Augustin Daly (1838-1899) was one of the most important and influential theatre managers of the nineteenth century and his famous company at the Fifth Avenue Theatre and later at Daly's Theatre set the standards of the day. Daly was also a prolific playwright and translator and one of the century's most respected American directors. The way he ran his famous repertory company, the disciplined way he approached rehearsals, and his talent for coordinating all the technical elements in a production gave American theatre a new respectability.

Alfred de Liagre, Jr. (1904-1987) produced and sometimes directed a variety of plays on Broadway from the 1930s through the 1970s, such as *The Voice of the Turtle* (1943), *The Madwoman of Chaillot* (1948), *J. B.* (1958), and *Deathtrap* (1978).

Charles Dillingham (1868-1934) was a beloved producer who presented some 200 plays and musicals on Broadway during the first three decades of the twentieth century. His shows were known for their opulence and good taste and few men in the business were better liked.

Mrs. John Drew (1820-1897) was a renowned actress known across the country but her greatest contribution was her management (from 1861 to 1892) of Philadelphia's Arch Street Theatre, one of the greatest ensembles in America.

William Dunlap (1766-1839) was a pioneering American playwright but he was also a significant manager and producer, running the famous Park Theatre in New York for many years.

A. E. Erlanger (1860-1930) was a ruthless businessman who rose through the ranks to be one of the most powerful men in America, heading the Theatrical Syndicate at the turn of the century and controlling hundreds of playhouses across the country.

Cy Feuer (1911-) and his producing partner **Ernest Martin** (1919-1995) were among the most successful of Broadway producers from the late 1940s through the 1960s, presenting many musical hits such as Frank Loesser's *Where's Charley?* (1948), *Guys and Dolls* (1950), and *How to Succeed in Business Without Really Trying* (1961).

Lew Fields (1867-1941) was, in addition to his celebrated career with Joe Weber as a performer and presenter of musical burlesques, a successful producer of plays and musicals, most notably the early efforts by the team of Rodgers and Hart and his son Herbert Fields.

Hallie Flanagan (1890-1969) was a highly experimental teacher and producer who headed the controversial Federal Theatre Project during its short but potent existence in the 1930s.

Charles Frohman (1860-1915) began his illustrious producing career with the hit *Shenandoah* (1888) and was a major force on Broadway and in London until his death on the *Lusitania* when it was sunk by a German submarine. In addition to introducing new American plays and bringing British classics to Broadway, Frohman nurtured the careers of such stars as Maude Adams, Ethel Barrymore, and Billie Burke.

Daniel Frohman (1851-1940), the brother of Charles Frohman, was a successful producer of American and foreign plays, as well as an astute theatre manager who built the Lyceum Theatre.

John Golden (1874-1955) was a Broadway lyricist who used his royalty earnings to go into producing in 1916. Among his many long-run hits were *Lightnin'* (1918), *The First Year* (1920), and *Seventh Heaven* (1922).

Max Gordon (1892-1978) was one of Broadway's most successful producers of both plays and musicals in the 1930s and 1940s. His hits ranged from *The Band Wagon* (1931) to *The Solid Gold Cadillac* (1953).

Arthur Hammerstein (1872-1955) rose from assistant for his father Oscar Hammerstein I's production company to an astute producer of musicals such as *The Firefly* (1912), *Rose-Marie* (1924), and *Sweet Adeline* (1929).

Oscar Hammerstein I (1847-1919) was a bigger-than-life impresario in theatre and opera who built several theatres, produced plays, lost theatres, and was always in the limelight. He was the grandfather of the lyricist/librettist Oscar Hammerstein II.

Sam Harris (1872-1941) was one of Broadway's most respected producers for his good taste and eye for spotting fine plays. He was the co-producing partner of George M. Cohan for some time then went on to a lucrative career as a solo producer.

Leland Hayward (1902-1971) was a former talent agent who became one of Broadway's busiest producers in the 1940s and 1950s. *A Bell for Adano* (1944), *Mister Roberts* (1948), *South Pacific* (1949), *Gypsy* (1952), and *The Sound of Music* (1959) were among his many hits.

Theresa Helburn (1887-1959) was the decisive executive director of the Theatre Guild for many years, producing some of their most famous Broadway productions.

Arthur Hopkins (1878-1950) was one of Broadway's most respected producers in the early decades of the century and he directed most of his famous productions himself. Hopkins had high standards and ambitious ideas for Broadway, as seen in his *The Jest* (1919), *Richard III* (1920), and *Hamlet* (1923), all three featuring John Barrymore, as well as *What Price Glory?* (1924), *Holiday* (1928), *The Petrified Forest* (1935) and many others. Hopkins also built the Plymouth Theatre in conjunction with the Shuberts.

Laura Keene (1826?-1873), one of the best actresses of the nineteenth century, was an early and determined theatre manager as well, presenting contemporary and classic plays in her famous company in New York in the 1850s and 1860s.

Marc Klaw (1858-1936) was a shrewd businessman who teamed up with Abe Erlanger in 1888 to create a powerful booking agency that eventually led to the Theatrical Syndicate.

Lawrence Langner (1890-1962) was a producer and theatre manager who helped found and/or run such theatre companies as the Washington Square Players, the Theatre Guild, Westport Country Playhouse, and the American Shakespeare Festival.

Eva Le Gallienne (1899-1991) was a remarkable dynamo of a woman: actress, manager, translator, and director. She directed many of the productions at her ambitious Civic Repertory Theatre in the 1920s and at the short-lived American Repertory Company, which she co-founded in 1946. Few American directors staged Ibsen and Chekhov as effectively as Le Gallienne.

Edwin Lester (1895-1990), the most impressive producer in West Coast theatre, helped found and/or manage such important companies as the Los Angeles Light Opera Festival, the San Francisco Light Opera Association, and the Los Angeles Light Opera Association.

Herman Levin (1907-1990) was a Broadway producer from the 1940s through the 1960s, most known for the long struggle he had in bringing *My Fair Lady* (1956) to light.

Thomas Maguire (1820?-1896), called the "Napoleon" of San Francisco theatre, built several theatres in that California city and was responsible for making it a booming theatre town in the mid-nineteenth century.

Elisabeth Marbury (1856-1933) was an influential agent for playwrights who was instrumental in creating the Princess Theatre musical series.

David Merrick (1911-), perhaps the last of the big-time controversial producers who were as famous as their productions, was the most successful Broadway producer of the 1960s. His many hits included musicals, dramas, and foreign imports, all produced with panache and very flamboyant marketing techniques. From *Fanny* (1954) to *State Fair* (1996), Merrick's career was one of the most colorful Broadway has ever seen.

Gilbert Miller (1884-1969) was a notable producer who presented many important plays on Broadway and in London from the 1920s through the 1950s. He was the son of the popular actor Henry Miller (1859-1926).

Oliver Morosco (1876-1945) was a West Coast theatre owner who started to produce plays and musicals in San Francisco and New York in order to fill his theatres. He also helped write many of his musical successes in the 1910s.

A. M. Palmer (1838?-1905) ran a famous theatre company out of the Union Square Theatre and later at the Madison Square Theatre, bringing superior acting and outstanding plays to New York audiences in the final decades of the nineteenth century.

Joseph Papp (1921-1991) did more than any other producer to develop Off Broadway into an exciting and artistically potent theatre movement. Through his New York Shakespeare Festival and later at the Public Theatre, Papp nurtured new American playwrights, promising actors, and experimental directors. Several of his productions, from Shakespeare revivals to new plays and musicals, transferred to Broadway with great success, none more so than *A Chorus Line* (1975).

Brock Pemberton (1885-1950) was a newspaper drama editor who turned to producing, providing several Broadway hits from the 1920s through the 1940s. His biggest success was the long-running *Harvey* (1944).

Harold Prince (1928-), with his producing partner **Robert Griffith** (1907-1961), presented some of the biggest musical hits of the 1950s, from *Pajama Game* (1954) to *Fiorello!* (1959). As a solo producer, Prince continued his string of successes, including *Fiddler on the Roof* (1964) and *Cabaret* (1966), until he started directing and eventually gave up producing altogether. He remains one of the most innovative and creative directors of musicals Broadway has ever seen and he is legendary for his bold approach to text, mastery at stage pictures and imagery, and his development of the concept musical. *Cabaret* (1966), *Company* (1970), *Sweeney Todd* (1979), *Phantom of the Opera* (1988), *Kiss of the Spider Woman* (1993), and the 1994 revival of *Show Boat* are among his many acclaimed productions.

Billy Rose (1899-1966) was a lyricist, theatre owner and manager, presenter of aquacades and shows for two World's Fairs, and a producer of Broadway plays and musicals, most memorably *Jumbo* (1935) and *Carmen Jones* (1943).

Arch Selwyn (1877?-1959) and his brother **Edgar Selwyn** (1875-1944) produced many Broadway plays in the 1910s and 1920s. They also built theatres and ran the American Play Company, a play brokerage firm.

The **Shubert Brothers** was an enterprising family of managers and producers who broke the power of the Theatrical Syndicate and created a large theatre monopoly of their own. The brothers Lee (1873?-1953), Sam (1876?-1905), and J. J. Shubert (1878?-1963) owned hundreds of theatres in New York and across the country and produced over 500 Broadway productions, mostly musicals "for the tired businessman."

Herman Shumlin (1898-1979) was the producer of many Broadway comedies but his reputation rests on the bold and controversial dramas he presented over his forty-year career. Among the most notable Shumlin productions were *Grand Hotel* (1930), *The Corn Is Green* (1940), and *The Deputy* (1964). Shumlin was also a director of important American plays on Broadway in the 1930s and 1940s, in particular Lillian Hellman's *The Children's Hour* (1934), *The Little Foxes* (1939), and *Watch on the Rhine* (1941).

Roger L. Stevens (1910-) produced many hit plays on Broadway, from *Bus Stop* (1955) to *Mary, Mary* (1961), as well as heading such distinguished companies as the Producers Theatre, the American Shakespeare Festival, and The Kennedy Center for the Performing Arts.

Michael Todd (1907-1958) was a colorful producer who loved to be in the news and was as famous as any of his productions. On Broadway he presented such diverse shows as the burlesque-like *Star and Garter* (1942) and Maurice Evans' *Hamlet* (1945).

George Tyler (1867-1946) was a busy producer at the turn of the century, presenting some 200 productions during a forty-year career, including *Sag Harbor* (1900), *Clarence* (1919), *Merton of the Movies* (1922) and others.

James William Wallack (1794-1864) formed his famous New York company in 1852 and, with management later taken over by his son **Lester Wallack** (1819-1888), for the next thirty-five years it was the finest ensemble in the nation. James emphasized British and Continental plays and under Lester's leadership more American works were presented. But consistent under each management was the superior quality of the acting ensemble.

Robert Whitehead (1916-) produced some fifty Broadway productions from the 1940s through the 1980s, as well as being an active producer at Lincoln Center, ANTA, and other theatre organizations. He is also a notable director, staging outstanding productions of *Medea* in 1947 and in 1982.

A. H. Woods (1870-1951) produced over 100 Broadway shows during the first decades of this century, many of them grisly melodramas at first, then later comedies and star vehicles.

Florenz Ziegfeld (1867-1932) remains America's most famous producer because his name still stands for a high quality kind of lavishness and glamour that was and is unique. In addition to his world-renowned *Follies* that he presented for the first time in 1907, Ziegfeld also produced many book shows, including *Sally* (1920), *Show Boat* (1927), *Rio Rita* (1927), *Whoopee* (1928) and others.

TOP DIRECTORS

Directing, that most misunderstood of theatre crafts, has gained in importance and respect over the past 100 years, and today the director is considered the single most influential person in a modern theatre production. This is a remarkable feat when one considers that theatre did very well without directors for 2,000 years. In the eighteenth and nineteenth centuries, most actor-managers rarely ran theatre companies as a director does today, trying to unify all the elements of a play and giving it a particular vision or interpretation. (Augustin Daly and A. M. Palmer were vibrant exceptions.) But even before America produced world-class playwrights, we did have remarkable directors who were respected and studied in Europe. Here are some of the finest American directors from the past.

George Abbott (1887-1995) directed dozens of musical and comedy hits in a career that lasted 80 years. His productions were known for their distinctive "Abbott touch," a razor-sharp sense of timing and building of intensity that did not seem forced or artificial. From his early smash *Broadway* (1926), which he co-wrote, to the successful revival of *On Your Toes* (1983), few directors ever had more hits than Abbott.

David Belasco See Colorful Producers earlier in this chapter.

Michael Bennett (1943-1987) did such startling things in his brief career that he managed to have a greater influence on the American musical theatre than many longtime veterans. Perhaps the most inspired of the director-choreographers who emerged in the 1970s, Bennett used dance, lighting, moving scenery, and exciting conceptual ideas vividly in such shows as *Follies* (1971), *A Chorus Line* (1975), and *Dreamgirls* (1981).

Abe Burrows (1910-1985) is mostly remembered for the brilliant librettos he wrote for musicals such as *Guys and Dolls* (1950) and *How To Succeed in*

Business Without Really Trying (1961) but he was also a superior director of musicals and comedies in the George Abbott style.

Gower Champion (1920-1980) was a choreographer-director who brought a playful sense of wit and charm to big Broadway musicals in the 1960s and 1970s. *Bye Bye Birdie* (1960), *Hello, Dolly!* (1964), and *42nd Street* (1980) were among his most popular shows.

Harold Clurman (1901-1980) was one of the founders of the Group Theatre and his staging of their influential works *Awake and Sing!* (1935) and *Golden Boy* (1937) illustrated a perceptive directorial touch. Clurman's later stage successes included *Member of the Wedding* (1950) and *Bus Stop* (1955).

George M. Cohan   See Colorful Producers earlier in this chapter.

Augustin Daly   See Colorful Producers earlier in this chapter.

Bob Fosse (1927-1987), a dancer-turned-choreographer-turned-director with a distinctive style in stage movement, directed such memorable musicals as *Sweet Charity* (1966), *Pippin* (1972), *Chicago* (1975), and *Dancin'* (1978). Fosse's stage work was very theatrical, sexy, often cynical and anti-romantic, but he did more than any other individual in the early 1970s to establish the role of the powerful director-choreographer.

Jed Harris (1900-1979) may have been the most hated man in twentieth-century American theatre, a ruthless producer and harsh director of actors with an outrageous behavior problem. Yet occasionally he staged superior productions and got exceptional performances out of his casts. Harris' most remembered Broadway hits include *The Green Bay Tree* (1933), *Our Town* (1938), *The Heiress* (1947), and *The Crucible* (1953).

Moss Hart (1904-1961) will always be remembered as one of our finest comic playwrights but in his day he was a much sought after director as well. Besides directing many of his own plays and musicals, Hart also was the guiding hand behind *Dear Ruth* (1944), *My Fair Lady* (1956), *Camelot* (1960) and others.

Arthur Hopkins   See Colorful Producers earlier in this chapter.

Margo Jones (1911-1955) just about single-handedly started the post-war Regional Theatre movement in America and the productions she directed at her innovative theatre in Dallas brought her attention rarely afforded to women directors. Jones reintroduced the arena stage to professional American theatre and her staging of classics and modern plays were written about across the country, especially her pre-Broadway productions of *Summer and Smoke* (1947) and *Inherit the Wind* (1955). Jones' most famous New York credits were directing Ingrid Bergman in *Joan of Lorraine* (1946) and co-directing the original *The Glass Menagerie* (1945).

George S. Kaufman (1889-1961), the prolific playwright collaborator, directed many of his own as well as others' productions. Kaufman's direction was unobtrusive, letting the play and performers get all the attention. But he guided many Broadway plays and musicals to success, from *The Front Page*

(1928) to *Guys and Dolls* (1950).

Elia Kazan (1909-) was a major force in the American theatre, from his days with the Group Theatre in the 1930s to his collaboration with our finest playwrights in the 1940s and 1950s. A meticulous director who guided new plays, kept detailed notebooks on his productions, and explored new approaches to performance (he co-founded the Actors Studio in 1947), Kazan was the single most influential director of American drama in the post-World War Two era. Many of the major plays by Tennessee Williams, Arthur Miller, and William Inge were first staged by Kazan, as well as such memorable productions as *The Skin of Our Teeth* (1942), *Tea and Sympathy* (1953), and *J. B.* (1958).

Eva Le Gallienne See Colorful Producers earlier in this chapter.

Robert Lewis (1909-) had a talent for directing a variety of plays, from thrillers to fanciful plays to musicals. Associated with the Group Theatre and the Theatre Guild, Lewis' varied productions include *My Heart's in the Highlands* (1939), *Brigadoon* (1947), *An Enemy of the People* (1950), *The Teahouse of the August Moon* (1953), *Witness for the Prosecution* (1954), and *On a Clear Day You Can See Forever* (1965).

Joshua Logan (1908-1988) was a Broadway favorite for his practical direction of many hit comedies and musicals. Logan was especially proficient in developing ways to move large, cumbersome musicals in a fluid, economic way. Among his many successes were *On Borrowed Time* (1938), *Annie Get Your Gun* (1946), *Mister Roberts* (1948), *South Pacific* (1949), and *Picnic* (1953).

Rouben Mamoulian (1898-1987) was a Russian-born stage and film director who had a vivid sense of movement and picturization in his productions. He started with the Theatre Guild and provided for them some of the most stunning stage direction seen in American musicals: *Porgy and Bess* (1935), *Oklahoma!* (1943), *Carousel* (1945), and *Lost in the Stars* (1949).

Guthrie McClintic (1893-1961) was a very prolific director, second only to George Abbott in the number of Broadway shows he staged during his long career. Today he is mostly remembered for the many plays he produced and directed for his wife, actress Katharine Cornell, *The Barretts of Wimpole Street* (1931) being the most famous.

Julian Mitchell (1854-1926) probably directed more Broadway musicals than any other director in a career that lasted from 1884 to 1925. It was Mitchell who helped develop the traditional female chorus line as it was seen for decades in American musicals. Among his notable productions were *A Trip to Chinatown* (1891), *The Wizard of Oz* (1903), *Babes in Toyland* (1903), and nine editions of the *Ziegfeld Follies*.

Philip Moeller (1880-1958) was an intuitive director who staged a variety of plays for the Theatre Guild using an "inspirational" method of working with actors. Among his many famous Guild productions were *They Knew What They Wanted* (1924), *Strange Interlude* (1928), *Elizabeth the Queen* (1930), *Biography* (1932), and *Ah, Wilderness!* (1933).

José Quintero (1924-) was a respected director of serious dramas and perhaps the finest interpreter of Eugene O'Neill's plays. Quintero directed the original *Long Day's Journey Into Night* (1956) and vibrant O'Neill revivals such as *The Iceman Cometh* (1956) and *A Moon for the Misbegotten* (1973).

Jerome Robbins (1918-) is the most famous choreographer-turned-director in modern American musical theatre and a master of blending plot, character, movement and visuals into an electrifying whole. Robbins choreographed several memorable musicals in the 1940s then moved on to directing in the 1950s, leaving behind a legacy of musical theatre classics: *Peter Pan* (1954), *West Side Story* (1957), *Gypsy* (1959), *Fiddler on the Roof* (1964) and others.

Alan Schneider (1917-1984) was responsible for introducing Albee, Pinter, Beckett, Kopit and other innovative dramatists to America in his regional and Broadway productions. Among the modern classics Schneider was the first to direct in the United States were *Waiting for Godot* (1956), *Endgame* (1958), *Who's Afraid of Virginia Woolf?* (1962), *Entertaining Mr. Sloane* (1967), and *The Birthday Party* (1967).

Hassard Short (1877-1956) was a master at staging musical plays and revues on Broadway, using moving scenery, mirrors, and lighting in ways not previously seen. In fact, he is credited with the elimination of footlights and replacing them with lights positioned in the balcony and around the proscenium. Among Short's most memorable shows were *Three's a Crowd* (1930), *The Band Wagon* (1931), *As Thousands Cheer* (1933), *Roberta* (1933), *Jubilee* (1935), and *Make Mine Manhattan* (1948).

Herman Shumlin See Colorful Producers earlier in this chapter.

Ned Wayburn (1874-1942), the pioneering director of musicals, was perhaps the first to try and coordinate all the elements of a production into a unified whole. Most of his musicals and revues are long forgotten now but the innovations he brought to staging, his promotion of tap dancing as a musical comedy staple, and his emphasis on tempo and picturization would become the basis for later musical theatre direction.

Margaret Webster (1905-1972) was a renowned actress who went on to stage some of the most innovative productions of Shakespeare yet seen in America. While some grumbled about Webster's mild tampering with the text, most found her Shakespeare productions bold and illuminating. She pioneered in the use of African-American actors in Shakespeare (her *Othello* in 1943 was the first Broadway production to use a black actor, Paul Robeson, in the title role) and she simplified the scenery so that the plays moved as quickly and smoothly as originally intended. Webster presented nine Shakespeare productions on Broadway, most of them commercial successes, as well as many others in regional playhouses, colleges, and overseas theatres.

Orson Welles (1915-1990) acted, produced, and directed in the theatre before going west for his celebrated film career. For the Federal Theatre Project and later his own Mercury Theatre, Welles staged such unforgettable productions as the black *Macbeth* (1936), *Doctor Faustus* (1937), *The Cradle Will Rock* (1937), a modern-dress *Julius Caesar* (1937), and *Danton's Death* (1938).

Robert Whitehead See Colorful Producers earlier in this chapter.

Today there are so many American directors of note working on and Off Broadway that any listing of them would have to be very selective and arguable. Here are some of the more interesting contemporary directors.

Joanne Akalaitis (1935-), an avant-garde director who co-founded the theatre group Mabou Mines in 1970, has presented a series of controversial plays in regional theatre and Off Broadway. Her *Endgame* (1984) and *The Balcony* (1986) are among her notable productions that use unconventional images, slow motion, and nontraditional sound effects.

Joseph Chaikin (1935-) founded the innovative Open Theatre in 1963, a troupe that used play text as the basis for exciting actor improvisation and exploration. The group's production of *The Serpent* (1967) was characteristic of Chaikin's bold approach to directing actors. He has staged many productions across the country and in regional theatre.

Richard Foreman (1937-) is an avant-garde playwright whose work is presented by the Ontological-Hysteric Theatre, which he founded in 1968, but he is more known as a director of startling originality. Foreman's use of odd imagery, striking tableaux with unusual perspective, and minimal use of actors have made his productions distinctive and controversial.

Gerald Gutierrez (1952-) is among the most accomplished young directors working in theatre today, known particularly for his sterling revivals of American plays. Recently he has been most associated with Lincoln Center Theatre where he directed outstanding productions of *Abe Lincoln in Illinois* (1993), *The Heiress* (1995), and *A Delicate Balance* (1996).

Marshall W. Mason (1940-) was associated with the Circle Repertory Theatre for many years and with the playwright Lanford Wilson, most of whose work he first directed. Among the most memorable Wilson-Mason collaborations were *The Hot L Baltimore* (1973), *Fifth of July* (1978), and *Talley's Folly* (1979).

Mike Nichols (1931-), the film director whose intermittent theatrical ventures have met with great success, made his name on Broadway for his expert direction of such comedies as *Barefoot in the Park* (1963), *Luv* (1964), and *The Odd Couple* (1965). He later expanded and directed such diverse New York hits as *The Little Foxes* (1967), *Uncle Vanya* (1973), *The Gin Game* (1977), *The Real Thing* (1984), and *Waiting for Godot* (1988).

Harold Prince See Colorful Producers earlier in this chapter.

Lloyd Richards (1923-) is the dean of African-American directors, a very accomplished director who, through his work at the Eugene O'Neill Theatre

Center and the Yale Repertory Theatre, has done much to promote new American playwrights. Richards directed the original *A Raisin in the Sun* (1959) and lately has directed all of the plays by August Wilson, from *Ma Rainey's Black Bottom* (1984) to *Seven Guitars* (1996).

Gene Saks (1921-) staged his first Broadway shows in the 1960s and soon proved to be one of the finest directors of comedy. Saks directed several Neil Simon plays, including the autobiographical trilogy *Brighton Beach Memoirs* (1983), *Biloxi Blues* (1985), and *Broadway Bound* (1986). Saks also directed several musicals.

John Tillinger (1939-), a New York actor who turned to directing, has staged several plays at the Long Wharf Theatre, the Manhattan Theatre Club, and many Off-Broadway theatres. He has directed such A. R. Gurney, Jr., plays as *The Perfect Party* (1986), *Sweet Sue* (1987), *Love Letters* (1988), and *Sylvia* (1995), as well as Terrence McNally's *The Lisbon Traviata* (1989), *Lips Together, Teeth Apart* (1991), and *A Perfect Ganesh* (1993).

Tommy Tune (1939-) gained attention as a performer-dancer then as a choreographer before turning to directing plays and musicals. Tune's early efforts were seen as slick and very clever but later his staging of musicals, such as *Nine* (1982) and *Grand Hotel* (1989), revealed an imaginative director-choreographer with a stunning sense of movement and picturization.

Robert Wilson (1941-), the avant-garde director who creates striking visual images in his work, calls his pieces operas because they employ a great deal of music, usually atonal as in his collaborations with Philip Glass. But Wilson's stage pieces are highly theatrical and he often approaches classic texts with intriguing new insight.

Jerry Zaks (1946-) has been directing only since 1979 and since that time he has proved himself an inspired interpreter of American musicals, comedies, and dramas. Zaks also has one of the most impressive track records for Broadway hits in so short a span of time. Among his credits are *The Foreigner* (1984), *Lend Me a Tenor* (1989), *Six Degrees of Separation* (1990), *Assassins* (1991), as well as the popular revivals *The House of Blue Leaves* (1986), *Anything Goes* (1987), *Guys and Dolls* (1992), and *A Funny Thing Happened on the Way to the Forum* (1996).

Since the rise of the regional theatre movement in America in the 1950s, it is possible for a director to have an accomplished career and stage dozens of admirable productions and not work in New York. Here are some of the notable American directors who have worked primarily outside of New York.

William Ball (1931-1991) directed outstanding productions of classics and modern plays in a half dozen different regional theatres but is most remembered for his fine work at San Francisco's American Conservatory Theatre, which he founded in 1964.

Arvin Brown (1940-) served as Artistic Director of the Long Wharf Theatre in New Haven from 1967 to 1996, directing over seventy productions there and sending a half dozen of them to Broadway.

Gordon Davidson (1933-) has mostly been associated with the Center Theatre Group at the Mark Taper Forum in Los Angeles where he has staged numerous new works over the years. *The Shadow Box* (1977), *Children of a Lesser God* (1979), and *Zoot Suit* (1979) are among the Davidson discoveries that he later brought to Broadway.

Adrian Hall (1927-) was the Artistic Director at the Trinity Square Repertory in Providence for 25 years where he staged many imaginative as well as controversial productions. Hall has also presented several stage adaptations over the years that he wrote or co-authored with others.

Mark Lamos (1946-) has directed many classical plays in his role as Artistic Director at Connecticut's Hartford Stage Company but he has also presented new works. Lamos is one of the finest interpreters of Shakespeare in America, directing unconventional but dazzling presentations filled with imaginative imagery and wit.

Des McAnuff was the Artistic Director of California's La Jolla Playhouse for several years where he directed a variety of classical, modern, and musical pieces. Among his productions to successfully transfer to Broadway are *Big River* (1985), *A Walk in the Woods* (1988), *The Who's Tommy* (1993), and the revival of *How To Succeed in Business Without Really Trying* (1995).

Gregory Mosher (1949-) is among the exciting new directors to come out of Chicago where he directed the original productions of plays by David Mamet, John Guare, Michael Weller and others. Mosher was long associated with the Goodman Theatre in Chicago and his New York credits include *American Buffalo* (1975) and *Edmond* (1982).

Jack O'Brien (1939-) has been Artistic Director of the Old Globe Theatre in San Diego since 1981 where he has staged both classics and new works with equal success. O'Brien's work is often seen on and Off Broadway as well, his most memorable credits are *Porgy and Bess* (1977), *The Cocktail Hour* (1988), *Two Shakespearean Actors* (1992), *Hapgood* (1994), and *Damn Yankees* (1994).

Peter Sellars (1957-), the controversial director of deconstructed opera productions, has staged many fascinating theatre productions since his notorious days as a student director at Harvard University. Working for various regional, New York, and international theatre companies, Sellars' bold and unconventional approach to theatre has delighted and infuriated many.

Daniel Sullivan (1940-) has directed revivals and new plays at the Seattle Repertory Theatre where he has served as Artistic Director. Among the Seattle premieres he directed that later went to New York were *The Heidi Chronicles* (1988), *The Sisters Rosensweig* (1992), and *Conversations With My Father* (1992).

Finally, here are some noted contemporary American playwrights who have also distinguished themselves as directors.

Edward Albee (1928-) has directed revivals of many of his plays over the years, in particular his early one-acts and the 1976 Broadway revival of *Who's Afraid of Virginia Woolf?* He has also directed plays by Samuel Beckett and others.

James Lapine (1949-) has staged Shakespeare and contemporary plays Off Broadway and in regional theatres but is most acclaimed for his superb direction of the musical productions that he has coauthored: *March of the Falsettos* (1981), *Sunday in the Park With George* (1984), *Into the Woods* (1987), *Falsettoland* (1990), and *Passion* (1994).

Arthur Laurents (1918-) directed his own *Anyone Can Whistle* (1964) and successful revivals of his *Gypsy* on Broadway in 1974 and 1989. Among the musicals by others that he staged were *I Can Get It for You Wholesale* (1962) and *La Cage aux Folles* (1983).

Richard Maltby, Jr. (1937-) has written a number of distinctive musicals and revues with David Shire and others but he has also directed such Broadway productions as *Ain't Misbehavin'* (1978) and *Song and Dance* (1985).

David Mamet (1947-) did not direct the initial productions of most of his plays but he has staged works by others, such as J. B. Priestly's *Dangerous Corner* (1995) Off Broadway. He has also directed films.

Emily Mann (1952-) is a respected playwright who stages her own work, as well as classical and contemporary pieces by others, at the McCarter Theatre in Princeton. *Twilight: Los Angeles 1992* (1994) and *Having Our Say* (1995) are among her acclaimed productions in regional theatre and later in New York.

Sam Shepard (1943-) has both acted in and directed productions of his plays, usually in regional theatres and Off Broadway. Shepard's most recent New York project was the direction of his own *Simpatico* (1994) at the Public Theatre.

George C. Wolfe (1954-) has directed his own productions, such as *The Colored Museum* (1986) and *Jelly's Last Jam* (1992), as well as plays by others, such as *Angels in America, Parts One & Two* (1993).

DISTINCTIVE CHOREOGRAPHERS

While audiences in general are not quite sure what a director does, they can see clearly what a choreographer does. American choreographers have been the envy of the world and few international productions capture the choreographic style that is uniquely Broadway. In addition to the director-choreographers Michael Bennett, Gower Champion, Bob Fosse, Jerome Robbins, Tommy Tune and Ned Wayburn discussed above, here are some of the theatre's other outstanding choreographers who have made an impact on Broadway past and present.

Robert Alton (1897-1957) was an innovative Broadway choreographer whose productions in the 1930s did much to change dancing in musicals from static chorus lines to interesting groupings of dancers with featured solo turns. Among Alton's successful shows were *Anything Goes* (1934), *Leave It To Me!* (1938), *DuBarry Was a Lady* (1939), *Pal Joey* (1940), and several editions of the *Ziegfeld Follies*.

George Balanchine (1904-1983), one of the finest classical choreographers of this century, did the dancing for sixteen Broadway musicals in the 1930s and 1940s and was responsible for bringing modern dance to the musical theatre. Among Balanchine's notable Broadway credits were *On Your Toes* (1936), in which his celebrated "Slaughter on Tenth Avenue" ballet was first seen, *Babes in Arms* (1937), *The Boys From Syracuse* (1938), *Cabin in the Sky* (1940), and *Where's Charley?* (1948).

Patricia Birch (1934-) has choreographed many musicals that are not considered dance shows but needed careful musical staging: *You're a Good Man, Charlie Brown* (1967), *The Me Nobody Knows* (1970), *A Little Night Music* (1973), *Pacific Overtures* (1976) and others. Birch, who sometimes directs as well, provided more traditional choreography for shows such as *Grease* (1972) and *Over Here* (1974).

Jack Cole (1914-1974) was an ingenious choreographer who used the sounds and forms of foreign cultures in his work, as well as a stylized, jazzy approach later seen in the work of Bob Fosse. Cole's particular talents were seen in such Broadway musicals as *Kismet* (1953), *Jamaica* (1957), *A Funny Thing Happened on the Way to the Forum* (1962), and *Man of La Mancha* (1965).

Graciela Daniele (1939-), a dancer-turned-choreographer who first gained attention for her dances in musicals at New York's Public Theatre, has also directed most of her productions since 1989. Daniele's credits include *The Pirates of Penzance* (1981), *The Mystery of Edwin Drood* (1981), *Once On This Island* (1990), and *Chronicle of a Death Foretold* (1995).

Danny Daniels (1924-) was an energetic featured dancer in Broadway musicals in the 1940s. He began choreographing in the 1960s but, despite his just-as-energetic choreography that was often applauded, very few of his shows were successes: *All American* (1962), *Best Foot Forward* (1963), *Walking Happy* (1966), *The Tap Dance Kid* (1983) and many others.

Agnes De Mille (1905-1993), the renowned choreographer for theatre and modern dance, did more than any other artist to bring narrative to Broadway choreography, as well as character-driven dance and psychologically motivated movement. De Mille came to the forefront of American choreographers with her musical numbers in *Oklahoma!* (1943) and showed similar wizardry in *One Touch of Venus* (1943), *Bloomer Girl* (1944), *Carousel* (1945), *Brigadoon*

(1947), *Allegro* (1947), *Juno* (1959) and others.

Ron Field (1934-1989) was a respected choreographer who also turned to directing later in his career. After dancing in several Broadway musicals in the 1940s and 1950s, Field began choreographing in 1962 and did such memorable musicals as *Cabaret* (1966), *Zorbá* (1968), *Applause* (1970) and others.

Peter Gennaro (1924-) is a recognized choreographer for Broadway, television, Radio City Music Hall, and other venues. His most notable Broadway musicals are *West Side Story* (1957) with Jerome Robbins, *Fiorello!* (1959), *The Unsinkable Molly Brown* (1960), *Bajour* (1964), *Irene* (1973), and *Annie* (1977).

Hanya Holm (1893-1992) was a versatile stage choreographer whose many musicals in London and New York point to no particular style but were all excellent. *Kiss Me, Kate* (1948), *Out of This World* (1950), *My Fair Lady* (1956), and *Camelot* (1960) are her most remembered Broadway credits.

Michael Kidd (1919-) is a film and stage choreograher-turned-director whose dances are known for their high energy and vitality. Kidd's first Broadway credit was *Finian's Rainbow* (1947) and he went on to choreograph *Love-Life* (1948), *Guys and Dolls* (1950), *Can-Can* (1953) and others. His directing credits include *Li'l Abner* (1956), *Destry Rides Again* (1959), *Wildcat* (1960), *The Rothschilds* (1970), and *The Goodbye Girl* (1993).

Joe Layton (1931-1994) was a director-choreographer who had a particular talent for creating magic out of thin material, as he did with *George M!* (1968) and *Barnum* (1980). Layton's other Broadway credits include choreography for *Once Upon a Mattress* (1959), *The Sound of Music* (1959), and *Sail Away* (1962), as well as direction and choreography for *No Strings* (1962), *The Girl Who Came to Supper* (1963), and *DearWorld* (1969).

Albertina Rasch (1896-1967) was known for her ballet sequences in musicals between 1925 and 1941. Among the twenty-six musicals she choreographed were *Rio Rita* (1927), *The Three Musketeers* (1928), *The Band Wagon* (1931), *Jubilee* (1935), and *Lady in the Dark* (1941).

Donald Saddler (1920-) was a dance soloist with some distinguished modern dance companies before he turned to choreographing Broadway musicals with *Wonderful Town* (1953). Saddler's other Broadway shows include *Milk and Honey* (1961), *The Robber Bridegroom* (1976), and the popular revivals of *No, No, Nanette* (1971) and *On Your Toes* (1983).

Susan Stroman first gained attention with her creative choreography for the Off-Broadway revue *And the World Goes Round* (1991), then went on to provide the award-winning choreography for *Crazy For You* (1992), *Show Boat* (1994), *A Christmas Carol* (1994), and *Big* (1996).

Lee Theodore (1933-1987), a dancer-turned-choreographer, created the role of Anybodys in *West Side Story* (1957) and danced in several other Broadway musicals before turning to choreography in the 1960s. In addition to such shows as *Baker Street* (1965), *Flora, the Red Menace* (1965), and *The Apple Tree*

(1966), Theodore founded the American Dance Machine, a company dedicated to preserving the choreography of American musicals.

Onna White created memorable dance sequences for film and theatre starting with the 1956 Broadway revival of *Carmen Jones*. Among her subsequent stage successes were *The Music Man* (1957), *Irma La Douce* (1960), *Mame* (1966), *1776* (1969), and *I Love My Wife* (1977).

BUSY DESIGNERS

Broadway in the past had the reputation for having the finest production values while road companies and regional theatres suffered in comparison. But today the top designers work all over and, while Broadway may have the biggest design budgets, excellent work can be found across the country. Here are some of the most notable twentieth-century scenic, costume, and lighting designers in America.

Ernest Albert (1857-1946) was truly a national scenic designer, with scene shops in St. Louis, Chicago, and Cedar Rapids, from which he designed hundreds of shows for New York and beyond. He was most known for his huge spectacle designs, such as in *Ben Hur* (1899) and *Hip Hip Hooray!* (1915) at the Hippodrome.

Theoni V. Aldredge (1932-) is one of Broadway's most gifted costume designers today with over 200 New York productions since 1957. Aldredge first gained attention for her many designs at the New York Shakespeare Festival and then went on to costume such Broadway shows as *Mary, Mary* (1961), *Much Ado About Nothing* (1972), *A Chorus Line* (1975), *Annie* (1977), *Dreamgirls* (1981), *La Cage Aux Folles* (1983), *The Secret Garden* (1991), and *Taking Sides* (1996).

Ralph Alswang (1916-1979) was a prolific designer who did sets, costumes, lighting, theatre restorations, and was even a theatre architect. From 1942 on he was represented on Broadway by such productions as *Jenny Kissed Me* (1948), *The Rainmaker* (1954), and *A Raisin in the Sun* (1959).

Boris Aronson (1900-1980), one of Broadway's most beloved and honored scenic designers, presented unique designs ranging from stark realism to bright fantasy to European expressionism for over eighty productions between 1927 and 1980. A Russian immigrant who started designing for the Yiddish Art Theatre, Aronson went on to do commercial productions such as *The Rose Tattoo* (1951), *J. B.* (1958), *Fiddler on the Roof* (1964), *Cabaret* (1966), *Company* (1970), *Follies* (1971), *A Little Night Music* (1973), and *Pacific Overtures* (1976).

Martin Aronstein (1936-) designed lights for many notable New York Shakespeare Festival productions, as well as regional, Broadway, and Off-Broadway productions since the 1960s. Aronstein's credits include such diverse

Broadway shows as *Tiny Alice* (1964), *George M!* (1968), *Moonchildren* (1972), *Noises Off* (1983), and *The Twilight of the Golds* (1993).

Lemuel Ayers (1915-1955) had a brief but striking career as a scenic and sometime costume and lighting designer in the 1940s and early 1950s. His spacious sets for *Oklahoma!* (1943) were his most famous but he did similarly excellent work for *Angel Street* (1941), *Bloomer Girl* (1944), *Kiss Me, Kate* (1948), *Out of This World* (1950), and *Camino Real* (1953).

Lucinda Ballard (1908-1993) was the first costume designer to receive a Tony Award for her efforts (she won the award for five plays she designed in the 1946-1947 season) and one of Broadway's most respected designers in the 1940s and 1950s. Among her fifty Broadway shows were *The Three Sisters* (1940), *I Remember Mama* (1944), *Annie Get Your Gun* (1946), *A Streetcar Named Desire* (1947), *Cat on a Hot Tin Roof* (1955), and *The Sound of Music* (1959).

Watson Barratt (1884-1962) was the Shuberts' favorite scenic designer, creating most of their shows in the 1920s, as well as over ninety other productions on Broadway between 1917 and 1955. His designs include *Blossom Time* (1921), *The Student Prince* (1924), *The Time of Your Life* (1940), and several editions of *The Passing Show* and *Artists and Models*.

Howard Bay (1912-1986) designed sets for over ninety Broadway productions between 1912 and 1986, presenting eleven shows in 1944 alone, and many times served as lighting and costume designer as well. Bay gained notoriety for his designs for *One Third of a Nation* (1937) and other Federal Theatre productions and went on to design *The Corn Is Green* (1940), *Come Back, Little Sheba* (1950), *The Music Man* (1957), *Man of La Mancha* (1965) and many others. With no one distinctive style, Bay excelled in a variety of forms and later wrote one of the finest books on stage design.

John Lee Beatty (1948-) is perhaps the finest purveyor of naturalism of the scenic designers working today. Among his memorable designs for Broadway are *The Innocents* (1976), *Talley's Folly* (1980), *Burn This* (1987), *Abe Lincoln in Illinois* (1993), and *A Delicate Balance* (1996).

Norman Bel Geddes (1893-1958) was a bold and adventurous scenic designer who experimented with breaking away from the proscenium and employing arena staging. He worked on Broadway, in regional playhouses, in opera, and was involved in the design of theatres around the world. Bel Geddes' massive cathedral set for Reinhart's *The Miracle* (1924), his distinctive *Hamlet* (1931) for Raymond Massey, and the unforgettable exterior set for *Dead End* (1935) are among his many memorable designs.

Aline Bernstein (1882-1955), Broadway's most prolific woman scenic designer, created the sets and costumes for over eighty productions between 1924 and 1950. Besides designing such shows as *Grand Hotel* (1930), *The Animal Kingdom* (1932), and *The Children's Hour* (1934), she co-founded the Museum of Costume Design, now housed at the Metropolitan Museum of Art.

Ken Billington (1946-) is a much-respected New York lighting designer who has lit many acclaimed Broadway productions since 1969. *On the Twentieth Century* (1978), *Sweeney Todd* (1979), *Meet Me in St. Louis* (1989), and *Sylvia* (1995) are among his representative works.

Stewart Chaney (1910-1969) is not so well known today but he designed over ninety Broadway productions between 1934 and 1964. His credits include *The Old Maid* (1935), *Life With Father* (1939), *Blithe Spirit* (1941), and *The Voice of the Turtle* (1943). Chaney was especially adept at realistic domestic interiors that looked and felt like people actually lived there.

Peggy Clark (Kelley) (1915-1996) started as a costume designer but soon moved into lighting, designing over sixty Broadway shows. Clark was one of the first women in the field and was instrumental in developing theatrical lighting as an independent art form. Her imaginative lighting was seen on Broadway in *Love Life* (1948), *Pal Joey* (1952), *Peter Pan* (1954), *Bye Bye Birdie* (1960), and *Gentlemen Prefer Blondes* (both the 1926 play and the 1949 musical).

Alvin Colt (1915-) has been a costume designer working on Broadway and across the country since 1940. His memorable New York productions include *On the Town* (1944), *Guys and Dolls* (1950), *The Lark* (1955), *Li'l Abner* (1956), *Here's Love!* (1963), *Sugar* (1972), *Accomplice* (1990) and *Forbidden Broadway Strikes Back!* (1996).

John Conklin (1937-) is a busy and inventive scenic and costume designer who has spent most of his time in regional theatre and opera but was represented on Broadway with *Tambourines to Glory* (1963), *Cat on a Hot Tin Roof* (1974), *The Philadelphia Story* (1980), *A Streetcar Named Desire* (1988) and others. He is particularly known for his bold designs for Mark Lamos' productions at the Hartford Stage in Connecticut.

Raoul Péne Du Bois (1914?-1985) was one of Broadway's most flamboyant costume designers, bringing a colorful European flair to his work in theatre, ballet, films, ice shows, and even aquacades. In addition to the costumes for *Jumbo* (1935), *Too Many Girls* (1938), *Gypsy* (1959) and others, Du Bois did both sets and costumes for several shows, including *Wonderful Town* (1953), *No, No, Nanette* (1971), *Irene* (1973), and *Sugar Babies* (1979).

William Eckert (1920-) and **Jean Eckert** (1921-1993), a successful husband and wife team, designed sets and sometimes costumes and lighting for several Broadway shows in the 1950s and 1960s. Their sets for *The Golden Apple* (1954), *She Loves Me* (1963), and *Mame* (1966) were particularly notable, as was their scenic, lighting, and costume designs for *Damn Yankees* (1955) and *Fiorello!* (1959).

Ben Edwards (1916-) was a designer of mostly non-musicals from the 1930s through the 1980s, doing sets and lights for many famous dramas and, in particular, for several O'Neill plays. His scenery had a solid, rustic feel to it and his atmospheric lighting was exemplary. Among his Broadway credits are *Medea* (1947 and 1982), *Anastasia* (1954), *A Touch of the Poet* (1958), *A Moon for the*

Misbegotten (1973), *Anna Christie* (1977), and *A Few Good Men* (1989).

A. H. Feder (1909-) was one of the pioneers who made theatrical lighting a designer's art rather than a technician's job. Abe Feder lit not only Broadway plays and musicals, but also operas, ballets, and interiors for museums, galleries, and art centers. *Macbeth* (1936), *Angel Street* (1941), *My Fair Lady* (1956), *On a Clear Day You Can See Forever* (1965), and *Carmelina* (1979) are among his superior lighting designs for Broadway.

Jules Fisher (1937-) is the most successful and honored lighting designer working in theatre today. In shows such as *Pippin* (1972), *Chicago* (1975), *Dancin'* (1978), *GrandHotel* (1989), *Jelly's Last Jam* (1992), *Angels in America* (1993), *A Christmas Carol* (1994), and *Bring in da Noise, Bring in da Funk* (1996), Fisher has found new and exciting ways to use light on stage.

Frederick Fox (1910-1991) designed scenery for over eighty Broadway shows between 1937 and 1961, including *Johnny Belinda* (1940), *Dear Ruth* (1944), *Light Up the Sky* (1948), and *Darkness at Noon* (1951). Fox also designed for operas and television and occasionally did lighting and costumes as well.

Paul Gallo (1953-) first gained attention with his intriguing lighting designs for Martha Clarke's dance-theatre pieces Off Broadway. He has been just as creative working on Broadway, lighting such shows as *The House of Blue Leaves* (1986), *City of Angels* (1989), *Crazy for You* (1992), and *Big* (1996).

John J. Gleason (1941-) was the lighting designer for many theatre productions at Lincoln Center in the 1960s and 1970s and he has lit some ninety Broadway shows as well. *The Great White Hope* (1968), *The Royal Family* (1975), and *The Mikado* (1993) are among his New York credits.

Mordecai Gorelik (1899-1990), the renowned author of many books and articles on theatre design, was a scenic designer for the Neighborhood Playhouse, the Provincetown Players, and the Group Theatre where his innovative sets were often as controversial as the plays. On Broadway he designed such dramas as *Thunder Rock* (1939), *All My Sons* (1947), and *A Hatful of Rain* (1955).

Jane Greenwood (1934-) is a British-born costume designer who came to Broadway via the Stratford Shakespeare Festival in Canada. She is particularly noted for her contemporary costumes but her period work is also expert. Among her many Broadway credits since her debut in 1963 are *The Prime of Miss Jean Brodie* (1968), *A Texas Trilogy* (1976), *Medea* (1982), *The Circle* (1989), *She Loves Me* (1993), *The Heiress* (1995), and *A Delicate Balance* (1996).

David Hays (1930-) has designed sets and/or lights for over fifty Broadway shows and nearly that many ballets as well. *Long Day's Journey Into Night* (1956), *Gideon* (1961), *No Strings* (1961), and *Platinum* (1978) are among his Broadway designs.

David Hersey (1939-) is an American-born lighting designer who has worked extensively in Europe, but his talented designs have been seen in New York in such imports as *The Life and Adventures of Nicholas Nickleby* (1981),

Cats (1982), *Les Misérables* (1987), and *Miss Saigon* (1991).

David Jenkins (1937-) is a busy scenic designer for television and film but he has done some memorable sets for regional theatre and Broadway, including *The Changing Room* (1973), *The Elephant Man* (1979), *Accomplice* (1990), and *Taking Sides* (1996).

George Clarke Jenkins (1911-) started as an assistant to Jo Mielziner then went on to design sets for many Broadway productions, such as *I Remember Mama* (1945), *The Immoralist* (1954), and *Wait Until Dark* (1966). He is also a much respected art decorator for films.

Robert Edmond Jones (1887-1954) did more than any other American designer to create and define the "New American Stagecraft" in the first half of the twentieth century. Between 1915 and 1951 he designed over 120 New York productions, including *The Man Who Married a Dumb Wife* (1915), *Anna Christie* (1921), *The Hairy Ape* (1922), *Desire Under the Elms* (1924), *Holiday* (1928), *Green Pastures* (1930), *Mourning Becomes Electra* (1931), and *The Enchanted* (1950). Jones' anti-realistic sets and lighting made powerful statements about the new directions American theatre should take, and his poetic writings and years of teaching were very influential around the world.

Marjorie Bradley Kellogg (1946-) has done much of her scenic design in regional theatre across the country but her New York credits have been very impressive. Her Broadway designs include *The Best Little Whorehouse in Texas* (1982), *American Buffalo* (1983), and *The Sea Gull* (1992).

Willa Kim (1930?-) has designed costumes for regional theatre, Off Broadway, film, ballet, and opera but she is most known for her vibrant and colorful designs for Broadway musicals, including *Dancin'* (1978), *Sophisticated Ladies* (1981), *The Will Rogers Follies* (1991), and *Grease* (1994).

Florence Klotz (1920?-) is a much-awarded costume designer whose work has been seen consistently since 1961. She is most remembered for her stunning costumes for several Harold Prince productions: *Follies* (1971), *A Little Night Music* (1973), *Pacific Overtures* (1976), *Grind* (1985), *Kiss of the Spider Woman* (1993), and *Show Boat* (1994).

Heidi Landesman (1951-) has designed scenery for many non-profit theatres Off Broadway and around the country, but she is best known for two designs that dazzled Broadway: *Big River* (1985) and *The Secret Garden* (1991).

Peter Larkin (1926-) designed the scenery for many Broadway shows in the 1950s, such as *The Teahouse of the August Moon* (1953) and *Peter Pan* (1954), and then divided his time designing for film and the occasional Broadway production, such as *Twigs* (1971), *Dancin'* (1979), and *The Rink* (1984).

Eugene Lee (1939-) did the sets and **Franne Lee** (1941-), his wife at the time, did the costumes for two unusual Broadway musicals: the environmental *Candide* revival in 1974 and *Sweeney Todd* (1979). Both have had distinctive careers designing in regional theatre, television, and film as well.

Ming Cho Lee (1930-) is one of America's most respected scenic designers as a result of his work in regional and educational theatre, opera, dance, and professional theatre in New York. In addition to such acclaimed Broadway designs as *Mother Courage and Her Children* (1963), *Much Ado About Nothing* (1972), *The Shadow Box* (1977), and *K2* (1983), Lee is a renowned educator in design and has influenced an entire generation of young designers.

Charles LeMaire (1897-1985) was the designer of lavish costumes for Broadway between 1919 and 1936 before he went to Hollywood. LeMaire designed for such illustrious revues as the *Ziegfeld Follies*, *George White's Scandals*, and *Earl Carroll's Vanities*, as well as such musicals as *Rose-Marie* (1924), *The New Moon* (1928), *Strike Up the Band* (1930), and *Of Thee I Sing* (1931).

William Ivey Long (1947-), a costume designer for theatre and opera, provided the superb costumes for *Nine* (1982), *Lend Me a Tenor* (1989), *Assassins* (1990), *Crazy for You* (1992), *Guys and Dolls* (1992), *Big* (1996) and others.

Santo Loquasto (1944-) designed sets and sometimes costumes for many famous productions at the New York Shakespeare Festival, including such Broadway transfers as *That Championship Season* (1972) and *Sticks and Bones* (1972). His set designs include *Singin' in the Rain* (1985) and *Grand Hotel* (1989). Loquasto is also one of the finest production designers working in films today.

Jo Mielziner (1901-1976) designed over 300 Broadway productions between 1924 and 1974, as well as lighting and costuming over 100 of them. Besides being the most prolific designer on record, Mielziner was also one of the most influential, bringing exciting new ideas to the scenic look of comedies, musicals, classics, and contemporary dramas. Some of his most memorable designs include the original productions of *Strange Interlude* (1928), *Of Thee I Sing* (1931), *Pal Joey* (1940), *The Glass Menagerie* (1945), *Death of a Salesman* (1949), *Cat on a Hot Tin Roof* (1955), *The King and I* (1951), *Look Homeward, Angel* (1957), and *1776* (1969). Mielziner's masterful style was neither realistic nor expressionistic, but a unique and poetic form that ushered in the Suggested Realism movement.

David Mitchell (1932-) is an imaginative scenic designer for ballet and Broadway whose credits include the award-winning designs for *Annie* (1977) and *Barnum* (1980), as well as *Brighton Beach Memoirs* (1983), *La Cage Aux Folles* (1983), *Tru* (1989), *Ain't Broadway Grand* (1993) and others.

Tharon Musser (1925-) has been a lighting designer of distinction on Broadway since 1956 when she lit the original *Long Day's Journey Into Night* (1956). In addition to designing over one hundred shows, including award-wining lighting for *Follies* (1971), *A Chorus Line* (1975), and *Dreamgirls* (1981), Musser was the first lighting designer to use a computer lighting system on Broadway.

Richard Nelson (1939-1996) designed lights for regional theatre, Off

Broadway, and Broadway where, from 1970 through the 1990s, he lit over forty productions. *Mornings at Seven* (1980), *Sunday in the Park With George* (1984), *Into the Woods* (1987), and *No Man's Land* (1994) are among his many notable productions.

Donald Oenslager (1902-1975) was a prolific scenic designer who also influenced generations of other designers as a long-time faculty member at the Yale School of Drama. He designed over 150 Broadway shows between 1925 and 1974, including *Girl Crazy* (1930), *Anything Goes* (1934), *You Can't Take It with You* (1936), *Born Yesterday* (1946), and *A Majority of One* (1959).

Nancy Potts is a costume designer who works in regional theatre, Off Broadway, and on Broadway. She gained attention for her costumes for several productions directed by Ellis Rabb, as well as *Hair* (1968), *Porgy and Bess* (1976), and *You Can't Take It With You* (1983).

William Ritman (1928?-1984) came from television in the 1950s and designed many Broadway non-musicals in the 1960s and 1970s. Ritman was particularly adept at interior box sets, such as seen in *Who's Afraid of Virginia Woolf?* (1962), *A Delicate Balance* (1966), *Play It Again, Sam* (1969), and *Deathtrap* (1978).

Carrie F. Robbins (1943-) was costume designer for Broadway shows such as *Grease* (1972), *Over Here* (1974), *Frankenstein* (1981), and *The Shadow Box* (1994). Her work has also been seen Off Broadway and in many regional theatres.

Jean Rosenthal (1912-1969) is perhaps America's premiere theatrical lighting designer, a pioneer who created a new art form in her over 200 ballets, operas, and Broadway shows. Rosenthal worked with the Neighborhood Playhouse, Martha Graham's dance company, the Federal Theatre Project, and Orson Welles' Mercury Theatre before her first Broadway design in 1938. Among her contributions to theatrical lighting was the use of flood lights to eliminate shadows and her development of the modern light plot. *Caesar and Cleopatra* (1949), *West Side Story* (1957), *Becket* (1960), *Fiddler on the Roof* (1964), *Cabaret* (1966), and *Plaza Suite* (1968) are among her many expert designs.

Ann Roth (1931-) is one of the theatre's busiest costume designers with over 100 Broadway shows to her credit since the early 1960s. Her designs were seen in *The Odd Couple* (1965), *Purlie* (1970), *The Royal Family* (1975), *The Best Little Whorehouse in Texas* (1978), *Biloxi Blues* (1985), and *What's Wrong With This Picture?* (1994).

Douglas Schmidt (1942-) is a much-sought after scenic designer in regional theatre, but Broadway has seen his work in *Veronica's Room* (1973), *Over Here* (1974), *The Threepenny Opera* (1977), *Frankenstein* (1981), *Porgy and Bess* (1983) and others.

Irene Sharaff (1910-1993) was the grande dame of American costume design with five decades of distinguished productions on Broadway, film, and ballet to her credit. Among her sixty-one Broadway productions, most remembered are *Alice in Wonderland* (1932), *On Your Toes* (1936), *The Boys From Syracuse* (1938), *Lady in the Dark* (1941), *The King and I* (1951), *Candide* (1956), *West Side Story* (1957), *Funny Girl* (1965), and *Irene* (1973).

Lee Simonson (1888-1967), the designer of many famous Theatre Guild productions, created scenic and costume designs for over eighty Broadway productions between 1919 and 1946. His memorable designs include *Liliom* (1921), *The Adding Machine* (1923), *Elizabeth the Queen* (1930), and *Idiot's Delight*. (1936). Simonson also authored several books on scenic design.

Thomas R. Skelton (1927-1994) was one of the country's top lighting designers for dance but his work was seen on Broadway in shows such as *Purlie* (1970), *Gigi* (1973), *Shenandoah* (1975), *Peter Pan* (1979), *Show Boat* (1983), and *A Few Good Men* (1989).

Oliver Smith (1918-1994) was Broadway's favorite scenic designer of musicals and the winner of seven Tony Awards with numerous nominations. Among his over 150 shows between 1942 and 1987 were *On the Town* (1944), *My Fair Lady* (1956), *West Side Story* (1957), *The Sound of Music* (1959), *Camelot* (1960), *Night of the Iguana* (1961), *Barefoot in the Park* (1963), and *Hello, Dolly!* (1964).

Raymond Sovey (1897-1966) did the scenic designs, and often the costumes as well, for over 180 shows between 1920 and 1958. Sovey was known for his plush interior sets as well as such Broadway productions as *The Front Page* (1928), *Green Grow the Lilacs* (1931), *Our Town* (1938), *Arsenic and Old Lace* (1941), and *Witness for the Prosecution* (1954).

Cleon Throckmorton (1897-1965) was associated with all the landmark theatre companies, from the Provincetown Players to the Civic Repertory Theatre to the Theatre Guild, and then later designed over 160 Broadway productions between 1921 and 1942. He contributed to the famous set design for *The Emperor Jones* (1920) and went on to design *In Abraham's Bosom* (1926), *Porgy* (1927), *Alien Corn* (1933) and many others.

Jennifer Tipton (1937-) is a respected lighting designer for dance, opera, and regional and international theatre, as well as a noted Broadway designer since 1969. Her designs were seen in *for colored girls who have considered suicide when the rainbow is enuf* (1976), *The Cherry Orchard* (1977), *Sophisticated Ladies* (1981), and *Jerome Robbins' Broadway* (1989).

Joseph Urban (1872-1933), the designer most associated with producer Florenz Ziegfeld, designed over ninety shows between 1910 and 1933. As well as designing several theatres, he created the sets for *Sally* (1920), *Rio Rita* (1926), *Show Boat* (1927), *Whoopee* (1928), and many editions of the *Ziegfeld Follies*.

Robin Wagner (1933-) is among the top scenic designers working today, particularly in the field of Broadway musicals. Wagner had his first design on Broadway in 1967 and has already presented over fifty productions, including

Hair (1968), *A Chorus Line* (1975), *On the Twentieth Century* (1978), *42nd Street* (1980), *Dreamgirls* (1983), *City of Angels* (1989), *Angels in America* (1993), and *Big* (1996).

Tony Walton (1934-), the English-born scenic designer who has become one of Broadway's most sought-after artists, debuted on Broadway in 1961 and has gone on to do over forty productions since then. Walton's credits include *Pippin* (1972), *Chicago* (1975), *The Real Thing* (1984), *Grand Hotel* (1989), *Lend Me a Tenor* (1989), *The Will Rogers Follies* (1991), *She Loves Me* (1993), and *A Christmas Carol* (1994).

Miles White (1914-) designed costumes for over forty Broadway shows since 1938. *Oklahoma!* (1943), *Carousel* (1945), *High Button Shoes* (1947), *Jamaica* (1957), *Bye Bye Birdie* (1960), and *Candida* (1970) are some of his representative credits.

Patricia Zipprodt (1925-) is the prolific and often-honored costume designer of Broadway, Off Broadway, film, ballet, and opera. Since 1957 she has dazzled Broadway with her costumes for such shows as *She Loves Me* (1963), *Fiddler on the Roof* (1964), *Cabaret* (1966), *1776* (1968), *Chicago* (1975), *Brighton Beach Memoirs* (1983), *Shogun* (1991), and *My Fair Lady* (1993).

BROADWAY'S THEATRE ARCHITECTS

The Theatre District in New York has been slowly moving uptown over the past 200 years, leaving behind theatres that were destroyed and architects that were forgotten. But most of our greatest designers of playhouses are still represented by existing theatres. In the present Theatre District, here are its most distinctive architects.

Henry B. Herts (1871-1933) designed over thirty theatres between 1900 and 1915. The New York theatres by Herts or his firm of Herts & Tallant still standing include the Lyceum, Booth, Sam S. Shubert, and Longacre Theatres. Gone are his Gaiety, Liberty, and old Helen Hayes Theatres but his lovely New Amsterdam Theatre is currently being restored. Herts also designed the celebrated Brooklyn Academy of Music and is credited with developing the cantilevered arch construction that allows balconies to be built without extensive use of pillars.

Herbert J. Krapp (1887-1973) was the most prolific theatre architect in America. As principle architect for the Shuberts, he designed twenty theatres in New York and another two dozen across the country. Krapp theatres currently still in use on Broadway include the Biltmore, Plymouth, Royale, Ambassador, Neil Simon, Broadhurst, Ethel Barrymore, Majestic, John Golden, Walter Kerr, Brooks Atkinson, Imperial, Richard Rodgers, Eugene O'Neill, and Ed Sullivan Theatres (though the last is now a television studio). He also designed the departed Morosco, Bijou, 49th Street, and Jolson's 59th Street Theatres.

Ironically, he did not design the Shubert's flagship theatre, the Sam S. Shubert Theatre.

Thomas Lamb (1871-1942) designed many theatres in New York but his only Broadway theatre still standing is the Mark Hellinger, which is currently leased as a church. His departed accomplishments include the Ziegfeld (with Joseph Urban), and the Harris and Eltinge Theatres, both now movie theatres. Lamb is also known for his many elegant movie theatre designs and as architect of the second Madison Square Garden.

John Bailey McElfatrick (1829-1906) and his firm J. B. McElfatrick designed over 100 theatres nationwide and is represented today in New York with the shuttered Republic Theatre on 42nd Street. Some of his long past theatres include the elegant Empire, Lyric, Hudson, Victoria, and Wallack's theatres.

Other notable architects of older or departed Broadway theatres include: William A. Swasey (the Princess, 48th Street, 39th Street, 44th Street, and Winter Garden theatres); George Keister (the Belasco, Earl Carroll, Astor, Selywn and George M. Cohan theatres); Eugene DeRosa (the Broadway, Vanderbilt, Klaw, New Yorker and Times Square theatres); and C. Howard Crane (the Music Box and Virginia theatres).

Architects of the Theatre District's more recent theatres include: Ralph Alswang (Gershwin Theatre), John C. Portland (Marquis Theatre), Allen Sayles (Circle in the Square uptown), and Kahn & Jacobs (Minskoff Theatre).

For further reading: Gerald Bordman's *Oxford Companion to American Theatre*, Ken Bloom's *Broadway: An Encyclopedic Guide to the History, People and Places of Times Square*, Mary Henderson's *Theatre in America*, Bobbi Owens' *Stage/Costume/Lighting Design on Broadway*, Don Wilmeth and Tice Miller's *Cambridge Guide to American Theatre*, *Notable Names in the American Theatre*, Samuel Leiter's *The Great Stage Directors*, and the *Best Plays* series.

6

MUSICALS

THE LONGEST RUNNING MUSICALS

Although its roots go deep into European operetta and ballad opera, the Broadway musical is a uniquely American concoction. The merging of song, dance, story, and spectacle into what we know as the musical is one of the theatre's most recent inventions, going back less than 150 years. But the new genre has come to dominate the American (and often international) theatre scene and most people imagine a musical when they think of a Broadway show.

Musicals are running longer than anyone ever thought a single show could run. Some of these long runs are more than a mere production; they have become an industry unto themselves. Here are the twenty longest-running Broadway musicals on record.

A Chorus Line (1975) by Hamlisch, Kleban, Bennett, Kirkwood, Dante (6,137 performances)
Cats (1982) by Webber, Eliot (5,990+ performances; still running)*
Oh! Calcutta! (1976 revival) by various authors (5,969 performances)
Les Misérables (1987) by Schönberg, Boublil, Kretzmer (4,100+ performances; still running)
Phantom of the Opera (1988) by Webber, Hart, Stilgoe (3,700+ performances; still running)
42nd Street (1980) by Warren, Dubin, Stewart, Bramble (3,486 performances)
Grease (1972) by Jacobs, Casey (3,388 performances)
Fiddler on the Roof (1964) by Bock, Harnick, Stein (3,242 performances)
Hello, Dolly! (1964) by Herman, Stewart (2,844 performances)
My Fair Lady (1956) by Loewe, Lerner (2,717 performances)
Annie (1977) by Strouse, Charnin, Meehan (2,377 performances)
Man of La Mancha (1965) by Leigh, Darion, Wasserman (2,328 performances)

* *Cats* will surpass *A Chorus Line* on June 19, 1997

Miss Saigon (1991) by Schönberg, Boublil, Maltby (2,300+ performances: still
     running)
Oklahoma! (1943) by Rodgers, Hammerstein (2,212 performances)
Pippin (1972) by Schwartz, Hirson (1,944 performances)
South Pacific (1949) by Rodgers, Hammerstein, Logan (1,925 performances)
The Magic Show (1974) by Schwartz, Randall (1,920 performances)
Dancin' (1978)* (1,774 performances)
La Cage aux Folles (1983) by Herman, Fierstein (1,761 performances)
Hair (1967) by MacDermot, Rado, Ragni (1,750 performances)**

Four of the record-holding musicals (*Cats, Les Misérables, Phantom of the
Opera*, and *Miss Saigon*) are imports from London. Only three on the above list
were produced before 1960; the majority of the long runs have been presented on
Broadway since 1970. Except for *Oh! Calcutta!, The Magic Show*, and *Dancin'*,
all continue to be produced regularly across the country or are likely to be once
they are available to regional groups.

Because the playhouses are smaller Off Broadway, it was sometimes possible
to run a musical for years when on Broadway the demand for tickets would be
satisfied in one season. But now it is difficult for a musical in an Off-Broadway
house to earn enough money to allow it to run profitably unless the overhead is
low. *The Fantasticks* is the happy example of a show that can sustain itself in a
small theatre. Listed below are the ten longest-running musicals Off Broadway.

The Fantasticks (1960) by Schmidt, Jones (14,000+ performances; still running)
Nunsense (1985) by Goggin (3,672 performances)
The Threepenny Opera (1955 revival) by Weill, Brecht, Blitzstein (2,611 perform-
     ances)
Forbidden Broadway (1982) by Alessandrini (2,332 performances)***
Little Shop of Horrors (1982) by Menken, Ashman (2,209 performances)
Godspell (1971) by Schwartz, Tebelak (2,124 performances)
Jacques Brel . . . (1968) by Brel, Blau, Shuman (1,847 performances)
Forever Plaid (1990) by Ross (1,811 performances)
You're a Good Man, Charlie Brown (1967) by Gesner (1,597 performances)
One Mo' Time (1980) by Bagneris (1,372 performances)

There are no foreign imports on this list, unless you consider *The Threepenny
Opera* and *Jacques Brel* as foreign plays; but both were conceived as American
productions and had lyric translations by Americans. It is worth pointing out

* no authors; various songs used
**Beauty and the Beast* , with over 1,000 performances and still playing to
     high numbers on Broadway, is likely to run long enough to be included in
     the top twenty someday.
***various editions ran between 1982 and 1987

that four of the ten musicals were revues: *Forbidden Broadway*, *Forever Plaid*, *Jacques Brel*, and *One Mo' Time*. Four of the musicals (*The Fantasticks*, *Godspell*, *Little Shop of Horrors*, and *You're a Good Man, Charlie Brown*) remain on the list of most produced musicals by school and community groups.

POPULAR NINETEENTH-CENTURY MUSICALS

Just as few nineteenth-century plays ran long enough in one location to make the list of long runs, there were several musicals from the 1800s not listed above that chalked up hundreds of performances in New York and on the road. While none of these musicals are revived today, they were sturdy entertainment vehicles in their day and sometimes left us notable songs and legendary performances. Here, in chronological order, is a selective list of some of the most popular American musicals from the last century.

The Black Crook (1866) is generally recognized as the first musical. It was definitely the most successful Broadway show up to that time and it combined plot, songs, dance, and spectacle in a way not previously seen. Charles M. Barras wrote the dark story about the villainous Herzog who tries to sell the soul of the painter Rudolf to the devil. Most of the score consisted of songs drawn from various sources and a French ballet troupe provided the dance and spectacle. Much of the original's success can be attributed to the chorus line of girls who wore "pink tights" and caused cries of outrage from pulpits and long lines at the box office. But the show was more than a curiosity. Audiences immediately accepted the unusual mixture of non-operatic music, balletic dance, and old-fashioned melodrama. *The Black Crook* was copied for decades afterward; a new theatre genre was born. In an era when a play that ran twenty performances was considered a profitable venture, *The Black Crook* ran 475 performances in its initial New York production and then returned to Manhattan no less than fifteen times.

Robin Hood (1891) was the first important American operetta and the most successful operetta of the nineteenth century. The show was based on the adventures of the legendary outlaw but the approach was more comic than swashbuckling. Reginald De Koven composed the bright score and Harry B. Smith provided the lyrics and libretto. Unlike most previous operettas that featured prima donnas in star turns, *Robin Hood* had a cast full of likable characters and memorable songs, including the interpolated "Oh, Promise Me." The operetta originated in Chicago and had a limited run of forty performances in New York. But *Robin Hood* returned to Broadway eight times, was a favorite on the road and, as late as 1944, was still a guaranteed crowd-pleaser.

A Trip to Chinatown (1891) can be considered America's first important musical comedy. A light-hearted frolic about the delightful confusions that occur when some youngsters evade the watch of their guardian and paint the town, *A Trip to Chinatown* allowed for comic turns and show-stopping production numbers. Percy Gaunt composed the sprightly score and Charles H. Hoyt wrote the lyrics and the frolicsome libretto. "Reuben and Cynthia" and "The Bowery" were the hits of the show and later the interpolated "After the Ball" swept the country and helped keep the musical popular for years. (657 performances)

Evangeline (1874) was an "American Opera-Bouffe Extravaganza" marginally based on Longfellow's poem. The heroine's adventures while searching the globe for her beloved Gabriel included a bevy of bare-legged chorus girls and a dancing cow. Audiences loved it. The musical originated in Boston and played for only sixteen performances in its initial New York run. But the show returned often during the next thirty years, most impressively in 1885 for 251 performances.

Adonis (1884) was the most successful Broadway production up to that time: a whopping 603 performances. The "musical burlesque" was a clever twist on the Pygmalion legend with a woman sculptor falling in love with her male creation. Unlike Eliza Doolittle, Adonis despairs of all the female adoration given him and asks to be returned to stone. The musical was a popular staple on the road for twenty years.

Wang (1891) had many successful elements to it: a witty story about a conniving Siamese Regent, a tuneful score with two runaway hits ("Ask the Man in the Moon" and "A Pretty Girl"), and delightful performances by the comic De Wolfe Hopper and the alluring Della Fox. The original Broadway production of *Wang* ran a satisfying 151 performances and was very popular in other cities on the road, becoming one of the biggest hits of its time.

The Passing Show (1894) ran a profitable 110 performances in New York but its importance lies in its descendant: the American musical revue, a genre that would reach its peak during the Depression. Instead of a disjointed vaudeville collection of acts, *The Passing Show* combined music, dance, and sketches in a uniformed production tied together with the thinnest of plots. Audiences approved of the concoction and revues would remain popular on Broadway for the next forty years.

El Capitan (1896) was a stirring operetta with music by John Philip Sousa and a plot filled with intrigue and action set among some rebel bands in South America. Many of the Sousa tunes were already familiar to audiences before the show opened and the musical was a favorite across the country after its 112-performance run on Broadway.

The Fortune Teller (1898) only stayed in New York for forty performances as part of its season-long national tour but the impact it made was great enough to establish Victor Herbert as America's premiere composer. The plot was one of mistaken identity involving a gypsy fortune teller and a wealthy heiress. The score included two hits ("Gypsy Love Song" and "Romany Life") that had all America caught up in the sound of gypsy romance. After its initial hit tour, *The Fortune Teller* was revived successfully for the next thirty years.

THE MOST POPULAR MUSICALS IN SCHOOLS

Musicals from Broadway have been a staple in high schools across the country since the late 1950s. The most produced musicals by high school groups, as reported by the International Thespian Society, are (in order of opening year):

> *Anything Goes* (1934)
> *Oklahoma!* (1943)
> *Brigadoon* (1947)
> *South Pacific* (1949)
> *Guys and Dolls* (1950)
> *Li'l Abner* (1956)
> *My Fair Lady* (1956)
> *The Music Man* (1957)
> *West Side Story* (1957)
> *Once Upon a Mattress* (1959)
> *The Sound of Music* (1959)
> *Bye Bye Birdie* (1960)
> *The Fantasticks* (1960)
> *Oliver!* (1963)
> *Fiddler on the Roof* (1964)
> *Hello, Dolly!* (1964)
> *You're a Good Man, Charlie Brown* (1967)
> *Godspell* (1971)
> *Grease* (1972)
> *Annie* (1977)
> *Little Shop of Horrors* (1982)

One must remember that some of the longest-running Broadway shows (e.g., *Phantom of the Opera* and *Cats*) have not yet been made available to schools and will probably be very popular once they are released.

MEMORABLE MUSICAL REVIVALS
ON AND OFF BROADWAY

While revivals of classic and contemporary plays have always been a mainstay of the Broadway season, revivals of musicals were rare. *The Black Crook* and other early musicals appeared on Broadway, went on a cross-country tour, then returned to New York for further performances. But these were not true revivals in that they were returns not reconceived productions. Some musical favorites toured for years in cut down productions based on the original. But for an older musical to be mounted on Broadway with a new production was not a common practice.

When *Show Boat* came back to Broadway in 1932 it was basically the same as the original 1927 production. But the 1946 Broadway production was a true revival and a sure sign that this musical was a great piece of American theatre and could be appreciated by succeeding generations. Since then we have seen many memorable revivals of classic and not-so-classic musicals. Here, in chronological order, are some of the most notable New York revivals of American musicals over the past forty-five years.

A Connecticut Yankee (1943)   This rewritten revival of Rodgers and Hart's 1927 hit musicalization of the Mark Twain tale was Lorenz Hart's last Broadway show. With Hart's mental and physical health failing, his partner Richard Rodgers was looking for a project that the lyricist could handle. They wrote six new songs for the new version, including the comic classic "To Keep My Love Alive" for Vivienne Segal to sing. Also in the cast were Dick Foran, Julie Warren, and Vera Ellen. The revival was a modest success but Hart died five days after opening night. (135 performances)

The Red Mill (1945)   This sprightly revival of the 1906 Victor Herbert comic operetta revived interest in the old genre and led the way for other operetta revivals in the 1940s. Just as comedians David Montgomery and Fred Stone made the original so popular, comic Eddie Foy, Jr., was the star that made the 1945 revival run. In fact, it ran nearly twice as long as the original. Also in the cast were Michael O'Shea, Odette Myrtil, and Dorothy Stone. (531 performances)

Show Boat (1946)   The 1927 musical theatre classic had returned to Broadway in 1932 but it was basically the same as the original production with some cast changes. It was this 1946 revival that proved that *Show Boat* was timeless and would always be with us. Authors Jerome Kern and Oscar Hammerstein produced the revival which included a new song ("Nobody Else But Me," the last song that Kern ever wrote), and Hammerstein directed with Hassard Short. The cast included Jan Clayton, Ralph Dumke, Carol Bruce, Charles Fredericks, Colette Lyons, and Buddy Ebsen. (418 performances)

Sweethearts (1947)   Because Eddie Foy, Jr., was so successful with a Broadway revival of Victor Herbert's *The Red Mill* two years earlier, it was decided to revive Herbert's *Sweethearts*, this time with comic Bobby Clark as the star. It worked and the revival ran almost twice as long as the 1913 original. (288 performances)

Pal Joey (1952)   While the original 1940 production of this Rodgers and Hart landmark musical ran a successful 374 performances, it took this revival to give the musical the recognition and appreciation it deserved. In fact, some of the same critics who found the show crude in 1940 praised its honesty in 1952. Vivienne Segal recreated the role of the jaded dowager and the heel Joey was played by Harold Lang this time. Also in the cast were Helen Gallagher, Elaine Stritch, and Lionel Stander. (540 performances)

Of Thee I Sing (1952)   Twenty-one years after this Pulitzer Prize winning satire opened, a Broadway revival opened with Jack Carson and Paul Hartman as the comic president and vice president. Co-librettist George S. Kaufman, who had directed the original, staged the revival as well. The cast featured Betty Oakes, J. Pat O'Malley, Lenore Lonergan, and Jack Whiting. Despite fine production values and some enthusiastic reviews, the revival did not seem to appeal to 1950s audiences and the run was disappointing.   (72 performances)

Porgy and Bess (1953)   The original 1935 production of this ambitious folk opera was considered a financial flop at only 124 performances and when it returned in 1942, with much the same cast, it managed to run a successful 286 performances. But the 1953 production that toured the states, as well as twenty-eight foreign countries, firmly established *Porgy and Bess* as an American masterpiece. Under the auspices of the State Department, this revival featured a rotating cast that included LeVern Hutcherson, Leontyne Price, Cab Calloway, John McCurry, and Helen Colbert. (305 performances)

Carousel (1957)   The New York City Center Light Opera Company presented this limited engagement of the Rodgers and Hammerstein classic and filled it with a superb cast: Howard Keel, Barbara Cook, Pat Stanley, Russell Nype, Bambi Linn and, in his final stage performance, Victor Moore as Starkeeper. (24 performances)

The Boy Friend (1958)   This Off-Broadway revival opened only four years after the original British import played Broadway and ran even longer. Ellen McCown, Gerrianne Raphael, and Bill Mullikin led the cast. (763 performances)

Leave It to Jane (1959)   Many were surprised when this Off-Broadway revival of the 1917 Princess Theatre musical ran two years. But they underestimated the timelessness of those early Jerome Kern-P. G. Wodehouse-Guy Bolton shows. Kathleen Murray played the title heroine and Larry Carra directed. (928 performances)

Anything Goes (1962)   Because this Off-Broadway revival of the Cole Porter favorite provided the first American cast recording of the show, for many years it was the most beloved production of *Anything Goes*. The vibrant cast included Hal Linden, Eileen Rodgers, and Mickey Deems. (239 performances)

The Boys From Syracuse (1963)   The cast recording of this Off-Broadway revival of the 1938 Rodgers and Hart musical endeared this production to the hearts of a generation of musical theatre lovers. The sparkling cast included Stuart Damon, Ellen Hanley, Rudy Tronto, Cathryn Damon, Danny Carroll, Karen Morrow, Clifford David, Julienne Marie, and Matthew Tobin. (500 performances)

Show Boat (1966)   This Music Theatre of Lincoln Center revival of the

Kern-Hammerstein classic was particularly noteworthy for its superb cast: Barbara Cook, Stephen Douglass, Constance Towers, David Wayne, and William Warfield. (63 performances)

No, No, Nanette (1971)   Before this revival, *No, No, Nanette* was considered ancient history by most in the business; an outdated show with one hit song, "Tea for Two." But this surprisingly popular revival put the show back in the performing repertoire, spawning road companies and hundreds of stock and school productions in the 1970s. Burt Shevelove rewrote some of the book and directed the lively production that featured vivid choreography by Donald Saddler and a cast including Susan Watson, Bobby Van, Helen Gallagher, Patsy Kelly, Jack Gilford and, in a brilliant nostalgic touch, Ruby Keeler. (861 performances)

A Funny Thing Happened on the Way to the Forum (1972)   This 1962 musical comedy classic was actually written with comic Phil Silvers in mind for the clever slave Pseudolus. Zero Mostel got the role but Silvers finally got to play the Roman con-man in this 1972 revival. Also in the cast were Larry Blyden, Mort Marshall, Carl Ballantine, and Reginald Owen. Co-author Burt Shevelove directed the popular production whose run was cut short by Silvers' illness. (156 performances)

Irene (1973)   There was no question that this revival of an early forgotten musical was an attempt to recreate the success of the *No, No, Nanette* revival in 1971. But the new *Irene* was plagued with problems and went through many staff changes before opening in 1973. Debbie Reynolds, in her Broadway debut, was the star and little of the original 1919 production remained except five songs and some of the plot. Despite weak reviews, *Irene* was able to run thanks to the box office power of Reynolds and, later, Jane Powell who succeeded her. (604 performances)

Candide (1973)   With major changes in the score and a whole new libretto by Hugh Wheeler, this innovative production of the 1956 beloved box office failure was much more than a mere revival. The exuberant Harold Prince directed production originated at the Chelsea Theatre Center of Brooklyn then went on to Broadway to prove that the Leonard Bernstein masterpiece could indeed work on stage. Prince staged the epic tale in an environmental setting and used a youthful cast instead of opera singers. Songs were rearranged, added, dropped, and Stephen Sondheim provided additional lyrics to those already written by Richard Wilbur, John Latouche, Dorothy Parker, and Bernstein himself. (740 performances)

Gypsy (1974)   This revival of the Jule Styne-Stephen Sondheim-Arthur Laurents Broadway favorite featuring Angela Lansbury originated in London, toured across the country and then arrived on Broadway. Librettist Laurents directed the production. (120 performances)

Very Good Eddie (1975)   The Goodspeed Opera House in rural Connecticut mounted this revival of the early Princess Theatre musical classic and brought it to Broadway where it ran nearly as long as the original 1915 production. The cast featured Charles Repole, Virginia Seidel, Cynthia Wells,

Spring Fairbank, Travis Hudson, and Nicholas Wyman. (304 performances)

Guys and Dolls (1976) This revival was memorable for its all-black cast that gave the Frank Loesser classic some vivid new sounds: gospel for "Sit Down, You're Rockin' the Boat," country for "A Bushel and a Peck," a jazzy "I'll Know," and so on. The fun cast included James Randolph, Norma Donaldson, Robert Guillaume, Ernestine Jackson, and Ken Page. (239 performances)

Oh! Calcutta! (1976) While mostly remembered today for its nudity and sexual subject matter, *Oh! Calcutta!* was actually a musical revue and played a successful 1,314-performance run starting in 1969. But more surprising was this 1976 Off-Broadway revival that ran an astounding thirteen years. Granted, the theatre was small and much of the clientele over the years were foreign visitors who responded to the multi-lingual advertising; but it still goes down as one of the most profitable revivals in the American theatre. (5,969 performances)

The Threepenny Opera (1976) Technically, the long-running 1955 Off-Broadway production of this Weill-Brecht master work was a revival because the musical was first produced on Broadway for a short run in 1933. But this 1976 Lincoln Center production was the first successful revival since the 1950s. Ralph Manheim and John Willett wrote a new, deliberately unpoetical translation and the abrasive production was staged by experimental director Richard Foreman. Raul Julia, Ellen Greene, Elizabeth Wilson, C. K. Alexander, Caroline Kava, and Blair Brown led the cast. (307 performances)

Porgy and Bess (1976) With musical sections restored and the recitative in tact, this acclaimed production by the Houston Grand Opera was the *Porgy and Bess* George Gershwin had originally envisioned. The mammoth production, directed by Jack O'Brien, featured Clamma Dale, Donnie Ray Albert and Larry Marshall. (76 performances)

Going Up (1976) The Goodspeed Opera House in Connecticut brought this 1917 Louis Hirsch-Otto Harbach musical about love and aviation back to Broadway. Bill Gile directed a cast that featured Pat Lysinger, Brad Blaisdell, Kimberly Farr, Maureen Brennan, and Walter Bobbie. (76 performances)

The King and I (1977) After becoming a star in the original 1951 production and starring in the 1956 film version, Yul Brynner toured across the country and to London in the Rodgers and Hammerstein musical and returned to Broadway with productions on a couple of occasions. This 1977 revival, with Constance Towers as his Anna, ran the longest. (696 performances)

Peter Pan (1979) If ever a show is destined to be revived regularly, it is this musicalization of the Barrie classic. The original 1954 production with Mary Martin only ran 152 performances on Broadway but seems immortal because of the television broadcast made of it. This 1979 revival, with Sandy Duncan as the high-flying boy-hero, is the longest recorded New York run of any version of *Peter Pan*. (551 performances)

On Your Toes (1983) This revival was one of those happy occasions when a musical, previously thought outdated and unproducable, returned to Broadway as a new success. Although he had unsuccessfully revived it in 1954, co-author George Abbott tried again in 1983 and he had a hit. The 1936 Rodgers and Hart score seemed fresh as ever and Peter Martins and Donald Saddler recreated George Balanchine's dynamic choreography, including the famous "Slaughter on Tenth Avenue" ballet. The cast included Natalia Makarova, Lara Teeter, George S. Irving, Christine Andreas, George de la Plena, and Dina Merrill. (505 performances)

My One and Only (1983)   What started out as a revival of the Gershwins' 1927 *Funny Face* went through so many book and song changes (not to mention several changes in artistic staff) that the show was given a new title. Tommy Tune, as star, director, and choreographer, was pretty much responsible for this lighthearted show but he was ably assisted by co-choreographer Thommie Walsh and cast members Twiggy, Charles "Honi" Coles, Bruce McGill, Denny Dillon, and Roscoe Lee Brown. (767 performances)

Zorbá (1983)   This revival was unusual in that its stars were Anthony Quinn and Lila Kedrova, two non-singers who had appeared in the 1964 film *Zorba the Greek* that inspired the original 1968 musical version. The revival toured before and after its New York engagement, which was longer than the original. (362 performances)

Show Boat (1983)   This fourth Broadway revival of the musical classic was mounted by the Houston Grand Opera and featured Donald O'Connor, Sheryl Woods, Ron Rains, Lonette McKee, and Bruce Hubbard. (73 performances)

Sweet Charity (1986)   The original 1966 production was a delightful vehicle for Gwen Verdon so it seemed unlikely that this show could be successfully revived without her. But this 1986 revival with Debbie Allen as the ever-hopeful Charity Valentine was fairly successful. Also in the cast were Bebe Neuwirth, Michael Rupert, Allison Williams, and Lee Wilkof.   (368 performances)

Anything Goes (1987)   The longest-running production of Cole Porter's nautical musical comedy, this Lincoln Center version featured Patti LuPone as Reno Sweeney. There were some book changes made and some Porter songs from other shows were interpolated (as they usually were with this show) but Jerry Zaks' direction was true to the spirit of the 1934 original. Also in the cast were Howard McGillin, Bill McCutcheon, Linda Hart, and Rex Everhart. Michael Shuin provided the memorable choreography. (804 performances)

Sweeney Todd, the Demon Barber of Fleet Street (1989)   This small-scale revival of the Stephen Sondheim musical thriller was much praised for its intimate production and fine cast. Beth Fowler and Bob Gunton starred and the powerful production was directed by Susan H. Schulman.   (189 performances)

Gypsy (1989)   This revival of the 1959 musical fable classic featured television star Tyne Daly as the indomitable Mama Rose. Both Daly and the production received plaudits from critics and audiences alike. (477 performances)

The Rothschilds (1990)   This Off-Broadway revival of a big Broadway show in a small space was a good example of a musical being reexamined and more fully-appreciated because of a later, more intimate production. The Jerry Bock-Sheldon Harnick 1970 musical was a large-scale work that managed to run 507 performances. This production by the American Jewish Theatre, directed by Lonny Price, featured Mike Burstyn as the family patriarch and many found it more involving than the original. (379 performances)

Crazy for You (1992)   This was another Gershwin revival that strayed so far from its original that a new title was used. Taking the basic plot and songs from the 1930 *Girl Crazy*, this "new Gershwin musical" interpolated Gershwin songs from a half dozen different sources. Ken Ludwig came up with the new libretto which, if no improvement on the original, was at least more palatable to modern audiences. Susan Stroman's choreography was the real star of the show. (1,622 performances)

Guys and Dolls (1992)   This production, the longest-running Broadway revival on record when it closed, did not tamper with the original material but, under Jerry Zaks' direction, seemed to make the Frank Loesser classic new all over again. The popular cast included Peter Gallagher, Josie de Guzman, Nathan Lane, Faith Prince, and Walter Bobbie. (1,144 performances)

She Loves Me (1993)   The original *She Loves Me* managed to run only 301 performances on Broadway in 1963 but it was always a beloved show with what is arguably Jerry Bock and Sheldon Harnick's finest score. Thirty years later the gentle musical romance was a hit on Broadway after originating at the Roundabout Theatre. Boyd Gaines, Judy Kuhn, Sally Mayes, Jonathan Freeman, and Howard McGillin led the delightful cast. (355 performances)

Grease (1994)   Even while the original 1972 production was still running, this musical became a favorite of stock companies and schools. So it did not seem too early for a Broadway revival in 1994, which actually got better reviews than the original. (1,000+ performances; still running)

Damn Yankees (1994)   Director Jack O'Brien rewrote some of the original 1955 libretto for this production that originated at the Old Globe Theatre in San Diego, but it was O'Brien's lively staging, Rob Marshall's exciting choreography, and the personable cast that made the show a hit all over again. Victor Garber, Bebe Neuwirth, and Jarrod Emick led the company; a year later Jerry Lewis joined the cast and made his Broadway debut. (510 performances)

Carousel (1994)   Although generally considered among Rodgers and Hammerstein's finest works, *Carousel* has never been as popular in revival. It took this production from Great Britain's Royal National Theatre to reestablish the 1945 musical's reputation and prove that the old Rodgers and Hammerstein works could be reexamined and reinterpreted without negating the originals. This stunning production, directed by Nicholas Hytner, played on the odd-shaped stage of the Vivian Beaumont Theatre in a way that revitalized the theatre as well. The dynamic American cast included Michael Hayden, Sally Murphy, Audra Ann McDonald, Eddie Korbich and Shirley Verrett. (337 performances)

Show Boat (1994) This most recent revival of the landmark musical classic originated in Toronto then came to New York with the largest cast and production Broadway had seen in many years. Harold Prince staged the mammoth musical, Susan Stroman devised the all-encompassing choreography, and the cast featured Rebecca Luker, John McMartin, Mark Jacoby, Elaine Stritch, Lonette McKee, and Michael Bell. (880+ performances; still running)

How to Succeed in Business Without Really Trying (1995) Film and stage actor Matthew Broderick starred in this lively revival of the Frank Loesser satire. Des McAnuff staged the production which also featured Megan Mullally, Ron Carroll, Jonathan Freeman and Jeff Blumenkrantz. (548 performances)

A Funny Thing Happened on the Way to the Forum (1996) Jerry Zaks, a master of comic direction, guided this Broadway revival with Nathan Lane, the star in Zaks' earlier *Guys and Dolls* revival, heading the bright and raucous production. Also in the cast were Mark Linn-Baker, Lewis J. Stadlen, Ernie Sabella, William Duell, Mary Testa, and Cris Groenendaal. (250+ performances; still running)

The King And I (1996) Although this Rodgers and Hammerstein favorite had returned to Broadway several times since the 1951 original, this production that originated in Australia made critics and audiences sit up and take notice. Director Christopher Renshaw found a sharper edge to the story and Donna Murphy and Lou Diamond Phillips brought out the darker aspects of the two title characters. (260+ performances; still running)

MUSICAL SEQUELS

Musical sequels are not very common and successful musical sequels are even more rare. Hit musicals like *Bye Bye Birdie*, *Annie*, and *The Best Little Whorehouse in Texas* became the flops *Bring Back Birdie*, *Annie II*, and *The Best Little Whorehouse Goes Public*. But here are a few instances of notable musical sequels.

Charles Gayler's play with songs, *Fritz, Our Cousin German* (1870), was a vehicle for J. K. Emmet and his portrayal of the lovable German immigrant Fritz spawned a series of sequels and similar vehicles that kept Emmet employed for the rest of his life. Among the descendants were *Fritz, the Bohemian*, *Fritz in Love*, *Fritz in Ireland*, *Fritz in Ireland and England*, *Fritz in Prosperity*, and *Fritz in Tammany Hall*.

Reginald De Koven's operetta *Robin Hood* (1891) was extremely popular so he returned to the Sherwood Forest characters for his operetta sequel *Maid*

Marian (1902). Despite some good reviews and a noteworthy score, the sequel only managed a modest sixty-four performances.

In the London import *The Girl From Kay's* (1903), Sam Bernard played the hilarious Mr. Hoggenheimer, an immigrant character that the audiences loved. So Americans Harry B. Smith and Ludwig Englander wrote the musical sequel *The Rich Mr. Hoggenheimer* (1906) for Bernard to star in. The result was one of the hits of the season with a superb comic performance by Bernard and some early song efforts by Jerome Kern that were interpolated into the score. Bernard also played Hoggenheimer in the later musicals *The Belle of Bond Street* (1914) and *Piggy* (1927), updated versions of the earlier two vehicles.

George M. Cohan's *Forty-five Minutes From Broadway* (1906) was a big success, due somewhat to Victor Moore's performance as Kid Burns. So Cohan wrote a sequel for Burns (and Moore) called *The Talk of New York* (1907) and it too was a hit.

If a show fails it is unlikely that a sequel will follow. But the unsuccessful musical *Pretty Mrs. Smith* (1914) introduced a character called Letitia Proudfoot and Charlotte Greenwood's hilarious portrayal of her led to five sequels: *Long, Lanky Letty* (1915), *So Long, Letty* (1916), *Linger Longer, Letty* (1919), *Let 'Er Go, Letty* (1921), and *Letty Pepper* (1922).

Of Thee I Sing (1931) was the most honored musical of its time: rave reviews, the first Pulitzer Prize for a musical, the first musical libretto to be published. Yet when the same authors, composer, and stars returned with the sequel *Let 'Em Eat Cake* two years later, the production met with lukewarm reviews and only managed to run ninety performances. Ironically, time has shown that the libretto by George S. Kaufman and Morrie Ryskind, the music by George Gershwin and the lyrics by Ira Gershwin are as potent as the original, but audiences in Depression-laden 1933 were not amused by a political satire showing America turning into a Fascist state and they stayed away.

William Finn wrote the Off-Broadway musical *In Trousers* in 1979 and introduced the character of the confused homosexual Marvin. He then developed the character and plot further and came up with *March of the Falsettos* (1981), which was a hit Off Broadway. A decade later he returned to Marvin and his friends with the sequel *Falsettoland* (1990). The last two shows were combined and produced on Broadway under the title *Falsettos* in 1992.

PROLIFIC COMPOSERS

Today it takes from two to six years to bring a musical from conception to Broadway opening night. So even our busiest contemporary composers have not been able to chalk up as many productions in their careers as the songwriters before the 1950s could. In the 1920s and 1930s, it was not unusual for a composer or lyricist in demand to be involved in three or four different musicals in one season. And many of them were also occupied with writing for Tin Pan Alley and Hollywood at the same time. Here are some of America's most prolific theatre composers of the past.

Irving Berlin (1888-1989) wrote the complete scores for some twenty Broadway musicals and contributed songs to others. But in a career that included hundreds of film and Tin Pan Alley songs, Berlin composed some 3,000 songs (about half of which were published), making him the most prolific and popular composer in American pop culture. His most remembered Broadway successes include *Watch Your Step* (1914), *As Thousands Cheer* (1933), *Louisiana Purchase* (1940), *Annie Get Your Gun* (1946), and *Call Me Madam* (1950).

George M. Cohan (1878-1942) not only wrote the scores for some two dozen musicals, but he usually wrote the librettos, directed, produced, and starred in them as well. Among his Broadway hits were *Little Johnny Jones* (1904), *Forty-Five Minutes From Broadway* (1906), *George Washington, Jr.* (1906), *Little Nellie Kelly* (1922), and *Billie* (1928). More than any other American composer, Cohan helped to define the American sound of popular music: brash, melodic, non-European tunes that were both catchy and contagious.

Reginald De Koven (1859-1920) was one of the most respected and popular American composers of the nineteenth century. Between 1887 and 1913, he composed the scores for twenty-four Broadway operettas, most memorably *Robin Hood* (1891).

Rudolf Friml (1879-1972) composed some twenty American operettas for Broadway, starting with his first effort, the hit *The Firefly* (1912), and continuing until the Depression killed off the genre in the 1930s. His most remembered shows include *Rose-Marie* (1924), *The Vagabond King* (1925), and *The Three Musketeers* (1928).

George Gershwin (1898-1937) managed to compose nearly twenty Broadway scores in his too-short life. More impressive is the all-encompassing range of music he wrote: musical comedy, satiric operetta, folk opera, as well as film scores and acclaimed concert pieces. From his early scores for the *George White's Scandals* in the 1920s to his stage masterpiece *Porgy and Bess* (1935), Gershwin is arguably the finest composer that Broadway has ever seen.

Ray Henderson (1896-1970), the composer of the team of DeSylva, Brown, and Henderson, wrote the scores for editions of *George White's Scandals*, *Good News!* (1927), *Hold Everything* (1928), *Flying High* (1930) and many other Broadway musicals.

Victor Herbert (1859-1924) is America's premiere composer of American operetta. Between 1894 and 1924, he composed forty-three Broadway operettas, most memorably *Babes in Toyland* (1903), *Mlle. Modiste* (1905), *The Red Mill* (1906), *Naughty Marietta* (1910), and *Sweethearts* (1913).

Jerome Kern (1885-1945), America's pioneering composer who brought a new-found sophistication to theatre music, wrote thirty-nine Broadway musicals between 1912 and when he went to Hollywood in 1934. Kern's innovative Princess Musicals in the 1910s opened up new possibilities for the Broadway musical and his *Show Boat* (1927) was the first true musical play. Other important Kern musicals include *The Girl From Utah* (1914), *Sally* (1920), *Sweet Adeline* (1929), and *The Cat and the Fiddle* (1931).

Cole Porter (1891-1964) scored twenty-four Broadway musicals in a career that stretched from 1916 to 1955. This most distinctive of American theatre composers retained an urbane and debonair style in his music and lyrics regardless of which decade he was writing in; yet the songs, if not most of the shows, seem curiously modern. Among the many Porter hits were *Fifty Million Frenchmen* (1929), *Anything Goes* (1934), *Leave It to Me!* (1938), *Panama Hattie* (1940), and *Kiss Me, Kate* (1948).

Richard Rodgers (1902-1979) had two distinctly different careers with two very different lyricists, Lorenz Hart and Oscar Hammerstein. With them, and with others after Hammerstein's death, Rodgers composed some fifty musicals for Broadway and the West End. From *The Garrick Gaieties* in 1925 to his last show *I Remember Mama* (1979) soon before he died, Rodgers was one of the most versatile of all composers with an endless talent for melody and innovative ways to use music on stage.

Sigmund Romberg (1887-1951) composed fifty-seven Broadway musicals between 1914 and 1951, most of them operettas that were considered the finest of the genre. Among his hits were *Maytime* (1917), *Blossom Time* (1921), *The Student Prince* (1924), *The Desert Song* (1926), and *The New Moon* (1928).

Jule Styne (1905-1994) scored some twenty Broadway musicals in a theatre career that lasted from 1947 to 1993. Working with a variety of lyricists, from Comden and Green to Stephen Sondheim, Styne composed such Broadway favorites as *High Button Shoes* (1947), *Gentlemen Prefer Blondes* (1949), *Peter Pan* (1954), *Bells Are Ringing* (1956), *Gypsy* (1959), and *Funny Girl* (1964).

OTHER COMPOSERS

Not wishing to put too much emphasis on the quantity rather than the quality of the work by American songwriters, here is a selective list of other distinguished theatre composers, past and present.

Richard Adler (1921-) scored two hits, *The Pajama Game* (1954) and *Damn Yankees* (1955), with his partner Jerry Ross, then went on to write interesting but unsuccessful shows on his own.

Harold Arlen (1905-1986), the celebrated composer who wrote film scores including *The Wizard of Oz* (1939), provided the music for several Broadway shows, often with lyricist E. Y. Harburg: *Hooray for What!* (1937), *Bloomer*

Girl (1944), *St. Louis Woman* (1946), *House of Flowers* (1954), *Jamaica* (1957) and others.

Leonard Bernstein (1918-1990), the internationally renowned composer and conductor, wrote only five Broadway musicals but each one was a marvel: *On the Town* (1944), *Wonderful Town* (1953), *Candide* (1956), *West Side Story* (1957), and the ill-fated *1600 Pennsylvania Avenue* (1976).

Eubie Blake (1883-1983) was the legendary African-American composer whose long career included pioneering the black musical form in such shows as *Shuffle Along* (1921), *Chocolate Dandies* (1924) and others.

Marc Blitzstein (1905-1964) wrote music and lyrics for such experimental musicals such as *The Cradle Will Rock* (1937), *Regina* (1949), and *Juno* (1959), as well as providing the famous translation/adaptation of Weill and Brecht's *The Threepenny Opera* (1954).

Jerry Bock (1928-) is the composer of such memorable Bock and Harnick musicals as *Fiorello!* (1959), *Tenderloin* (1960), *She Loves Me* (1963), *Fiddler on the Roof* (1964), *The Apple Tree* (1966), and *The Rothschilds* (1970), all written with lyricist Sheldon Harnick.

David Braham (1838-1905) was one of the first composers on Broadway to write in the more popular style rather than for operetta. He scored the famous Harrigan and Hart *Mulligan Guards* musicals in the 1870s and 1880s, as well as other Broadway shows.

Ivan Caryll (1861-1921) was a reliable composer in the 1910s and 1920s who wrote the music for such shows as *The Pink Lady* (1911), *Chin-Chin* (1914), *Jack o' Lantern* (1917), and *Tip Top* (1920).

Cy Coleman (1929-) is the tuneful Broadway composer who has provided the vibrant music for *Little Me* (1962), *Sweet Charity* (1966), *I Love My Wife* (1977), *On the Twentieth Century* (1978), *Barnum* (1980), *City of Angels* (1989), *The Will Rogers Follies* (1991) and others.

Vernon Duke (1903-1969) was the composer of several musicals from the 1930s through the 1950s, experimenting with all kinds of jazz and blues, as in his *Cabin in the Sky* (1940).

William Finn (1952-) is the contemporary composer-lyricist who has written such offbeat musicals as *In Trousers* (1979), *March of the Falsettos* (1981), and *Falsettoland* (1990).

Stephen Flaherty (1960-) is the promising young composer of such accomplished musical scores as *Lucky Stiff* (1988), *Once on This Island* (1990), and *My Favorite Year* (1992).

Nancy Ford (1935-) is the composer of the female songwriting team of Cryer and Ford. She has provided the music for such innovative musicals as *Now Is the Time for All Good Men* (1967), *The Last Sweet Days of Isaac* (1970), and *I'm Getting My Act Together and Taking It on the Road* (1978).

Micki Grant (1941-), the African-American composer-lyricist who wrote a series of musicals about the black experience in the 1970s, contributed music to

Don't Bother Me, I Can't Cope (1971), *Your Arms Too Short to Box With God* (1976), *Working* (1978) and other Broadway musicals.

Marvin Hamlisch (1944-) has had an uneven but interesting career on Broadway, writing the music for *A Chorus Line* (1975), *They're Playing Our Song* (1979), *Smile* (1982), and *The Goodbye Girl* (1993).

Jerry Herman (1932-) is the tremendously successful composer-lyricist of the Broadway megahits *Hello, Dolly!* (1964), *Mame* (1966), and *La Cage aux Folles* (1983). He has also written fine scores for *Milk and Honey* (1961), *Dear World* (1969), *Mack and Mabel* (1974) and other musicals.

Louis Hirsch (1881-1924) was an up-and-coming composer who wrote the scores for several Broadway and London musicals before his untimely death. *Going Up* (1917), *Mary* (1920), and editions of the *Ziegfeld Follies* are among his limited Broadway credits.

Karl Hoschna (1877-1911) was a promising composer who died young but left a handful of accomplished musicals written with lyricist Otto Harbach, such as *Three Twins* (1908) and *Madame Sherry* (1910).

John Kander (1927-) is the composer of the successful team of Kander and Ebb who have provided several memorable musicals, such as *Flora, the Red Menace* (1965), *Cabaret* (1966), *The Happy Time* (1968), *70, Girls, 70* (1971), *Chicago* (1975), *The Act* (1977), *Woman of the Year* (1984), *The Rink* (1984), and *Kiss of the Spider Woman* (1993).

Burton Lane (1912-), the successful film and theatre composer, provided the music for *Finian's Rainbow* (1947), *On a Clear Day You Can See Forever* (1965) and other musicals and revues.

Frank Loesser (1910-1969) only composed five Broadway shows but each one was distinctive and superior: *Where's Charley?* (1948), *Guys and Dolls* (1950), *The Most Happy Fella* (1956), *Greenwillow* (1960), and *How to Succeed in Business Without Really Trying* (1961).

Frederick Loewe (1904-1988) composed some of Broadway's most romantic music as part of the celebrated team of Lerner and Loewe. *Brigadoon* (1947), *Paint Your Wagon* (1951), *My Fair Lady* (1956), and *Camelot* (1960) are his most memorable scores.

Alan Menken (1949-), the hugely successful film composer, started in theatre and often returns to the stage. His theatre scores include *Little Shop of Horrors* (1982), *Weird Romance* (1992), *Beauty and the Beast* (1994), and *A Christmas Carol* (1994).

Bob Merrill (1921-), the composer-lyricist who has had several hits on Broadway, sometimes writes the full score for a show, sometimes just the lyrics. His Broadway credits include *New Girl in Town* (1957), *Take Me Along* (1959), *Carnival* (1961), *Funny Girl* (1964), and *Sugar* (1972).

Harold Rome (1908-1993) wrote both music and lyrics for the famous labor musical revue *Pins and Needles* (1937), then went on to provide the scores for several Broadway shows, including *Call Me Mister* (1946), *Wish You Were*

Here (1952), *Fanny* (1954) and *I Can Get It for You Wholesale* (1962).

Jerry Ross (1926-1955) wrote music and lyrics with collaborator Richard Adler for the Broadway hits *The Pajama Game* (1954) and *Damn Yankees* (1955) before his untimely death.

Harvey Schmidt (1929-) has written music for Tom Jones' lyrics and librettos for *The Fantasticks* (1960), *110 in the Shade* (1963), *I Do! I Do!* (1966), *Celebration* (1969) and other musicals.

Arthur Schwartz (1900-1984) composed music for many revues and musicals with such lyricists as Ira Gershwin, Dorothy Fields, and Howard Dietz. Among his many Broadway credits are *The Little Show* (1929), *The Band Wagon* (1931), *Flying Colors* (1932), *Revenge With Music* (1934), *At Home Abroad* (1935), *A Tree Grows in Brooklyn* (1951), and *The Gay Life* (1961).

Stephen Schwartz (1948-) has written music and lyrics for Broadway, the West End, and film. His early successes *Godspell* (1971), *Pippin* (1972), and *The Magic Show* (1974) were followed by shows less successful but just as accomplished: *The Baker's Wife* (1976), *Working* (1978) and others.

David Shire (1937-), as the composer for the team of Maltby and Shire, has written the music for such revues and musicals as *Starting Here, Starting Now* (1977), *Baby* (1983), *Closer Than Ever* (1989), and *Big* (1996).

Baldwin Sloane (1872-1925) composed over two dozen musicals between 1896 and 1912, including *The Mocking Bird* (1902), *The Wizard of Oz* (1903), and *Tillie's Nightmare* (1910).

Stephen Sondheim (1930-) is the premiere composer-lyricist working in the theatre today and a recognized innovator of the musical theatre form since 1957. He was lyricist for such Broadway shows as *West Side Story* (1957) and *Gypsy* (1959) before writing both music and lyrics for *A Funny Thing Happened on the Way to the Forum* (1962), *Anyone Can Whistle* (1964), *Company* (1970), *Follies* (1971), *A Little Night Music* (1973), *Sweeney Todd* (1979), *Sunday in the Park With George* (1984), *Into the Woods* (1987), *Passion* (1994) and others.

John Philip Sousa (1854-1932), America's celebrated "March King," also composed a handful of Broadway musicals, most memorably *El Capitan* (1896), *The Bride Elect* (1898), and *Chris and the Wonderful Lamp* (1900).

Charles Strouse (1928-) is a respected composer of many Broadway musicals including popular hits and colorful flops. *Bye Bye Birdie* (1960), *All American* (1962), *Golden Boy* (1964), *Applause* (1970), *Annie* (1977), *Rags* (1986), and *Nick and Nora* (1991) are among his Broadway credits.

Elizabeth Swados (1951-) wrote music and lyrics for *Nightclub Cantata* (1977), *Alice in Concert* (1980), *The Haggadah* (1981), *Doonesbury* (1983) and other unconventional musicals Off Broadway and on.

Kurt Weill (1900-1950) had a distinctive career in Germany writing music dramas such as *The Threepenny Opera* (1928) with Bertolt Brecht, and then an equally accomplished career on Broadway where he wrote the music for

Knickerbocker Holiday (1938), *Lady in the Dark* (1941), *One Touch of Venus* (1943), *Street Scene* (1947), *Lost in the Stars* (1949) and others.

Meredith Willson (1902-1984) wrote both music and lyrics for three Broadway musicals in the tuneful Cohan style: *The Music Man* (1957), *The Unsinkable Molly Brown* (1960), and *Here's Love* (1963).

Maury Yeston (1945-) is a composer-lyricist who has written such intriguing musicals as *Nine* (1982), *Grand Hotel* (1989), and his own version of *Phantom of the Opera* called *Phantom*.

Vincent Youmans (1898-1946) was the innovative composer who experimented with jazz and rhythm in his Broadway musicals *Two Little Girls in Blue* (1921), *Wildflower* (1923), *No, No, Nanette* (1925), *Hit the Deck* (1927), *Take a Chance* (1932) and others.

(See Chapter 4 for lyricists and librettists.)

SONGS ALMOST LOST

Many musical hits of the past have fallen into obscurity because their librettos have not aged well. But the individual songs from even the most forgotten musicals sometime have a life of their own and live on in new recordings and performances. How ironic that many of America's favorite songs almost did not see the light of day or were quickly forgotten, only to be rediscovered later. Here are some memorable American theatre songs that were almost lost to us.

"After the Ball" (Charles K. Harris)   One of the most popular songs of the nineteenth century and still a recognized favorite, it was first heard in vaudeville in 1892 but the singer forgot some of the words and the song failed to get any notice. When the composer paid the singing star J. Aldrich Libby to insert the song into the musical *A Trip to Chinatown* in Milwaukee in 1892, the audience sat stunned for a few moments then cheered for five minutes. "After the Ball" was used in all productions of the show after that and it was put into *Show Boat* (1927) years later as an accurate period piece for the story.

"Ah, Sweet Mystery of Life" (Victor Herbert/Rida Johnson Young) This rhapsodic duet that epitomizes operetta cliché was in the score of *Naughty Marietta* (1910) but no one thought it would become popular; it was listed simply as "Finale" in the program. But audiences picked it out immediately and it went on to be one of the most played and recorded of all operetta songs.

"All the Things You Are" (Jerome Kern/Oscar Hammerstein) Kern wrote this lovely song in such an unusual key and used such odd changes in harmony that he was convinced it could never be popular. And the show it was written for, *Very Warm for May* (1939), only ran fifty-nine performances so it seemed the song had little chance for longevity. But "All the Things You Are" was picked up by recording artists and orchestras and has always remained a favorite. In a 1964 poll, American composers chose this song most often as their all-time favorite.

"Always" (Irving Berlin)   This sentimental favorite was written for the Marx Brothers' Broadway musical *The Cocoanuts* (1925) but librettist George S. Kaufman disliked it so much and he had it cut from the score. (He mockingly called it "I'll Be Loving You-- Thursday.") Berlin gave the song to his bride Ellin MacKay as a wedding present and it eventually became a Tin Pan Alley hit.

"As Time Goes By" (Herman Hupfeld)   This standard was written for a Broadway musical called *Everybody's Welcome* (1931), which was a modest success but no one paid any attention to the song, even after crooner Rudy Vallee made a recording of it. Not until a decade later when Dooley Wilson sang "As Time Goes By" in the film *Casablanca* (1942) did the song catch on with the public. It remains one of the most recorded songs in popular American culture.

"Autumn in New York" (Vernon Duke)   Although written as the finale for *Thumbs Up!* (1934), this famous ballad received little attention. It was not until a recording years later by Louella Hogan that the song became popular.

"Bewitched, (Bothered and Bewildered)" (Richard Rodgers/Lorenz Hart)   This hit song from *Pal Joey* (1940) took a long time to become nationally popular. Because of the sordid tone of the lyric, the song was denied radio play. Even with expurgated lyric changes, it was not heard because of a fight being waged at the time between ASCAP and the radio stations. Ironically, the song first caught on in France in the 1940s and not until the early 1950s did it become a hit in America.

"Bill" (Jerome Kern/P. G. Wodehouse)   One of the finest of all torch songs, "Bill" was dropped from a handful of musicals before it was heard on Broadway. Originally written for the Princess musical *Oh, Lady! Lady!!* (1918), the song was cut because it did not fit the dashing and likable character of Bill in the story. Kern and Wodehouse put "Bill" in the musical *Sally* (1920) for star Marilyn Miller to sing but it was not her type of song and was cut. Kern suggested the song as a nightclub number for the dissipated Julie (Helen Morgan) to sing in *Show Boat* (1927) and that was how the standard was introduced to the public.

"Brother, Can You Spare a Dime?" (Jay Gorney/E. Y. Harburg)   Here is a case where a song was deliberately blocked from the public because of political reasons. The biting Depression song was written for the Broadway revue *Americana* (1932) but the producers felt it was too heavy for the light-hearted show and planned to cut it. The songwriters got the song back into the show and audiences, now at the lowest point of the Depression, immediately were caught up in it. Republican officials, facing an election in a few months, got the controversial song barred from radio play. But recordings by Bing

Crosby, Al Jolson and others were bought up by the public and the song became the unofficial theme song of the Depression era.

"Can that Boy Foxtrot" (Stephen Sondheim) Considered one of the slyest of all songs in the Sondheim repertoire, this number was written for *Follies* (1971) but was cut and replaced with "I'm Still Here." The song was later heard in the revue *Side By Side By Sondheim* (1977) and has been a cult favorite ever since.

"Come Down, Ma Evening Star" (John Stromberg/Robert B. Smith) This song, associated with Lillian Russell for many years, is one of the theatre's true swan songs. Stromberg wrote the music for Russell to sing in *Twirly Whirly* (1902) but changed his mind before showing it to anyone. A few weeks later he committed suicide in his apartment and the sheet music was found in his pocket. The song was added to the score with Smith's lyric. Russell broke down on stage when she sang it on opening night and the ballad remained her signature song throughout her career.

"Easy to Love" (Cole Porter) Porter wrote this gentle love song for William Gaxton and Bettina Hall to sing in *Anything Goes* (1934) but Gaxton had trouble hitting the high notes and insisted on a new number. Porter then wrote "All Through the Night" to replace it and "Easy to Love" wasn't heard until the film musical *Born to Dance* (1936) where James Stewart sang it, having trouble with those same high notes but no one minded.

"Fugue for Tinhorns" (Frank Loesser) This delightful opening song for three horseplayers in *Guys and Dolls* (1950) was originally conceived as a trio for Nathan Detroit (Sam Levene), Sky Masterson (Robert Alda), and Sarah Brown (Isabel Bigley). For various reasons (including the fact that Levene could not sing anything that was musically complex) the number was cut and Loesser used the melody for a new lyric about horse racing.

"How Long Has This Been Going On?" (George Gershwin/Ira Gershwin) Originally conceived as a duet for the young lovers Adele Astaire and Stanley Ridges in *Funny Face* (1927), this poignant song about the discovery of love was cut when Ridges was cut from the cast. The Gershwins replaced it with "He Loves and She Loves" but the original song was soon heard on stage in *Rosalie* (1928) where Bobbe Arnst sang it. The number got little notice and just about disappeared until decades later when recordings by Peggy Lee and Lee Wiley made it popular.

"I Guess I'll Have to Change My Plan" (Arthur Schwartz/Howard Dietz) The melody for this song goes back to the early 1920s when Schwartz and Lorenz Hart worked at a summer camp and wrote a number called "I Love to Lie Awake in Bed." Schwartz resurrected the music years later for *The Little Show* (1929) where Dietz wrote the present lyric and Clifton Webb sang it. Surprisingly, the song did not catch on. Not until the number became popular in England as "The Blue Pajama Song" did it gain attention here.

"I'll Be Seeing You" (Sammy Fain/Irving Kahal) This World War Two favorite just escaped being lost forever. It was written for and first heard in *Right This Way* (1938), a fourteen-performance flop. For five years the song sat unpublished and unrecorded. But when it was finally recorded by Hildegarde, Frank Sinatra and others, it stayed on the Hit Parade charts for twenty-four weeks and became the most wistful song of longing during that era.

"I've Confessed to the Breeze" (Vincent Youmans/Otto Harbach) This coy love song was written for *No, No, Nanette* (1925) but dropped before opening. Luckily it was added to the long-running London production and gained popularity in England and, eventually, America. The song was not heard on Broadway until the 1970 revival of *No, No, Nanette*.

"I've Got a Crush on You" (George Gershwin/Ira Gershwin) This romantic standard was conceived as a glib and rapid tempo number for the ensemble in *Treasure Girl* (1928). When that show quickly flopped, the Gershwins put it in their *Strike Up the Band* (1930) where it caught on, still as a sassy and lively number. It was not until years later, when Lee Wiley recorded "I've Got a Crush on You" in a slower, more sincere tempo, did it emerge as the love song we know today.

"Let the Sunshine In" (Galt MacDermot/Gerome Ragni/James Rado) Originally titled "The Flesh Failures," this number from *Hair* (1968) was sung by the ensemble as the show's finale. When the Fifth Dimension recorded it as "Let the Sunshine In," the song became a best-seller and the song we know today.

"Let's Misbehave" (Cole Porter) One of Porter's naughtiest but most delightful songs, it was cut from *Paris* (1928) and replaced by the more ambiguous "Let's Do It (Let's Fall in Love)." But "Let's Misbehave" was published and caught on after it was heard in a Paris nightclub and recorded by Irving Adamson and His Commanders.

"Love for Sale" (Cole Porter) The most censored of all of Porter's songs, "Love for Sale" was the unsentimental cry of a quartet of prostitutes in *The New Yorkers* (1930). Not open to any innocent interpretations, the song was denied radio play for many years. Eventually recordings by Libby Holman, Billie Holiday and others made the song well known.

"The Man I Love" (George Gershwin/Ira Gershwin) This beloved torch song was put in and pulled out of more shows than any other Gershwin number. Adele Astaire was to sing the song at the top of *Lady, Be Good!* (1924) but it was deemed too somber for such a jazz-flavored show and was cut. "The Man I Love" was next put into the 1927 version of *Strike Up the Band*, which closed out of town and the song was missing from the score when the revised version opened on Broadway in 1930. Ira Gershwin rewrote some of the song's lyric so that it could be put into the score for *Rosalie* (1928) but it was cut in rehearsals. The number was published in 1928 as a Tin Pan Alley item and it slowly caught on, especially after Helen Morgan performed it everywhere.

"Meadowlark" (Stephen Schwartz) This lovely ballad, a favorite of female singers, was written for *The Baker's Wife*, which closed in 1976 during its pre-Broadway tour. Producer David Merrick insisted the song was too long and shortened it then cut it completely at one point of the tour but it was replaced and eventually recorded with much of the rest of the score. For a song that never made it to Broadway, "Meadowlark" is sung and recorded often.

"Mr. Monotony" (Irving Berlin)   This odd but fascinating song may hold the record for being cut from more shows than any other. Berlin wrote it for the 1948 film *Easter Parade* and Judy Garland recorded it and filmed it but the sequence was left on the cutting room floor. The song was then added to the Broadway score of *Miss Liberty* (1949) where Jerome Robbins choreographed it but it was soon cut. Ethel Merman sang it in *Call Me Madam* (1950) for awhile but it was cut before opening night. "Mr. Monotony" was finally heard on Broadway in *Jerome Robbins' Broadway* (1989). Ironically, a few weeks after that revue opened, the producers decided to trim the lengthy show and once again "Mr. Monotony" was cut out.

"My Cup Runneth Over" (Harvey Schmidt/Tom Jones)   This hit ballad from *I Do! I Do!* (1966) was giving stars Mary Martin and Robert Preston trouble in rehearsal because of the long sustained high notes at the end of the song. The number was cut but was so sorely missed that Schmidt simplified some of the music and it was reinstated during the Boston tryouts.

"On the Street Where You Live" (Frederick Loewe/Alan Jay Lerner)   Hard to believe, but this wonderful ballad from *My Fair Lady* (1956) did not go over well in previews and the song was almost cut out of the score. But Lerner dearly loved it and set out to find why the audience was so restless and inattentive while Freddy (John Michael King) was singing the song. After asking around, he found that the audience did not recognize the character of Freddy from his two earlier scenes and were confused by the song. Lerner rewrote some of the dialogue leading up to the song and changed the verse slightly and the song immediately became a highlight of the score.

"People" (Jule Styne/Bob Merrill)   One of the biggest hits to come from Broadway in the 1960s, this ballad was nearly cut from *Funny Girl* (1964) because it was felt it slowed down the action and was not necessary to the plot or the character of Fanny Brice. But Barbra Streisand recorded the song before rehearsals began and the record's growing popularity made it impossible to remove from the score.

"A Simple Melody" (Irving Berlin)   This delightful number, often known as "Play a Simple Melody," was one of the first contrapuntal (or double) songs of the American theatre. Berlin wrote it for *Watch Your Step* (1914) and it was a hit with the audience. But it never became popular outside of the theatre and soon seemed to completely disappear. Not until forty years later did it resurface and become a nationwide hit, due mostly to a 1950 recording by Bing and Gary Crosby that was a best-seller.

"Smoke Gets in Your Eyes"   (Jerome Kern/Otto Harbach)   Kern wrote the melody of this song as a lively soft shoe number for *Show Boat* (1927) but it was never used in the show. Six years later Harbach wrote the bewitching lyric and the song became the hit of *Roberta* (1933).

"Sometimes I'm Happy" (Vincent Youmans/Clifford Grey/Irving Caesar) This exciting rhythm ballad was first heard as "Come On and Pet Me" with a lyric by Oscar Hammerstein and William Cary Duncan and written for *Mary Jane McKane* (1923) but it was cut out of town. With a new lyric by Grey and Caesar, and now called "Sometimes I'm Happy," the song was put in *A Night Out* (1925) but that show closed out of town. It was finally heard in *Hit the Deck!* (1927) where it became a hit.

"Supper Time" (Irving Berlin) One of the most penetrating songs ever written about racial prejudice, this song was written for the revue *As Thousands Cheer* (1933). The producers felt such a heavy number would be out of place in the show and considered cutting it. But Ethel Waters' heartbreaking rendition of the song was so potent that they kept it in.

"There Won't Be Trumpets" (Stephen Sondheim) This captivating cult favorite was written for the experimental musical *Anyone Can Whistle* (1964) but was cut before opening. The number was later heard in the Broadway revue *Side By Side By Sondheim* 1977) and in the Off-Broadway musical *Marry Me a Little* (1981).

"There's No Business Like Show Business" (Irving Berlin) Hard to believe that this unofficial anthem for the entertainment business was nearly lost forever. Berlin wrote it for *Annie Get Your Gun* (1946) to cover a scenery change. When he played it for the producers he thought they disliked it, so Berlin discarded the sheet music. When the producers insisted they did like it and that it should be put into the score, Berlin could not find the sheet music in his cluttered office. A secretary finally found it a few days later under a phone book and the rest is history.

"You Say the Nicest Things, Baby" (Jimmy McHugh/Harold Adamson) This ballad and "I Got Lucky in the Rain" both became hits despite heavy odds. Both were written for *As the Girls Go* (1948) but, because of an ASCAP strike at the time, none of the score could be recorded. But both numbers eventually found an audience with later recordings.

BROADWAY DIVAS

In the theatre, the true star is usually a female star. Americans have always been more fascinated by the ability an actress has to hold an audience than they are with most male performers. Opera has its divas but the female star of a musical is no less worshipped, imitated and argued about. Most of the beloved theatre divas have been highly mannered, often less than beautiful, and always bigger than life. Here is a selective list of some renowned American female stars of the Broadway musical, past and present.

Adele Astaire (1898-1981) was the more celebrated member of the brother-sister act in vaudeville and in Broadway musicals in the 1920s. Adele had a pleasant soprano voice but her superior talents were her comic timing and her agile dancing abilities. With her brother Fred she starred in such shows as *Lady, Be Good!*(1924), *Funny Face* (1927), and *The Band Wagon* (1931). She retired in 1931 at the peak of her career to marry Lord Cavendish of England.

Lauren Bacall (1924-) only appeared in two Broadway musicals, *Applause* (1970) and *Woman of the Year*(1981), but was a full-fledged star in both hit shows. The model-turned-movie star had limited singing and dancing abilities but carried her shows with guts and glamour.

Pearl Bailey (1918-1990) was a singing comedienne who always stole the show in the musicals that featured her, such as *St. Louis Woman* (1946), *Arms and the Girl* (1950), and *House of Flowers* (1954). Her greatest triumph was as Dolly Levi in the 1967 all-black revival of *Hello, Dolly!*

Nora Bayes (1880-1928) starred in several forgotten Broadway musicals between 1908 and 1922 but she introduced and was long associated with several songs that are still with us: "Shine On, Harvest Moon," "Has Anybody Here Seen Kelly?," "Take Me Out to the Ball Game," "Japanese Sandman" and others.

Fanny Brice (1891-1951) was one of vaudeville and Broadway's most beloved comediennes but also a singer who could just as easily move an audience to tears with a torch song. She was featured in Broadway revues between 1910 and 1936, most memorably several editions of the *Ziegfeld Follies*. Although she rarely appeared in book musicals, she developed an array of distinct characters that she performed on stage and on the radio. Her life and career was the basis for the bio-musical *Funny Girl* (1964).

Helen Broderick (1891-1959) was a sly comic actress who appeared in Broadway plays and musicals until 1934 when she left for a notable career in Hollywood. Her most remembered performances were in the musicals *Fifty Million Frenchmen* (1929), *The Band Wagon* (1931), and *As Thousands Cheer* (1933).

Betty Buckley (1947-) is an accomplished singer-actress who often replaced the original stars in such musicals as *I'm Getting My Act Together . . .* (1978) and *Sunset Boulevard* (1994). She did get to originate major roles in *1776* (1969), *Cats* (1982), and *The Mystery of Edwin Drood* (1985).

Carol Burnett (1933-), the popular television comedienne, first gained attention in the Broadway musical *Once Upon a Mattress* (1959) and went on to *Fade Out--Fade In* (1964) before concentrating on television and films.

Marie Cahill (1870-1933) was a temperamental but lively singer-comedienne who appeared in several forgotten musicals around the turn of the century. In *Sally in Our Alley* (1902) she got to introduce the hit song "Under the Bamboo Tree."

Irene Castle (1893-1969) and her husband Vernon revolutionized ballroom dancing in Europe and America. Before Vernon's premature death, they appeared in vaudeville and on Broadway, most memorably in Irving Berlin's *Watch My Step* (1914).

Carol Channing (1921-), the distinctive singing comedienne, has been a Broadway musical star for nearly fifty years. Her most beloved roles are the flapper Lorelei Lee in *Gentlemen Prefer Blondes* (1949) and the matchmaking Dolly Levi in *Hello, Dolly!* (1964).

Barbara Cook (1927-), one of the finest voices ever heard on the Broadway stage, originated the role of Marian Paroo in *The Music Man* (1957). Her other Broadway credits are as leading lady in unsuccessful but beloved musicals such as *Flahooley* (1951), *Candide* (1956), *She Loves Me* (1963), and *The Grass Harp* (1971).

Edith Day (1896-1971) captivated audiences in musicals such as *Going Up* (1917) and as the title role in *Irene* (1919) before going to London where she was known as the Queen of Drury Lane for her leading roles in American musicals.

Ruth Etting (1907-1978) was an acclaimed torch singer of nightclubs who appeared in several Broadway musicals. She is most remembered for her performances in *Whoopee* (1928) where she sang "Love Me or Leave Me" and *Simple Simon* (1930) where she introduced "Ten Cents a Dance."

Nanette Fabray (1922-) never achieved the stardom on Broadway that she deserved but was always praised for her warm performances in musicals such as *High Button Shoes* (1947), *Love Life* (1948), and *Arms and the Girl* (1950).

Della Fox (1871-1913) was a very popular musical star on Broadway at the turn of the century though her singing and dancing talents were questionable. She appeared in a number of forgotten musicals and revues riding on her considerable stage presence and rapport with an audience.

Helen Gallagher (1926-) never quite achieved stardom on Broadway but she was the undisputed highlight of many musicals between 1944 and 1971. Her most remembered roles were in *Hazel Flagg* (1953), *Sweet Charity* (1966), and the revivals of *Pal Joey* in 1952 and *No, No, Nanette* in 1971.

Betty Garrett (1919-), a sly comedienne and vivacious singer, was featured in such Broadway musicals as *Something for the Boys* (1943), *Call Me Mister* (1946), and *Meet Me in St. Louis* (1989).

Tamara Geva (1907-) was a Russian-born ballerina who lit up many musical revues and introduced the "Slaughter on Tenth Avenue" ballet in *On Your Toes* (1936).

Lulu Glaser (1874-1958) made a spectacular debut in 1891 when she moved from the chorus of *The Lion Tamer* to play the lead when the star fell ill. Glaser went on to star in several musicals over the next twenty years, most memorably in *Erminie* (1893), *Sweet Ann Page* (1900), and *Dolly Varden* (1902).

Dolores Gray (1924-), a brash singer and comedienne, never made it to super stardom on Broadway but always got enthusiastic reviews. Her musical credits include *Two on the Aisle* (1951), *Destry Rides Again* (1959), and *Sherry!* (1967).

Charlotte Greenwood (1893-1978) was a leggy comedienne who stared in several musicals built around a character she created called "Letty." Her unique dancing style made her a favorite in vaudeville and in musical revues between 1905 and 1950.

Tammy Grimes (1934-) is equally at home in musicals, contemporary plays, and the classics. The uniquely voiced star's musicals include *The Unsinkable Molly Brown* (1960), *High Spirits* (1964), and *42nd Street* (1980).

Louise Groody (1897-1961) was a musical comedy favorite in the 1920s. She originated the title character in *No, No, Nanette* (1925) and introduced "Sometimes I'm Happy" in *Hit the Deck!* (1927).

Juanita Hall (1901-1968) rarely played the leading role but often stole the show playing ethnic types in such musicals as *St. Louis Woman* (1946), *South Pacific* (1949) as Bloody Mary, *The House of Flowers* (1954), and *Flower Drum Song* (1958).

Anna Held (1873-1918) was a coquettish singer from Paris who Florenz Ziegfeld introduced to Broadway with much fanfare in 1896. The great beauty appeared in some forgotten musicals at the turn of the century then starred in vaudeville. Several suggestive songs were long associated with her, including "It's Delightful to Be Married" and "Won't You Come and Play With Me?"

Evelyn Herbert (1898-1975) was an acclaimed star of operettas on Broadway between 1923 and 1934. The gifted singer's shows include *Stepping Stones* (1923), *My Maryland* (1926), and *The New Moon* (1928).

Libby Holman (1906-1971) was a renowned torch singer who provided unforgettable moments in such Broadway musicals as *The Little Show* (1929), *Three's a Crowd* (1930), and *Revenge With Music* (1934).

May Irwin (1862-1938) was a beloved stage singer and comic, once dubbed "the female Falstaff." She appeared in vaudeville and in Broadway musicals between 1883 and 1925. Her rendition of "The Bully Song" in *The Widow Jones* (1895) made her a star and kept her on top for the next decade.

Helen Kane (1904-1966) was known as the "Boop-Boop-a-Doop Girl" with her baby singing voice and her famous rendition of "I Wanna Be Loved By You." She was featured in musicals and vaudeville shows in the 1920s.

Patti LuPone (1949-), the dynamic leading lady of musicals since the 1970s, brings a brash and passionate temperament to all her roles. She is most remembered as the fiery title character in *Evita* (1979) and as Reno Sweeney in the 1987 revival of *Anything Goes*. She is also popular in London where she was in the original productions of *Les Misérables* (1985) and *Sunset Boulevard* (1993).

Mary Martin (1913-1990) was one of the most beloved of Broadway stars and the originator of several of the musical theatre favorite roles, including

Nellie Forbush in *South Pacific* (1949), *Peter Pan* (1954), and Maria Von Trapp in *The Sound of Music* (1959). More versatile than most musical stars, she captivated audiences through her perky characterizations rather than showmanship or glamour.

Ethel Merman (1908-1984) was, with Mary Martin, the reigning queen of Broadway musicals between the 1930s and the 1960s. The very definition of a Broadway belter, Merman usually played brassy and cynical broads as opposed to the usual innocent ingenue of earlier musicals. After a smashing debut in *Girl Crazy* (1930), she starred in many musicals by the Gershwins, Cole Porter, and Irving Berlin, introducing dozens of song standards. Merman's greatest acting achievement was as Mama Rose in the original *Gypsy* (1959).

Marilyn Miller (1898-1936) was Broadway's favorite musical comedy star in the 1920s and she was still at her peak when she died prematurely at thirty-eight. A talented actress, singer, and dancer, the petite star was featured in such Broadway hits as *Sally* (1920), *Sunny* (1925), *Rosalie* (1928), and *As Thousands Cheer* (1933), as well as in revue series such as *The Passing Show* and the *Ziegfeld Follies*.

Liza Minnelli (1946-), the popular film and concert star, has returned to Broadway in a handful of musicals, such as *The Act* (1977) and *The Rink* (1984). Coming from a show business family, she first gained attention Off and on Broadway and is one of the few celebrities with considerable box office draw.

Helen Morgan (1900-1941) was one of America's most heartbreaking torch singers and was featured in such musicals as *Show Boat* (1927), where she originated the role of Julie and sang the torch song classic "Bill," and *Sweet Adeline* (1929), in which she sang her signature song "Why Was I Born?" Unlike traditional torch singers, her voice was a high soprano with a wispy quality.

Ann Pennington (1894?-1971) was a beloved, dimple-kneed dancer who lit up the stage in several editions of the *Ziegfeld Follies* and *George White's Scandals*. In the 1926 edition of the *Scandals* she introduced the "Black Bottom," a dance that swept the country.

Bernadette Peters (1948-) is one of the most versatile of today's musical theatre stars, graduating from bubbly ingenues to mature and complex roles. Her credits include *Dames at Sea* (1968), *George M* (1968), *Mack and Mabel* (1974), *Sunday in the Park With George* (1984), *Song and Dance* (1985), and *Into the Woods* (1987).

Blanche Ring (1876?-1961) was a petite song belter who was featured in dozens of musicals between 1892 and 1938. While the shows she performed in are mostly forgotten, she did introduce several song standards, such as "I've Got Rings on My Fingers," "Waltz Me Around Again, Willie," and "Come, Josephine, in My Flying Machine."

Chita Rivera (1933-) is the enduring musical theatre star who has regularly appeared on Broadway since 1955 in both successful shows and notorious bombs; yet she has always managed to get great reviews. Her credits include *West Side Story* (1957), as the original Anita, *Bye Bye Birdie* (1960), *Chicago* (1975), *The Rink* (1984), and *Kiss of the Spider Woman* (1993).

Lillian Russell (1861-1922) was the American musical theatre's first great musical star. Starting in Gilbert and Sullivan operettas in the 1880s, she reached the peak of her popularity in the 1890s when she appeared in dozens of shows written expressly for her. Russell's singing voice was proficient enough and her renowned hour-glass figure and expert comic timing endeared her to audiences two decades into the next century.

Julia Sanderson (1887-1975) was a leading lady in musicals between 1904 and 1927. Her doll-like features and lyrical singing voice made her popular in such musicals as *The Girl from Utah* (1914), in which she introduced Jerome Kern's "They Didn't Believe Me," and *Tangerine* (1921).

Vivienne Segal (1897-1992) was perhaps the most adaptable of musical theatre stars, succeeding in operetta, Princess musicals, and cynical musical comedy. She gained prominence in *The Blue Paradise* (1915) and remained a star for thirty years. Her other musicals include *Oh, Lady! Lady!* (1918), *The Desert Song* (1926), *I Married an Angel* (1938), and *Pal Joey* (1940 and the 1952 revival). Segal's success lay in her charming voice, comic abilities, and superb acting talent.

Elaine Stritch (1925-), the raspy-voiced singing comedienne, has been stealing the show on Broadway since 1947. Although she was the leading lady in *Goldilocks* (1958) and *Sail Away* (1961), she is equally remembered for her pungent supporting performances in *Angel in the Wings* (1947), *Pal Joey* (1952 revival), *Company* (1970), and *Show Boat* (1994 revival).

Fay Templeton (1865-1939) has one of the longest stage careers on record (over sixty years) and was a favorite in various kinds of musical shows. She is most remembered for her comic performances in the Weber and Fields burlesques, as Mary in George M. Cohan's *Forty-five Minutes From Broadway* (1906) and, near the end of her career, as Aunt Minnie in *Roberta* (1933).

Gwen Verdon (1926-), the singing-dancing star of several Bob Fosse musicals, first gained attention in a supporting role in *Can-Can* (1953), then went on to star in *Damn Yankees* (1955), *New Girl in Town* (1957), *Sweet Charity* (1966), *Chicago* (1975) and others. Verdon is unique in her use of dance to portray sexy, tough characters with a heart of gold.

Nancy Walker (1921-1992) was an accomplished comedienne who rarely found success when she starred in a show but was always the highlight of musicals that she was featured in. Her most remembered performances were in *Best Foot Forward* (1941), *On the Town* (1944), and *Do Re Mi* (1960).

Ethel Waters (1900?-1977) was a versatile black actress singer who exuded warmth and power in her performances. She highlighted Broadway revues, such as *Blackbirds of 1930*, *As Thousands Cheer* (1933), and *At Home Abroad* (1935), and was the leading lady in the book musical *Cabin the the Sky* (1940).

Of course, some of Broadway's favorite musical divas have come from Britain. Here are the four most famous examples.

Julie Andrews (1935-) first caught Broadway's attention when she came to America in the British import *The Boy Friend* (1954). Her impeccable performances as Eliza Doolittle in *My Fair Lady* (1956), as Guenevere in *Camelot* (1960), and the title role(s) in *Victor/Victoria* (1995) made her a Broadwaylegend.

Angela Lansbury (1925-) began her musical theatre career late in life but made up for lost time with a string of unforgettable performances, including *Anyone Can Whistle* (1964), the title role in *Mame* (1966), *DearWorld* (1969), *Gypsy* (1974 revival), and Mrs. Lovett in *Sweeney Todd* (1979).

Gertrude Lawrence (1898-1952) first came to Broadway in *Charlot's Revue* (1924) and immediately became an audience favorite here where she appeared in musicals and plays over the next twenty-eight years. Her most remembered musical appearances were in *Oh, Kay!* (1926), *Lady in the Dark* (1941), and *The King and I* (1951).

Beatrice Lillie (1894-1989) was generally considered the funniest stage comedienne on either side of the Atlantic. Starting with *Andre Charlot's Revue* in 1924, she made many memorable Broadway appearances in revues and book musicals. Her musical credits include *The Third Little Show* (1931), *Walk a Little Faster* (1932), *At Home Abroad* (1935), *Seven Lively Arts* (1944), *Inside U.S.A.* (1948), and *High Spirits* (1964).

(Some Broadway musical leading men are included in the Other Popular Actors of Yesterday in Chapter 3.)

BEST PLAYS MUSICALS

Burns Mantle, the original and long-time editor of the *Best Plays* series, argued often that musicals should not be considered as candidates for the ten best plays each season because the scripts for musicals, separated from their music, were not meant to stand alone. Fourteen volumes of the series went by before a musical was included in the top ten: *Of Thee I Sing*. But even Mantle noticed a trend for more literate musical scripts starting with *Oklahoma!* in 1943 and more musicals started to appear on the list in the 1940s. When John Chapman took over as editor in the late 1940s, he seemed more disposed to musicals (and the librettos were indeed getting better) and by the 1960s, when the golden age for musicals had past, rarely a year's edition went by without one or two musicals on the list.

Looking back as far as 1919, it is interesting to note the classic musicals in the 1920s and 1930s that were not cited simply because they were musicals:

Rose-Marie, The Boys From Syracuse, The Desert Song, Good News!, Anything Goes, and *Show Boat.* But it is surprising to notice later works that somehow did not get chosen: *Carousel, Finian's Rainbow, Kiss Me, Kate, Pal Joey, South Pacific, Annie Get Your Gun, The King and I, The Music Man, West Side Story,* and *Gypsy.* The omission of such shows illustrates how dangerous top ten lists can be. Here, in chronological order, are the *Best Plays* editions that selected musicals that season:

1932-1933	*Of Thee I Sing*
1942-1943	*Oklahoma!*
1945-1946	*Lute Song*
1946-1947	*Brigadoon*
1947-1948	*Allegro*
1949-1950	*Lost in the Stars*
1950-1951	*Guys and Dolls*
1952-1953	*Wonderful Town*
1953-1954	*The Golden Apple*
1954-1955	*The Boy Friend*
1955-1956	*My Fair Lady*
1956-1957	*Candide*
1959-1960	*Fiorello!*
1961-1962	*How to Succeed in Business Without Really Trying*
1962-1963	*Stop the World -- I Want to Get Off*
	She Loves Me
1963-1964	*Hello, Dolly!*
1964-1965	*Fiddler on the Roof*
1965-1966	*Man of La Mancha*
	It's a Bird, It's a Plane, It's Superman
1966-1967	*The Apple Tree*
	Cabaret
	You're a Good Man, Charlie Brown
1967-1968	*Your Own Thing*
1968-1969	*Celebration*
	1776
1969-1970	*Applause*
	Company
1970-1971	*Follies*
1972-1973	*A Little Night Music*
1974-1975	*A Chorus Line*
1975-1976	*Chicago*
	Pacific Overtures
1976-1977	*Annie*
1977-1978	*The Best Little Whorehouse in Texas*
1978-1979	*Sweeney Todd*
1980-1981	*42nd Street*
1981-1982	*Nine*

1982-1983	*Cats*
	My One and Only
1983-1984	*La Cage aux Folles*
	Sunday in the Park With George
1985-1986	*The Mystery of Edwin Drood*
1986-1987	*Les Misérables*
	Three Postcards
1987-1988	*Into the Woods*
1989-1990	*Grand Hotel*
	City of Angels
	Once On This Island
1990-1991	*Falsettoland*
	Miss Saigon
1991-1992	*Crazy for You*
1992-1993	*Wings*
	Kiss of the Spider Woman
1993-1994	*Passion*
1994-1995	*Sunset Boulevard*

THE MOST INFLUENTIAL BROADWAY MUSICALS

Here is a list that cannot help but cause argument: the most influential musicals of the American theatre. These are not necessarily the best or most successful, but the American shows that opened up new possibilities and laid the groundwork for important movements in the genre.

The Black Crook (1866) See Popular Nineteenth Century Musicals earlier in this chapter.

The Brook (1879) is little known today but this musical, subtitled *A Jolly Day at the Picnic*, is the grandfather of farce-comedy in the American musical. The plot was loosely held together by the premise of a troupe of performers on a picnic who pull costumes and props out of their picnic baskets. What resulted was a riotous vaudeville of sorts but both critics and audiences accepted the pretense and demanded more of the farcical approach rather than spectacles like *The Black Crook*. The show ran for an estimated thirty-two performances, returned the next season for three weeks and spawned several imitations.

The Mulligan Guard Ball (1879) was the most popular of the seven *Mulligan Guard* musical farces that Edward Harrigan and Tony Hart presented in their successful series of shows about brawling immigrants in New York. David Braham provided the music for this wild musical farce about the group rivalry between the Irish Mulligan Guard and the Negro Skidmore Guard, all ending in slapstick chaos. The use of all-American ethnic types would lay the groundwork for George M. Cohan and others. (153 performances)

Robin Hood (1891) See Popular Nineteenth Century Musicals earlier in this chapter.

A Trip to Chinatown (1891) See Popular Nineteenth Century Musicals earlier in this chapter.

The Passing Show (1894) See Popular Nineteenth Century Musicals earlier in this chapter.

Little Johnny Jones (1904) was George M. Cohan's first Broadway hit and the first truly American musical comedy. Forsaking European models and operatic pretensions, Cohan introduced the brash and slangy kind of musical that is still with us. Cohan co-produced, directed, wrote, and starred in this musical tale about an American jockey accused of throwing the Derby in England. Critics complained of the unpoetic nature of the songs and the coarse characters but audiences embraced the patriotic show and wanted more; Cohan brought the musical back for a return engagement a few months later. (52 performances)

Very Good Eddie (1915) was the first Princess Theatre musical to become a hit and it launched a new trend for intimate, sophisticated musical comedy. Jerome Kern and a variety of lyricists provided the delightful score and Guy Bolton and Philip Bartholomae wrote the libretto about two honeymooning couples trying to cruise up the Hudson River. The musical eschewed spectacle, chorus lines of showgirls and disjointed comic turns. Instead it provided literate comedy and the songs contributed to the free-and-easy plotting. Although P. G. Wodehouse would later join the team and some of the subsequent Princess shows would boast even finer scores, *Very Good Eddie* is the show that started it all. (341 performances)

Show Boat (1927) is the American theatre's first musical play and perhaps the most enduring of all musical works. Wider in scope, deeper into character, and dealing with more complex issues than ever thought possible in a musical, *Show Boat* revealed the genre as more than mere entertainment; a true art form was born. Jerome Kern's music remains a highpoint in musical theatre history and Oscar Hammerstein's knowing lyrics and perceptive libretto have not dated. In addition to being revived continually over the decades, *Show Boat* made it possible for the musical to mature and grow. (575 performances)

Of Thee I Sing (1931) brought a literary respect to the musical that it had not previously enjoyed. In addition to being the first musical to win the Pulitzer Prize for Drama, the witty Gershwins-Kaufman-Ryskind satire proved that musicals could be as literate and perceptive as the most telling plays. *Of Thee I Sing* utilized comic operetta techniques but was also brash musical comedy, as it commented on American government, lifestyle, attitudes, and illusions. (441 performances)

Porgy and Bess (1935) was America's first and (still possibly finest) world-class opera, a towering work that its authors chose to present on Broadway in a theatre rather than in an opera house. The work, labeled a "folk opera" but always argued about as to its true classification, uses elements of grand opera yet has a musical theatre feel to it, especially in its plotting, subplots, and comic relief. George and Ira Gershwin worked with playwright Dubose Heyward to create a landmark musical that is still very unique. (124 performances)

Pal Joey (1940) taught the American musical to grow up. Unrelentless in its cynicism and totally unsentimental in its approach to love and sex, *Pal Joey* paved the way for musicals that approach life realistically, such as *West Side Story* and *Cabaret*. John O'Hara's libretto and the Rodgers and Hart score were thought too abrasive at first but *Pal Joey* eventually became a model for tougher, more contemporary kinds of musical plays. (374 performances)

Oklahoma! (1943) was the American theatre's first fully integrated musical and it set the format for musicals for the next forty years. For the first time, plot, characters, song and even dance all combined to create a unified whole. The Rodgers and Hammerstein work also eschewed an urban, glitzy setting (the usual milieu for musicals) and emphasized simplicity and sincerity over the jokes and spectacle. (2,212 performances)

West Side Story (1957) may have been traditional in its plotting but was a major innovation in its use of dance to create tension and mood rather than mere entertainment diversion. Leonard Bernstein's music and Jerome Robbins' choreography went beyond theatre dance or even traditional ballet to create a new form of dance theatre. Also important in the show was the way Bernstein and lyricist Stephen Sondheim used opera techniques in a score that was contemporary musical theatre. (734 performances)

Hair (1967) was the first successful use of rock music in a Broadway musical. While the thin plotting by authors Gerome Ragni and James Rado was more celebratory than causal, the show spoke crudely and directly to audiences in a way not previously experienced in a Broadway theatre. Galt MacDermot composed the popular music and the score opened up the way musicals could sound. Another innovation of *Hair*, like it or not, was the use of electronic instrumentation and the necessity for microphones on stage; rock musicals are hardly the norm these days but these two features, alas, are. (1,836 performances)

Company (1970) was not the first concept musical (the idea pops up intermittently in shows since the 1940s) but it was the first to successfully approach its subject matter conceptually rather than through traditional plotting and characterization. George Furth's book was episodic and collage-like and Stephen Sondheim's score was revealing and contemporary. *Company* would make it possible for later concept musicals, such as *A Chorus Line*, to be easily accepted. (706 performances)

For further reading: Gerald Bordman's *The Oxford Companion to American Theatre* and *American Musical Theatre: A Chronicle*, Stanley Green's *Encyclopedia of Musical Theatre*, Thomas Hischak's *Stage It With Music: An*

Encyclopedic Guide to the American Musical Theatre, and *The American Musical Theatre Song Encyclopedia,* *Lissauer's Encyclopedia of Popular Music*, Ken Bloom's *American Song: The Complete Musical Theatre Companion.*

7

AWARDS

THE TONY AWARDS

What started as a chummy in-house awards banquet in 1947 has developed into a big-time commercial circus that sometimes resembles more a beauty pageant than an arts affair. But the Tony Awards, Broadway's version of the Oscars, still mean something special and are still considered an honor. Sponsored by the American Theatre Wing and named after former Wing chairman Antoinette Perry, the Tonys were established to recognize outstanding work on Broadway. Initially the nominees were never announced so there were no "winners" or "losers." But the awards grew in importance, nominations were made public starting in 1956 and what resulted was a contest. When the ceremony itself was televised for the first time in 1967, the show also became a powerful marketing tool for Broadway.

The Tonys have always had their inconsistencies and controversies and it is no different today. How people and plays are nominated, the questionable classifications of Best Actors and Best Featured Actors, and the continued exclusion of Off-Broadway productions are issues that seem to be forever unresolved. But still the award has its status.

Here, by category, are the Tony Award winners to date, with commentary following each section.

Best Plays and Musicals

	Play	Musical
1947	No award	No award
1948	*Mister Roberts*	No award
1949	*Death of a Salesman*	*Kiss Me, Kate*
1950	*The Cocktail Party*	*South Pacific*

1951	The Rose Tattoo	Guys and Dolls
1952	The Fourposter	The King and I
1953	The Crucible	Wonderful Town
1954	The Teahouse of the August Moon	Kismet
1955	The Desperate Hours	The Pajama Game
1956	The Diary of Anne Frank	Damn Yankees
1957	Long Day's Journey Into Night	My Fair Lady
1958	Sunrise at Campobello	The Music Man
1959	J. B.	Redhead
1960	The Miracle Worker	Tie: Fiorello! and The Sound of Music
1961	Becket	Bye Bye Birdie
1962	A Man for All Seasons	How to Succeed in Business Without Really Trying
1963	Who's Afraid of Virginia Woolf?	A Funny Thing Happened On the Way to the Forum
1964	Luther	Hello, Dolly!
1965	The Subject Was Roses	Fiddler on the Roof
1966	Marat/Sade	Man of La Mancha
1967	The Homecoming	Cabaret
1968	Rosencrantz and Guildenstern Are Dead	Hallelujah, Baby!
1969	The Great White Hope	1776
1970	Borstal Boy	Applause
1971	Sleuth	Company
1972	Sticks and Bones	Two Gentlemen of Verona
1973	That Championship Season	A Little Night Music
1974	The River Niger	Raisin
1975	Equus	The Wiz
1976	Travesties	A Chorus Line
1977	The Shadow Box	Annie
1978	Da	Ain't Misbehavin'
1979	The Elephant Man	Sweeney Todd
1980	Children of a Lesser God	Evita
1981	Amadeus	42nd Street
1982	Nicholas Nickleby	Nine
1983	Torch Song Trilogy	Cats
1984	The Real Thing	La Cage Aux Folles
1985	Biloxi Blues	Big River
1986	I'm Not Rappaport	The Mystery of Edwin Drood
1987	Fences	Les Misérables
1988	M. Butterfly	Phantom of the Opera
1989	The Heidi Chronicles	Jerome Robbins' Broadway
1990	The Grapes of Wrath	City of Angels
1991	Lost in Yonkers	The Will Rogers Follies
1992	Dancing at Lughnasa	Crazy for You
1993	Angels in America: Part One	Kiss of the Spider Woman
1994	Angels in America: Part Two	Passion

| 1995 | *Love! Valor! Compassion!* | *Sunset Boulevard* |
| 1996 | *Master Class* | *Rent* |

Of all the Best Play winners, sixteen have been British or Irish productions. Only six winners of the Best Musical award were from abroad, but all six have been from London and all since 1980, capturing a third of all the Best Musical Tonys. This constitutes, in many minds, a British invasion.

The most frequently winning playwright of non-musicals is the British Tom Stoppard who has won the Best Play three times (*Rosencrantz and Guildenstern Are Dead, Travesties* and *The Real Thing*). Fellow Englishman Peter Shaffer has won twice but so have Americans Neil Simon, Arthur Miller, Terrence McNally, and Tony Kushner.

An interesting footnote: while most of the Best Play and Best Musical Tony winners were later made into films, only four went on to win Best Picture Oscars: *My Fair Lady, The Sound of Music, A Man for All Seasons,* and *Amadeus.*

Many notable plays written since 1947 fail to appear on the above list for various reasons. Plays presented Off Broadway or beyond are not eligible for the Tony. With five nominees for Best Play each year, there are bound to be years when too many superior plays opened in one season. Consider the 1956 awards that honored *The Diary of Anne Frank* and had to pass up *Cat on a Hot Tin Roof, The Chalk Garden, Tiger at the Gates,* and *Bus Stop.* Even with five nominees, some fine plays have gone unnoticed. While Neil Simon's *Biloxi Blues* won in 1985, another play in his trilogy, *Brighton Beach Memoirs,* was not even nominated the season it opened. Here are some plays since 1947 that qualified for but were not nominated for a Best Play Tony Award.

After the Fall
American Buffalo
Brighton Beach Memoirs
Burn This
Conversations With My Father
A Few Good Men
Gemini
A Hatful of Rain
The Lion in Winter
Look Homeward, Angel
Loose Ends
Love Letters
Mary, Mary
The Matchmaker
A Moon for the Misbegotten
On Golden Pond
Sweet Bird of Youth

A Texas Trilogy
A View From the Bridge

Because the number of new musicals each season has been declining since the 1940s, most musicals of significance have been acknowledged with at least a Tony nomination. But there have been some curious choices for Best Musical over the years. For example, the Tony voters chose *Two Gentlemen of Verona* over *Follies* or even *Grease* in 1972. Here are some other memorable musicals since 1947 that did not win the Best Musical Tony.

Beauty and the Beast
Bring in da Noise, Bring in da Funk
Carnival
Chicago
Dreamgirls
Falsettos
Grand Hotel
Gypsy
Hair
Jelly's Last Jam
The Most Happy Fella
Peter Pan
The Secret Garden
She Loves Me
Sunday in the Park With George
Sweet Charity
West Side Story
Where's Charley?

Best Revivals

As fewer and fewer new plays and musicals opened on Broadway, it was felt in 1977 that a Tony should be given for "best reproduction of a play or musical." Before that date a special Tony was given if the committee felt an exceptional revival appeared on Broadway. Starting in 1994, separate awards were given for play and for musical revivals. Here are the winners of the Best Revival since the inception of the new category.

1977	*Porgy and Bess*
1978	*Dracula*
1979	No award
1980	*Morning's at Seven*
1981	*The Pirates of Penzance*
1982	*Othello*

1983	*On Your Toes*
1984	*Death of a Salesman*
1985	*Joe Egg*
1986	*Sweet Charity*
1987	*All My Sons*
1988	*Anything Goes*
1989	*Our Town*
1990	*Gypsy*
1991	*Fiddler on the Roof*
1992	*Guys and Dolls*
1993	*Anna Christie*
1994	*An Inspector Calls, Carousel*
1995	*The Heiress, Show Boat*
1996	*A Delicate Balance, The King and I*

Best Actresses: Plays

It is the personalities, more than the plays, that have always made the Tony Awards so interesting. Best Actor and Actress competition is usually a more interesting race than titles or authors. The American Theatre has always shone a preference for actresses over actors and the quintessential Broadway star is a female star. Here are the winning ladies for plays.

	Best Actress	Best Featured Actress
1947	Tie: Ingrid Bergman, *Joan of Lorraine;* Helen Hayes, *Happy Birthday*	No award
1948	Tie: Judith Anderson, *Medea;* Katharine Cornell, *Antony and Cleopatra;* Jessica Tandy, *A Streetcar Named Desire*	No award
1949	Martita Hunt, *The Madwoman of Chaillot*	Shirley Booth, *Goodbye, My Fancy*
1950	Shirley Booth, *Come Back, Little Sheba*	No award
1951	Uta Hagen, *The Country Girl*	Maureen Stapleton, *The Rose Tattoo*
1952	Julie Harris, *I Am a Camera*	Marian Winters, *I Am a Camera*
1953	Shirley Booth, *Time of the Cuckoo*	Beatrice Straight, *The Crucible*
1954	Audrey Hepburn, *Ondine*	Jo Van Fleet, *The Trip to Bountiful*
1955	Nancy Kelly, *The Bad Seed*	Patricia Jessell, *Witness for the Prosecution*
1956	Julie Harris, *The Lark*	Una Merkel, *The Ponder Heart*
1957	Margaret Leighton, *Separate Tables*	Peggy Cass, *Auntie Mame*
1958	Helen Hayes, *Time Remembered*	Anne Bancroft, *Two for the Seesaw*

1959	Gertrude Berg, *A Majority of One*	Julie Newmar, *The Marriage-Go-Round*
1960	Anne Bancroft, *The Miracle Worker*	Anne Revere, *Toys in the Attic*
1961	Joan Plowright, *A Taste of Honey*	Colleen Dewhurst, *All the Way Home*
1962	Margaret Leighton, *The Night of the Iguana*	Elizabeth Ashley, *Take Her, She's Mine*
1963	Uta Hagen, *Who's Afraid of Virginia Woolf?*	Sandy Dennis, *A Thousand Clowns*
1964	Sandy Dennis, *Any Wednesday*	Barbara Loden, *After the Fall*
1965	Irene Worth, *Tiny Alice*	Alice Ghostley, *The Sign in Sidney Brustein's Window*
1966	Rosemary Harris, *The Lion in Winter*	Zoe Caldwell, *Slapstick Tragedy*
1967	Beryl Reid, *The Killing of Sister George*	Marian Seldes, *A Delicate Balance*
1968	Zoe Caldwell, *The Prime of Miss Jean Brodie*	Zena Walker, *Joe Egg*
1969	Julie Harris, *Forty Carats*	Jane Alexander,*The Great White Hope*
1970	Tammy Grimes, *Private Lives*	Blythe Danner, *Butterflies Are Free*
1971	Maureen Stapleton, *The Gingerbread Lady*	Rae Allen, *And Miss Reardon Drinks a Little*
1972	Sada Thompson, *Twigs*	Elizabeth Wilson, *Sticks and Bones*
1973	Julie Harris, *The Last of Mrs. Lincoln*	Leora Dana, *The Last of Mrs. Lincoln*
1974	Colleen Dewhurst, *A Moon for the Misbegotten*	Frances Sternhagen, *The Good Doctor*
1975	Ellen Burstyn, *Same Time, Next Year*	Rita Moreno, *The Ritz*
1976	Irene Worth, *Sweet Bird of Youth*	Shirley Knight, *Kennedy's Children*
1977	Julie Harris, *The Belle of Amherst*	Tarzana Beverly, *for colored girls who have considered suicide when the rainbow is enuf*
1978	Jessica Tandy, *The Gin Game*	Ann Wedgeworth, *Chapter Two*
1979	Tie: Constance Cummings, *Wings* Carole Shelley, *The Elephant Man*	Joan Hickson, *Bedroom Farce*
1980	Phyllis Frehlich, *Children of a Lesser God*	Dinah Manoff, *I Ought to Be in Pictures*
1981	Jane Lapotaire, *Piaf*	Swoosie Kurtz, *Fifth of July*
1982	Zoe Caldwell, *Medea*	Amanda Plummer, *Agnes of God*
1983	Jessica Tandy, *Foxfire*	Judith Ivey, *Steaming*
1984	Glenn Close, *The Real Thing*	Christine Baranski, *The Real Thing*
1985	Stockard Channing, *Joe Egg*	Judith Ivey, *Hurlyburly*
1986	Lily Tomlin, *The Search for Signs of Intelligent Life in the Universe*	Swoosie Kurtz, *The House of Blue Leaves*
1987	Linda Lavin, *Broadway Bound*	Mary Alice, *Fences*

1988	Joan Allen, *Burn This*	L. Scott Caldwell, *Joe Turner's Come and Gone*
1989	Pauline Collins, *Shirley Valentine*	Christine Baranski, *Rumors*
1990	Maggie Smith, *Lettice & Lovage*	Margaret Tyzack, *Lettice & Lovage*
1991	Mercedes Ruehl, *Lost in Yonkers*	Irene Worth, *Lost in Yonkers*
1992	Glenn Close, *Death and the Maiden*	Brid Brennan, *Dancing at Lughnasa*
1993	Madeline Kahn, *The Sisters Rosensweig*	Debra Monk, *Redwood Curtain*
1994	Diana Rigg, *Medea*	Jane Adams, *An Inspector Calls*
1995	Cherry Jones, *The Heiress*	Frances Sternhagen, *The Heiress*
1996	Zoe Caldwell, *Master Class*	Audra McDonald, *Master Class*

Julie Harris is the most honored actress with five Tony Awards. She is followed in the non-musical category by Zoe Caldwell with four awards and Jessica Tandy, Irene Worth, and Shirley Booth, each with three awards (although Booth appeared in musicals as well). The great actresses from the 1930s and 1940s (Ina Claire, Lynn Fontanne, Laurette Taylor, etc.) missed out on winning Tonys because their careers concluded about the time the award was established; but the durable Helen Hayes did manage to win two Tonys before she retired from the stage.

Best Actors: Plays

	Best Actor	Best Featured Actor
1947	Tie: José Ferrer, *Cyrano de Bergerac* Fredric March, *Years Ago*	No award
1948	Tie: Henry Fonda, *Mister Roberts* Paul Kelly, *Command Decision* Basil Rathbone, *The Heiress*	No award
1949	Rex Harrison, *Anne of the Thousand Days*	Arthur Kennedy, *Death of a Salesman*
1950	Sidney Blackmer, *Come Back, Little Sheba*	No award
1951	Claude Rains, *Darkness at Noon*	Eli Wallach, *The Rose Tattoo*
1952	José Ferrer, *The Shrike*	John Cromwell, *Point of No Return*
1953	Tom Ewell, *The Seven Year Itch*	John Williams, *Dial M for Murder*
1954	David Wayne, *The Teahouse of the August Moon*	John Kerr, *Tea and Sympathy*
1955	Alfred Lunt, *Quadrille*	Francis L. Sullivan, *Witness for the Prosecution*
1956	Paul Muni, *Inherit the Wind*	Ed Begley, *Inherit the Wind*
1957	Fredric March, *Long Day's Journey Into Night*	Frank Conroy, *The Potting Shed*

1958	Ralph Bellamy, *Sunrise at Campobello*	Henry Jones, *Sunrise at Campobello*
1959	Jason Robards, Jr., *The Disenchanted*	Charlie Ruggles, *The Pleasure of His Company*
1960	Melvyn Douglas, *The Best Man*	Roddy McDowall, *The Fighting Cock*
1961	Zero Mostel, *Rhinoceros*	Martin Gabel, *Big Fish, Little Fish*
1962	Paul Scofield, *A Man for All Seasons*	Walter Matthau, *A Shot in the Dark*
1963	Arthur Hill, *Who's Afraid of Virginia Woolf?*	Alan Arkin, *Enter Laughing*
1964	Alec Guinness, *Dylan*	Hume Cronyn, *Hamlet*
1965	Walter Matthau, *The Odd Couple*	Jack Albertson, *The Subject Was Roses*
1966	Hal Holbrook, *Mark Twain Tonight!*	Patrick Magee, *Marat/Sade*
1967	Paul Rogers, *The Homecoming*	Ian Holm, *The Homecoming*
1968	Martin Balsam, *You Know I Can't Hear You When the Water's Running*	James Patterson, *The Birthday Party*
1969	James Earl Jones, *The Great White Hope*	Al Pacino, *Does a Tiger Wear a Necktie?*
1970	Fritz Weaver, *Child's Play*	Ken Howard, *Child's Play*
1971	Brian Bedford, *The School for Wives*	Paul Sand, *Story Theatre*
1972	Cliff Gorman, *Lenny*	Vincent Gardenia, *The Prisoner of Second Avenue*
1973	Alan Bates, *Butley*	John Lithgow, *The Changing Room*
1974	Michael Moriarty, *Find Your Way Home*	Ed Flanders, *A Moon for the Misbegotten*
1975	John Kani and Winston Ntshona, *Sizwe Banzi Is Dead* and *The Island*	Frank Langella, *Seascape*
1976	John Wood, *Travesties*	Edward Herrman, *Mrs. Warren's Profession*
1977	Al Pacino, *The Basic Training of Pavlo Hummel*	Jonathan Pryce, *Comedians*
1978	Bernard Hughes, *Da*	Lester Rawlins, *Da*
1979	Tom Conti, *Whose Life Is It Anyway?*	Michael Gough, *Bedroom Farce*
1980	John Rubenstein, *Children of a Lesser God*	David Rounds, *Morning's at Seven*
1981	Ian McKellen, *Amadeus*	Brian Backer, *The Floating Light Bulb*
1982	Roger Rees, *Nicholas Nickleby*	Zakes Mokae, *Master Harold . . . and the Boys*
1983	Harvey Fierstein, *Torch Song Trilogy*	Matthew Broderick, *Brighton Beach Memoirs*
1984	Jeremy Irons, *The Real Thing*	Joe Mantegna, *Glengarry Glen Ross*
1985	Derek Jacobi, *Much Ado About Nothing*	Barry Miller, *Biloxi Blues*

1986	Judd Hirsch, *I'm Not Rappaport*	John Mahoney, *The House of Blue Leaves*
1987	James Earl Jones, *Fences*	John Randolph, *Broadway Bound*
1988	Ron Silver, *Speed-the-Plow*	B. D. Wong, *M. Butterfly*
1989	Philip Bosco, *Lend Me a Tenor*	Boyd Gaines, *The Heidi Chronicles*
1990	Robert Morse, *Tru*	Charles Durning, *Cat on a Hot Tin Roof*
1991	Nigel Hawthorne, *Shadowlands*	Kevin Spacey, *Lost in Yonkers*
1992	Judd Hirsch, *Conversations With My Father*	Larry Fishburne, *Two Trains Running*
1993	Ron Leibman, *Angels in America, I*	Stephen Spinella, *Angels in America, I*
1994	Stephen Spinella, *Angels in America, II*	Jeffrey Wright, *Angels in America, II*
1995	Ralph Fiennes, *Hamlet*	John Glover, *Love! Valor! Compassion!*
1996	George Gizzard, *A Delicate Balance*	Ruben Santiago-Hudson, *Seven Guitars*

These awards have been spread out so broadly over the years that no one actor has ever won more than two Best Actor awards in a non-musical. No wonder the female race is always more exciting. It is worth pointing out that Ralph Fiennes is the only actor to win a Tony Award for playing that most demanding role of Hamlet, though many have been nominated for their efforts.

Best Actress: Musicals

	Best Actress	Best Featured Actress
1947	No award	No award
1948	Grace Hartman, *Angel in the Wings*	No award
1949	Nanette Fabray, *Love Life*	No award
1950	Mary Martin, *South Pacific*	Juanita Hall, *South Pacific*
1951	Ethel Merman, *Call Me Madam*	Isabel Bigley, *Guys and Dolls*
1952	Gertrude Lawrence, *The King and I*	Helen Gallagher, *Pal Joey*
1953	Rosalind Russell, *Wonderful Town*	Sheila Bond, *Wish You Were Here*
1954	Dolores Gray, *Carnival in Flanders*	Gwen Verdon, *Can-Can*
1955	Mary Martin, *Peter Pan*	Carol Haney, *The Pajama Game*
1956	Gwen Verdon, *Damn Yankees*	Lotte Lenya, *The Threepenny Opera*
1957	Judy Holliday, *Bells Are Ringing*	Edith Adams, *Li'l Abner*
1958	Tie: Thelma Ritter, Gwen Verdon, *New Girl in Town*	Barbara Cook, *The Music Man*
1959	Gwen Verdon, *Redhead*	Tie: Pat Stanley, *Goldilocks,* and the cast of *La Plume de Ma Tante*
1960	Mary Martin, *The Sound of Music*	Patricia Neway, *The Sound of Music*

1961	Elizabeth Seal, *Irma La Douce*	Tammy Grimes, *The Unsinkable Molly Brown*
1962	Tie: Anna Maria Alberghetti, *Carnival;* Diahann Carroll, *No Strings*	Phyllis Newman, *Subways Are for Sleeping*
1963	Vivien Leigh, *Tovarich*	Anna Quayle, *Stop the World, I Want to Get Off*
1964	Carol Channing, *Hello, Dolly!*	Tessie O'Shea, *The Girl Who Came to Supper*
1965	Liza Minnelli, *Flora, the Red Menace*	Maria Karnilova, *Fiddler on the Roof*
1966	Angela Lansbury, *Mame*	Beatrice Arthur, *Mame*
1967	Barbara Harris, *The Apple Tree*	Peg Murray, *Cabaret*
1968	Tie: Patricia Routledge, *Darling of the Day;* Leslie Uggams, *Hallelujah, Baby!*	Lillian Hayman, *Hallelujah, Baby!*
1969	Angela Lansbury, *Dear World*	Marian Mercer, *Promises, Promises*
1970	Lauren Bacall, *Applause*	Melba Moore, *Purlie*
1971	Helen Gallagher, *No, No, Nanette*	Patsy Kelly, *No, No, Nanette*
1972	Alexis Smith, *Follies*	Linda Hopkins, *Inner City*
1973	Glynis Johns, *A Little Night Music*	Patricia Elliott, *A Little Night Music*
1974	Virginia Capers, *Raisin*	Janie Sell, *Over Here!*
1975	Angela Lansbury, *Gypsy*	Dee Dee Bridgewater, *The Wiz*
1976	Donna McKechnie, *A Chorus Line*	Kelly Bishop, *A Chorus Line*
1977	Dorothy Loudon, *Annie*	Dolores Hall, *Your Arms Too Short to Box With God*
1978	Liza Minnelli, *The Act*	Nell Carter, *Ain't Misbehavin'*
1979	Angela Lansbury, *Sweeney Todd, the Demon Barber of Fleet Street*	Carlin Glynn, *The Best Little Whorehouse in Texas*
1980	Patti LuPone, *Evita*	Priscilla Lopez, *A Day in Hollywood*
1981	Lauren Bacall, *Woman of the Year*	Marilyn Cooper, *Woman of the Year*
1982	Jennifer Holliday, *Dreamgirls*	Liliane Montevecchi, *Nine*
1983	Natalia Makarova, *On Your Toes*	Betty Buckley, *Cats*
1984	Chita Rivera, *The Rink*	Lila Kedrova, *Zorbá*
1985	No award	Leilani Jones, *Grind*
1986	Bernadette Peters, *Song and Dance*	Bebe Neuwirth, *Sweet Charity*
1987	Maryann Plunkett, *Me and My Girl*	Frances Ruffelle, *Les Misérables*
1988	Joanna Gleason, *Into the Woods*	Judy Kaye, *Phantom of the Opera*
1989	Ruth Brown, *Black and Blue*	Debbie Shapiro, *Jerome Robbins' Broadway*
1990	Tyne Daly, *Gypsy*	Randy Graff, *City of Angels*
1991	Lea Salonga, *Miss Saigon*	Daisy Eagan, *The Secret Garden*
1992	Faith Prince, *Guys and Dolls*	Tonya Pinkins, *Jelly's Last Jam*
1993	Chita Rivera, *Kiss of the Spider Woman*	Andrea Martin, *My Favorite Year*
1994	Donna Murphy, *Passion*	Audra Ann McDonald, *Carousel*
1995	Glenn Close, *Sunset Boulevard*	Gretha Boston, *Show Boat*

| 1996 | Donna Murphy, *The King and I* | Ann Duquesnay, *Bring in da Noise, Bring in da Funk* |

Angela Lansbury and Gwen Verdon are the record holders in this category with four Tonys each. This is quite a remarkable feat for Lansbury when you consider she has only appeared in five musicals. Verdon has been nominated six times and managed to win four times, another impressive record. Perennial favorite Mary Martin comes in third with three awards, the same number Glenn Close has won although only one of those Tonys was for a musical.

Best Actor: Musicals

	Best Actor	Best Featured Actor
1947	No award	No award
1948	Paul Hartman, *Angel in the Wings*	No award
1949	Ray Bolger, *Where's Charley?*	No award
1950	Ezio Pinza, *South Pacific*	Myron McCormick, *South Pacific*
1951	Robert Alda, *Guys and Dolls*	Russell Nype, *Call Me Madam*
1952	Phil Silvers, *Top Banana*	Yul Brynner, *The King and I*
1953	Thomas Mitchell, *Hazel Flagg*	Hiram Sherman, *Two's Company*
1954	Alfred Drake, *Kismet*	Harry Belafonte, *John Murray Anderson's Almanac*
1955	Walter Slezak, *Fanny*	Cyril Ritchard, *Peter Pan*
1956	Ray Walston, *Damn Yankees*	Russ Brown, *Damn Yankees*
1957	Rex Harrison, *My Fair Lady*	Sydney Chaplin, *Bells Are Ringing*
1958	Robert Preston, *The Music Man*	David Burns, *The Music Man*
1959	Richard Kiley, *Redhead*	Tie: Russell Nype, *Goldilocks*, and the cast of *La Plume de Ma Tante*
1960	Jackie Gleason, *Take Me Along*	Tom Bosley, *Fiorello!*
1961	Richard Burton, *Camelot*	Dick Van Dyke, *Bye Bye Birdie*
1962	Robert Morse, *How to Succeed in Business Without Really Trying*	Charles Nelson Reilly, *How to Succeed in Business Without Really Trying*
1963	Zero Mostel, *A Funny Thing Happened on the Way to The Forum*	David Burns, *A Funny Thing Happened on the Way to the Forum*
1964	Bert Lahr, *Foxy*	Jack Cassidy, *She Loves Me*
1965	Zero Mostel, *Fiddler on the Roof*	Victor Spinetti, *Oh, What a Lovely War*
1966	Richard Kiley, *Man of La Mancha*	Frankie Michaels, *Mame*
1967	Robert Preston, *I Do! I Do!*	Joel Grey, *Cabaret*
1968	Robert Goulet, *The Happy Time*	Hiram Sherman, *How Now Dow Jones*
1969	Jerry Orbach, *Promises, Promises*	Ronald Holgate, *1776*
1970	Cleavon Little, *Purlie*	René Auberjonois, *Coco*

1971	Hal Linden, *The Rothschilds*	Keene Curtis, *The Rothschilds*
1972	Phil Silvers, *A Funny Thing Happened on the Way to the Forum*	Larry Blyden, *A Funny Thing Happened on the Way to the Forum*
1973	Ben Vereen, *Pippin*	George S. Irving, *Irene*
1974	Christopher Plummer, *Cyrano*	Tommy Tune, *Seesaw*
1975	John Cullum, *Shenandoah*	Ted Ross, *The Wiz*
1976	George Rose, *My Fair Lady*	Sammy Williams, *A Chorus Line*
1977	Barry Bostwick, *The Robber Bridegroom*	Lenny Baker, *I Love My Wife*
1978	John Cullum, *On the Twentieth Century*	Kevin Kline, *On the Twentieth Century*
1979	Len Cariou, *Sweeney Todd, the Demon Barber of Fleet Street*	Henderson Forsythe, *The Best Little Whorehouse in Texas*
1980	Jim Dale, *Barnum*	Mandy Patinkin, *Evita*
1981	Kevin Kline, *The Pirates of Penzance*	Hinton Battle, *Sophisticated Ladies*
1982	Ben Harney, *Dreamgirls*	Cleavant Derricks, *Dreamgirls*
1983	Tommy Tune, *My One and Only*	Charles "Honi" Coles, *My One and Only*
1984	George Hearn, *La Cage aux Folles*	Hinton Battle, *The Tap Dance Kid*
1985	No award	Ron Richardson, *Big River*
1986	George Rose, *The Mystery of Edwin Drood*	Michael Rupert, *Sweet Charity*
1987	Robert Lindsay, *Me and My Girl*	Michael Maguire, *Les Misérables*
1988	Michael Crawford, *Phantom of the Opera*	Bill McCutcheon, *Anything Goes*
1989	Jason Alexander, *Jerome Robbins' Broadway*	Scott Wise, *Jerome Robbins' Broadway*
1990	James Naughton, *City of Angels*	Michael Jeter, *Grand Hotel*
1991	Jonathan Pryce, *Miss Saigon*	Hinton Battle, *Miss Saigon*
1992	Gregory Hines, *Jelly's Last Jam*	Scott Waara, *The Most Happy Fella*
1993	Brent Carver, *Kiss of the Spider Woman*	Anthony Crivello, *Kiss of the Spider Woman*
1994	Boyd Gaines, *She Loves Me*	Jarrod Emick, *Damn Yankees*
1995	Matthew Broderick, *How to Succeed in Business Without Really Trying*	George Hearn, *Sunset Boulevard*
1996	Nathan Lane, *A Funny Thing Happened on the Way to the Forum*	Wilson Jermaine Heredia, *Rent*

Hinton Battle is the only actor to have won more than two Tony Awards for performing in a musical; he has won three in the Featured Actor category. Zero Mostel has won three Tonys as well but one of them was for a non-musical.

Memorable Double Winners

Some roles must be lucky (or too good to ignore) for they earned Tony Awards for more than one actor or actress playing them. Zero Mostel, Phil Silvers, and Nathan Lane all won for playing the sly slave Pseudolus in productions of *A Funny Thing Happened on the Way to the Forum.* (Jason Alexander played Pseudolus in one musical number in *Jerome Robbins' Broadway* and he also won.) Both Angela Lansbury and Tyne Daly won for playing Mama Rose in *Gypsy*, while both José Ferrer and Christopher Plummer won playing the title role in *Cyrano de Bergerac* (though Plummer's Tony was for a musical version). Robert Morse and Matthew Broderick each won for playing the ambitious Finch in *How to Succeed in Business Without Really Trying* and both Gertrude Lawrence and Donna Murphy won for playing Anna in *The King and I.*

Judith Anderson, Zoe Caldwell, and Diana Rigg all won for playing *Medea* and Ingrid Bergman and Julie Harris both were honored for playing Joan of Arc; Bergman in *Joan of Lorraine* and Harris in *The Lark.* Stephen Spinella is the only actor to win two Tony Awards for playing the same role in two different plays, *Angels in America: The Millennium Approaches* and *Perestroika.* And, in a switch from the usual order of things, Lila Kedrova won an Oscar for playing Hortence in the film *Zorbá the Greek* then later won a Tony for playing the same role in the Broadway revival of the musical *Zorbá.*

Memorable Losers

Because there can only be one Best Actor or Actress winner in each category each season (although ties in voting do occur), many memorable performances have failed to win Tony Awards. Sometimes it is just a case of bad timing. Ethel Merman's legendary performance as Mama Rose in *Gypsy* lost to Mary Martin's Maria Von Trapp in *The Sound of Music* in 1959; but, as Merman wisely stated, "you can't buck a nun." Here are some other indelible Broadway performances since 1947 that did not win a Tony.

> Julie Andrews in *My Fair Lady*
> Barbara Bel Geddes in *Cat on a Hot Tin Roof*
> Vivian Blaine and Sam Levene in *Guys and Dolls*
> Marlon Brando in *A Streetcar Named Desire*
> Georgia Brown in *Oliver!*
> Carol Burnett in *Once Upon a Mattress*
> Richard Burton in *Hamlet*
> Sid Caesar in *Little Me*
> Carol Channing in *Gentlemen Prefer Blondes*

Lee J. Cobb in *Death of a Salesman*
Alfred Drake in *Kiss Me, Kate*
Frances Eldridge in *Long Day's Journey Into Night*
Henry Fonda in *Clarence Darrow*
Joel Grey in *George M!*
Julie Harris in *A Member of the Wedding*
Lena Horne in *Jamaica*
Josephine Hull in *The Solid Gold Cadillac*
Burl Ives in *Cat on a Hot Tin Roof*
Deborah Kerr in *Tea and Sympathy*
Alfred Lunt and Lynn Fontanne in *The Visit*
Claudia McNeil and Sidney Poitier in *A Raisin in the Sun*
Laurence Olivier in *The Entertainer*
Jason Robards in *A Moon for the Misbegotten*
Rosalind Russell in *Auntie Mame*
Barbra Streisand in *Funny Girl*
Elaine Stritch in *Company*
Gwen Verdon in *Sweet Charity*

Best Musical Authors

While the Tony committee has consistently given awards to the authors of musical librettos (or books, as most like to call them) since 1949, there have been various ways of handling composers and lyricists. Sometimes only composers are recognized, sometimes composing and lyric writing are honored separately, and, more recently, the two have been combined in a Best Score category. Such inconsistencies made for some embarrassing gaps, such as Oscar Hammerstein's exceptional lyrics for *South Pacific* and Alan Jay Lerner's superior lyrics for *My Fair Lady* not even being nominated.

1947   No awards
1948   No awards
1949   Book: Bella and Samuel Spewack, *Kiss Me, Kate*
        Score: Cole Porter, *Kiss Me, Kate*
1950   Book: Oscar Hammerstein, Josuha Logan, *South Pacific*
        Composer: Richard Rodgers, *South Pacific*
1951   Book: Jo Swerling, Abe Burrows, *Guys and Dolls*
        Score: Frank Loesser, *Guys and Dolls*
1952   No awards
1953   Book: Joseph Fields, Jerome Chodorov, *Wonderful Town*
        Composer: Leonard Bernstein, *Wonderful Town*
1954   Book: Charles Lederer, Luther Davis, *Kismet*
        Composer: Alexander Borodin, *Kismet*
1955   Book: George Abbott, Richard Bissell, *The Pajama Game*
        Score: Richard Adler, Jerry Ross, *The Pajama Game*

1956   Book: George Abbott, Douglass Wallop, *Damn Yankees*
        Score: Richard Adler, Jerry Ross, *Damn Yankees*
1957   Book: Alan Jay Lerner, *My Fair Lady*
        Composer: Frederick Loewe, *My Fair Lady*
1958   Book: Meredith Willson, Franklin Lacey, *The Music Man*
        Score: Meredith Willson, *The Music Man*
1959   Book: Herbert & Dorothy Fields, Sidney Sheldon, David Shaw, *Redhead*
        Composer: Albert Hague, *Redhead*
1960   Book: (Tie) Jerome Weidman, George Abbott, *Fiorello!* and Howard
            Lindsay, Russel Crouse, *The Sound of Music*
        Composer: (Tie) Jerry Bock, *Fiorello!* and Richard Rodgers, *The Sound of
            Music*
1961   Book: Michael Stewart, *Bye Bye Birdie*
        Score: No award
1962   Book: Abe Burrows, Jack Weinstock, Willie Gilbert, *How to Succeed in
            Business Without Really Trying*
        Composer: Richard Rodgers, *No Strings*
1963   Book: Burt Shevelove, Larry Gelbart, *A Funny Thing Happened on the Way
            to the Forum*
        Score: Lionel Bart, *Oliver!*
1964   Book: Michael Stewart, *Hello, Dolly!*
        Score: Jerry Herman, *Hello, Dolly!*
1965   Book: Joseph Stein, *Fiddler on the Roof*
        Score: Sheldon Harnick, Jerry Bock, *Fiddler on the Roof*
1966   Book: No award
        Score: Mitch Leigh, Joe Darion, *Man of La Mancha*
1967   Book: No award
        Score: Jule Styne, Betty Comden, Adolph Green, *Hallelujah, Baby!*
1969   No awards
1970   No awards
1971   Book: George Furth, *Company*
        Lyrics: Stephen Sondheim, *Company*
        Composer: Stephen Sondheim, *Company*
1972   Book: John Guare, Mel Shapiro, *Two Gentlemen of Verona*
        Score: Stephen Sondheim, *Follies*
1973   Book: Hugh Wheeler, *A Little Night Music*
        Score: Stephen Sondheim, *A Little Night Music*
1974   Book: Hugh Wheeler, *Candide*
        Score: Frederick Loewe, Alan Jay Lerner, *Gigi*
1975   Book: James Lee Barrett, Peter Udell, Philip Rose, *Shenandoah*
        Score: Charlie Smalls, *The Wiz*
1976   Book: James Kirkwood, Nicholas Dante, *A Chorus Line*
        Score: Marvin Hamlisch, Edward Kleban, *A Chorus Line*
1977   Book: Thomas Meehan, *Annie*
        Score: Charles Strouse, Martin Charnin, *Annie*

1978 Book: Betty Comden, Adolph Green, *On the Twentieth Century*
      Score: Cy Coleman, Betty Comden, Adolph Green, *On the Twentieth Century*
1979 Book: Hugh Wheeler, *Sweeney Todd, the Demon Barber of Fleet Street*
      Score: Stephen Sondheim, *Sweeney Todd, the Demon Barber of Fleet Street*
1980 Book: Tim Rice, *Evita*
      Score: Andrew Lloyd Webber, Tim Rice, *Evita*
1981 Book: Peter Stone, *Woman of the Year*
      Score: John Kander, Fred Ebb, *Woman of the Year*
1982 Book: Tom Eyen, *Dreamgirls*
      Score: Maury Yeston, *Nine*
1983 Book: T. S. Eliot, *Cats*
      Score: Andrew Lloyd Webber, T. S. Eliot, *Cats*
1984 Book: Harvey Fierstein, *La Cage aux Folles*
      Score: Jerry Herman, *La Cage aux Folles*
1985 Book: William Hauptman, *Big River*
      Score: Roger Miller, *Big River*
1986 Book: Rupert Holmes, *The Mystery of Edwin Drood*
      Score: Rupert Holmes, *The Mystery of Edwin Drood*
1987 Book: Alain Boublil, Claude-Michel Schönberg, *Les Misérables*
      Score: Alain Boublil, Claude-Michel Schönberg, Herbert Kretzmer, *Les Misérables*
1988 Book: James Lapine, *Into the Woods*
      Score: Stephen Sondheim, *Into the Woods*
1989 No awards
1990 Book: Larry Gelbart, *City of Angels*
      Score: Cy Coleman, David Zippel, *City of Angels*
1991 Book: Marsha Norman: *The Secret Garden*
      Score: Cy Coleman, Betty Comden, Adolph Green, *The Will Rogers Follies*
1992 Book: William Finn, James Lapine, *Falsettos*
      Score: William Finn, *Falsettos*
1993 Book: Terrence McNally, *Kiss of the Spider Woman*
      Score: (Tie) John Kander, Fred Ebb, *Kiss of the Spider Woman,* and Pete Townsend, *Tommy*
1994 Book: James Lapine, *Passion*
      Score: Stephen Sondheim, *Passion*
1995 Book: Don Black, Christopher Hampton, *Sunset Boulevard*
      Score: Andrew Lloyd Webber, Don Black, Christopher Hampton, *Sunset Boulevard*
1996 Book: Jonathan Larson, *Rent*
      Score: Jonathan Larson, *Rent*

Composer/lyricist Stephen Sondheim is the undisputed winner here with seven Tony Awards to date. Sondheim is a Tony favorite these days. Consider, however, that they did not even nominate his score for *A Funny Thing Happened on the Way to the Forum* in 1963 but went ahead and voted it Best Musical. Next in frequency, the lyricist/librettist team of Comden and Green have won four times. Ironically, their finest set of lyrics, written for *Wonderful Town*, were not even nominated because only composers were honored that year. Composers Richard Rodgers, Cy Coleman, and Andrew Lloyd Webber, librettists Hugh Wheeler and George Abbott, and the songwriting team of Kander and Ebb have all won three times. Sadly, composer Jule Styne and composer/lyricist Frank Loesser only won one Tony each; a meager total considering that all of their Broadway shows were produced since the inception of the Tony Award.

Best Directors

The Tony for Director has always been problematic; too many times the best play or musical failed to win the Tony for director, continuing the long-felt suspicion that most people do not know what a theatre director actually does. We hear the script, see the actors, and soak up the designs. But the director's talents are elusive. Often the award is given for impressive staging (e.g., Harold Prince) or comic timing (e.g., Mike Nichols) but few Tony voters (or audience members, for that matter) have figured out the all encompassing role the director plays in theatre today.

	Plays	Musicals
1947	Elia Kazan, *All My Sons*	No award
1948	No award	No award
1949	Elia Kazan, *Death of a Salesman*	No award
1950	No award	Joshua Logan, *South Pacific*
1951	No award	George S. Kaufman, *Guys and Dolls*
1952	José Ferrer, *The Shrike, The Fourposter, Stalag 17*	No award
1953	Joshua Logan, *Picnic*	No award
1954	Alfred Lunt, *Ondine*	No award
1955	Robert Montgomery, *The Desperate Hours*	No award
1956	Tyrone Guthrie, *The Matchmaker, Six Characters in Search on an Author, Tamburlaine the Great*	No award
1957	No award	Moss Hart, *My Fair Lady*
1958	Vincent J. Donehue, *Sunrise at Campobello*	No award
1959	Elia Kazan, *J. B.*	No award
1960	Arthur Penn, *The Miracle Worker*	George Abbott, *Fiorello!*
1961	John Gielgud, *Big Fish, Little Fish*	Gower Champion, *Bye Bye Birdie*
1962	Noel Willman, *A Man for All Seasons*	Abe Burrows, *How to Succeed in Business Without Really Trying*

1963	Alan Schneider, *Who's Afraid of Virginia Woolf?*	George Abbott, *A Funny Thing Happened On the Way to the Forum*
1964	Mike Nichols, *Barefoot in the Park*	Gower Champion, *Hello, Dolly!*
1965	Mike Nichols, *Luv* and *The Odd Couple*	Jerome Robbins, *Fiddler on the Roof*
1966	Peter Brook, *Marat/Sade*	Albert Marre, *Man of La Mancha*
1967	Peter Hall, *The Homecoming*	Harold Prince, *Cabaret*
1968	Mike Nichols, *Plaza Suite*	Gower Champion, *The Happy Time*
1969	Peter Dews, *Hadrian VII*	Peter Hunt, *1776*
1970	Joseph Hardy, *Child's Play*	Ron Field, *Applause*
1971	Peter Brook, *A Midsummer Night's Dream*	Harold Prince, *Company*
1972	Mike Nichols, *Prisoner of Second Avenue*	Harold Prince and Michael Bennett, *Follies*
1973	A. J. Antoon, *That Championship Season*	Bob Fosse, *Pippin*
1974	José Quintero, *A Moon for the Misbegotten*	Harold Prince, *Candide*
1975	John Dexter, *Equus*	Geoffrey Holder, *The Wiz*
1976	Ellis Rabb, *The Royal Family*	Michael Bennett, *A Chorus Line*
1977	Gordon Davidson, *The Shadow Box*	Gene Saks, *I Love My Wife*
1978	Melvin Bernhardt, *Da*	Richard Maltby, Jr., *Ain't Misbehavin'*
1979	Jack Hofsiss, *The Elephant Man*	Harold Prince, *Sweeney, Todd, the Demon Barber of Fleet Street*
1980	Vivian Matalon, *Morning's at Seven*	Harold Prince, *Evita*
1981	Peter Hall, *Amadeus*	Wilford Leach, *The Pirates of Penzance*
1982	Trevor Nunn and John Caird, *Nicholas Nickleby*	Tommy Tune, *Nine*
1983	Gene Saks, *Brighton Beach Memoirs*	Trevor Nunn, *Cats*
1984	Mike Nichols, *The Real Thing*	Arthur Laurents, *La Cage aux Folles*
1985	Gene Saks, *Biloxi Blues*	Des McAnuff, *Big River*
1986	Jerry Zaks, *The House of Blue Leaves*	Wilford Leach, *The Mystery of Edwin Drood*
1987	Lloyd Richards, *Fences*	Trevor Nunn and John Caird, *Les Misérables*
1988	John Dexter, *M. Butterfly*	Harold Prince, *Phantom of the Opera*
1989	Jerry Zaks, *Lend Me a Tenor*	Jerome Robbins, *Jerome Robbins' Broadway*
1990	Frank Galati, *The Grapes of Wrath*	Tommy Tune, *Grand Hotel*
1991	Jerry Zaks, *Six Degrees of Separation*	Tommy Tune, *The Will Rogers Follies*
1992	Patrick Mason, *Dancing at Lughnasa*	Jerry Zaks, *Guys and Dolls*

1993	George C. Wolfe, *Angels in America, I*	Des McAnuff, *Tommy*
1994	Stephen Daldry, *An Inspector Calls*	Nicholas Hytner, *Carousel*
1995	Gerald Gutierrez, *The Heiress*	Harold Prince, *Show Boat*
1996	Gerald Gutierrez, *A Delicate Balance*	George C. Wolfe, *Bring in da Noise, Bring in da Funk*

Harold Prince holds the record for Directing Tonys, eight to date and all for musicals. It is probably fitting that he leads the list because his productions in the 1960s and 1970s did much to revitalize the musical theatre. Mike Nichols, with five Tonys, comes in second, which is more impressive when one realizes how few plays he has staged on Broadway. Similarly impressive is newcomer Jerry Zaks with four Tonys for a career that did not start on Broadway until the mid-1980s. Elia Kazan, perhaps the most influential post-War director, won three times, as did Tommy Tune and Gower Champion; although the last two have won several Tonys for Choreography as well.

Best Choreographers

Since the rise of the director-choreographer in the 1960s, the fine line between the two jobs has become practically invisible. In *Fiddler on the Roof*, for instance, who can say where Jerome Robbins the director lets off and Jerome Robbins the choreographer takes over? Before *Oklahoma!* there was no problem telling when book stopped and dancing started. But today it is often a puzzle. For example, dance and movement in *Follies* was so essential to the whole piece that director Harold Prince listed choreographer Michael Bennett as co-director. Here are the winners for the Choreography Tonys.

1947	Tie: Agnes de Mille, *Brigadoon;* Michael Kidd, *Finian's Rainbow*
1948	Jerome Robbins, *High Button Shoes*
1949	Gower Champion, *Lend an Ear*
1950	Helen Tamiris, *Touch and Go*
1951	Michael Kidd, *Guys and Dolls*
1952	Robert Alton, *Pal Joey*
1953	Donald Saddler, *Wonderful Town*
1954	Michael Kidd, *Can-Can*
1955	Bob Fosse, *The Pajama Game*
1956	Bob Fosse, *Damn Yankees*
1957	Michael Kidd, *Li'l Abner*
1958	Jerome Robbins, *West Side Story*
1959	Bob Fosse, *Redhead*
1960	Michael Kidd, *Destry Rides Again*
1961	Gower Champion, *Bye Bye Birdie*
1962	Tie: Agnes de Mille, *Kwamina;* Joe Layton, *No Strings*

1963   Bob Fosse, *Little Me*
1964   Gower Champion, *Hello, Dolly!*
1965   Jerome Robbins, *Fiddler on the Roof*
1966   Bob Fosse, *Sweet Charity*
1967   Ron Field, *Cabaret*
1968   Gower Champion, *The Happy Time*
1969   Joe Layton, *George M!*
1970   Ron Field, *Applause*
1971   Donald Saddler, *No, No, Nanette*
1972   Michael Bennett, *Follies*
1973   Bob Fosse, *Pippin*
1974   Michael Bennett, *See Saw*
1975   George Faison, *The Wiz*
1976   Michael Bennett, Bob Avian, *A Chorus Line*
1977   Peter Gennaro, *Annie*
1978   Bob Fosse, *Dancin'*
1979   Michael Bennett, Bob Avian, *Ballroom*
1980   Tommy Tune, Thommie Walsh, *A Day in Hollywood/A Night in the Ukraine*
1981   Gower Champion, *42nd Street*
1982   Michael Bennett, Michael Peters, *Dreamgirls*
1983   Tommy Tune, Thommie Walsh, *My One and Only*
1984   Danny Daniels, *The Tap Dance Kid*
1985   No award
1986   Bob Fosse, *Big Deal*
1987   Gillian Gregory, *Me and My Girl*
1988   Michael Smuin, *Anything Goes*
1989   Cholly Atkins, Henry Le Tang, Frankie Manning, Fayard Nicholas, *Black and Blue*
1990   Tommy Tune, *Grand Hotel*
1991   Tommy Tune, *The Will Rogers Follies*
1992   Susan Stroman, *Crazy for You*
1993   Wayne Cilento, *Tommy*
1994   Kenneth MacMillan, *Carousel*
1995   Susan Stroman, *Show Boat*
1996   Savion Glover, *Bring in da Noise, Bring in da Funk*

The undisputed winner here is Bob Fosse with eight Best Choreographer Tonys (plus another for directing). Michael Kidd, Gower Champion, and Michael Bennett each won five Tonys in the category and the last two also won directing Tonys as well. Relative-newcomer Tommy Tune has won four Tonys (plus three for directing). Renowned choreographer Jerome Robbins has won three for choreography (plus two for directing) and theatre dance pioneer Agnes De Mille won only twice.

Best Designers

Because the costumes, sets, and lights for musicals usually seem to overshadow those for plays, it is not surprising that most Tonys in these categories have gone to musicals over the years. Not to demean the wonderful designs listed below, you will not find much subtlety or many understated designs in the winning group. Tony voters know the power of impressive scenery and costumes and usually award them accordingly. Lighting, which was not added as a category until 1970, is the most difficult to award. The old adage that the best lighting never draws attention to itself has never won a designer a Tony.

1947   Costumes: Lucinda Ballard, *Street Scene* and other plays; David Ffolkes, *Henry VIII*
1948   Costumes: Mary Percy Schenck, *The Heiress*
        Sets: Horace Armistead, *The Medium*
1949   Costumes: Lemuel Ayers, *Kiss Me, Kate*
        Sets: Jo Mielziner, *Death of a Salesman* and other plays
1950   Costumes: Aline Bernstein, *Regina*
        Sets: Jo Mielziner, *The Innocents*
1951   Costumes: Miles White, *Guys and Dolls*
        Sets: Boris Aronson, *The Rose Tattoo* and other plays
1952   Costumes: Irene Sharaff, *The King and I*
        Sets: Jo Mielziner, *The King and I*
1953   Costumes: Miles White, *Hazel Flagg*
        Sets: Raoul Pene du Bois, *Wonderful Town*
1954   Costumes: Richard Whorf, *Ondine*
        Sets: Peter Larkin, *Ondine* and other plays
1955   Costumes: Cecil Beaton, *Quadrille*
        Sets: Oliver Messel, *House of Flowers*
1956   Costumes: Alvin Colt, *Pipe Dream*
        Sets: Peter Larkin, *Inherit the Wind* and other plays
1957   Costumes: Cecil Beaton, *My Fair Lady*
        Sets: Oliver Smith, *My Fair Lady*
1958   Costumes: Motley, *The First Gentleman*
        Sets: Oliver Smith, *West Side Story*
1959   Costumes: Rouben Ter-Arutunian, *Redhead*
        Sets: Donald Oenslager, *A Majority of One*
1960   Costumes: Cecil Beaton, *Saratoga*
        Sets (musical): Oliver Smith, *The Sound of Music*; Sets (drama): Howard Bay, *Toys in the Attic*
1961   Costumes (musical) Adrian, Tony Duquette, *Camelot*; Costumes (drama): Motley, *Becket*
        Sets (musical): Oliver Smith, *Camelot*; Sets (drama): Oliver Smith, *Becket*

1962   Costumes: Lucinda Ballard, *The Gay Life*
           Sets: Will Steven Armstrong, *Carnival*
1963   Costumes: Anthony Powell, *The School for Scandal*
           Sets: Sean Kenny, *Oliver!*
1964   Costumes: Freddy Wittop, *Hello, Dolly!*
           Sets: Oliver Smith, *Hello, Dolly!*
1965   Costumes: Patricia Zipprodt, *Fiddler on the Roof*
           Sets: Oliver Smith, *Baker Street*
1966   Costumes: Gunilla Palmstierna-Weiss, *Marat/Sade*
           Sets: Howard Bay, *Man of La Mancha*
1967   Costumes: Patricia Zipprodt, *Cabaret*
           Sets: Boris Aronson, *Cabaret*
1968   Costumes: Desmond Heeley, *Rosencrantz & Guildenstern Are Dead*
           Sets: Desmond Heeley, *Rosencrantz & Guildenstern Are Dead*
1969   Costumes: Louden Sainthill, *Canterbury Tales*
           Sets: Boris Aronson, *Zorbá*
1970   Costumes: Cecil Beaton, *Coco*
           Sets: Jo Mielziner, *Child's Play*
           Lighting: Jo Mielziner, *Child's Play*
1971   Costumes: Raoul Pene du Bois, *No, No, Nanette*
           Sets: Boris Aronson, *Company*;
           Lighting: H. R. Poindexter, *Story Theatre*
1972   Costumes: Florence Klotz, *Follies*
           Sets: Boris Aronson, *Follies*
           Lighting: Tharon Musser, *Follies*
1973   Costumes: Florence Klotz, *A Little Night Music*
           Sets: Tony Walton, *Pippin*;
           Lighting: Jules Fisher, *Pippin*
1974   Costumes: Franne Lee, *Candide*
           Sets: Franne and Eugene Lee, *Candide*
           Lighting: Jules Fisher, *Ulysses in Nighttown*
1975   Costumes: Geoffrey Holder, *The Wiz*
           Sets: Carl Toms, *Sherlock Holmes*
           Lighting: Neil Peter Jampolis, *Sherlock Holmes*
1976   Costumes: Florence Klotz, *Pacific Overtures*
           Sets: Boris Aronson, *Pacific Overtures*
           Lighting: Tharon Musser, *A Chorus Line*
1977   Costumes: Theoni V. Aldredge, *Annie*
           Sets: David Mitchell, *Annie*
           Lighting: Jennifer Tipton, *The Cherry Orchard*
1978   Costumes: Edward Gorey, *Dracula*
           Sets: Robin Wagner, *On the Twentieth Century*
           Lighting: Jules Fisher, *Dancin'*
1979   Costumes: Franne Lee, *Sweeney Todd*
           Sets: Eugene Lee, *Sweeney Todd; the Demon Barber of Fleet Street*
           Lighting: Roger Morgan, *The Crucifier of Blood*

1980	Costumes: Theoni V. Aldredge, *Barnum*
	Tie: Sets: David Mitchell, *Barnum*, and John Lee Beatty, *Talley's Folly*
	Lighting: David Hersey, *Evita*
1981	Costumes: John Bury, *Amadeus*
	Sets: John Bury, *Amadeus*
	Lighting: Willa Kim, *Sophisticated Ladies*
1982	Costumes: William Ivey Long, *Nine*
	Sets: John Napier, Dermot Hayes, *Nicholas Nickleby*
	Lighting: Tharon Musser, *Dreamgirls*
1983	Costumes: John Napier, *Cats*
	Sets: Ming Cho Lee, *K2*
	Lighting: David Hersey, *Cats*
1984	Costumes: Theoni V. Aldredge, *La Cage aux Folles*
	Sets: Tony Straiges, *Sunday in the Park With George*
	Lighting: Richard Nelson, *Sunday in the Park With George*
1985	Costumes: Florence Klotz, *Grind*
	Sets: Heidi Landesman, *Big River*
	Lighting: Richard Riddell, *Big River*
1986	Costumes: Patricia Zipprodt, *Sweet Charity*
	Sets: Tony Walton, *The House of Blue Leaves*
	Lighting: Pat Collins, *I'm Not Rappaport*
1987	Costumes: John Napier, *Starlight Express*
	Sets: John Napier, *Les Misérables*
	Lighting: David Hersey, *Les Misérables*
1988	Costumes: Maria Bjornson, *Phantom of the Opera*
	Sets: Maria Bjornson, *Phantom of the Opera*
	Lighting: Andrew Bridge, *Phantom of the Opera*
1989	Costumes: Claudio Segovia, Hector Orezzoli, *Black and Blue*
	Sets: Santo Loquasto, *Cafe Crown*
	Lighting: Jennifer Tipton, *Jerome Robbins' Broadway*
1990	Costumes: Santo Loquasto, *Grand Hotel*
	Sets: Robin Wagner, *City of Angels*
	Lighting: Jules Fisher, *Grand Hotel*
1991	Costumes: Willa Kim, *The Will Rogers Follies*
	Sets: Heidi Landesman, *The Secret Garden*
	Lighting: Jules Fisher, *The Will Rogers Follies*
1992	Costumes: William Ivey Long, *Crazy for You*
	Sets: Tony Walton, *Guys and Dolls*
	Lighting: Jules Fisher, *Jelly's Last Jam*
1993	Costumes: Florence Klotz, *Kiss of the Spider Woman*
	Sets: John Arnone, *Tommy;*
	Lighting: Chris Parry, *Tommy*
1994	Costumes: Ann Hould-Ward, *Beauty and the Beast*
	Sets: Rick Fisher, *An Inspector Calls*
	Lighting: Bob Crowley, *Carousel*

1995   Costumes: Florence Klotz, *Show Boat*
           Sets: John Napier, *Sunset Boulevard*
           Lighting: Andrew Bridge, *Sunset Boulevard*
1996   Costumes: Roger Kirk, *The King and I*
           Sets: Brian Thomson, *The King and I*
           Lighting: Jules Fisher, Peggy Eisenhauer, *Bring in da Noise, Bring in da Funk*

Oliver Smith received more Tony Awards than any other designer, seven for scenic design between 1957 and 1965. Other multiple set designer winners include Boris Aronson with six Tonys, and Jo Mielziner, Cecil Beaton, and John Napier with four each. The costume designers have pretty much spread the awards evenly over the years, with Theoni V. Aldredge, Franne Lee, and Patricia Zipprodt each with three Tonys, but Florence Klotz has managed to win six, all for musicals. Jules Fisher, with seven Tonys, has won more lighting awards than any other designer. Lighting designers John Hersey and Tharon Musser have each won three times. Jean Rosenthal, perhaps the most influential of all theatrical lighting designers and the person most responsible for developing the role of the lighting designer as separate from scenic and costume designers, never won a Tony despite her over 200 Broadway shows.

The Tony Champ

Producer/director Harold Prince has won the most Tony Awards, sixteen as of this writing. Here is an accounting of his winning trophies over the past five decades.

        1955   *The Pajama Game* (co-producer)
        1956   *Damn Yankees* (co-producer)
        1960   *Fiorello!* (co-producer)
        1965   *Fiddler on the Roof* (two awards: as producer for the Best Musical and as Best Producer; go figure that one out)
        1967   *Cabaret* (two awards: producer, director)
        1971   *Company* (two awards: producer, director)
        1972   *Follies* (co-director)
        1973   *A Little Night Music* (producer)
        1974   *Candide* (director)
        1979   *Sweeney Todd, the Demon Barber of Fleet Street* (director)
        1980   *Evita* (director)
        1988   *Phantom of the Opera* (director)
        1995   *Show Boat* (director)

Special Tonys

For various reasons, the Tony committee has bestowed special, non-category Tony Awards over the years. Sometimes these honors were for individuals making a special appearance on Broadway that season who did not fit into the traditional Best Actor or Best Actress category. Sometimes a production, usually a visiting program from abroad, was honored. Other times whole organizations were singled out. Before they established a category for revival productions, the Tony committee sometimes honored exceptional revivals on Broadway that season. Since 1977 the committee has annually recognized a regional theatre company.

American actors and actresses who have received special Tony Awards (and the year they were honored) include:

Vera Allen (1948)
Joe E. Brown (1948)
Mary Martin (1948)
June Lockhart (1948)
James Whitmore (1948)
Judy Garland (1952)
Danny Kaye (1953)
Burgess Meredith (1960)
Eva Le Gallienne (1964)
Carol Channing (1968 and 1995)
Pearl Bailey (1968)
Carol Burnett (1969)
Barbra Streisand (1970)
Alfred Lunt (1970)
Lynn Fontanne (1970)
Ethel Merman (1972)
Liza Minnelli (1974)
Bette Midler (1974)
Lily Tomlin (1977)
Barry Manilow (1977)
Diana Ross (1977)
Henry Fonda (1979)
Mary Tyler Moore (1980)
Lena Horne (1981)
Yul Brynner (1985)
Jackie Mason (1987)
Alfred Drake (1990)
Jessica Tandy (1994)
Hume Cronyn (1994)

Foreign actors and actresses who received special Tony Awards (and the year they were honored) include:

>Maurice Evans (1950)
>Charles Boyer (1952)
>Beatrice Lillie (1953)
>John Gielgud (1959)
>Audrey Hepburn (1968)
>Marlene Dietrich (1968)
>Maurice Chevalier (1968)
>Rex Harrison (1969)
>Peter Cook (1963 and 1974)
>Dudley Moore (1963 and 1974)
>Richard Burton (1976)

Playwrights and composers who have received special Tony Awards include:

>Arthur Miller (1947)
>Kurt Weill (1947)
>Howard Lindsay and Russel Crouse (1959)
>James Thurber (1960)
>Richard Rodgers (1962)
>Irving Berlin (1963)
>Leonard Bernstein (1969)
>Neil Simon (1975)

Plays that have received special Tony Awards (and the year they were bestowed) include:

>*The Threepenny Opera* (1956)
>*A Thurber Carnival* (1960)
>*Fiddler on the Roof* (1972)
>*A Moon for the Misbegotten* (1974)
>*Candide* (1974)
>*La Tragedie de Carmen* (1984)
>*The Fantasticks* (1992)
>*Oklahoma!* (1993)

Theatres and theatre organizations that received special Tony Awards include:

>Theatre Collection of the New York Public Library (1956)
>American Shakespeare Festival (1957)
>New York Shakespeare Festival (1958 and 1970)
>The Theatre Guild (1961 and 1972)
>APA-Phoenix Theatre (1968)
>National Theatre of Great Britain (1969)

Negro Ensemble Company (1969)
Actors' Fund of America (1973 and 1982)
Shubert Organization (1973)
Theatre Development Fund (1973)
Mark Taper Forum (1977)
National Theatre for the Deaf (1977)
Equity Library Theatre (1977)
Long Wharf Theatre (1978)
American Conservatory Theatre (1979)
Eugene O'Neill Memorial Theatre Center (1979)
Actors Theatre of Louisville (1980)
Goodspeed Opera House (1980 and 1995)
Trinity Square Repertory Company (1981)
Guthrie Theatre (1982)
Oregon Shakespeare Association (1983)
Theatre Collection, Museum of the City of New York (1983)
San Diego Old Globe Theatre (1984)
New York State Council on the Arts (1985)
Steppenwolf Theatre (1985)
American Repertory Theatre (1986)
San Francisco Mime Troupe (1987)
Brooklyn Academy of Music (1988)
South Coast Repertory Company (1988)
Hartford Stage Company (1989)
Seattle Repertory Theatre (1990)
Yale Repertory Theatre (1991)
Goodman Theatre (1992)
La Jolla Playhouse (1993)
McCarter Theatre (1994)
Alley Theatre (1996)

Special Tony Awards have also been given to: producers David Merrick (1961 and 1968), Gilbert Miller (1965), and Roger L. Stevens (1971); cartoonist Al Hirschfeld (1975 and 1984); critics Brooks Atkinson (1962) and Elliott Norton (1971); orchestrator Robert Russell Bennett (1957); directors Franco Zeffirelli (1962) and George Abbott (1987); *Playbill* Magazine (1971); scenic designer Oliver Smith (1965); restaurant owner Vincent Sardi, Sr. (1947); New York City Mayor John Lindsay (1973) and New York State Governor John D. Rockefeller, 3rd (1960).

THE PULITZER PRIZE FOR DRAMA

Although considered conservative and outdated at times, the Pulitzer Prize for Drama is still regarded as the most prestigious award for plays. It is the oldest of all the awards and, because there is only one category, it still carries considerable weight. The script rather than the production is honored so it is in effect a playwriting award. The prize is awarded each spring by the Graduate School of Journalism at Columbia University.

The play must be American and not be based on another play (thereby disqualifying most musicals). Initially the play had to be produced in the New York City area during the calendar year preceding the award date. But that has been altered and regional theatre productions now qualify. The Pulitzer Committee may decline to offer an award if it feels no play that year merits the honor. This has, on occasion, caused some bitterness on the part of the theatre community. Here are the winning plays and playwrights since the award's establishment in 1917.

1917	No award
1918	*Why Marry?*, Jesse Lynch Williams
1919	No award
1920	*Beyond the Horizon*, Eugene O'Neill
1921	*Miss Lulu Bett*, Zona Gale
1922	*Anna Christie*, Eugene O'Neill
1923	*Icebound*, Owen Davis
1924	*Hell Bent fer Heaven*, Hatcher Hughes
1925	*They Knew What They Wanted*, Sidney Howard
1926	*Craig's Wife*, George Kelly
1927	*In Abraham's Bosom*, Paul Green
1928	*Strange Interlude*, Eugene O'Neill
1929	*Street Scene*, Elmer Rice
1930	*The Green Pastures*, Marc Connelly
1931	*Alison's House*, Susan Glaspell
1932	*Of Thee I Sing*, Ira Gershwin, George S. Kaufman, Morrie Ryskind
1933	*Both Your Houses*, Maxwell Anderson
1934	*Men in White*, Sidney Kingsley
1935	*The Old Maid*, Zoe Akins
1936	*Idiot's Delight*, Robert E. Sherwood
1937	*You Can't Take It With You*, George S. Kaufman, Moss Hart
1938	*Our Town*, Thornton Wilder
1939	*Abe Lincoln in Illinois*, Robert E. Sherwood
1940	*The Time of Your Life*, William Saroyan
1941	*There Shall Be No Night*, Robert E. Sherwood
1942	No award
1943	*The Skin of Our Teeth*, Thornton Wilder

1944	No Award
1945	*Harvey*, Mary Chase
1946	*State of the Union*, Howard Lindsay, Russel Crouse
1947	No award
1948	*A Streetcar Named Desire*, Tennessee Williams
1949	*Death of a Salesman*, Arthur Miller
1950	*South Pacific*, Richard Rodgers, Oscar Hammerstein, Joshua Logan
1951	No award
1952	*The Shrike*, Joseph Kramm
1953	*Picnic*, William Inge
1954	*Teahouse of the August Moon*, John Patrick
1955	*Cat on a Hot Tin Roof*, Tennessee Williams
1956	*Diary of Anne Frank*, Frances Goodrich, Albert Hackett
1957	*Long Day's Journey Into Night*, Eugene O'Neill
1958	*Look Homeward, Angel*, Ketti Frings
1959	*J. B.*, Archibald MacLeish
1960	*Fiorello!*, George Abbott, Jerry Bock, Sheldon Harnick, Jerome Weidman
1961	*All the Way Home*, Tad Mosel
1962	*How to Succeed in Business Without Really Trying*, Abe Burrows, Frank Loesser
1963	No award
1964	No award
1965	*The Subject Was Roses*, Frank D. Gilroy
1966	No award
1967	*A Delicate Balance*, Edward Albee
1968	No award
1969	*The Great White Hope*, Howard Sackler
1970	*No Place to Be Somebody*, Charles Gordone
1971	*The Effect of Gamma Rays on Man-in-the-Moon Marigolds*, Paul Zindel
1972	No award
1973	*That Championship Season*, Jason Miller
1974	No award
1975	*Seascape*, Edward Albee
1976	*A Chorus Line*, Michael Bennett, Nicholas Dante, James Kirkwood, Edward Kleban, Marvin Hamlisch
1977	*The Shadow Box*, Michael Cristofer
1978	*The Gin Game*, D. L. Coburn
1979	*Buried Child*, Sam Shepard
1980	*Talley's Folly*, Lanford Wilson
1981	*Crimes of the Heart*, Beth Henley
1982	*A Soldier's Play*, Charles Fuller
1983	*'night, Mother*, Marsha Norman
1984	*Glengarry Glen Ross*, David Mamet
1985	*Sunday in the Park With George*, James Lapine, Stephen Sondheim
1986	No award
1987	*Fences*, August Wilson
1988	*Driving Miss Daisy*, Alfred Uhry

1989   *The Heidi Chronicles*, Wendy Wasserstein
1990   *The Piano Lesson*, August Wilson
1991   *Lost in Yonkers*, Neil Simon
1992   *The Kentucky Cycle*, Robert Schenkkan
1993   *Angels in America: Millennium Approaches*, Tony Kushner
1994   *Three Tall Women*, Edward Albee
1995   *The Young Man from Atlanta*, Horton Foote
1996   *Rent*, Jonathan Larson

It is worth noting that George Gershwin's name does not appear among the authors of *Of Thee I Sing*. The committee ruled that the composition of music was not a literary form and therefore only mentioned the librettists and lyricist in the award. This was later changed and composers shared in future awards.

Eugene O'Neill still holds the record for Pulitzer Prizes in Drama with four awards, followed by Robert E. Sherwood and Edward Albee each with three. Two-time winners include Tennessee Williams, August Wilson, Thornton Wilder, and George S. Kaufman. Some distinguished American playwrights who have never won a Pulitzer in the category of drama: Robert Anderson, Philip Barry, S. N. Behrman, Clare Boothe, Paddy Chayefsky, Rachel Crothers, Edna Ferber, John Guare, A. R. Gurney, Lillian Hellman, Lorraine Hansberry, Terrence McNally, Clifford Odets, and Paul Osborn.

Add to that list Irving Berlin, Leonard Bernstein, Cole Porter, Lerner and Loewe, and all the other creators of musicals who were never recognized. Rarely have musical plays been honored with a Pulitzer; in fact, only seven times. It was not until sixteen years after the inception of the award that a musical was honored: *Of Thee I Sing*. Since then there has been one musical winner for each decade: *South Pacific*, *Fiorello!*, *How to Succeed in Business Without Really Trying*, *A Chorus Line*, *Sunday in the Park With George*, and *Rent*.

The Pulitzer Prize has had more than its share of controversy over the years. Before the Tony Awards were established in 1947, the Pulitzers got a great deal of attention and there was often an outcry in the press over some of the committee's choices. In 1925 both *Desire Under the Elms* and *What Price Glory?* were bypassed in favor of the melodramatic *They Knew What They Wanted*. Many were not pleased with the tepid *Alison's House* winning over *Elizabeth the Queen* and *Once in a Lifetime* in 1931. Dissatisfaction with the Pulitzer choice was so strong in 1935 that it gave rise to a new award. That year saw *The Children's Hour*, *Petrified Forest*, *Valley Forge*, and *Awake and Sing*, yet the committee chose to honor *The Old Maid*. In reaction to the decision, the drama critics founded their own theatre prize, the New York Drama Critics Circle Award.

Harvey has remained a perennial favorite but many were upset in 1945 when it was chosen over *The Glass Menagerie*. Just as disturbing were the years when no award was given and some superior plays were ignored. In 1946 both *All My Sons* and *The Iceman Cometh* were snubbed with a "no award" decision by the committee. In 1950 *The Rose Tattoo, The Country Girl*, and *Guys and Dolls* were all deemed undeserving of a Pulitzer and no award was given. The worst upset came in 1963 when Columbia issued no award for drama, slighting the powerful (and controversial) *Who's Afraid of Virginia Woolf?* by Edward Albee. Committee members John Mason Brown and John Gassner resigned over that decision and the Pulitzer Prize was labeled old fashioned and conservative for some years after. (The committee honored Albee four years later with an award for the less-successful *A Delicate Balance*.) Here are the plays that have won both the Tony Award for Best Play or Musical and the Pulitzer Prize for Drama:

Death of a Salesman
South Pacific
The Teahouse of the August Moon
The Diary of Anne Frank
Long Day's Journey Into Night
J. B.
Fiorello!
How to Succeed in Business Without Really Trying
The Subject Was Roses
The Great White Hope
That Championship Season
A Chorus Line
The Shadow Box
Fences
The Heidi Chronicles
Lost in Yonkers
Angels in America: Millennium Approaches
Rent

NEW YORK DRAMA CRITICS CIRCLE AWARDS

Like the Pulitzer Prize, these awards emphasize plays over performers, directors, and designers. The award was first established in 1935 in reaction to the poor decisions often made by the Pulitzer committee. Unlike the Tony Awards, the Circle honors plays both on Broadway and Off Broadway and, unlike the Pulitzer Prize, recognizes foreign plays as well. If the committee feels the best play is an American one, then it is honored and a second award is given to best foreign play. If a foreign play is deemed best, a second award is cited for Best American Play. Musicals were added as a separate category in 1945. Listed below are the Drama Critics Circle's best American plays and musicals:

	Plays	Musicals
1936	*Winterset*	
1937	*High Tor*	
1938	*Of Mice and Men*	
1939	No American award	
1940	*The Time of Your Life*	
1941	*Watch on the Rhine*	
1942	No American award	
1943	*The Patriots*	
1944	No American award	
1945	*The Glass Menagerie*	
1946	No American award	*Carousel*
1947	*All My Sons*	*Brigadoon*
1948	*A Streetcar Named Desire*	
1949	*Death of a Salesman*	*South Pacific*
1950	*Member of the Wedding*	*The Consul*
1951	*Darkness at Noon*	*Guys and Dolls*
1952	*I Am a Camera*	*Pal Joey*
1953	*Picnic*	*Wonderful Town*
1954	*The Teahouse of the August Moon*	*The Golden Apple*
1955	*Cat on a Hot Tin Roof*	*The Saint of Bleeker Street*
1956	*The Diary of Anne Frank*	*My Fair Lady*
1957	*Long Day's Journey Into Night*	*The Most Happy Fella*
1958	*Look Homeward, Angel*	*The Music Man*
1959	*A Raisin in the Sun*	
1960	*Toys in the Attic*	*Fiorello!*
1961	*All the Way Home*	*Carnival*
1962	*The Night of the Iguana*	*How to Succeed in Business Without Really Trying*
1963	*Who's Afraid of Virginia Woolf?*	
1964	No American award	*Hello, Dolly!*
1965	*The Subject Was Roses*	*Fiddler on the Roof*
1966	No American award	*Man of La Mancha*
1967	No American award	*Cabaret*
1968	No American award	*Your Own Thing*
1969	*The Great White Hope*	*1776*
1970	*The Effect of Gamma Rays on Man-in-the-Moon Marigolds*	
1971	*The House of Blue Leaves*	*Follies*
1972	*That Championship Season*	*Two Gentlemen of Verona*
1973	*The Hot l Baltimore*	*A Little Night Music*
1974	*Short Eyes*	*Candide*
1975	*The Taking of Miss Janie*	*A Chorus Line*
1976	*Streamers*	*Pacific Overtures*
1977	*American Buffalo*	*Annie*

1978	No American award	Ain't Misbehavin'
1979	The Elephant Man	Sweeney Todd, the Demon Barber of Fleet Street
1980	Talley's Folly	
1981	Crimes of the Heart	
1982	A Soldier's Play	
1983	Brighton Beach Memoirs	Little Shop of Horrors
1984	Glengarry Glen Ross	Sunday in the Park With George
1985	Ma Rainey's Black Bottom	
1986	A Lie of the Mind	
1987	Fences	
1988	Joe Turner's Come and Gone	Into the Woods
1989	The Heidi Chronicles	
1990	The Piano Lesson	City of Angels
1991	Six Degrees of Separation	The Will Rogers Follies
1992	Two Trains Running	
1993	Angels in America: Millennium Approaches	Kiss of the Spider Woman
1994	Three Tall Women	
1995	No American award	
1996	Seven Guitars	Rent

The contemporary playwright August Wilson and the composer-lyricist Stephen Sondheim have received the most Drama Critics Circle awards; Sondheim has won six times (Follies, A Little Night Music, Pacific Overtures, Sweeney Todd, Sunday in the Park With George, and Into the Woods) and Wilson has also won six times (Ma Rainey's Black Bottom, Fences, Joe Turner's Come and Gone, The Piano Lesson, Two Trains Running, and Seven Guitars). Tennessee Williams has won four times and John Guare and Frank Loesser have won three times each.

In many ways the New York Drama Critics Circle Awards are the most thorough and satisfying of all the different awards because they include all kinds of plays: American, foreign, musicals, Broadway, and Off Broadway. But, being critics, they do have their prejudices. Neil Simon, not always a critics' favorite, has won only once. And the Circle has been rather strict about their musical awards. There seems to be little explanation why such musicals as West Side Story, Gypsy, Company, and Kiss Me, Kate were not honored. But all in all, the list of winners is a fairly comprehensive look at the best New York theatre has offered over the years.

To win the Tony Award, Pulitzer Prize, and New York Drama Critics Circle Award for the same play is considered the American theatre's Triple Crown. The fifteen plays to date that have won all three awards are:

Death of a Salesman
South Pacific

The Teahouse of the August Moon
The Diary of Anne Frank
Long Day's Journey Into Night
Fiorello!
How To Succeed in Business Without Really Trying
The Subject Was Roses
The Great White Hope
That Championship Season
A Chorus Line
Fences
The Heidi Chronicles
Angels in America: Millennium Approaches
Rent

THE NOBEL PRIZE

The Nobel Prize for Literature, given annually by the Nobel Foundation in Sweden since 1901, has been awarded to only one American dramatist, Eugene O'Neill, in 1936. The American-born British author T. S. Eliot won the literature prize in 1948 but it was for his poetry rather than his playwriting.

THE OSCARS

The Academy of Motion Picture Arts and Sciences has given a Best Picture "Oscar" annually since 1928. The following Best Picture winners were based on plays that won either the Best Play/Musical Tony Award or the Pulitzer Prize for Drama.

You Can't Take It With You (1938) from the 1937 Pulitzer winner
My Fair Lady (1964) from the 1956 Tony winner
The Sound of Music (1965) from the 1959 Tony co-winner
A Man for All Seasons (1966) from the 1961 Tony winner
Amadeus (1980) from the 1980 Tony winner
Driving Miss Daisy (1987) from the 1987 Pulitzer winner

OTHER NEW YORK AWARDS

The **Clarence Derwent Awards** are given to newcomers in the field of acting. Derwent was a British-born actor who appeared in numerous (and often supporting) roles on Broadway between 1915 and 1948, and was president of Actors Equity for two terms. The awards, which have been given by Actors

Equity since 1945, are for two actors in supporting roles either on Broadway or Off Broadway.

The **Drama Desk Awards** are given by New York drama reporters, editors, and critics in a variety of categories, including such overlooked areas as orchestrations, solo performances, special effects, and music written for a play. The Drama Desk, a group that also sponsors luncheon discussion programs, has been giving out the awards since the 1954-1955 season.

The **George Jean Nathan Award** is for dramatic criticism and was provided for in the will of the critic when he died in 1958. Since that year the award has been given annually, the sole winner being determined by the heads of the English Departments of Cornell, Yale, and Princeton Universities.

The **Lucille Lortel Awards** are named after Off Broadway's pioneering producer and are sponsored by the League of Off-Broadway Theatres and Producers. As expected, the awards honor achievement in Off-Broadway productions in various categories since 1986. Lortel herself is usually on the panel of judges.

The **Obie Awards** are Off Broadway's equivalent to the Tonys. The awards were established in 1956 by *The Village Voice* to recognize achievements in the new alternative theatre arising in Greenwich Village. Categories have changed over the years but awards have been given to performers, plays, directors, designers, and theatre companies appearing Off Broadway. The Obies do not limit the number of winners in any one category so coverage is usually pretty thorough.

The **Outer Circle Awards** are annual awards for New York theatre given by journalists who review plays for the out-of-town newspapers and national publications. The Circle was founded by critics John Gassner, Charles Freeman, and Joseph Kaye in 1950 and awards are given for both performers and plays on Broadway and Off Broadway.

The **Theatre World Awards** recognize outstanding new acting talent in the New York theatre. The awards, given to usually a dozen new faces to the theatre scene, are given by the *Theatre World* editor John Willis and a committee of critics, and have been an annual event since 1945.

Other awards given in New York include the **William Inge Award** for lifetime achievement in theatre; the **Annual Drama League Awards**; the **Joseph Kesselring Prize** for new plays; the **Astaire Award** for dance; the **Robert Whitehead Award** for producing; the **American Theatre Wing Design Awards**; the **Annual Jujamcym Theatre Awards** for developing new talent; the **Mr. Abbott Award** for directing; and the **New York Dance and Performance Awards**, also known as the Bessies.

Some New York awards no longer given include the **Donaldson Awards** (1944-1955), named after W. H. Donaldson, founder of *Billboard* Magazine; the **Marharam Awards** for scenic design (1964-1985); and the **Page One**

Awards (1945-1965) given by New York City journalists.

REGIONAL AWARDS

The **Annual ACTA New Play Award** is given for an outstanding new work in cross-country theatre. The award has been given by the American Theatre Critics Association since 1985.

The **Barrymore Awards** are the most recent regional awards, first presented in 1995 to recognize superior theatre in the Philadelphia area. The award is named after the famous Barrymore family of actors who hailed from Philadelphia.

The **Boston Theatre Awards** (formerly the Elliott Norton Awards named after the famous Boston theatre critic) have been given for Boston area theatre productions since 1982.

The **Helen Hayes Awards** have been presented by the Washington Theatre Awards Society since 1983 to recognize theatre in the District of Columbia area. They are named after the beloved actress who was a Washington native.

The **Joseph Jefferson Awards** have been given annually since 1968 for achievement in theatre in the Chicago area. The award is named for the famed nineteenth-century actor.

The **Los Angeles Critics Circle Awards** have been given for Los Angeles area theatre productions since 1969.

For further reading: Lee Alan Morrow's *The Tony Award Book*, Isabelle Stevenson's *The Tony Award*, John L. Toohey's *A History of the Pulitzer Prize Plays*, and the *Best Plays* Series.

8

THEATRICAL ODDS AND ENDS

THEATRICAL AUTOBIOGRAPHIES

Theatre folk, by their nature, love to tell a good story. They are also notorious for spicing up a tale that may be a little too routine or ordinary. So one always has to read a theatrical autobiography with a grain of salt. But when the writer is as succinct and entertaining as a Moss Hart or a Joseph Jefferson, the result can be delicious. Listed below are some of the memoirs written over the past 150 years by American theatre celebrities and artists. Many of these autobiographies were written with other writers, though often they are not credited.

George Abbott (1887-1995), prolific director/playwright of musicals and comedies with one of the longest theatre careers on record: *Mister Abbott* (1963).

Richard Adler (1921-), composer/lyricist of *Damn Yankees* and other musicals: *You Gotta Have Heart* (1990).

Fred Allen (1894-1956), popular radio comedian who appeared in vaudeville and several Broadway revues: *Much Ado About Me* (1956).

John Murray Anderson (1886-1954), director and producer of many Broadway revues: *Out Without My Rubbers* (1954).

Mary Anderson (1859-1940), beautiful and beloved actress of the late nineteenth century: *A Few Memories* (1896).

Eve Arden (1912-1990), wise-cracking character actress of stage, film, and television: *Three Phases of Eve* (1985).

George Arliss (1868-1946), popular stage and screen actor of sinister roles: *Up the Years from Bloomsbury* (1927).

Fred Astaire (1899-1987), debonair stage and film dancing star: *Steps in Time* (1959).

Lauren Bacall (1924-), model-turned-film star who later appeared in Broadway plays and musicals: *By Myself* (1978).

Pearl Bailey (1918-1990), singing comedienne who appeared intermittently in Broadway musicals: *The Raw Pearl* (1968), *Talking to Myself* (1971).

Tallulah Bankhead (1903-1968), throaty actress of Broadway melodramas and comedies:*Tallulah* (1952).

Henry Clay Barnabee (1833-1917), renowned comic singer-actor who appeared in several Gilbert and Sullivan American premieres and other musicals: *My Wanderings* (1913).

Ethel Barrymore (1879-1959), renowned actress from a theatrical dynasty: *Memories* (1955).

Lionel Barrymore (1878-1954), versatile character actor of the Barrymore clan:*We Barrymores* (1951).

S. N. Behrman (1893-1973), stylish playwright of American comedy of manners: *People in a Diary* (1972).

Norman Bel Geddes (1893-1958), innovative Broadway scenic designer: *Miracle in the Evening* (1960).

William Brady (1863-1950), colorful producer of regional and Broadway plays at the turn of the century: *Showman* (1937).

Billie Burke (1885-1970), distinctive comedienne of stage and film: *With a Feather on My Nose* (1949).

Abe Burrows (1910-1985), successful author of comedies and musical comedies: *Honest Abe* (1980).

Eddie Cantor (1892-1964), singer-comedian favorite of Broadway, radio, and film: *My Life Is in Your Hands* (1927), *Take My Life* (1957).

Irene Castle (1893-1969), influential ballroom dancer and Broadway performer: *Castles in the Air* (1958).

George M. Cohan (1878-1942), multi-talented composer, author, director, and performer who helped define the American musical comedy: *Twenty Years on Broadway* (1924).

Betty Comden (1915-), prolific Broadway lyricist and librettist: *Off Stage* (1995).

Marc Connolly (1890-1981), popular playwright and sometime collaborator with George S. Kaufman: *Voices Offstage* (1968).

Katharine Cornell (1893-1974), beloved actress in contemporary and classic plays on Broadway and on tour: *I Wanted to Be an Actress* (1939).

William H. Crane (1845-1928), popular comic stage actor of the nineteenth century: *Footprints and Echoes* (1927).

Cheryl Crawford (1902-1986), distinguished Broadway producer associated with the Theatre Guild and the Group Theatre: *One Naked Individual* (1977).

Hume Cronyn (1911-), versatile stage and film character actor: *A Terrible Liar: A Memoir* (1991).

Owen Davis (1874-1956), author of popular Broadway melodramas: *I'd Like to Do It Again* (1931), *My First Fifty Years in the Theatre* (1950).

Jefferson De Angelis (1859-1933), acrobatic comic and character actor: *A*

Vagabond Trouper (1931) with Alvin E. Harlow.

Agnes De Mille (1905-1993), famed Broadway choreographer: *Dance to the Piper* (1951), *And Promenade Home* (1956), *Speak to Me, Dance With Me* (1973), *Reprieve: A Memoir* (1981)

Howard Dietz (1896-1983), distinctive lyricist and frequent partner of composer Arthur Schwartz: *Dancing in the Dark* (1974).

Marie Dressler (1869-1934), overpowering comic actress of Broadway and films: *The Life Story of an Ugly Duckling* (1924), *My Own Story* (1934).

John Drew (1853-1927), distinguished actor of the Barrymore clan: *My Years on the Stage* (1922).

Mrs. John Drew (1820-1897), grande dame actress of the Drew-Barrymore family dynasty: *Autobiographical Sketch of Mrs. John Drew* (1899).

Vernon Duke (1903-1969), distinctive Broadway and film composer: *Passport to Paris* (1955).

William Dunlap (1766-1839), early American playwright, producer, and historian: *Diary of William Dunlap* (1930).

Rose Eytinge (1835-1911), popular but temperamental nineteenth-century stage actress: *The Memories of Rose Eytinge* (1905).

Frank Fay (1897-1961), beloved character actor mostly remembered from *Harvey*: *How to Be Poor* (1935).

Henry Fonda (1905-1982), film star who often returned to Broadway: *Fonda: My Story* (1981).

Eddie Foy (1856-1928), popular vaudeville and Broadway comic: *Clowning Through Life* (1928).

Daniel Frohman (1851-1940), successful Broadway producer and respected theatre philanthropist: *Memories of a Manager* (1911), *Daniel Frohman Presents* (1935).

Mrs. George Henry Gilbert (1821-1904), most popular stage comedienne of the nineteenth century: *The Stage Reminiscences of Mrs. Gilbert* (1904).

Lillian Gish (1893-1993), pioneering film actress who often returned to Broadway: *Dorothy and Lillian Gish* (1973).

John Golden (1874-1955), lyricist-turned-producer who had many hits on Broadway: *Stage-Struck John Golden* (1930) with Viola Brothers Shore.

Nat Goodwin (1857-1919), beloved comic actor on Broadway around the turn of the century: *Nat Goodwin's Book* (1914).

Max Gordon (1892-1978), highly successful Broadway producer: *Max Gordon Presents* (1963) with Lewis Funke.

Ruth Gordon (1896-1985), versatile stage and film actress: *Myself Among Others* (1971), *My Side* (1976).

Charlotte Greenwood (1893-1978), lanky comedienne favorite in both musicals and comedies: *Never Too Tall* (1947).

Marvin Hamlisch (1944-), Broadway and movie composer: *The Way I*

Was (1992).

Jed Harris (1900-1979), notoriously temperamental director and producer who had many Broadway hits: *A Dance on the High Wire* (1979).

Moss Hart (1904-1961), ingenious playwright and director: *Act One* (1959).

June Havoc (1916-), indomitable singing star of vaudeville and Broadway: *Early Havoc* (1980).

Helen Hayes (1900-1993), distinguished "first lady of the American Theatre": *My Life in Three Acts* (1990).

Ben Hecht (1894-1964), famous playwright of Broadway comedies and films, often in collaboration with Charles MacArthur: *A Child of the Century* (1954).

Theresa Helburn (1887-1959), powerful producer associated with the Theatre Guild: *A Wayward Quest* (1960).

Katharine Hepburn (1907-), renowned film actress who often returned to the stage: *Me* (1991).

Jerry Herman (1932-), successful composer/lyricist of *Hello, Dolly!* (1964) and other hits: *Showtune* (1996) with Marilyn Stasio.

Arthur Hopkins (1878-1950), prolific Broadway producer and director: *To a Lonely Boy* (1937).

De Wolf Hopper (1858-1935), commanding singing comic in many hit plays and musicals over a fifty-year career: *Once a Clown, Always a Clown* (1927) with Wesley Winan Stout.

John Houseman (1902-1988), the distinguished director and producer associated with the Mercury Theatre and the Acting Company: *Run-Through* (1972), *Front and Center* (1979), *Final Dress* (1983).

Elsie Janis (1889-1956), beloved star of plays and vaudeville and a favorite of the Armed Forces during World War One: *So Far, So Good!* (1932).

George Jessel (1898-1981), vaudeville comic and famed toastmaster who appeared in several plays on Broadway: *So Help Me* (1943), *This Way, Miss* (1955).

Joseph Jefferson (1829-1905), most popular comic actor of the nineteenth century: *Autobiography of Joseph Jefferson* (1890).

James Earl Jones (1931-), powerful African-American actor of stage and film: *James Earl Jones: Voices and Silences* (1993) with Penelope Niven.

Walter C. Kelly (1873-1939), pudgy comedian of vaudeville, films, and Broadway: *Of Me I Sing* (1953).

Lawrence Langner (1890-1962), the producer and sometime playwright associated with the Theatre Guild and other theatre groups: *The Magic Curtain* (1951).

Eva Le Gallienne (1899-1991), distinguished actress, producer, director, and translator: *At 33* (1934), *With a Quiet Heart* (1953).

Alan Jay Lerner (1918-1986), leading Broadway lyricist and librettist: *On* *the Street Where I Live* (1978).

Joshua Logan (1908-1988), successful director and author of Broadway plays and musicals: *Josh: My Up and Down, In and Out Life* (1976), *Movie Stars, Real People and Me* (1978).

Elisabeth Marbury (1856-1933), influential dramatists' agent and founder of the Princess Musicals series: *My Crystal Ball* (1924).

Mary Martin (1913-1990), queen of Broadway musical comedy: *My Heart Belongs* (1976).

Guthrie McClintic (1893-1961), successful producer and director who often worked with his wife Katharine Cornell: *Me and Kit* (1955).

Ethel Merman (1908-1984), the Broadway musical's favorite belter and comedienne: *Merman* (1978) with George Eells.

George Middleton (1880-1967), a playwright and co-founder of the Dramatists Guild: *These Things Are Mine* (1947).

Arthur Miller (1915-), leading American post-war playwright: *Time Bends* (1987).

Helena Modjeska (1840-1909), Polish-born actress whose notable career was in America: *Memories and Impressions of Helena Modjeska* (1910).

Clara Morris (1848-1925), popular nineteenth-century actress: *Life on the Stage* (1901).

Anna Cora Mowatt (1819-1870), early American playwright and actress: *Autobiography of an Actress; or Eight Years on the Stage* (1854).

Elliott Nugent (1899-1980), popular playwright and actor: *Events Leading Up to the Comedy* (1965).

Molly Picon (1898-1992), favorite character actress of vaudeville, the Yiddish Theatre, and Broadway: *So Laugh a Little* (1962).

Channing Pollock (1880-1946), a playwright and dramatic critic on Broadway in the early decades of the century: *Harvest of My Years* (1943).

James T. Powers (1862-1943), grotesque-looking comedian on Broadway and in vaudeville: *Twinkle Little Star* (1939).

Harold Prince (1928-), prolific and innovative producer and director of Broadway musicals: *Contradictions: Notes on 26 Years in the Theatre* (1974).

José Quintero (1924-), distinguished director of Eugene O'Neill plays and other dramas: *If You Don't Dance, They Beat You* (1972).

Elmer Rice (1892-1967), author of *The Adding Machine, Street Scene* and other distinguished dramas: *Minority Report* (1963).

Harry Richman (1895-1972), a classy singing star of many Broadway revues: *A Hell of a Life* (1966).

Paul Robeson (1898-1976), powerful actor-singer and political activist: *Here I Stand* (1971).

Edward G. Robinson (1893-1973), versatile character actor of films and stage: *All My Yesterdays* (1973).

Richard Rodgers (1902-1979), dean of American musical theatre composers:

Musical Stages (1975).

Will Rogers (1879-1935), beloved humorist who appeared in vaudeville and Broadway revues: *Autobiography of Will Rogers* (1949).

Alan Schneider (1917-1984), famed director of plays by Edward Albee, Samuel Beckett and others: *Entrances: An American Director's Journey* (1986).

Neil Simon (1927-), extremely popular playwright and screenwriter, *Rewrites: A Memoir* (1996).

Lee Simonson (1888-1967), influential scenic and costume designer: *Part of a Lifetime* (1943).

Otis Skinner (1958-1942), popular leading man in exotic roles: *Footlights and Spotlights* (1924).

Cornelia Otis Skinner (1901-1979), playwright and actress: *Family Circle* (1948).

Walter Slezak (1902-1983), musical comedy star who later turned to films: *What Time's the Next Swan?* (1962).

Harry B. Smith (1860-1936), prolific lyricist and librettist of Broadway musicals: *First Nights and First Editions* (1931).

E. H. Sothern (1859-1933), popular American Shakespearean actor at the turn of the century: *The Melancholy Tale of Me* (1916).

John Philip Sousa (1854-1932), favorite march composer who also scored Broadway musicals and operettas: *Marching Along* (1928).

Maureen Stapleton (1925-), versatile character actress of stage and film: *A Hell of a Life* (1995) with Jane Scovell.

Fred Stone (1873-1959), popular comic actor in vaudeville and on Broadway, often with his partner David Montgomery: *Rolling Stone* (1945).

Augustus Thomas (1857-1934), ground-breaking American playwright: *The Print of My Remembrance* (1922).

Sophie Tucker (1884-1966), brassy singing star of vaudeville and Broadway: *Some of these Days* (1945).

John Van Druten (1901-1957), urbane playwright, author of *I Am a Camera* and other plays: *The Widening Circle* (1957).

Bayard Veiller (1869-1943), author of popular stage thrillers: *The Fun I've Had* (1941).

Ethel Waters (1900?-1977), versatile African-American actress and singer: *His Eye Is on the Sparrow* (1951) with Charles Samuels and *To Me It's Wonderful* (1972).

Mae West (1892-1980), the notorious actress and sometime playwright: *Goodness Had Nothing to Do With It* (1959).

Tennessee Williams (1911-1983), leading American dramatist: *Memoirs* (1975).

Meredith Willson (1902-1984), composer/lyricist of *The Music Man* and other shows: *But He Doesn't Know the Territory* (1959).

P. G. Wodehouse (1881-1975), influential lyricist and librettist: *Bring On* *the Girls! The Improbable Story of Our Life in Musical Comedy* (1953) with Guy Bolton.

Peggy Wood (1892-1978), operetta star who also appeared in plays and on television: *How Young You Look* (1940).

FAMOUS THEATRE FAMILIES

America may not have royalty but often in the theatre there are dynasties. Families of actors were particularly prominent in the nineteenth century and in the first decades of the twentieth century. Listed below are some theatrical families and theatre personalities who are related.

Adler: Jacob P. Adler (1855-1926), premiere actor of the Yiddish-American theatre.

Stella Adler (1902-1992), renowned actress on Broadway and in the Yiddish theatre and later an influential acting teacher, the daughter of Jacob Adler.

Luther Adler (1903-1984), powerful Broadway actor long associated with the Group Theatre, son of Jacob and brother to Stella Adler.

Albee: E. F. Albee (1857-1930), entrepreneur who, with B. F. Keith, monopolized the nation's vaudeville circuit by buying theatres and booking acts.

Edward Albee (1928-), the renowned American playwright, the adopted grandson of E. F. Albee.

Bateman: H. L. Bateman (1812-1875), actor-turned-playwright who later wrote plays for and promoted the careers of his daughters Kate and Ellen.

Kate Bateman (1842-1917), child prodigy actress who later was popular on Broadway, particularly in *Evangeline*, written by her mother Sidney Francis Bateman (1823-1881).

Bel Geddes: Norman Bel Geddes (1893-1958), innovative scenic and lighting designer on Broadway.

Barbara Bel Geddes (1922-), versatile stage, film, television actress, daughter of Norman Bel Geddes.

Booth: Junius Brutus Booth (1796-1852), erratic but distinguished classical actor.

Junius Brutus Booth, Jr. (1821-1883), actor turned successful producer, son of Junius Booth.

Agnes Booth (1846-1910), much respected tragic actress, wife of Junius Booth, Jr.

Edwin Booth (1833-1893), classical actor and probably finest American actor of the nineteenth century, son of Junius Booth, Sr.

John Wilkes Booth (1839-1865), dashing actor and infamous assassin of

Abraham Lincoln, son of Junius Booth, Sr.

Chodorov: Edward Chodorov (1904-1988), playwright-director on Broadway in the 1930s and 1940s.

Jerome Chodorov (1911-), film and theatre author who wrote *My Sister Eileen, Wonderful Town, Junior Miss* and others, brother of Edward Chodorov.

Davenport: E. L. Davenport (1815-1877), versatile actor and successful theatre manager on Broadway and on tour.

Fanny Davenport (1850-1898), regal beauty who was one of the most beloved actresses of her day, daughter of E. L. Davenport.

May Davenport (1856-1927), actress popular in theatres in Philadelphia and Boston, daughter of E. L. Davenport.

Edgar L. Davenport (1862-1918), actor long associated with Boston theatres, son of E. L. Davenport.

Harry Davenport (1866-1949), versatile stage and film actor, son of E. L. Davenport.

De Mille: Henry C. De Mille (1855?-1893), successful Broadway playwright, often in collaboration with David Belasco.

Beatrice De Mille (?-1923), influential playwright's agent, wife of Henry C. De Mille.

William C. De Mille (1878-1955), playwright of popular melodramas at the turn of the century, later a director and writer of films, son of Henry and Beatrice De Mille.

Cecil B. De Mille (1881-1959), stage actor and director who later became more famous for his films, son of Henry and Beatrice De Mille.

Agnes De Mille (1905-1993), influential Broadway choreographer and director, daughter of William C. De Mille.

Drew/Barrymore: Mrs. John Drew (1820-1897), British-born actress who managed Philadelphia's Arch Street Theatre and presented distinguished repertory productions.

John Drew (1827-1862), Dublin-born actor known for colorful Irish characters in America, married Louisa Lane (Mrs. John Drew).

John Drew (1853-1927), colorful actor of classical roles, son of Louisa and John Drew.

Maurice Barrymore (1849-1905), erratic but commanding actor on Broadway.

Georgiana Drew Barrymore (1856-1893), tall, elegant actress in Philadelphia and New York, daughter of Louisa and John Drew and married to Maurice Barrymore.

Lionel Barrymore (1878-1954), renowned character actor of stage and film, son of Georgiana and Maurice Barrymore.

Ethel Barrymore (1879-1959), statuesque actress and one of the early purveyors of naturalistic acting in America, daughter of Georgiana and Maurice Barrymore.

John Barrymore (1882-1942), mesmerizing actor of stage and film and probably the most gifted actor of his generation, son of Georgiana and Maurice Barrymore.

Duff: John Duff (1787-1831), powerful classical actor in New York, Boston, and Philadelphia.

Mrs. John Duff (1794-1857), renowned classical actress, married to John Duff.

Mary Duff (1811?-1852), popular classical actress in Philadelphia and New York, daughter of John Duff.

Fields: Lew Fields (1867-1941), popular and influential comic who, with his partner Joe Weber, perfected a unique ethnic quality in vaudeville and Broadway musicals.

Joseph Fields (1895-1966), author of comedies and musicals, son of Lew Fields.

Herbert Fields (1897-1958), innovative author of musical librettos with Cole Porter, Rodgers and Hart and others, son of Lew Fields.

Dorothy Fields (1905-1974), versatile lyricist and librettist with a long and varied career on Broadway and in Hollywood, daughter of Lew Fields.

Foy: Eddie Foy (1856-1928), popular comic in vaudeville and on Broadway, famous for the act Eddie Foy and the Seven Little Foys.

Eddie Foy, Jr. (1905?-1983), comic performer of *The Pajama Game* and other Broadway musicals, son of Eddie Foy.

Frohman: Daniel Frohman (1851-1940), influential Broadway producer.

Gustave Frohman (1855-1930), theatre manager and producer, brother of Daniel and Charles Frohman.

Charles Frohman (1860-1915), successful producer and creator of many Broadway stars, brother of Daniel and Gustave Frohman.

Gershwin: Ira Gershwin (1896-1983), distinctive and versatile Broadway and film lyricist.

George Gershwin (1898-1937), possibly America's most accomplished Broadway composer, brother of Ira Gershwin.

Gish: Lillian Gish (1896-1993), legendary film actress who often returned to the stage.

Dorothy Gish (1898-1968), actress on film from her youth but with many stage appearances as well, sister of Lillian Gish.

Hallam: Lewis Hallam (1714-1756), actor-manager who first brought professional theatre to the colonies in 1752.

Mrs. Lewis Hallam (?-1773), classical actress who came to America, becoming its first popular actress, married to Lewis Hallam.

Lewis Hallam, Jr. (1740-1808), actor-manager who founded the American Company, the first resident troupe in the colonies, son of Lewis Hallam.

Isabella Hallam (1746-1826), member of the Hallam family who remained in England and became a popular actress, daughter of Lewis Hallam, Sr.

Hammerstein: Oscar Hammerstein I (1847-1919), colorful impresario and producer of theatre and opera.

Arthur Hammerstein (1872-1955), successful Broadway producer of musicals and operettas, son of Oscar Hammerstein I.

Oscar Hammerstein II (1895-1960), America's most influential and beloved lyricist of Broadway musicals, grandson of Oscar Hammerstein I and nephew of Arthur Hammerstein.

William Hammerstein (1918-), succesful theatre producer, son of Oscar Hammertein II.

James Hammerstein (1931-), successful theatre director and producer, son of Oscar Hammerstein II.

Harris: William Harris, Sr. (1844-1916), pioneering theatre owner and producer who helped found the Theatrical Syndicate.

William Harris, Jr. (1884-1946), successful Broadway producer on Broadwayin the 1920s, son of William Harris, Sr.

Henry Harris (1886-1912), promising Broadway producer who died at the peak of his career in the sinking of the *Titanic*, son of William Harris, Sr.

Herne: James A. Herne (1839-1901), pioneering author of potent Ibsen-like plays such as *Margaret Fleming*.

Crystal Herne (1883-1950), popular actress in Broadway dramas, daughter of James A. Herne.

Jefferson: Joseph Jefferson (1774-1832), accomplished comic actor born in England who came to America and was a popular favorite at Philadelphia's Chestnut Street Theatre.

Joseph Jefferson, Jr. (1804-1842), actor and scenic painter, son of Joseph Jefferson.

Joseph Jefferson (1829-1905), the most beloved comic actor of the nineteenth century, famous for playing in his own adaptation of *Rip Van Winkle*, son of Joseph Jefferson, Jr.

Kelly: Walter C. Kelly (1873-1939), favorite comic actor in vaudeville and on Broadway.

George Kelly (1887-1974), distinctive playwright of satirical comedies such as*The Show-Off* and *Craig's Wife*, brother of Walter Kelly.

Grace Kelly (1928-1982), stage actress-turned movie star-turned Princess of Monaco, niece of George Kelly.

MacKaye: Steele MacKaye (1842-1894), innovative nineteenth-century playwright, actor-manager, and educator.

Percy MacKaye (1875-1956), playwright of unusual plays and forerunner of the non-commercial theatre, son of Steele MacKaye.

Marx: Chico (b. Leonard) Marx (1886-1961), eldest of performing comic Marx Brothers of vaudeville, Broadway, and film.

Harpo (b. Arthur) Marx (1888-1964), silent, harp-playing brother of the team.

Groucho (b. Julius) Marx (1890-1977), wise-cracking member of the Marx Brothers, later popular on radio and television.

Gummo (b. Milton) Marx (1893-1977), brother performer in vaudeville, later a successful theatrical agent.

Zeppo (b. Herbert) Marx (1901-1979), occasional straight man in the celebrated comedy team of brothers.

Al Shean (1868-1949), member of the renowned vaudeville comedy team of Gallagher and Shean, brother to Minnie Marx and uncle to her children, the five Marx brothers.

Miller: Henry Miller (1859-1926), versatile actor and sometime producer-director who built his own theatre.

Gilbert Miller (1884-1969), successful producer of plays in New York and London from the 1920s through the 1950s, son of Henry Miller.

Minnelli: Vincente Minnelli (1903-1986), imaginative director and designer on Broadway, later a successful film director.

Judy Garland (1922-1969), vaudeville performer-turned movie star with infrequent Broadway concert appearances, wife of Vincente Minnelli.

Liza Minnelli (1946-), popular Broadway, concert, and film actress-singer, daughter of Vincente Minnelli and Judy Garland.

O'Neill: James O'Neill (1847-1920), classical actor, later a famous matinee idol on Broadway and on tour.

Eugene O'Neill (1888-1953), America's most experimental and accomplished playwright, son of James O'Neill.

Perkins: Osgood Perkins (1892-1937), versatile character actor on Broadway, best remembered for *The Front Page*.

Anthony Perkins (1932-1992), distinctive actor on Broadway and in films, son of Osgood Perkins.

Plummer: Christopher Plummer (1929-), Canadian-born classical actor on Broadway and in films.

Tammy Grimes (1934-), gravel-voiced actress popular in musicals, plays, and the classics, wife of Christopher Plummer.

Amanda Plummer (1957-), unusual leading lady in films and on Broadway, daughter of Christopher Plummer and Tammy Grimes.

Power: Tyrone Power (1797-1841), Irish-born actor popular in America for his character roles on stage.

Tyrone Power (1869-1931), versatile character actor on Broadway, grandson of the above.

Tyrone Power (1913-1958), dashing leading man on stage who spent most of his career in films, grandson of the above.

Shubert: Lee Shubert (1873?-1953), theatrical producer and theatre owner, head of the Shubert Brothers' nationwide empire.

Sam S. Shubert (1876?-1905), financial manager of the Shubert monopoly, brother of Lee and J. J. Shubert.

J. J. Shubert (1878?-1963), partner in the Shubert empire who specialized in producing musicals and operettas, brother of Lee and Sam Shubert.

Skinner: Otis Skinner (1858-1942), dashing leading man known for exotic roles in *Kismet, Blood and Sand* and other plays.

Cornelia Otis Skinner (1901-1979), author, playwright, and actress most known for her phenomenal one-woman shows, daughter of Otis Skinner.

Smith: Harry B. Smith (1860-1936), Broadway's most prolific lyricist and librettist, author of Broadway musicals and operettas.

Robert B. Smith (1875-1951), Broadway librettist and lyricist, brother of Harry B. Smith.

Sothern: E. A. Sothern (1826-1881), popular comic actor in the mid-nineteenth century.

E. H. Sothern (1859-1933), accomplished Shakespearean actor, son of E. A. Sothern.

Wallack: Henry Wallack (1790-1870), British-born actor on stage in New York, Philadelphia, and Baltimore.

James Wallack (1794-1864), actor-manager who led America's most accomplished theatre company of the nineteenth century, brother of Henry Wallack.

James William Wallack, Jr. (1818-1873), popular tragic actor in New York and on national tours, son of Henry Wallack.

Lester Wallack (1819-1888), producer and dashing leading man in classical and contemporary plays, son of James William Wallack.

UNUSUAL THEATRE TERMS

Every profession has its own distinct jargon and theatre is no different. Here are some less familiar theatre terms from the past, some of which are still used, others rather archaic.

aisle sitters American slang for a newspaper drama critic. Back when critics had strict deadlines to submit copy for New York's many daily papers, they were usually issued aisle seats so that they could make a quick getaway at the end of the play. It also suggested an advantageous place to sit if the play was dull and one wanted to unobtrusively leave during a break in the action.

angels Since the 1920s, a term for a financial backer of a play. Originally the expression referred to an investor in a political campaign. But theatre started using the term and it is rarely heard in political jargon today.

Annie Oakley A complimentary ticket or pass to a play. An expression not used much today, the free ticket was probably named after the famous sharpshooter because the holes punched in the ticket resembled bullet holes.

balloon Actors' slang meaning to forget one's lines. A similar expression is to "go up" on lines.

The Big Four A term of respect and admiration during the nineteenth century for the four stars of Daly's Theatre: John Drew, James Lewis, Ada Rehan and Mrs. G. H. Gilbert.

blood and thunder A slang term for a melodrama, especially the lurid and sensational types common in the mid-1800s.

boffo Journalists' slang for a hit play. The word is probably some kind of abbreviation for "box office."

chew the scenery To overact. The expression has uncertain origins but the phrase to "chew up" scenery was popularized by Dorothy Parker who, in a 1930 review, wrote that an actor was "more glutton than artist . . . he commences to chew up the scenery."

claptrap A cheap or overused ruse to get applause from an audience.

count the house When an actor stares out into an audience while on stage. While it does not mean the actor is actually counting bodies in the seats, the effect seems to suggest it.

daddy Slang for a stage manager.

deadwood The tickets left unsold in the box office after the performance.

do you recognize the profession? An old-fashioned way actors used to ask at the box office for a free ticket.

don't call us, we'll call you A popular phrase for not-so-subtle rejection. It probably originated soon after the popular use of the telephone but in the 1940s directors first found it a terse way of getting rid of unwanted auditionees.

double in brass An archaic term for an actor who also plays an instrument in the orchestra. Unions put a stop to that; today it means playing two roles in the same production.

dress the house A box office term for leaving empty seats between patrons when you sell tickets so that the audience will seem to be larger than it really is.

fake An actor's term for ad libbing on stage, usually to cover a mistake or mishap.

George Spelvin A fictitious name used in a program or in billing to disguise the true identity of an actor. Sometimes an actor who plays two roles in a play will use "George Spelvin" for the lesser role. Actors working illegally (an Equity actor in a non-Equity production) will sometimes use the name as well. Producers sometimes use George Spelvin for a role that does not exist, such as the supporting characters in *Sleuth*. The female equivalent is Georgina Spelvin and in England they use Walter Plinge.

ghost Slang for the theatre's treasurer. The expression "the ghost walks" means to get paid.

go to Cain's Old-fashioned way of saying a play has closed. For over fifty years, Cain's Warehouse bought scenery from closed shows and sold or rented it to road companies.

The Great White Way A trite and archaic expression for the street Broadway and, indirectly, the theatre business. The term originated in the late 1890s when electric light was first used on the exteriors of the theatres. Today the phrase is usually used in a mocking way.

green room A backstage room where actors wait before going onstage. There are many theories of where the expression came from and why the color green, none of them fully satisfactory. It is likely the term is simply derived from "scene room."

green umbrella A seldom used term for a prop or gesture or other hook that an actor uses to discover his characterization of a role. The term originated with the actor Alfred Lunt who struggled to find the key to playing Henry Higgins in a *Pygmalion* tour until he decided that the character would carry a green umbrella.

handcuffed Slang for an audience that is hesitant to applaud a play. A similar expression meaning the same thing is "to sit on one's hands."

hold up the scenery Demeaning term for what actors with small roles are expected to do onstage. They do not literally hold up scenery but they may as well for all their role has to offer them.

Joe Blatz Slang for an average, all-American theatregoer. George M. Cohan originated the phrase, saying he wrote all his shows with a Joe Blatz in mind.

lay an egg Show business term for failure. For actors it usually means to say a funny line and not get any response from the audience.

milestone When a production reaches its one hundredth performance. In today's theatrical economy, that hardly means a hit; but it used to be quite a feat.

nut The amount of money it takes to keep a show on the boards for one week. If a play earns as much as its weekly running costs, it is said to "make the nut." The expression probably goes back hundreds of years to when traveling players toured small towns. The sheriff (or sometimes the innkeeper) would remove the axle nut from the troupe's wagon and not return it until all the bills were paid.

paper the house Box office slang for giving out free passes so the theatre does not look so empty to the spectators who paid for their tickets. Papering the house on opening night, for example, is common practice.

peanut gallery Originally the cheap seats in a theatre, often a second balcony. The more uncouth patrons would sit there and throw peanuts at the actors if they were not enjoying the show. Since the 1950s TV show *Howdy Doody*, the term has come to mean an audience of children.

resting A euphemism used by actors to say that they are unemployed at the moment. Similar expressions include "to be between engagements" or being "at liberty."

Rialto An old-fashioned name for the theatre district in New York. The original Rialto was the business district in Venice. Shakespeare originated the phrase "news from the Rialto" in *The Merchant of Venice* and the expression was often used in reference to theatre news.

send in the clowns An old expression meaning to keep the show going even though something has gone wrong. It originated in the circus where clowns were sent in to amuse the crowd if an accident or mishap occurred. Because of the popular Stephen Sondheim song "Send in the Clowns," it now means something more wistful or resigned.

straw-hat theatre Because fashion called for straw hats in the summer months, especially in rural areas where vacationing was popular, summer stock theatre became known as straw-hat theatre around the turn of the century. To "do the straw-hat circuit" still means to tour a show at various summer theatres.

subway circuit A slang expression for touring productions of Broadway shows that played in theatres in the other boroughs after the Manhattan run. The policy ceased in the 1950s and the term became obscure.

tab shows Touring shows that hit the smaller towns and even the carnival circuit were labeled tabs. They were usually cut-down versions of an original Broadway musical or revue but sometimes tabs were original works. After film came in, the term was used to describe short, live entertainment pieces that were performed in movie houses as part of the film program.

Ten-Twent'-Thirt' Slang for a show that charged thirty cents for the best seats, twenty for the medium seats and only a dime for the cheap seats. It could refer to an inexpensive tour that played in poor neighborhoods or a local theatre with low prices.

Tin Pan Alley While this term referred to the music publishing business in America, it was specifically a group of music publishers' offices situated on a few blocks of 28th Street around Fifth Avenue and Broadway. The name derived from the tinny sound coming from the offices as song pluggers played new songs for salesmen and distributors.

turkey The widely used theatrical expression for a deserved Broadway flop. The term probably originated from the old practice of a producer opening a show he knew was awful around Thanksgiving time, hoping to benefit from the early Christmas box office rush for entertainment.

winging it This popular expression, that today means to improvise on the spot and deal with the situation as it occurs, comes from the nineteenth-century repertory theatre when actors had to learn roles very quickly and often opened with little or no rehearsal. This practice forced actors to sometimes tack up written lines in the wings so they could study them before each scene.

THEATRE CRITICS

Theatre criticism, as we know it today, originated in Restoration England. Written theatre critiques were printed in American publications from the earliest days of play production. Newspaper criticism was thinly disguised advertising at first but by the early 1800s some reputable critics emerged. By the turn of the century, when New York City boasted many daily newspapers and weekly publications, theatre criticism flourished. Today, with only a few papers left and with less opportunity to develop their craft because of fewer productions, drama critics are often more powerful than their background warrants. Here are some of the notable theatre critics from the print media over the years.

Kelcey Allen (1875-1951) was the long-time critic for the New York *Clipper, Women's Wear Daily,* and the *Daily News Record*, reviewing Broadway when he was only 18 years old and attending over 6,000 opening nights before he retired.

John Anderson (1896-1943) reviewed for the New York *Evening Post* and *Journal American*, as well as writing several books on theatre.

Brooks Atkinson (1894-1984) was the dean of American theatre critics, reviewing plays for the New York *Times* from 1924 to 1960. An astute yet gentle critic, he also wrote some distinguished books on theatre.

Clive Barnes (1927-) is a British-born dance critic who became the drama critic for the New York *Times* in 1967 amidst much controversy. For the next ten years he was the most powerful reviewer in America, then he moved to the New York *Post* where he still writes theatre reviews.

Robert Benchley (1889-1945) is still widely read for his delightful humorous pieces but he was also a well-read theatre critic for *Life* throughout the 1920s and for *The New Yorker* throughout the 1930s.

Whitney Bolton (1900-1969) was drama critic for the New York *Herald Tribune* and the *Morning Telegraph* in the 1920s and 1930s before going to Hollywood where he scripted several movies. He rejoined the *Telegraph* in 1949.

Heywood Broun (1888-1939) was a clever and direct theatre reviewer for the New York *World* and *Vanity Fair* in the 1920s and a popular wit on the lecture circuit.

John Mason Brown (1900-1969) was a much-respected author of books on drama and an editor of *Theatre Arts Monthly* but he also wrote drama reviews for such publications as the *Evening Post, World-Telegram*, and the *Saturday Review of Literature*.

T. Allston Brown (1836-1918) was a theatre manager who also was drama editor of the New York *Clipper* and the author of several books on the history of the American theatre.

Claudia Cassidy (1900-1996) was a severe but knowledgeable drama critic for the Chicago *Sun* and *Tribune* throughout the 1940s and 1950s until 1965. Her continual criticisms of third-rate theatre did much to stop Broadway producers from sending inferior touring productions to the Midwest.

John Chapman (1900-1972) was drama editor and reviewed plays for the New York *Daily News* from 1929 through 1971. He edited the *Best Plays* from 1947 to 1952.

Henry Austin Clapp (1841-1904) was a drama critic based in Boston where he wrote for the *Advertiser* and the *Herald*, but his incisive writing appeared in several New York papers and he was also a Shakespeare scholar and popular lecturer.

Richard Coe (1916-1995), who reviewed theatre for the Washington *Post* from 1936 to 1981, was one of the most influential critics outside of New York City and his opinions and suggestions were so useful they were actually sought out by producers.

Edward A. Dithmar (1854-1917) started as a theatre critic at the *Evening Post* but in 1876 became the reviewer for the *Times* where his "impressionistic" way of reviewing a play was read for the next thirty years.

Gilbert Wolf Gabriel (1890-1952) was a magazine writer, playwright, and drama critic for the *New York American* and *Cue Magazine*.

John Gassner (1903-1967) is remembered today as the respected teacher and editor of many books on world drama but he also served as drama critic on such magazines as *Time*, *New Theatre Magazine*, *Forum*, and *Direction*.

Jack Gaver (1902-1974), a drama critic and author, reviewed for the United Press International for over thirty years starting in 1929.

Wolcott Gibbs (1902-1958) was *The New Yorker*'s drama critic from 1939 until his death, writing intelligent and revealing reviews in the magazine's witty style. He also wrote the successful comedy *Season in the Sun* (1950).

Rosamond Gilder (1891-1986) was a talented writer who sat on the boards of many theatre organizations, such as the Federal Theatre Project and ANTA, and she edited and reviewed plays for *Theatre Arts Magazine* for over twenty years.

Percy Hammond (1873-1936) was a Chicago newspaper critic who became the reviewer for the New York *Tribune* (later *Herald Tribune*) in 1921. His homey and unacademic observations were widely read for the next fifteen years.

Henry Hewes (1917-) reviewed drama for the *Saturday Review* for many years, as well editing the *Best Plays* and working on regional theatre productions.

William Dean Howells (1837-1920) was a distinguished man of letters who wrote many plays, few of them successes. But his writing about theatre helped bring attention to several emerging American playwrights.

J. W. S. Hows (1841-1926) was a widely read theatre critic for the *Albion* and he wrote several books on drama and poetry.

James Huneker (1859?-1921) was a farsighted music then drama critic who championed the causes of Ibsen and Shaw in his writings for the New York *Sun* and *Times*.

Lawrence Hutton (1843-1904) was a drama critic for the New York *Evening Mail* in the 1870s and later, as literary editor of *Harper's Magazine*, did much to develop interest in American theatre history.

Washington Irving (1783-1859), the early American master of short stories, biographies, and histories, co-authored plays, mostly unsuccessful, and his works were often dramatized by others, mostly successfully. But it was Irving's letters, articles, and contemporary accounts of actors and plays that make him an early and valuable American drama critic.

Edith Isaacs (1878-1956) reviewed drama for *Ainslee's Magzine* in the 1910s and edited some important theatre books, but she was most influential as editor of *Theatre Arts* magazine from 1918 to 1946, making it the premiere theatre publication of this century.

Walter Kerr (1913-1996), one of America's most famous critics and the author of several books about the theatre, was one of the few theatre critics to be actively involved in writing, producing, and directing plays. Kerr served as theatre reviewer for *Commonweal*, the *Herald Tribune*, and the *Times*.

Louis Kronenberger (1904-1980) was *Time* magazine's drama critic from 1938 to 1961, also writing for the newspaper *PM* in the 1940s. He was an editor for *Fortune* magazine and a handful of other publications. He edited the *Best Plays* from 1952 to 1961.

Richard Lockridge (1898-1982) was the drama critic at the New York *Sun* throughout the 1920s and 1930s. He was also a successful novelist, writing the Mr. and Mrs. North books with his wife Frances Lockridge.

Burns Mantle (1873-1948) was a drama critic from Denver and Chicago newspapers who reviewed Broadway for the *Evening Mail* and the *Daily News* for many years. He is most remembered as the founder and, from 1919 to 1947, editor of the *Best Plays* series that still chronicles theatre activities in New York and elsewhere.

John McClain (1904-1967) was a screenwriter who, at various times in his career, was drama critic for the New York *Sun* and the *Journal American*.

Ward Morehouse (1899-1966) wrote several books and plays but was most known as the drama critic for the Newhouse newspapers in the 1950s.

Hobe Morrison (1904-) started as a drama writer for newspapers in Philadelpia before joining *Variety* in 1937 where he reviewed plays for over forty years.

George Jean Nathan (1882-1958) was a much-respected but sometimes cruel critic and champion for new American dramatists such as Eugene O'Neill and William Saroyan. In addition to writing several books and co-editing with H. L. Menken *The Smart Set* and *The American Mercury*, Nathan reviewed plays for *Vanity Fair*, *The Saturday Review of Literature*, *The Bohemian* and others. Before his death, Nathan established the George Jean Nathan Award that is still given to authors of superior theatre criticism.

Elliott Norton (1903-) was the longtime Boston drama critic who wrote for the Boston *Post* and the *Record American* (later the *Herald American*). For nearly fifty years Norton was one of the most respected and intelligent critics outside of New York City.

Dorothy Parker (1893-1967), the caustic American wit, poet, and short story writer, was a frequent and much-quoted drama critic for *The New Yorker* for several years.

Henry Taylor Parker (1867-1934) was a New York and Boston critic who was greatly respected for his in-depth reviews of plays. He wrote for the Boston *Transcript* and the New York *Globe*.

Frank Rich (1949-), the controversial drama critic for the New York *Times* in the 1980s, was the most powerful critical voice on Broadway and, consequently, much reviled by theatre people and even other critics. He was known to strongly promote shows that he liked and his writing was often intelligent.

Sime Silverman (1873-1933) was a critic for the New York *Daily American* and *Morning Telegraph* before founding *Variety* in 1905 and editing it until his death.

Ashton Stevens (1872-1951) was one of Chicago's most outspoken and influential theatre critics, writing for the Chicago *Herald* and *Examiner* from 1910 to his death forty-one years later.

Howard Taubman (1907-1996) was a theatre and music editor and reviewer for the New York *Times* from the 1930s through the 1960s. He also wrote books on music.

J. Rankin Towse (1854-1933) was a conservative drama critic who wrote for the New York *Evening Post* for over fifty years, condemning the new American works at the turn of the century and wishing for the return of the old stock companies of the mid-1800s.

Richard Watts, Jr. (1898-1981) was a drama critic who reviewed for the *Herald-Tribune* and the New York *Post* during a newspaper career that lasted sixty years.

A. C. Wheeler (1835-1903) was a drama critic and sometime playwright who wrote for the New York *World*, *Leader*, *Sun*, and the young *Times* under such bizarre pseudonyms as "Trinculo" and "Nym Crinkle."

William Winter (1836-1917) wielded more power than any other New York theatre critic in the last four decades of the nineteenth century. Writing for the *Albion* and then the *Tribune* for over forty years, Winter was a perceptive critic and a champion of David Belasco and other emerging American writers. But as Ibsen-like realism started to be produced, he ranted and condemned the new form and its American imitators.

Alexander Woollcott (1887-1943) is remembered as the colorful wit of the Algonquin Round Table, a radio favorite and the inspiration for *The Man*

Who Came to Dinner; but he was also a longtime critic for the New York *Times*, *Herald*, *Sun*, and *World*. Woollcott was a controversial critic in his younger days, a sentimental caricature in his later years.

Stark Young (1881-1963), a noted translator and author of theatre books, served as drama critic on such papers as the *New Republic*, the New York *Times*, and *Theatre Arts* magazine.

HISTORIC THEATRES ACROSS THE COUNTRY

There are over forty operating playhouses across the country that have been designated as "historic" by the League of Historic American Theatres, an organization founded in 1977 to preserve and protect old theatres that have historical and architectural significance. Add to that the many historic theatres no longer with us and one realizes the breadth of fine old theatres outside of New York that this country has possessed. Here is a selection of some of the more notable American historic theatres across the country, some from long gone and others still operating today.

Arch Street Theatre (Philadelphia) Built in 1828 when Philadelphia theatre was thriving enough to support several playhouses, the Arch Street Theatre has seen perhaps more great actors and managers than any theatre outside of New York. Its managers have included William Forrest (who brought his brother Edwin Forrest for many engagements), William Burton, William Wheatley and, most famous of all, Mrs. John Drew whose stock company remained at the Arch Street for thirty-one years. This was the home of the celebrated Drew-Barrymore clan and their productions rivaled any to be found in the nation. The grand old playhouse was demolished in 1936.

Baldwin Theatre (San Francisco) The finest touring house on the West Coast, this theatre opened in 1875 and saw most major national tours on its stage until it burnt down in 1898. Gambler Elias Jackson "Lucky" Baldwin built the theatre on Market Street and three years later built a hotel around it that encompassed a whole city block. The playhouse never housed a resident company but its temporary tenants were the best in American theatre.

Bella Union (San Francisco) This theatre-saloon-gambling house, built in 1849 on Portsmouth Square, had a reputation for being a rough house from the first opening night when an audience member died in a shootout after the show. But audiences loved going to the "Belly Union" even after gambling was outlawed in 1856. After a few fires and being rebuilt each time, the theatre became a museum in 1895 and then was destroyed one final time in the earthquake of 1906.

Boston Museum (Boston) The cultured name for this theatre was necessary in order for the Puritanical Bostonians to attend a play without go to a playhouse. In reality, the 1841 theatre housed one of the finest resident companies in the country and offered quality theatre there until it closed in 1893.

California Theatre (San Francisco)   Two different playhouses named the California Theatre stood on Bush Street at different times. The first theatre was built in 1869 to provide a home for the popular actors John McCullough and Lawrence Barrett and soon a first-class resident company developed that was considered by some as the best away from the East Coast. When that playhouse was demolished in 1888, another with the same name was built on the same site and, though no equal to the original's company, housed quality theatre until it was destroyed in the 1906 earthquake.

Chestnut Street Theatre (Philadelphia)   This lovely theatre, copied from the plans of the Theatre Royal in Bath, England, was called the New Theatre when it opened in 1793. By the next year a full season of plays was offered and it soon became the leading theatre in Philadelphia, housing the finest plays and players of the day. In 1816 it was the first American theatre to install gas lighting. By the middle of the century, the theatre was suffering from competition and, after a few fires and rebuilding, was eventually demolished in 1913.

Dock Street Theatre (Charleston, South Carolina)   One of the earliest pemanent theatres in America, the Dock Street has sketchy records and long periods of mystery. It opened in 1736 and operated until 1749 when it was sold and remained inactive for some time. It is thought the building burned and was rebuilt twice but documents are incomplete. We do know that a theatre on that location was restored by the Federal Works Administration in 1937.

Elitch's Gardens Theatre (Denver)   This lovely theatre set amidst thirty-two acres of gardens is America's oldest operating summer theatre. Actor John Elitch planned the wooden, octagonal theatre but died before its completion in 1890. Since that time it has housed vaudeville, touring companies, and its own stock company.

Federal Street Theatre (Boston)   A handsome playhouse designed by famed architect Charles Bulfinch in 1794, this theatre (also called the Boston Theatre during its long history) was Boston's first permanent theatre. For thirty years it was Boston's premiere playhouse and survived until the 1870s.

Folger Shakespeare Memorial Library (Washington, DC)   Inside this 1932 library built by oil magnate Henry Clay Folger lies a reasonable facsimile of the Globe Theatre that is still used for performances. For a time it housed a resident company called Shakespeare Theatre at the Folger.

Ford's Theatre (Washington, DC)   One of America's most famous theatres because it is the site of Lincoln's assassination in 1865, Ford's Theatre has had more than its fair share of misfortunes but still survives as a lovely playhouse. John T. Ford converted a church on the site into a playhouse in 1861. It burned down a year later but Ford rebuilt it, enlarging the house to 1,700 seats, and reopened it as the New Ford's Theatre in 1863. The War Office closed the theatre after the assassination and converted the building into offices, only to have disaster strike again in the 1870s when parts of the structure collapsed and several government employees died. For nearly a century the building was empty until 1968, after a three-year restoration, it reopened as an operating theatre. Elegant and comfortable with only 741 seats, Ford's Theatre has been in use regularly since then.

Goodspeed Opera House (East Haddam, Connecticut) A Victorian Gothic playhouse built in 1876 by William H. Goodspeed as a local theatre, this gem from the past is an excellent example of an old theatre doing new and exciting things. The playhouse flourished until 1920 when it was closed and ignored for forty years. When it was slated for demolition, concerned citizens saved the Goodspeed, restored it to its original glamour and opened it in 1963 as an operating theatre. Since then it has housed revivals of old plays and musicals and originated new ones, some of which have gone on to Broadway.

Hedgerow Theatre (Moylan, Pennsylvania) Set in a converted mill near Philadelphia, the Hedgerow opened in 1923 as the home of a resident repertory company that flourished until 1956, even boasting a first-class theatre school. The school remains and the theatre still houses a summer theatre.

Holliday Street Theatre (Baltimore) Sometimes called the New Theatre or the Baltimore Theatre, locals always referred to this 1794 playhouse as the "Holliday" after its address. The original wooden structure was replaced by brick in 1813 and it was here that the "Star Spangled Banner" received its first public performance in 1819. Burned and rebuilt in the 1870s, the Holliday remained a leading playhouse until it was finally demolished in 1917.

Howard Athenaeum (Boston) While the Boston Museum was the home to renowned stock companies, this venerable playhouse, converted from a church in 1846, saw the great touring productions for the next twenty-five years. In the 1870s it went from a vaudeville theatre to a burlesque house in the 1920s. Plans to restore the old theatre were scuttled when it burned down in 1960.

National Theatre (Washington, DC) When the National Theatre was built on E Street in 1835 it was the first legitimate theatre to be built in our nation's capital. Since then five different theatres, all called the National, have stood on roughly the same spot. Perhaps the most beautiful of the Nationals was one designed by J. B. McElfatrick in 1885 and operated until it burned in 1922, the year the current theatre was built.

St. Louis Municipal Outdoor Theatre (St. Louis) One of the largest outdoor theatres in the world, the "Muny" (as the locals call it) is a large amphitheatre built in 1919 to stage operettas in the summer months. Today musicals are the usual fare in the 12,000-seat theatre.

Southwark Theatre (Philadelphia) America's first permanent theatre building, the South Street Theatre, as locals often called it, was a 1766 brick structure lit by oil. *The Prince of Parthia* (1767), the first professionally produced American play, was done here, as well as many pioneering productions of the eighteenth century. In 1821 the Southwark ceased to function as a theatre and in 1912 it was demolished.

Tivoli Opera House (San Francisco) One of the first theatres built to house musical theatre, the Tivoli started as a beer garden in the early 1870s that featured musical shows. The idea caught on and a bigger theatre was built in 1878, providing a home for early American musicals until it burned in the 1906 earthquake.

Walnut Street Theatre (Philadelphia) This venerable 1811 playhouse is the oldest operating theatre in America today. Built as a circus, it soon converted to plays and saw the great stars and companies that vied for the public in Philadelphia in its heyday. For decades it was a major touring house and today it houses a regional theatre company.

REGIONAL THEATRES

There are hundreds of professional, semi-professional, and community theatres operating across the country. In many ways this network of playhouses, producing new works and revivals, is our national theatre. Here are some of the most notable professional theatre companies outside of New York.

Actors Theatre of Louisville (Kentucky) A professional resident company since it was founded in 1964, the ATL has a reputation for finding exciting new plays, several of which went on to Broadway and Pulitzer Prizes. Artistic director Jon Jory has been the creative force behind the theatre company since 1969.

Alley Theatre (Houston) Nina Vance was the powerhouse producer who guided this amateur group from its 1947 beginnings to a landmark theatre instigating the post-war regional theatre movement. The company went professional in 1954.

American Conservatory Theatre (San Francisco) This company, founded by William Ball in Pittsburgh in 1964, moved a few times before settling at the Geary Theatre in San Francisco. The company is one of the few in North America that performs in true repertory.

American Repertory Theatre (Cambridge, Massachusetts) In 1979 Robert Brustein founded this company dedicated to new plays and new approaches to classic pieces. The theatre, located at Harvard University, has a reputation for bold and controversial productions directed by non-traditionalists such as Joanne Akalaitis and Robert Wilson.

American Shakespeare Festival Theatre (Stratford, Connecticut) Founded in 1950 and housed in a replica of the original Globe, this theatre company performed Shakespeare's works in a lovely setting for over twenty years.

The theatre has had a troubled history since the 1970s and still exists on the books but few productions have been seen recently.

Arena Stage (Washington, DC)   Under the guidance of co-founder Zelda Fichandler, this company started presenting professional theatre in various locations in the capital in 1950. Since 1961 it has been housed in its three-theatre complex, which offers varied theatre productions in varied performance spaces.

Barter Theatre (Abingdon, Virginia)   Since 1932, a resident company, housed in a theatre high in the hills of Virginia, has performed a repertory of new and old plays. The theatre was founded by Robert Porterfield and in the lean Depression years tickets could be purchased with foodstuffs, hence the name Barter Theatre. In 1946 it was declared the official State Theatre of Virginia, the first company to be so recognized by a state.

Center Stage (Baltimore)   Founded in 1963 and located at its current site since 1975, Baltimore's LORT theatre has enjoyed a fine reputation for new and old plays, some of which went on to Broadway.

Cleveland Playhouse (Cleveland, Ohio)   One of America's oldest operating theatre companies, the Cleveland Playhouse was founded in 1915 and has been providing professional theatre since 1921.

Dallas Theatre Center (Texas)   A professional acting company since 1959, the Dallas Theatre Center has the distinction of performing in two theatre spaces designed by Frank Lloyd Wright, the only playhouses he ever devised.

Eugene O'Neill Memorial Theatre (Waterford, Connecticut)   Much more than just a producing theatre, the O'Neill, founded in 1963, is also a conference center, a Eugene O'Neill research library, an instigator for workshops and seminars, and the birthplace of the National Playwrights Conference, the National Theatre of the Deaf and other institutions.

Goodman Theatre (Chicago)   Founded in 1925 as the Goodman Theatre Center of the Art Institute of Chicago, the Goodman offered productions in the Windy City until the Depression forced it to close down. The theatre was reactivated in 1969 and has been a vital producing company since then.

Guthrie Theatre (Minneapolis)   Here is a theatre that started as an idea and then went and looked for a place to build it. Co-founder Tyrone Guthrie conceived the idea of a professional repertory company outside of New York and, after careful study of statistics and a generous offer from the Walker Art Center, decided on Minneapolis. The company premiered in 1963 in a unique thrust stage theatre designed by Guthrie and Tanya Moiseiwitsch and it has been a leading regional theatre ever since.

Hartford Stage Company (Hartford, Connecticut)   This esteemed theatre company was founded in 1964 and in 1977 moved into its own thrust stage facility where, under the artistic direction of Mark Lamos, innovative productions of new and classic plays have been presented.

Kennedy Center for the Performing Arts (Washington, DC)   Conceived in 1958 as the National Cultural Center, the arts complex opened in 1971 with the late president's name as the official title and has been providing a space for theatre, opera, music, and dance ever since. Used mostly for touring shows, the Kennedy Center has developed some outstanding new productions that went on to national fame.

Long Wharf Theatre (New Haven, Connecticut) Actually situated in a warehouse near the waterfront, the Long Wharf has been presenting quality revivals and new plays since 1965. Under the artistic direction of Arvin Brown since 1967, the theatre has sent several of its productions to Broadway and Off Broadway.

Mark Taper Forum Theatre (Los Angeles) This professional company, housed in a very modern arts complex that opened in 1967, has premiered many plays, some of which have gone on to additional success elsewhere. Gordon Davidsdon is the guiding hand behind the company, which also presents plays in two other locations in the Los Angeles area.

McCarter Theatre Company (Princeton, New Jersey) Emily Mann has kept this theatre company in the forefront of regional theatres with her experimental productions of new scripts and reconsidered classics. The McCarter company, founded in 1960, was the first professional theatre in the country to be under the jurisdiction of a university.

National Theatre of the Deaf (Chester, Connecticut) Primarily a touring company, this internationally acclaimed institution using deaf and speaking actors began at the Eugene O'Neill Center in 1966.

Old Globe Theatre (San Diego) This theatre organization goes back to 1937 and today is a major professional company operating year around in two theatre spaces. Classics, new works, and musicals have all flourished here, some of them moving successfully to Broadway.

Oregon Shakespearian Festival (Ashland, Oregon) One of the oldest Shakespeare producing companies in the world, this theatre has been presenting the Bard's productions in an outdoor setting since 1935. Today it operates three theatres and offers non-Shakespearean plays as well.

Pasadena Community Playhouse (Pasadena, California) Founded in 1918 and eventually building its own theatre, this amateur theatre company had a national reputation for exciting revivals and new plays, as well as a famous school. The company fell apart in the late 1960s but reopened as the Pasadena Playhouse in 1986.

Pittsburgh Playhouse (Pittsburgh, Pennsylvania) Serving Western Pennsylvania since 1933, this amateur theatre was known throughout the country for its professional-like productions, often using New York directors and guest actors. In the 1960s it faltered, was briefly a professional company, then returned under the ownership of Point Park College. Today it offers a mixture of professional and educational theatre.

Steppenwolf Theatre Company (Chicago) Since 1976 this adventurous group has presented difficult plays in excellent productions, developing along the way several actors and directors who later reached national prominence.

Trinity Square Repertory Company (Providence, Rhode Island) One of the finest repertory companies in the country, the Trinity Square was started in 1964 and for many years was under the artistic direction of Adrian Hall.

Yale Repertory Theatre (New Haven, Connecticut) An outgrowth of the Yale School of Drama, this professional theatre founded by Robert Brustein in 1966 has introduced several outstanding directors, actors, and playwrights over the years. Its subsequent artistic directors have been Lloyd Richards and Stan Wojewodski, Jr.

While they are not resident companies as such, the drama clubs at certain universities have been producing theatre for many decades. Many of these academic theatre groups have been presenting plays longer than any regional professional company. Here are the most famous of these university groups.

Harvard Dramatic Club (Harvard University) Founded in 1908 to showcase plays written by students and alumni, this theatre group expanded its repertory in 1917 to include the classics and new foreign plays. Recently the group joined Radcliffe's dramatic club and, working with the American Repertory Theatre, still presents productions.

Hasty Pudding Club (Harvard University) One of the oldest performing troupes in the country, this social club founded in 1795 presented mock trials for the first decades of its existence, then moved into more traditional theatricals in the 1850s. Since 1884 the presentations have been original musical spoofs and over the years many future dramatists got their start in Hasty Pudding shows. The club continues the tradition of men playing the female roles even though Harvard is co-ed today.

Mask and Wig Club (University of Pennsylvania) A quaint old Philadelphia clubhouse/theatre still houses this annual musical spoof written and performed by male students. The club was founded in 1889 and still takes its productions on tour.

Triangle Club (Princeton University) Begun in 1888 as the Princeton Dramatic Association, this social-theatrical club started producing original musicals in 1890 and three years later changed its name to the Triangle Club. A handful of the members over the years went on to fame in theatre and literature.

While the complete selection of regional theatres currently operating is too long to mention, no less describe, here is a representative list that hints at the breadth of theatre in America today.

Actor's Express (Atlanta)
Alabama Shakespeare Festival (Montgomery)

Alliance Theatre Company (Atlanta)
American Music Theatre Festival (Philadelphia)
American Stage Festival (Milford, New Hampshire)
American Theatre Company (Tulsa, Oklahoma)
Antenna Theatre (Sausalito, California)
Arizona Theatre Company (Tuscon)
Arkansas Repertory Theatre (Little Rock)
Asolo Theatre Company (Sarasota, Florida)
Bailiwick Repertory (Chicago)
Berkeley (California) Repertory Theatre
Berkshire Theatre Festival (Stockbridge, Massachusetts)
Birmingham (Alabama) Children's Theatre
Boarshead: Michigan Public Theatre (Lansing)
California Theatre Center (Sunnyvale)
Capital Repertory Company (Albany, New York)
The Children's Theatre Company (Minneapolis)
Childsplay, Inc. (Tempe, Arizona)
City Theatre Company (Pittsburgh)
Cincinnati Playhouse in the Park
Clarence Brown Theatre Company (Knoxville, Tennessee)
Coconut Grove Playhouse (Miami)
The Colony Studio Theatre (Los Angeles)
A Contemporary Theatre (Seattle)
Cornerstone Theatre Company (Santa Monica, California)
Court Theatre (Chicago)
Creede (Colorado) Repertory Theatre
Crossroads Theatre Company (New Brunswick, New Jersey)
Delaware Theatre Company (Wilmington)
Denver Theatre Center Company
Detroit Repertory Theatre
East West Players (Los Angeles)
The Empty Space Theatre (Seattle)
Ensemble Theatre of Cincinnati
Eureka Theatre Company (San Francisco)
Florida Studio Theatre (Sarasota)
Fulton Theatre Company (Lancaster, Pennsylvania)
George Street Playhouse (New Brunswick, New Jersey)
Geva Theatre (Rochester, New York)
Goodspeed Opera House (East Haddam, Connecticut)
Great Lakes Theatre Festival (Cleveland)
Honolulu Theatre for Youth
Huntington Theatre Company (Boston)
Illusion Theatre (Minneapolis)
Indiana Repertory Theatre (Indianapolis)
Intiman Theatre Company (Seattle)
La Jolla (California) Playhouse
Madison (Wisconsin) Repertory Theatre

Magic Theatre (San Francisco)
Meadow Brook Theatre (Rochester, Michigan)
Merrimack Repertory Theatre (Lowell, Massachusetts)
Metro Theatre Company (St. Louis)
Milwaukee Repertory Theatre
Missouri Repertory Theatre (Kansas City)
Mixed Blood Theatre Company (Minneapolis)
Nebraska Repertory Theatre (Lincoln)
New American Theatre (Rockford, Illinois)
New Jersey Shakespeare Festival (Madison)
New Stage Theatre (Jackson, Mississippi)
Odyssey Theatre Ensemble (Los Angeles)
Olney (Maryland) Theatre
Omaha Magic Theatre
Paper Mill Playhouse (Millburn, New Jersey)
Pegasus Players (Chicago)
Pennsylvania Stage Company (Allentown)
People's Light and Theatre Company (Malvern, Pennsylvania)
Perseverance Theatre (Douglas, Alaska)
Philadelphia Drama Guild
Philadelphia Festival Theatre for New Plays
The Philadelphia Theatre Company
Phoenix (Arizona) Theatre
Pioneer Theatre Company (Salt Lake City)
Pittsburgh Public Theatre
Playhouse on the Square (Memphis)
Playmakers Repertory Company (Chapel Hill, North Carolina)
Portland (Oregon) Repertory Theatre
Portland (Oregon) Stage Center
Portland (Maine) Stage Company
Remains Theatre (Chicago)
The Repertory Theatre of St. Louis
Round House Theatre (Silver Spring, Maryland)
Sacramento (California) Theatre Company
San Diego (California) Repertory Theatre
San Jose (California) Repertory Theatre
Santa Monica (California) Playhouse
Seattle Children's Theatre
Seattle Repertory Company
Shakespeare and Company (Lenox, Massachusetts)
The Shakespeare Tavern (Atlanta)
The Shakespeare Theatre (Washington, DC)
Society Hill Playhouse (Philadelphia)
Source Theatre Company (Washington, DC)
South Coast Repertory (Costa Mesa, California)
St. Louis Black Repertory Company
Stage One: The Louisville Children's Theatre

Stage West (Fort Worth, Texas)
Stagewest (Springfield, Massachusetts)
Stamford (Connecticut) Theatre Works
Studio Arena Theatre (Buffalo, New York)
The Studio Theatre (Washington, DC)
Syracuse Stage
Tennessee Repertory Theatre (Nashville)
Unicorn Theatre (Kansas City, Missouri)
Victory Gardens Theatre (Chicago)
Virginia Stage Company (Norfolk)
Walnut Street Theatre Company (Philadelphia)
Williamstown (Massachusetts) Theatre Festival
Wilma Theatre (Philadelphia)
Wisdom Bridge Theatre (Chicago)
Woolly Mammoth Theatre Company (Washington, DC)

THEATRE ORGANIZATIONS

In addition to producing companies, there are many theatre organizations with many different purposes and goals. Also, there are about a dozen trade unions that are concerned with the operation of professional theatre. Here is a selected list of some of these organizations past and present.

Actors' Equity Association (AEA), perhaps the strongest union in commercial theatre today, handles contracts, working conditions, and other areas dealing with actors, singers, and dancers in the theatre. The AEA was founded in 1912 as a reaction to the miserable conditions actors found themselves in under the Theatrical Syndicate. A famous strike in 1919 proved the young union's power and it grew in importance during the New Deal in the 1930s. Today controversy still surrounds some Equity decisions and it still has more unemployed members than any other theatre union.

Actors' Fidelity Association was formed by George M. Cohan and other producers as a reaction to the actors' strike of 1919. The group attracted some distinguished actors but the majority sided with Actors' Equity and the group soon disbanded.

Actors' Fund of America is a benevolent organization dedicated to helping needy theatre professionals. The group was formed in 1881, as an American version of Britain's Actors' Benevolent Fund, and is still very active today.

American Federation of Musicians, or simply the Musicians' Union, is the organization that provides live music for each Broadway theatre, whether a musical is playing there or not. In a controversial union rule, the size of the theatre dictates the minimum number of musicians that must be hired, even if they do not perform.

American Guild of Variety Artists (AGVA) started as an organization for vaudeville performers in 1938 and soon developed into a trade union handling vaudeville, circuses, burlesque, rodeos, and so on. Today the union represents performers in nightclubs and cabarets, casinos, concert venues, ice shows, and similar specialty acts.

American National Theatre and Academy (ANTA) has been a producing agency, a theatre owner, a source for advisement and a school during its long history. Founded in 1935 by an act of Congress but never receiving funds from the government, ANTA has had an uneven history but continues to sponsor events on occasion.

American Society of Composers, Authors and Publishers (ASCAP) was founded in 1914 to protect the rights of songwriters whose work was often performed and published without any payment to its creators. Not limited to theatre music, ASCAP and its equivalent society, **Broadcast Music, Inc. (BMI)**, still count all the major songwriters as their members.

American Theatre Association (ATA) was a large organization that divided itself into separate areas for college, community, and children's theatre, as well as theatre performed at military installations. The ATA held regional and national conventions, workshops, and even a placement service before it suddenly went bankrupt in 1986.

American Theatre Critics Association (ATCA) was formed in 1974 when drama critics across the country united to uphold the standards of theatre criticism and promote quality critical writing about the drama. The ATCA gives a Tony Award each year to a regional theatre and submits a new play from the resident theatres to be cited in the annual *Best Plays* volume.

American Theatre Wing is a very active organization that sponsors seminars on theatre, provides performances for school groups, and presents the Tony Awards each year. The Wing was founded in 1939 by Rachel Crothers and a group of other women active in professional theatre. During World War Two they ran the popular Stage Door Canteen for military servicemen.

Association for the Promotion and Protection of an Independent Stage in the United States was the long-winded name of a short-lived group of actors who fought against the Theatrical Syndicate in the 1890s. Mrs. Fiske, Richard Mansfield, James O'Neill, and Helena Modjeska were among the actors who founded the organization and vowed not to perform in Syndicate theatres in an effort to break the theatre monopoly.

Association for Theatre in Higher Education (ATHE) was formed by heads of drama in colleges and universities when the American Theatre Association went bankrupt in 1986. It holds conventions annually, publishes the scholarly *Theatre Journal*, and promotes resident companies on campuses, working with the **University/Resident Theatre Association (U/RTA)**.

Association of Theatrical Press Agents and Managers (ATP-

AM) is the union, started in 1938, that handles advance press agents, publicists, house managers, and company managers.

Council of Stock Theatres (COST) and its sister agency, the **Council of Resident Stock Theatres (CORST)**, handles contracts for professional dinner theatres, stock companies, and outdoor theatres. COST deals with theatres that book touring shows or theatres that hire staff per show, whereas CORST handles theatres that hire a resident company and staff for the season.

Drama Desk sponsors discussion luncheons on different theatre topics and awards the Drama Desk Awards each year. The group was founded in 1949 and became a non-profit organization in 1974.

Dramatists Guild, Inc. is the union for playwrights, composers and lyricists that grew out of several earlier attempts to protect the rights of theatre authors. The Guild was founded as a separate entity in 1919 but did not start writing contracts for authors until 1926. The Guild today negotiates contracts, provides employment information for playwrights, and sponsors seminars and play contests.

Federal Theatre Project was America's bold and unsuccessful venture into a federally subsidized theatre program. Established by Congress in 1935 as part of the Works Progress Administration (WPA) with the intention of giving employment to theatre personnel during the Depression and providing low-cost performances for the public, the Federal Theatre was an exciting and provocative program with hundreds of productions across the country and an audience in the millions. But the left-wing nature of some of the plays displeased many conservative politicians and the project was abolished suddenly in 1939.

Institute of Outdoor Drama is an organization headquartered in Chapel Hill, North Carolina, that advises and provides services for groups that wish to pursue theatre outdoors.

International Alliance of Theatrical Stage Employees (IATSE) is the union for the carpenters, stagehands, electricians, property and sound crew in playhouses that offer professional theatre.

International Thespian Society is made up of high school theatre groups and offers conventions and conferences, as well as the monthly *Dramatics* magazine.

League of American Theatres and Producers was instituted in 1930 as a way to cut down on ticket scalping and disreputable ticket speculation, but the organization's goals grew to include theatre contracts and labor relations. The League originally concentrated on Broadway theatre (it was first called the **League of New York Theatres**) but expanded its title and scope in 1985.

League of Historic American Theatres seeks to protect and nurture historic operating theatres across the country. The League was founded in 1977 by Michael P. Price of the Goodspeed Opera House and today has some fifty member playhouses.

League of Resident Theatres (LORT) is the organization that oversees contracts and classifies the various professional regional theatres across the nation. LORT was founded in 1965 as the network of professional resident theatres was growing and a consistent basis for writing labor contracts became necessary. The sixty-some member theatres are categorized as either LORT A, LORT B, LORT C, or LORT D theatres, based on their budgets and other factors.

National Endowment for the Arts and its twin agency, the **National Endowment for the Humanities**, are Federal government-sponsored organizations that provide money for a variety of art forms as well as education, social programs, and fellowships. Like past programs that used taxpayers' money for the arts, the Endowment is often subject to political pressure and criticism from special interest groups.

Society of American Dramatists and Composers was an early effort to deal with piracy of plays and musicals in the nineteenth century and to establish minimum royalties for playwrights. Founded in 1890 by playwrights Bronson Howard and David Belasco, the Society did not last long but it did manage to exert enough pressure to have anti-piracy laws enacted.

Society of Stage Directors and Choreographers is more a bargaining group than an actual union but it does represent its members in matters of contract and setting minimum fees for directors and choreographers at professional theatres. The Society was founded in 1959, the last group of theatre professionals to organize.

Theatre Communications Group (TCG) was founded in 1961 to assist non-profit professional theatre across the country. TCG offers seminars, workshops, consulting, and job placement services, and publishes plays and a monthly magazine *American Theatre*.

Theatre Development Fund (TDF) is a non-profit organization promoting theatre in New York. TDF provides tickets to help small theatres find an audience and it runs the Costume Collection that enables non-profit and educational theatres to rent quality costumes at low rates. The Fund was founded in 1967. Its most successful and visible venture has been the institution and running of the TKTS booth on Times Square, which sells theatre tickets at reduced rates.

Theatre Library Association is a 1937 wing of the American Library Association that serves to compile and preserve theatre books, photographs, designs and playbills in libraries and museums across the country.

United Scenic Artists of America (USAA), the union for scenic, costume and lighting designers, negotiates wages, work conditions, and royalties. USAA was founded in 1912 and one still needs to pass vigorous examinations in order to be admitted to the union.

THEATRE MAGAZINES AND PERIODICALS

Publications about theatre have come and gone over the years and even the best of them have a relatively short life span. But some of the efforts have been glorious. Here is a selective list of past and current theatre publications.

American Theatre is a monthly magazine published by the Theatre Communications Group since 1984. Its articles concentrate on non-profit professional theatre, listings across the country, and the complete text of selected new plays.

Backstage is a weekly show business tabloid that has been providing news, reviews, casting notices, and lists of upcoming productions for theatre, television, and film actors since 1960.

Billboard was originated in 1884 as a trade sheet covering theatre, later adding music, carnivals, and circuses. Today it concentrates on the popular music business.

Broadside is the quarterly publication by the Theatre Library Association, emphasizing theatre books, photographs, and playbills since 1973.

The Clipper started in 1853 as a sporting and theatrical trade paper but soon concentrated on vaudeville. It was absorbed into *Variety* in 1924.

The Drama Review is a scholarly quarterly that has looked at the newest trends in theatre since 1955. It was called the *Tulane Drama Review* until 1967 when it was housed at the New Orleans university. Today the periodical comes out of New York University's School of the Arts and is often known as *TDR*.

Dramatic Mirror was the leading trade paper for theatre before *Variety*. Founded in 1884 as the *New York Mirror*, the periodical covered business news as well as gossip and crusading editorials on theatre business. It started to emphasize film in 1915 and ceased publication in 1922.

Dramatics is the monthly magazine put out by the International Thespian Society since 1929. Its articles relate to high school theatre production.

Dramatists Guild Quarterly is the periodical for playwrights, composers, and lyricists that the Dramatist Guild has put out since 1964. It has articles by and for playwrights, as well as a thorough listing of productions by members across the country and in foreign countries.

The Green Book Magazine offered novelizations of contemporary plays, as well as photographs, articles, and biographical sketches. The periodical was published between 1909 and 1921.

Kurt Weill Newsletter is dedicated to the Americanized composer Weill and productions of his theatre and concert works. The periodical is published twice a year by the Kurt Weill Foundation.

National Theatre Critics Reviews began in 1943 as the *New York Theatre Critics' Reviews*, reprinting all the print reviews by the major Broadway critics. The field was later expanded and, since the monthly publication adopted its new name in 1995, it now covers reviews from different media across the country.

New York Star was a trade sheet that emphasized vaudeville news. It was published from 1920 to 1930, sometimes as the *Vaudeville News*.

The Passing Show is a periodical put out by the Shubert Foundation regarding the history of past Broadway productions, Shubert shows in particular. The free magazine has been published twice a year since 1977.

Performing Arts Magazine is an arts monthly that has provided information on theatre, film, and music events since 1967.

Performing Arts Journal focuses on contemporary theatre, dance, and music. It has published three times a year since 1976.

Playbill is the magazine that includes the theatre program for most Broadway playhouses. The operation was founded in 1884 by Frank Vance Strauss to provide reading material in theatre programs. In 1911 it was given the title *Strauss Magazine Theatre Program* which was changed to *Playbill* in 1934. Today there is also a national monthly version that patrons can subscribe to.

Plays, self-described as the "drama magazine for young people," has printed royalty-free plays and skits for schools and children's theatres since 1941.

Show Business is a New York weekly trade sheet geared to the acting profession, offering casting news and articles related to actors in different media.

Show Music, a relatively recent quarterly that concerns itself with theatre music, has offered articles, reviews, and commentary since 1981.

The Sondheim Review is a periodical dedicated to the past and present work of composer/lyricist Stephen Sondheim. It contains news about national and international Sondheim productions as well as articles, reviews, and listings.

Stages is a national monthly tabloid on theatre that offers production and book reviews. It was founded in 1984.

Theatre is the scholarly journal that is published three times a year by the Yale School of Drama and the Yale Repertory Theatre. It contains articles, reviews, and play scripts.

Theatre Arts was a favorite of theatregoers across the nation with its catchy articles, plentiful pictures, and a full play text included in most issues. The magazine was founded in 1916 as a quarterly and went monthly soon after, publishing many colorful issues until its cessation in 1964.

Theatre Crafts has been a favorite publication of designers since 1967, covering Broadway, national, and international news and articles about scenic, costume, and lighting design, as well as props, stage construction, and sound. In 1992 *Theatre Crafts* merged with *Theatre Crafts International* and today the monthly magazine is simply known as *TCI*.

Theatre Design and Technology is a quarterly published by the U. S. Institute for Theatre Technology. The publication, started in 1965, is now known simply as *T D & T*.

Theatre Journal is a quarterly that is published by the Association for Theatre in Higher Education, presenting articles on theatre scholarship and criticism. The periodical, started in 1949 as the *Educational Theatre Journal*, also contains critiques by college faculty of productions around the world.

Theatre Magazine was a popular monthly magazine that entertained its readers with photos and articles on stage performers much as a fan magazine for films. The periodical was published from 1901 to 1931.

Theatre Studies is a scholarly annual published by the Theatre Research Institute since 1955.

Theatre Survey is a semi-annual academic periodical about American theatre history published by the American Society for Theatre Research since 1960.

Theatre Week was founded in 1987 as a weekly magazine about commercial and regional theatre. It has since expanded its coverage to include educational and foreign theatre as well but much of its emphasis is still on New York theatre.

The Thespian Mirror was a short-lived but historically important journal published by John Howard Payne in New York in 1805-1806, one of the earliest theatre periodicals on record.

The Thespian Oracle is the earliest known theatre-related periodical in America. Little is known about it except its first (and possibly last) issue published in Philadelphia in 1798.

Variety, the "Bible of Show Business," has been published weekly since 1905 and still carries the most up-to-date information on the commercial theatre. The trade paper emphasized vaudeville at first (hence, its name), but legitimate theatre and later film began to dominate its pages. Today the theatre section is the smallest as television and film get most of the coverage, but its theatre financial figures, reports on projects, and pragmatic reviews are still noteworthy.

For further reading: Ken Bloom's *Broadway: An Encyclopedic Guide to the History, People and Places of Times Square*, Steven Suskin's *Opening Night on Broadway*, Don Wilmeth and Tice Miller's *Cambridge Guide to American Theatre*, Gerald Bordman's *Oxford Companion to American Theatre*, and the *Best Plays* series.

BIBLIOGRAPHY

Alpert, Hollis. *Broadway: 125 Years of Musical Theatre*. New York: Arcade
    Publishers, 1991.
Atkinson, Brooks. *Broadway*, Rev. ed. New York: MacMillan Publishing Co.,
    1974.
Barlow, Judith. *Plays By Women*. New York: Avon Books, 1981.
Berney, K. A., ed. *Contemporary Dramatists*. 5th ed. Detroit: Gale Research,
    Inc., 1993.
The Best Plays. 78 editions. Editors: Garrison and John Chapman (1894-1919);
    Burns Mantle (1919-1947); John Chapman (1947-1952); Louis
    Kronenberger (1952-1961); Henry Hewes (1961-1964); Otis Guernsey
    (1964-1985); Otis Guernsey and Jeffrey Sweet (1985-1995). New York:
    Dodd, Mead & Co., 1894-1988; New York: Applause Theatre Book
    Publishers, 1988-1993; New York: Limelight Editions, 1994-1995.
Bloom, Ken. *American Song: The Complete Musical Theatre Companion,*
    1877-1995, 2nd ed. New York: Schirmer Books, 1996.
_____. *Broadway: An Encyclopedic Guide to the History, People and Places*
    of Times Square. New York: Facts on File, Inc., 1991.
Blum, Daniel. *Great Stars of the American Stage: A Pictorial Record*. New
    York: Grosset & Dunlap Publishers, 1954.
Blum, Daniel, and John Willis. *A Pictorial History of the American Theatre,*
    1860-1980. 5th ed. New York: Crown Publishers, 1981.
Bordman, Gerald. *American Musical Theatre: A Chronicle*, 2nd ed. New York:
    Oxford University Press, 1992.
_____ . *American Theatre: A Chronicle of Comedy and Drama, 1869-1914*.
    New York: Oxford University Press, 1994.
_____. *American Theatre: A Chronicle of Comedy and Drama, 1914-1930*.
    New York: Oxford University Press, 1995.

_____. *American Theatre: A Chronicle of Comedy and Drama, 1930-1969.* New York: Oxford University Press, 1996.

_____. *The Oxford Companion to American Theatre.* 2nd ed. New York: Oxford University Press, 1992.

Botto, Louis. *At This Theatre: An Informal History of New York's Legitimate Theatres.* New York: Dodd, Mead & Co., 1984.

Brewer's Theatre: A Phrase and Fable Dictionary. New York: Harper Collins Publishers, Inc., 1994.

Brockett, Oscar G., and Robert R. Findlay. *Century of Innovation: A History of European and American Theatre and Drama Since 1870.* Englewood Cliffs, NJ: Prentice-Hall, Inc., 1973.

_____. *History of the Theatre.* 7th ed. Boston: Allyn and Bacon, 1995.

Bronner, Edwin J. *The Encyclopedia of the American Theatre, 1900-1975.* San Diego: A. S. Barnes and Company, Inc., 1980.

Brown, T. Allston. *A History of the New York Stage: From First Performance in 1732 to 1901.* 3 vols. Reissue of 1903 ed. New York: Benjamin Blom, Inc., 1964.

Brown-Guillory, Elizabeth. *Their Place on Stage: Black Women Playwrights in America.* Westport, CT: Greenwood Press, 1988.

Cerf, Bennett, and Van H. Cartnell, eds. *S.R.O.: The Most Successful Plays of the American Stage.* New York: Doubleday & Co., Inc., 1944.

Chinoy, Helen Krich, and Linda Walsh Jenkins, eds. *Women in American Theatre.* New York: Crown Publishers, 1981.

Churchill, Allen. *The Great White Way.* New York: E. P. Dutton & Co., Inc., 1962.

Clurman, Harold. *The Fervent Years.* New York: Alfred A. Knopf, 1945.

Engel, Lehrman. *The American Musical Theatre: A Consideration.* New York: CBS Legacy Collection Books, 1967.

_____. *Their Words Are Music: The Great Theatre Lyricists and Their Lyrics.* New York: Crown Publishers, 1975.

Epstein, Lawrence, ed. *A Guide to Theatre in America.* New York: MacMillan Publishing Co., 1985.

Ewen, David. *American Songwriters.* New York: H. W. Wilson Co., 1987.

_____. *New Complete Book of the American Musical Theatre.* New York: Henry Holt & Co., 1976.

Flannagan, Hallie. *Arena: The History of the Federal Theatre.* Reissue of 1940 ed. New York: Benjamin Blom, Inc., 1965.

France, Rachel. *A Century of Plays by American Women.* New York: Richards Rosen, 1979.

Frick, John W., and Carlton Ward. *Directory of Historic American Theatres.* Westport, CT: Greenwood Press, 1987.

Furia, Philip. *The Poets of Tin Pan Alley: A History of America's Great Lyricists.* New York: Oxford University Press, 1990.

Ganzl, Kurt, and Andrew Lamb. *Ganzl's Book of the Musical Theatre*. New York: Schirmer Books, 1989.

_____ . *Ganzl's Encyclopedia of the Musical Theatre*. New York: Schirmer Books, 1993.

Goldman, William. *The Season*. New York: Harcourt Brace and World, 1969.

Goldstein, Malcolm. *The Political Stage*. New York: Oxford University Press, 1974.

Gorelik, Mordecai. *New Theatres for Old*. New York: Samuel French, Publishers, 1957.

Gottfried, Martin. *Broadway Musicals*. New York: Harry N. Abrams, 1980.

_____ . *More Broadway Musicals*. New York: Harry N. Abrams, 1991.

Green, Stanley. *Broadway Musicals Show By Show*. 4th ed. Milwaukee: Hal Leonard Publishing Corp., 1995.

_____ . *Encyclopedia of the Musical Theatre*. New York: Dodd, Mead & Co., 1976.

_____ . *The World of Musical Comedy*. 4th ed. New York: A. S. Barnes & Co., 1980.

Greenberg, Jan Weingarten. *Theatre Business: From Auditions Through Opening Night*. New York: Holt, Rinehart and Winston, 1981.

Griffiths, Trevor R., and Carole Woodis, eds. *The Back Stage Theatre Guide*. New York: Back Stage Books (Watson-Guptill), 1991.

Grose, B. Donald, and O. Franklin Kenworthy. *A Mirror to Life: A History of Western Theatre*. New York: Holt, Rinehart and Winston, 1985.

Guernsey, Otis L. (ed.). *Curtain Times: The New York Theatre, 1965-1987*. New York: Applause Theatre Book Publishers, 1987.

_____ . *Playwrights, Lyricists, Composers on Theatre*. New York: Dodd, Mead & Co., 1974.

Henderson, Mary C. *The City and the Theatre: New York Playhouses from Bowling Green to Times Square*. Clifton, NJ: James T. White & Co., 1973.

_____ . *Theatre in America*. 2nd ed. New York: Harry N. Abrams, 1996.

Herbert, Ian (ed.). *Who's Who in the Theatre*. Detroit: Gale Research Company, 1981.

Hischak, Thomas S. *The American Musical Theatre Song Encyclopedia*. Westport, CT: Greenwood Press, 1995.

_____ . *Stage It With Music: An Encyclopedic Guide to the American Musical Theatre*. Westport, CT: Greenwood Press, 1993.

_____ . *Word Crazy: Broadway Lyricists from Cohan to Sondheim*. New York: Praeger Press, 1991.

Hixon, Don L., and Dan A. Hennessee. *Nineteenth Century American Drama: A Finding Guide*. Metuchen, NJ: Scarecrow Press, 1977.

Hoyt, Harlowe R. *Town Hall Tonight: Intimate Memories of the Grassroots Days of the American Theatre*. New York: Bramhall House, 1955.

Ireland, Joseph N. *Records of the New York Stage From 1750 to 1860.* 2 vols. Reprint of 1866 ed. New York: Benjamin Blom, 1966.

Langley, Stephen. *Theatre Management and Production in America.* New York: Drama Book Publishers, 1990.

Laufe, Abe. *Broadway's Greatest Musicals.* New York: Funk and Wagnalls, 1977.

_____. *The Wicked Stage: A History of Theatre Censorship and Harassment in the United States.* New York: Frederick Ungar Publishing Co., 1978.

Leiter, Samuel L. *The Encyclopedia of the New York Stage, 1920-1930.* Westport, CT: Greenwood Press, 1985.

_____. *The Encyclopedia of the New York Stage, 1930-1940.* Westport, CT: Greenwood Press, 1989.

_____. *The Encyclopedia of the New York Stage, 1940-1950.* Westport, CT: Greenwood Press, 1992.

_____. *The Great Stage Directors.* New York: Facts on File, Inc., 1994.

_____. *Ten Seasons: New York Theatre in the Seventies.* West-port, CT: Greenwood Press, 1986.

Leon, Ruth. *Applause: New York's Guide to the Performing Arts.* New York: Applause Theatre Book Publishers, 1991.

Lewine, Richard, and Alfred Simon. *Songs of the Theatre.* New York: H. W. Wilson Company, 1984.

Lissauer, Robert. *Lissauer's Encyclopedia of Popular Music.* 2nd ed. New York: Facts on File Publications, 1996.

Little, Stuart W. *Off-Broadway: The Prophetic Theatre.* New York: Coward, McCann & Geoghegan, Inc., 1972.

Little, Stuart W., and Arthur Cantor. *The Playmakers.* New York: E. P. Dutton & Co., Inc., 1970.

Lynes, Russell. *The Lively Audience: A Social History of the Visual and Performing Arts in America, 1890-1950.* New York: Harper & Row, 1985.

Mandelbaum, Ken. *Not Since Carrie: Forty Years of Broadway Musical Flops.* New York: St. Martin's Press, 1991.

Mates, Julian. *America's Musical Stage:Two Hundred Years of Musical Theatre.* Westport, CT: Greenwood Press, 1985.

Mordden, Ethan. *The American Theatre.* New York: Oxford University Press, 1981.

_____. *Better Foot Forward: The History of American Musical Theatre.* New York: Grossman Publishers, 1976.

_____. *Broadway Babies: The People Who Made the American Musical.* New York: Oxford University Press, 1983.

Morehouse, Ward. *Matinee Tomorrow: Fifty Years of Our Theatre.* New York: McGraw-Hill Book Co., 1949.

Morley, Sheridan. *The Great Stage Stars*. New York: Facts on File Publications, 1986.

Morrow, Lee Alan. *The Tony Award Book*. New York: Abbeville Press, 1987.

Moses, Montrose J., and John Mason Brown. *The American Theatre as Seen by Its Critics, 1752-1934*. New York: W. W. Norton & Co., Inc., 1934.

_____. *Famous Actor-Families in America*. Reprint of 1906 ed. New York: Greenwood Press, 1968.

Odell, George C. D. *Annals of the New York Stage*. 15 vols. New York: Columbia University Press, 1927-1949.

Owen, Bobbi. *Costume Designer on Broadway: Designers and Their Credits, 1915-1985*. Westport, CT: Greenwood Press, 1987.

_____. *Lighting Design on Broadway: Designers and Their Credits, 1915-1990*. Westport, CT: Greenwood Press, 1991.

_____. *Stage Design on Broadway: Designers and Their Credits, 1915-1990*. Westport, CT: Greenwood Press, 1991.

Quinn, Arthur Hobson. *A History of the American Drama*. New York: Harper and Brothers, 1927.

_____. *Representative American Plays: From 1767 to the Present Day*. 7th ed. New York: Appleton-Century-Crofts, 1953.

Rigdon, Walter, ed. *The Biographical Encyclopedia and Who's Who of the American Theatre*. New York: James H. Heineman, Inc., 1966.

Robinson, Alice M., Vera Mowry Roberts, and Milly S. Barranger, eds. *Notable Women in the American Theatre*. Westport, CT: Greenwood Press, 1989.

Rosenberg, Bernard and Ernest Harburg. *The Broadway Musical: Collaboration in Commerce and Art*. New York: New York University Press, 1993.

Saylor, Oliver M. *Our American Theatre*. Reissue of 1923 ed. New York: Benjamin Blom, Inc., 1971.

Seilhamer, George O. *History of the American Theatre*. Reprint of 1891 ed. New York: Greenwood Press, 1968.

Seldes, Gilbert. *The Seven Lively Arts*. New York: Sagamore Press, Inc., 1957.

Seller, Maxine Schwartz. *Ethnic Theatre in the United States*. Westport, CT: Greenwood Press, 1983.

Shafer, Yvonne. *American Women Playwrights, 1900-1950*. New York: Peter Lang Publishing, Inc., 1995.

Sheward, David. *It's a Hit: The Backstage Book of Longest-Running Broadway Shows*. New York: Watson-Guptill Publications-BPI Communications, Inc., 1994.

Stevenson, Isabelle, ed. *The Tony Award: A Complete Listing With a History of the American Theatre Wing*. New York: Crown Publishers, 1995.

Suskin, Steven. *Opening Night on Broadway: A Critical Quotebook of the Golden Era of the Musical Theatre*. New York: Schirmer Books, 1990.

Taubman, Howard. *The Making of the American Theatre*. New York: Coward

McCann, Inc., 1965.

Theatre World. 49 editions. Editors: Daniel Blum (1944-1964); John Willis (1964-1993); New York: Greenburg, 1944-1957; Philadelphia: Chilton, 1957-1964; New York: Crown Publishers, 1964-1990; New York: Applause Theatre Book Publishers, 1991-1993.

Toll, Robert C. *On With the Show: The First Century of Show Business in America.* New York: Oxford University Press, 1976.

Toohey, John L. *A History of the Pulitzer Prize Plays.* New York: The Citadel Press, 1967.

Turner, Mary M. *Forgotten Leading Ladies of the American Theatre.* Jefferson, North Carolina: McFarland & Company, Inc., 1990.

Weales, Gerald. *The Jumping-Off Place: American Drama in the 1960s, from Broadway to Off-Off-Broadway to Happenings.* New York: MacMillan Publishing Co., 1969.

Williams, Jay. *Stage Left.* New York: Charles Scribner's Sons, 1974.

Wilmeth, Don B., and Tice Miller, eds. *Cambridge Guide to American Theatre.* New York: Cambridge University Press, 1993.

Wilson, Edwin, and Alvin Goldfarb. *Living Theatre: A History.* New York: McGraw-Hill, Inc., 1994.

Wilson, Garff B. *Three Hundred Years of American Drama and Theatre,* Englewood Cliffts, NJ: Prentice-Hall, Inc., 1973.

Young, William C. *Documents of American Theatre History: Famous American Playhouses, 1716-1971.* Chicago: American Library Assoc., 1973.

INDEX

About the Author

THOMAS S. HISCHAK is Professor of Theatre at the State University of New York College at Cortland. He is the author of several plays published by Samuel French, Inc., Dramatic Publishing Co., Baker's Plays, and others. His books include *The American Musical Theatre Song Encyclopedia* (Greenwood, 1995), *Stage It with Music: An Encyclopedic Guide to the American Musical Theatre* (Greenwood, 1993), and *Word Crazy: Broadway Lyricists from Cohan to Sondheim* (Praeger, 1991).